BARRY ROSE

SITTING ON A PIN

A MUSICAL MEMOIR

Barry Rose sat on a pin – Barry ROSE!

– a chant often aimed at me during my school days

© Barry Michael Rose, 2021

Published by Barry Michael Rose

A CIP catalogue record for this book is available from the British Library.

ISBN: 978-1-3999-0667-8

Book design by Beth Truesdale
Back and front cover design by Simon Blake – www.simonblakestudio.com

Prepared and printed by:

York Publishing Services Ltd.,
64 Hallfield Road,
Layerthorpe,
York YO31 7ZQ

Telephone: 01904 431213

Website: www.yps-publishing.co.uk

Dedicated to my wife Elizabeth (Buffie),
without whom I am nothing,
and most of what follows could never have been possible.

Contents

THE CATHEDRAL, GUILDFORD D14544

As we walked around the east end of the unfinished
Guildford Cathedral on that summer afternoon in 1959,
I turned to my friend and said,
'One day, some lucky bloke is going to be Organist here...'

Prelude

Everyone has a unique story to tell, and musicians are no exception. For many years I've fought shy of committing mine to paper, asking myself, 'Who wants to read about a boy from an east London suburb who, against all the odds, tried to make a career in music after giving up a secure job in the world of commerce?'

A journey from playing the harmonium in a small, corrugated iron mission church to the so-called heady heights of the grand organs in three of our great Cathedrals might seem like the stuff of dreams. Maybe it was, but dreams don't always come true, and there are often nightmares along the way.

Perhaps I wasn't cut out to be the archetypal Cathedral organist – something pointed out to me quite forcibly when I turned up at Westminster Abbey to practise for a celebrity organ recital the following evening. Met by the Dean's verger, he barked, 'Who are you, and what are you doing here?' Stammering, I replied, 'I'm Barry Rose, Organist of the new Guildford Cathedral.' Back came the reply, 'You, a Cathedral organist? You can't be, you don't look like one.'

He may have been right, and having been given the awesome responsibility of creating a new musical foundation at a new Cathedral, I was more than aware that the eyes of the church music 'establishment' were keenly monitoring this unknown and unqualified 25-year-old. Those early days at Guildford were a journey of faith, and Faith, and if, as I believe, our lives are governed by a greater Being, my musical pilgrimage would take me elsewhere – St. Paul's Cathedral, the BBC, The King's School Canterbury, and finally to the Cathedral and Abbey Church at St. Albans.

I'm very aware that any memoir can seem to be nothing but a string of names, dates and places, and mine is no exception, though I hope there might be something else along the way to inform and interest you.

Whatever our age or experience, all of us need help and encouragement, and I owe such a great debt of gratitude to so many people. Some are mentioned by name in the narrative that follows, but countless others have also been so influential, and that includes every singer and every organist with whom I have ever worked. The toils, tears and occasional triumphs of a long musical life are documented in this book, though it wouldn't have been completed without the encouragement of my wife and children, and the editorial skill and print preparation by Graeme McCullough and Beth Truesdale.

A few weeks after the Consecration of Guildford Cathedral, I happened to meet the Archdeacon of Surrey, who rather pompously enquired, 'And when is your next *big* Service?' He was somewhat taken aback when I answered, 'Evensong today.'

It may be a transient offering, but that's what musicians do – we give of our best, whatever the day, time or occasion and, as I've never ceased to remind my choirs, in Worship only the best is good enough for God.

Thank you for coming this far – and now, please join me at the very start of my musical journey.

Barry Rose
Somerset – October 2021

Special thanks to:

Simon Blake – for his original caricature and inventive design of the front cover.

Malcolm Archer, Canon Michael McCarthy, Canon Stephen Shipley and *Hilary Davan Wetton* – for their generous contributions to the back cover.

Simon Gaunt, Jeremy Jackman, David Ireson, Andrew Parnell, Margaret (Miggi) Sharp, and *Richard Tanner* – for reading through some of the original drafts.

Nicolas (Nick) Ware – for so many photographs.

Rob Ruutel – for his skill in resurrecting and preparing old graphics for publication.

Andy Russell – for much initial advice and help.

In the Beginning
London E4 1934-1946

Chingford (E4) lies at the very eastern edge of London. Divided into two, South Chingford adjoins Walthamstow, whilst the northern boundary of North Chingford is Epping Forest, designated as the 'People's Forest' following a visit by Queen Victoria in 1882 when she declared, 'It gives me the greatest satisfaction to dedicate this beautiful forest to the use and enjoyment of my people for all time.'

No-one seems sure as to how the name of Chingford originated. Some think it describes the bridge over the River Ching. Others point towards the Domesday Book (1086), which describes the area as *Cingefort*, which could refer to the King's Ford. There were certainly some royal connections – the oldest building in the borough is a hunting lodge built for King Henry VIII in 1543, later renamed Queen Elizabeth's Hunting Lodge.

It was in Woodland Road, North Chingford, on 24th May 1934 – Empire Day – that I was born, the only son of Gladys Mildred Rose (née Barker) and Stanley George Rose. Christened Barry Michael, I was the second of three children – Wendy Pamela, born a year earlier on 13th May 1933, and Jillian Barbara seven years later on 20th June 1941. Wendy and I often speculated on our parents' choice of names and wondered if they might have been influenced by J.M. Barrie's popular book *Peter Pan*, in which the heroine is called Wendy.

Both parents had been brought up in South Hackney, London, where my mother's mother, Louisa Mary Barker, was a member of the congregation and parish clerk of St. John's Church; her deceased husband having been a lay reader. One of two daughters, Gladys met Stanley through local music-making, he as a violinist and she as a pianist. Stanley's father, George Durrant Rose, had two boys and one girl, and was an executive in the firm of Bishop and Brooke, suppliers to the bakery industry. Their head office was in Cock Lane in the centre of the City of London, with branches in various towns and cities throughout England.

At some stage the family migrated to the leafier surrounds of North Chingford. George Rose, his wife and daughter were living in an executive-style house in Connaught Avenue, whilst his elder son, Harold, was a few streets away in the comparably desirable Mount View Road. My parents' house in Woodland Road was more modest, but in 1934 they moved to the more spacious Beresford Road, a quiet street a short distance from Chingford Plains and the edge of Epping Forest. The back gardens of the houses on our side of the road abutted the railway tracks that led into Chingford Station, the end of the commuter line from Liverpool Street.

My father described himself as a haulage contractor, which in reality meant that he drove a lorry for his father's firm, delivering supplies to the branches of Bishop and Brooke. Often we would hear him say that he would be going to Hitchin, Bedford, Kettering and Leicester that day, and sometimes he would even go as far afield as Newport, South Wales.

At the age of ten I can remember being taken on the occasional run to Chichester. To this young boy, the slow climb up Duncton Hill was not just exciting, but also quite frightening in a fully laden lorry which would often have to make the ascent in first gear. The local office of Bishop and Brooke was in one of the streets that radiated from the Market Cross, and their warehouse was down by the canal basin (now the partially restored Chichester Canal). After delivering his load, he would take me next door to the wholesale ice-cream store for a delicious free snack.

My earliest clear memories of Beresford Road are of the start of World War II in 1939, by which time I was five. It had been a hot, dry summer, and on the evening of Sunday 3rd September, I can remember us standing in the back garden as dusk drew in, as our parents tried to explain the implications of war to Wendy and me.

In the garden at Beresford Road, 1941

Outside 85 Beresford Road, c. 1940

At that time we were both at the local Roman Catholic Convent School in Forest View. A year or so later I was moved to King's Road Church School, where we sat in rows of old-fashioned desks and learned to write with chalk on small blackboard slates. My memories of that school are of formal learning, strict discipline, and unquestioning respect for our teachers.

King's Road School, Chingford, 1941. I am in the third row up, second from the right.

In mid-1941 our father received his 'call-up' papers and was due to be drafted into the army. The bombing of London had already begun in September of the previous year. Night after night the sky was lit up with the distant glow of burning buildings, and the house shook every time a bomb fell several miles away. Our parents decided that it might be safer if we moved out of London on a temporary basis, though how long 'temporary' would be, no-one seemed quite sure. Wendy and I wondered why it was necessary when my father had gone to the trouble of having a substantial brick air-raid shelter built in the back garden, complete with blast wall in front of the entrance door. But for us it would be an adventure.

One night, we were piled into the back of his lorry with a few personal belongings and driven to the village of Beedon, in the remote Berkshire countryside, where friends from Chingford had some relations. My memories of the cottage in which we stayed were of the total blackness and quiet, the only illumination being the paraffin lamps we had to carry up the rickety stairs when we went to bed. With all those strange shadows, it was an exciting and ghostly experience for a seven-year-old.

A month or so later we returned home. I went back to King's Road School and Wendy stayed at home – the convent she had been attending had been requisitioned as a billet for the army.

Bombs were now falling on Chingford, and as well as being regularly woken in the middle of the night and herded into the air-raid shelter, we began to hear a strange new word: evacuation. A government initiative begun in 1938, the object was to move children away from areas threatened by bombing. We were to be evacuated to the Cheshire countryside, far away from London.

The process began with a name tag firmly tied to one of our coat buttonholes, and the obligatory gas mask in its cardboard container hung around our necks. There was an emotional farewell as we piled onto a coach to Euston Station, and there we boarded a special train and were soon steaming away from bomb-scarred London. I was nearly eight and had never heard of Macclesfield (Cheshire), but that was to be our destination. When we arrived, we were met by a reception committee, waiting in small groups until we heard our names read out. We were then introduced to our surrogate parents who would be looking after us for the foreseeable future.

Wendy and I were allocated to the village of Bollington, just four miles from Macclesfield, though we were placed in separate households. I went to No. 10 Highfield Road, a handsome 1930s semi-detached house, as the guest of Mr. and Mrs. Waterhouse. The Waterhouses were devout Methodists, and on Sunday mornings we would always be in church, with me hoping that the sermon would soon end – it was usually far too long for my boyhood patience. Wendy was placed with a family about half a mile away, and after a few weeks it became obvious that she was not going to settle. She desperately wanted to return to Chingford, and though I went with her, it was not because of any unhappiness on my part.

By then our father was in the army, and it was left to my mother to provide for us and to arrange schooling. She was also looking after a new arrival in the family: Jillian, our younger sister, had been born on 20th June 1941. Added to that, her own mother's house

Mrs. Waterhouse outside No. 10 Highfield Road, Bollington

in Church Crescent, South Hackney, had been destroyed by bombing, and with what was left of her belongings, she came to live with us at Chingford. At least there were now two adults, and some extra financial support for our mother who was coping with three children.

What about our schooling? Wendy was sent to Richmond House School, a small fee-paying school in a private house in Richmond Road, a few streets off Station Road, North Chingford's main street. The founder and Principal was Mrs. T.F. Hardy, a stern yet kindly lady whose husband worked behind the counter in a nearby grocery shop. Richmond House pupils were easily identified by their grey uniform with red trimmings and RHS on the blazer pocket. They advertised that their pupils would be well prepared for the 11-plus examination that Wendy would sit in 1944.

For me, school was to be much closer to home. Crescent Road was a few streets away, and it was to there that the Roman Catholic boys' school, St. Egbert's College, had transferred when their large premises in The Ridgeway, known as The Chantry, had been commandeered for troop accommodation. It was strictly a boys-only school, and I use the word 'strictly' with good reason. Run and staffed by the Brothers of our Lady of Mercy – a misnomer if ever there was one – the headmaster was the fearsome Brother Isidore. Bespectacled and balding, he was a towering figure over us small boys, and thought nothing of administering a thrashing for the pettiest offences, academic or behavioural. For some reason I seemed to be one of his favourites, so I never experienced the pain of his cane.

On our way to lunch in the small school refectory we would pass Brother Isidore's study, and there, outside, would be the queue of unfortunate miscreants, waiting their turn to be punished. On one occasion Brother Isidore invited me in, put his arm around me, and asked how I was. Now, in later life, and with a string of much-publicised lawsuits against the Roman Catholic Church, I'm tempted to think that maybe I should have been worried by that private and personal attention.

Our uniform was a bright green blazer with red piping around the collar and lapels, together with a striped tie of the same colours. Play times were often spent amongst the trees – the houses in Crescent Road face the edge of Epping Forest – or making our way towards the Royal Forest Hotel and Warren Pond, searching for shrapnel from exploded bombs.

Memories of music lessons from those days at St. Egbert's are still vivid, so perhaps the musical genes were beginning to be activated at the age of eight and nine, as we sang *O Soldier, soldier, won't you marry me* at the annual school concert, complete with actions.

Our class music was in the one room that had a piano, and it was Miss Rosa Larcombe LRAM who had us all dutifully singing the words that A.P. Herbert had set to the central section of Sir Edward Elgar's *Pomp and Circumstance March No. 4*: '*All men must be free / March for liberty with me / Brutes and braggarts may have their little way / We will never bow the knee…*'

That was the first time I had ever heard Elgar's music, and what a deep impression it made on this young lad, as did Ron Presnall's singing of Schubert's *Die Forelle* (*The Trout*) at another of the school concerts. These took place in the ballroom of the nearby Queen Elizabeth public house, and my abiding memory is of Ron striding onto the stage, looking very tall and grown-up in his long trousers, and then producing the most amazing treble voice, accompanied by Miss Larcombe's nimble technique at the piano.

Family life had been turned upside down by the sudden reappearance of our father, who had been invalided out of the army after some sort of nervous breakdown. He did not come back to Chingford for long, but instead was admitted to a mental hospital at Shenley, in Hertfordshire, where he remained for the best part of a year. Our visits involved what seemed to be an interminable journey on two buses, often not connecting with each other. The hospital was a grim and forbidding place to us children, and often we were witness to scenes of violence and restraint, all very unsettling to young and impressionable minds.

By early 1944 our father had returned home from hospital and was beginning to pick up the threads of his previous life, driving the lorry for his father's firm. It may have been for financial reasons that I was transferred from St. Egbert's College to Richmond House School, or it may have been with one eye to the 11-plus examination early the following year. If I passed I would gain a place at a grammar school and thus receive free education, rather than my parents continuing to pay fees for the senior part of St. Egbert's College.

Richmond House School had moved to larger premises in The Ridgeway. Our mixed classes were quite small, and the timetable included some music in the form of class singing, taken by Mrs. Hardy, the Principal. I remember one occasion when Michael Cousins, one of my friends, decided he would spontaneously rewrite the words of Thomas Morley's *Now is the month of Maying*. The lines in question were *Each with his bonny lass, upon the greeny grass.*

Up sang Michael, as loud as he could, *Each with his bonny lass, a-wiping of his arse…* The singing stopped. There was dead silence. Mrs. Hardy's finger beckoned. Michael went to the front of the class and received a fearsome smack around his head. Justice was summary, and you soon learned not to misbehave again!

We also had elocution lessons, taken by Mrs. Bailey. With her impeccable sense of diction, we were dragged through communal poetry recitations: *Three jolly farmers once bet a pound, Each dance the others would off the ground…* We would dutifully chant Walter de la Mare's poem in unison, whilst also taking the opportunity to misbehave the moment Mrs. Bailey's attention was elsewhere.

The war was still on, and bombing was still a daily occurrence, though now in a new and sinister form: the V-1 flying bomb. Powered by a basic jet engine which sounded a bit like a throaty motorcycle, each day hundreds were launched towards London – Chingford being well within the target range.

One morning in 1944, waiting for the bus to school, I was standing looking in a shop window when I heard the engine of a V-1 flying bomb cut out. Shortly it would crash to the ground and destroy the area wherever it hit. It might have been instinct, but I moved away from the shop seconds before the nearby explosion shattered the window, sending shards of glass flying in all directions. Had I been standing there I would have been cut to pieces.

But amid all this wartime horror there was music, and although I did not realise it, at home, at school, and at church, the seeds were being sown for my future career. My mother often played the piano and my father occasionally played the violin, so it was not surprising that Wendy and I were sent to have piano lessons. I was ten, and our teacher was Mrs. Humphries, a redoubtable North Country lady, who would sit by the side of me, ruler in hand, ready to rap my knuckles each time I made a mistake. 'Don't baNG!' she would say, emphasising the last syllable with a broad nasal twang that made it sound rather like 'banger'. I often wondered if there was a Mr. Humphries, and if his knuckles also got rapped by the ruler. I was never studious with my practice, and scales seemed to be a bit of a waste of time, so it was learning pieces such as *Glow Worm* that interested me more than working at those boring scales and arpeggios – something I was to regret in later life.

But there was an upside to the lessons. Wendy and I had been sent to the local Sunday school of the parish church of St. Peter and St. Paul. Known as Children's Church, each Sunday morning we would make our way to No. 4 Crown Buildings, a parade of shops facing the church. Through a corridor and out of the back door we would come to a hut, where our local lay reader, Mr. T.F. Brooks, would take the Service. Hymns and choruses were sung from *Golden Bells*, and each week the piano was played in turn by one of two girls – Audrey Neville or June Porter. It was Audrey who caught my eye and my boyhood affection, with her long flowing auburn hair and delicate poise; probably the first time I had fallen for the opposite sex. She was older and more sophisticated than me, but, joy of joys, she lived opposite my grandparents in Connaught Avenue, and whilst visiting them, I would catch an occasional glimpse of her arriving at or leaving her house.

Sunday school in Chingford turned out to be the beginning of a lifetime in church music. Someday, I thought, I might be allowed to play the hymns at Children's Church,

and it was not long before I was taking a copy of *Golden Bells* to Mrs. Humphries'
lessons, and was surprised and encouraged by her patience and enthusiasm for hymns.

It was at my grandparents' home in Connaught Avenue that I made my first acquaintance with recorded church music. Helping to lay the table for a family Sunday
lunch, I discovered some 12-inch gramophone records in a sideboard drawer. One
of them was Ernest Lough's recording of Mendelssohn's *Hear My Prayer*, which I
was able to play over and over on the wind-up gramophone in the
adjoining drawing room. Little did I realise that some 30 years
later I would succeed choirmaster George Thalben-Ball at
the BBC and discuss this very recording with the great man
himself.

If there were serious musicians in the family at this
time, they were on my mother's side. Her sister, Nell
(Ellen), was married to George Elmitt, and they lived in
Watford. Both were keen string players – Nell on the violin and George on the viola. Their three children, Pauline,
Mavis (later to become Kate) and Martin were all musically
gifted. Pauline played the violin, Mavis the piano and Martin
the cello. They were the studious ones, acquiring success in local
music festivals and Associated Board examinations.

In some ways the Chingford branch of the family was being left behind musically.
My parents wanted me to do better – or maybe they omitted to tell me that they were
trying to keep up with the Elmitts – so they decided that I should change teachers. I
was sent to Miss Phyllis Hiscox LRAM, a fearsome grey-haired spinster who lived in
an imposing house in Eglington Road. No *Golden Bells* allowed there. She was determined that scales and arpeggios were going to feature large in our lessons. To make
sure you learned the right fingering pattern for each key, she would produce a card
table covered in green baize, and there I would sit playing scales on the green surface
with no sound to guide me, struggling to find the right fingering and wrist position.

It didn't last long. I began to skip lessons, preferring to walk further up the road to
spend the time with Brian Gibbons, a school friend. Many years later, it might have
been this playing truant that caused my mother to lament loudly after a performance
of Handel's *Messiah* that I had conducted in St. Paul's Cathedral, 'All that money I
wasted on your piano lessons.'

Children's Church soon outgrew the small hut at the back of Crown Buildings, and
our new home was the parish hall in The Ridgeway, beside the leafy and curiously
named Organ Lane. I was now on the rota of Sunday morning pianists, though, sadly
for me, Audrey was no longer one of them.

Meanwhile, a new curate had arrived in the Chingford parish. The Reverend Reginald Box, later to become Brother Reginald SSF, was put in charge of St. Anne's, a dual-purpose corrugated iron mission hut in Chingford Hatch, about a mile away from our Beresford Road home. Someone had told him that I played hymns on the piano, and he asked my parents if I might be available to play the harmonium for the Services at St. Anne's. A few weeks later, towards the end of 1946, I made my very first appearance as a church organist, and at the end of twelve months I was handed an envelope in which there was a £1 note: my first salary as a musician. Riches indeed!

Situated near the local railway level crossing, St. Anne's wasn't really a church building in the usual style. At one end there was a set of sliding shutters enclosing a small sanctuary, and at the opposite end was a stage. A hall during the week, it was used by the local scouts and cubs (the 7th Chingford troop) for their weekly meetings. I was soon persuaded to join them, and during those years I went on camping trips to the coastal wilds of Essex and to Guernsey (Channel Islands), as well as gaining useful performing experience as a pianist for several of their 'Gang Shows'.

St. Anne's Church, Chingford Hatch, c. 1948

Near the front of the hall, and up against the wall adjacent to the window in the picture at left, was a worn-out harmonium, which, on Sundays, was pushed out and turned around, so that I could see the sanctuary as I played for the Services. Our hymn book was *The English Hymnal,* very different from *Golden Bells*, with a mixture of plainsong melodies and adapted folk tunes, most of which were then new to me. This was to be my musical world for several years. There was no choir, and I, a boy of 12 and a non-singer, was not in the least bit interested in starting one.

2

E4 to E17
1945–1950

Early in 1945, I sat the 11-plus examination to determine which school I would attend after Richmond House. A year earlier, Wendy had contracted rheumatic fever and was in no fit state to pass the exam. She went to the local secondary modern school in Wellington Avenue, but was not happy there and moved to the Technical College in Walthamstow.

Meanwhile, I managed to get into the school of my parents' choice, Sir George Monoux (pronounced 'Monarchs') Grammar School, Walthamstow E17, some four miles from where we lived in Chingford. The examination took place at the local Chingford County High School, where at one time I thought I would like to go. But it was co-educational, and with my none-too-good behavioural record at co-ed Richmond House School, my parents thought that the discipline and ethos of an all-boys school would suit me better.

As it so happened, I was to miss the start of the new school in September; that week we were on a family holiday in Folkestone, Kent. How well I remember turning up at Sir George Monoux after all the new boys had started and finding that they were already into the school routine. I had no textbooks and had to sit at a rickety old desk that others had tried and decided they didn't want. Not an auspicious start.

The forms were divided into M, G, and S (**M**onoux **G**rammar **S**chool), and it was said that the brightest boys were in the M form, the not-quite-so-brights in the G form, and, as we used to

Early September 1945, on the beach at Folkestone. I am wearing my new school tie!

put it somewhat indelicately, the 'no-hopers' in the S form. I was put into Form 1M, where our form mistress was Miss James, who also taught us the basics of French with a delightfully gentle and friendly approach.

This was the period when male teachers were either still in the Forces or gradually returning after demobilisation, and it was the military approach, style and gait of T.C. Taylor (Tubby Taylor to us) that struck fear into our young hearts. Striding down the stone-flagged corridor in his demobilisation-issue raincoat, and still holding his Major's stick of authority, his voice would boom out, 'Quick test – take down what is given,' and before he was halfway through the classroom door, we would be frantically writing down his instructions (6 x 13, or 3/5 of 60 etc.), hoping that some of the answers to the ten questions might be correct. There was no way of cheating since our books had to be passed to another boy for marking. Strangely enough, I was quite adept at mental arithmetic and managed to keep my head above water, though I was to flounder later on when faced with more complex mathematical problems.

We might have been terrified of Tubby Taylor, but that was nothing like the fear we were later to experience from the Latin master, Dr. P.G. Reaney. Known to all the boys as 'Kip', he had seriously damaged one eye in what we were told was a rugby playing accident, and it was a terrifying bloodshot sight to us 12-year-olds. He would think nothing of walking up and down between the rows of desks and unmercifully pulling the hair of any miscreant (such as myself).

Latin and I did not get on together, and a couple of years later I was able to give it up and concentrate on music as a subject for my General Schools Certificate. Of the other subjects, French seemed to be my strongest, and science (chemistry, physics, and biology) my weakest. Somewhere in the middle were English, geography, and history, but none of my results in these really justified my remaining in the M class, though somehow I did until the end of my time at the school.

With the help of friends, I usually managed to present a better school report than the one given to me to take home to my parents on the last day of term. We'd retreat to a suitably quiet place in nearby Lloyd Park, and get to work with Sloan's Ink Eradicator and a supply of fountain pens filled with different shades of blue and black ink. With them we were able to delete the lowly D and E grades and substitute Bs and Cs, even though we couldn't always successfully alter the comments that followed. The headmaster's comments at the foot of each report were usually written in red ink (for good work), blue ink (for average work), or green ink (for poor work), and it required considerable skill with the ink eradicator to alter these successfully. Somehow we succeeded in substituting a different colour ink and slightly changing his wording.

But the original report was correct. I was not working hard enough. I was lazy, badly behaved and always seemed to be in Saturday morning detention. As Mr. Stirrup, the Headmaster, read out the list of Saturday detentions at our Thursday morning assembly, he would come to my name, '… and Rose has the most detentions… Five…' he would say. 'What we've come to expect,' he would add with a resigned tone to his voice.

The company I kept was doubtful. We were the rebels against the system; we were the ones who would absent ourselves from lessons and hide in the toilets; we were the ones who would use our dinner money to buy cigarettes; we were the ones who would play truant; we were the ones who would alter our school reports so that our parents would think that our grades were better than they actually were. And often, we were downright dishonest, stealing other people's belongings, and stealing from shops as well. Homework was left undone, and far too often I was standing outside Mr. Stirrup's office, waiting for him to administer the cane where it hurt most – six of the best across the palms of my hands. In some strange way this gave me some 'street cred' amongst the rest of the class. My hands may have been covered in weals and too red and tingling to hold a pen properly, but I was one of the select few who had survived a visit to the dreaded H.M.'s study!

∾

Music began to play a larger part in my life through meeting John Forsdyke at school. John came from a family of musical brothers, and since his voice had broken, he had taken up the flute and had also come to St. Anne's mission church to try to recruit some youngsters to form a choir. He gathered a small group of boys who met after school one day each week. In those days it was relatively easy to attract boys to a choir, and John soon had them in cassocks and surplices, ready to sing at the Sunday Service. He did not stay at St. Anne's for very long, and at that stage I had no knowledge of choir training, nor was I inclined (or able) to take on a group of boys nearly of my own age. The boys gradually drifted away, and we were back to congregational singing at the Services.

John had introduced me to Leo, one of his two elder brothers, and that introduction was to influence the course of music in my life throughout those impressionable years. Leo was a student at the Royal College of Music in London, where his principal study was piano, and his second study was organ with Osborne Peasgood, Sub-Organist of Westminster Abbey. Leo also attended appreciation-of-music classes given by the distinguished composer, Herbert Howells – once smuggling me into one of them; not that I understood much of what Dr. Howells was saying.

The Forsdyke house in Dudley Road became a second home. I was fascinated by the grand piano in the front room, as well as Leo's large collection of 78 rpm records (the usual format in those days). These were played on an HMV record player, on which the pick-up head used Imhof fibre needles, sharpened after each playing by a small grindstone driven by contact with the turntable.

But more than all these new delights, I made my first acquaintance with piano duets, providing a rather inept lower part to Leo's expertise in the upper part. We'd play movements from the piano duet versions of Peter Warlock's *Capriol Suite*; Gabriel Fauré's *Dolly Suite*; Claude Debussy's *Petite Suite*; Edward Elgar's own transcription of his *Serenade for Strings*; as well as the extended and more difficult duet version of Roger Quilter's *Children's Overture*. To say that I was inadequate in technique (and also sight-reading) is a bit of an understatement, but I dare to think that Leo could sense some sort of innate musicality within me, and he was not only patience personified, but also always encouraging to this young would-be musician.

Leo was also an avid concertgoer, and as well as taking me to many Henry Wood Promenade Concerts at the Royal Albert Hall, we also went on trips to Cambridge, where we attended Evensong in King's College Chapel. This was the great awakening for me. Aside from a few 78 rpm gramophone records, I'd never heard singing of that quality. It was like being in heaven, and that special King's sound from Boris Ord's choir would be indelibly imprinted in my brain for many years to come.

Then there was the music in the school, both in class lessons and some short piano recitals given in the school hall. Mr. L.C. Belchambers (no prizes for guessing his nickname – Belchie) was the school's music master. Ageing and grey-haired, he was noted for putting his hand in his pocket during classes and apparently fiddling with his private parts. He was also adept at throwing the board-rubber with deadly accuracy, but apparently oblivious to the mayhem in the class when he sat behind the upright piano, hoping that we would join in such songs as: *Sir Eglamore, that valiant knight, fa-la, lanky-down dilly*. Not much chance of me taking part. I still had no interest in singing whatsoever.

Once a week, just before break, we'd have a short mid-morning piano recital in the school hall, usually given by H.J. 'Lizzie' Hyde, the French teacher. An able musician with a prodigious keyboard technique, he could race through a Chopin Polonaise as well as many professional pianists. His French lessons were lively and participative, and occasionally he would trot out his favourite motto: 'Rose,' he would ask, 'what is life?' He would immediately answer with a knowing smile, 'It all depends upon the liver.' Some of the boys appreciated this *double entendre*, though we often wondered if he might be a secret drinker.

There were also some outstanding musicians among the boys in the school: Donald Purchese was an accomplished clarinettist and went on to form his own jazz quintet, often featuring in BBC radio broadcasts; the two Alans – Brown and Hemmings – were fine pianists, and both contributed to the mid-morning music recitals. Alan Brown

went on to the Guildhall School of Music, whilst in 1952, Alan Hemmings was elected
to the coveted organ scholarship at St. John's College, Cambridge. Former pupils of
the school also include the conductor Sir John Pritchard, the legendary jazz musician
Sir John Dankworth, the accompanist Richard Nunn, and the pianist and composer
Michael Nyman.

And where was young Rose amongst this plethora of talent? Nowhere. That is,
until February 1949, when the headmaster decided to hold a Founder's Day Service in
the local parish church of St. Mary, Walthamstow, and I was invited to play the organ
for it. The news that a 14-year-old was to
play the three-manual pipe organ for the
Service was picked up by the local newspaper, *The Walthamstow Guardian*, and
from there it was featured in the *London
Evening News*. I had sort of 'arrived' as
a musical personality in the school, even
though I was still getting up to five detentions every week!

The Organist

A 14-YEAR-OLD boy, Barry Rose,
official organist of St. Anne's
Church, Chingford Hatch, is to
play at the Founders' Day service
at his school, the Sir George
Monoux Grammar School, Walthamstow

The London Evening News, *February 1949*

In mid-1950 there was great excitement at St. Anne's: we were to have a new
priest-in-charge and he would be living in a house that the diocese had just purchased.
Simeon Robert (Bob) Birchnall had been a curate at St. Wilfrid's Church, Harrogate,
which, as I later discovered, had a choir programme very much on the lines of English
cathedrals. I was just 16 when he and his wife Sheila turned up in a tiny old Austin 7,
and it soon became obvious that Bob was not just a priest, but also an accomplished
singer.

The first thing he did was to form a small church choir. Bob sang tenor and Sheila
sang alto, and soon he'd built up an eight-voice group, all from the parish or nearby.
It was my very first experience of watching and learning how to take a choir practice,
and soon the choir was singing a short anthem at Evensong each Sunday.

At the church's 1951 Carol Service I would make my very first gramophone recordings, accompanying the choir on the piano (by then the old worn-out harmonium
was no longer usable). Ever since seeing and hearing Leo's vast collection of 78 rpm
records, I'd wondered how these were made, and by chance I discovered a firm in
London's Piccadilly that offered recording facilities on a mobile basis. They would
come and record you, for a suitable fee, of course.

I had won a small amount of money in a Festival of Britain talent competition,
and with that and the annual payment I was receiving from St. Anne's, I was able to
pay for the firm to come and record our Carol Service, exactly as it took place. There
was no chance of a rehearsal or balance test. They turned up an hour or so before the

St. Anne's Church Choir, c. 1950. I am on the extreme left of the middle row

Service, placed a microphone on a stand near the choir, and one in front of the lectern from where the lessons would be read. Wires trailed to their van parked outside, and the carols, together with some of the readings, were cut directly onto soft shellac discs. If any of the choir wanted to listen, we'd have to pass them around. The problem with the discs was that the coating was extremely soft, and most pick-ups in those days used steel needles which gradually gouged out the surface, causing endless crackle, clicks and bumps at the next playing. By the time they were returned to me it was difficult to hear any of the music above the surface noise. But what those records had done was to kindle a fascination in the art of recording which would stay with me for the rest of my life.

I was now spending more and more time with Leo at Dudley Road, often staying overnight, where three of us – Leo, his younger brother Tony, and I – would share a bed. Leo had been appointed Organist and Choirmaster of nearby St. Luke's Church in Walthamstow, and on one occasion was invited to play at St. Saviour's Church, a mile or so away in Markhouse Road. St. Saviour's had sustained bomb damage during the war and had been refurbished, including a new two-manual organ by Henry Willis. Still clear in my memory is that recital, in which Leo was joined by two fellow students from the Royal College of Music, both singers, and both to become world famous in their field: Gerald English (tenor) and Maurice Bevan (baritone). At that time both Gerald and Maurice were members of St. Paul's Cathedral Choir, and as I sat in the audience on that evening, little did I realise that nearly 30 years later, Maurice would be singing in the choir that I would be directing at St. Paul's.

Meanwhile, back in Chingford, my young life had been turned upside down by adolescent love. In the congregation at St. Anne's was a very pretty fair-haired girl about my age. I found out that her name was Jill and that she lived in Ashdown Road, a few streets away from St. Anne's. Every Sunday evening she would be sitting in the same spot waiting for Evensong to begin, and here was this young organist, hoping to ask her for a date. It turned out that her father was a colleague of one of my uncles, and in the end that opened the door to an introduction.

This was the first serious romance in my life and was to last for more than five years. Jill and I had many happy times together, though I was far too slow and shy to take our relationship seriously. In the end she fell for a handsome young man called Tony, married him, and emigrated to Canada, whilst I turned my admiring glances towards her sister Jackie. Somehow you never forget your first real sweetheart, and many years later when we were both in our late 60s, Jill and I made contact again by email, meeting up in Charleston, South Carolina, where I was then working.

Music of another kind also came into my life, at the Regal Cinema, Highams Park, about three miles from my home, and just down the road from St. Anne's – one of two cinemas owned and run by the Brooke-Green family from nearby Woodford; the second being our local cinema in Chingford – the Doric.

A cinema organ was a whole new world to me, and I managed to get access to it in a very roundabout way. Raymond Grogan, a school friend, had a part-time job as a projectionist at the Doric, and sometimes he managed to smuggle me up into the cinema's projection room. There, I would help to rewind the large reels of film as they came off the projector and lace up the next reel of film, or simply hang around on the outside parapet, watching the long queues waiting for the next showing.

The head projectionist was Ted Cummings, a rough and ready character, and a heavy smoker. He spent his time between the two cinemas, and for some reason he took a liking to me, offering me the chance to go to the projection room at the Regal, provided I brought him some cigarettes. It was there that I got my first sight of the cinema organ. Built by the local firm of R. Spurden Rutt, it came up from the pit on its motorised lift, lights flashing and changing colour in their glass case, as Mr. Brooke-Green himself played popular melodies of the day until the next film began.

After the harmonium at St. Anne's, here was something completely different both in sight and sound (and especially in the sound), with its many orchestral effects – including most of the percussion section: bells, xylophone, celesta, snare drum, cymbal etc. – all controlled by the organist's feet. Mr. Brooke-Green was a most able

The R. Spurden Rutt organ from the Regal Cinema, Highams Park

player and allowed me access to the organ on some Saturday mornings. After his brilliant demonstrations, my efforts were very amateurish. Nevertheless, he invited me to play at the Regal during the week, between the end of a film and the start of the newsreel or the trailers for forthcoming attractions. By doing this I instinctively learned to modulate from one key to another, so that there would be a seamless join between the music at the end of one film and the Metro-Goldwyn-Mayer fanfare at the start of the next.

It was my mother who introduced me to great choral works. Once or twice a year the Chingford United Choir would perform a well-known oratorio in the local Methodist Church, accompanied by organ and piano, usually in duet. The organ was played by the church Organist, Ethel Butcher, and the piano by Frank Rushton FRCO (Fellow of the Royal College of Organists), a well-known local teacher. It was the first time I heard such works as Handel's *Messiah* and Mendelssohn's *Elijah*, and the enterprising choir committee brought nationally renowned soloists to sing, including Isobel Baillie (soprano), Richard Lewis (tenor), and Owen Brannigan (bass). I would sit in the pew following my score, little realising that I, too, would one day conduct these very works. The same is true of John Stainer's *The Crucifixion*, a work with which I would become closely associated in later years. Every Good Friday it was sung in the parish church, and either my mother or my father would take me there, give me a vocal score and help me to follow it.

We now had a harmonium in the front room at home. My father had bought it from an antique shop on one of his trips for Bishop and Brooke, and later it would be moved to St. Anne's to accompany the Services. Although I was not taking the piano seriously, my mother and father arranged for me to have lessons with the Organist of Chingford Parish Church, L.W. Tracey-Arkell ARCO, in the hope that I might learn to play at least one instrument reasonably well.

The problem in learning the organ is having access to a suitable instrument for practice, and since my Saturday morning lessons were on the parish church organ, that was the obvious instrument to use. The No. 38 bus from school in Walthamstow arrived back in Chingford around 4.45 p.m., by which time, in the autumn and winter months, it was dark. Apart from the light on the organ console, a large, dark and empty church is a frightening place to be alone, and I had no idea who was coming in and out when the doors creaked open and shut.

Chingford Parish Church

A charge was made for practising on the organ. The money was put into an envelope, in which was a card you signed, saying how much time you'd spent at the organ. Initially, I paid up, but soon began not only to spend my own practice money on cigarettes etc. but also to take some money out of the envelope as well. The parish clerk was a rather severe and tall lady called Miss Hart, and she would suddenly appear from nowhere, looking like some sort of witch in her black cloak and biretta-style hat. Though she was puzzled by the lack of money in the practice-time envelope, mercifully she never caught me red-handed, though I think she had her suspicions. Later, a new combination padlock appeared on the organ. The console was locked, and only those allowed to practise knew the combination. It was time to be more careful.

Dutifully I ploughed my way through John Stainer's tutor *The Organ*, graduating from there to J.S. Bach's *Eight Short Preludes and Fugues*, some not-too-difficult Rheinberger, and a set of preludes and postludes by F.W. Wadely, who was then Organist of Carlisle Cathedral. Mr. Arkell was a patient and kind teacher, and several years later we met again, this time in Alton, Hampshire, to where he had retired, and where I, as the Organist of Guildford Cathedral, was giving a celebrity recital in the local parish church. He was in the audience that evening, and afterwards we had a long chat, during which I was able to thank him for the start he had given me.

One of the other names on the practice-money card at church was F.G. Fillmore, and one day when I was practising, Mr. Fillmore appeared, listened appreciatively and struck up a conversation. Fred Fillmore must have been all of 60 years of age and had recently retired from his full-time job as a telephone engineer. An enthusiastic amateur organist, he and his wife lived in New Road, about two miles from my Beresford Road home. Some Saturdays we would go on an 'organ crawl', usually on the No. 38 bus route, to such places as Clapton Park Congregational Church, known as The Round Chapel, and Holy Trinity Church, Cloudesley Square, Islington, where we would spend a happy afternoon playing on the three-manual Henry Speechly organ. Since I didn't have much money, all of these trips were generously financed by Fred, and afterwards we'd usually go back to his house in Chingford for supper.

Perhaps his greatest coup was in July 1950, when he gained access to the mighty organ in London's Royal Albert Hall. I had seen and heard it when Leo had taken me to the Henry Wood Promenade Concerts, but never did I think I would have the opportunity to play it. One Thursday afternoon we had an hour on the huge instrument. I shudder to think what it cost Fred, but he was always generosity itself to this young 16-year-old would-be organist. Someone (I guess it might have been him) tipped off the local paper that we'd been at the Albert Hall, and about a week later a column appeared, with the heading, 'Chingford's "genius" fulfilled ambition'!

Chingford's "Genius Fulfilled Ambition

SIXTEEN - YEAR - OLD Barry Rose, of 85, Beresford-road, Chingford, who has been described by many experienced organists as a genius, fulfilled his greatest ambition on Thursday. He had the singular honour of being allowed to play on the great organ at the Albert Hall.

The Walthamstow Guardian,
July 1950

On a summer Saturday, with nothing much to do, I caught the bus to High Beach, a small village in the very heart of Epping Forest. As I walked past the church, I heard the sound of organ music. Naturally I went in to listen, and met the church Organist, Sidney Carlton Roberts, who, it turned out, also lived in Chingford. 'Can you play the organ?' he asked. 'Yes,' I replied, so he let me try out the lovely two-manual Father Willis instrument, situated at floor level at the back of the nave. We got talking, and he asked if I might be available to play for some Sunday morning Services on days when he needed to be away. I said yes, and so began an association with the church which was to last for a few years.

I had a bicycle, but somehow it never seemed to be in working order, and though there was a Sunday bus service available in the summer months, the only answer in winter was to walk to High Beach, over three miles from Chingford by road, or about one and a half miles by cutting through Epping Forest. As time progressed, I was asked if I could stay and also play for their Evensong. In the summer months it wasn't possible because of the 6.30 p.m. Evensong at St. Anne's, but during the winter, Evensong at High Beach was brought forward to 3.00 p.m. and that would allow me to be back in time to play at St. Anne's.

By the end of a November or December Evensong it was dark – very dark. There was no street lighting of any kind between the church and the road where I lived in Chingford: nearly two miles of pitch black to negotiate through the middle of Epping Forest, sometimes without a torch. After leaving church, and having walked a few yards down the road, I would come to a small refreshment kiosk bathed in a welcome pool of gaslight, where I fortified myself for the journey ahead with a warming cup of OXO. The owners of the kiosk were members of the congregation, and I think they took pity on this young man who then had to do the lonely trek through the forest.

It was terrifying. The ground was often sodden underfoot, your shoes filled with water and you couldn't see overhanging branches and brambles until they had bruised or cut you. Getting back

High Beach Church organ

to Chingford in time for tea was not so much a matter of navigational skills, but more of blind panic and instinct. Sometimes you could hear the foxes or deer scuttling away as you approached, and every twig you trod on sounded like some forest demon taking a pot-shot at you.

Organists of High Beach Church

But whatever the disadvantages of the long trek there and back, playing the organ at High Beach was a joy, and somehow I felt more at home there than I did in my local parish church in Chingford. The association with High Beach would cease when I joined the RAF in 1952, though I did return there later with the choir of St. Anne's to make another set of recordings. My name is still inscribed on the list of Organists – from 1951 to 1952 – by which time I'd left school and set out on a career in insurance. As my father had said: 'A proper job'.

3

A Proper Job
1950-1951

In the summer of 1950 I sat the School Certificate examination, the precursor of the GCSE examinations that started the following year. The grades offered to successful candidates were Pass, Credit, and Distinction. Five or more credits or distinctions would offer matriculation exemption and a presumed later entry into university.

There was no way I was going to achieve that level, but after a crash-course of revision in the garden at 85 Beresford Road, I managed to achieve credits in English, French and music, with passes in mathematics and religious instruction. My scores were a partial rebuttal of the headmaster's closing remark on my school report of that term:

'I think it is doubtful whether he has done enough work to satisfy the examiners.'

The results were not enough to justify my staying on at Sir George Monoux School, and neither did they want me to stay. So, in July 1950, at the age of 16 years and two months, I left school with no career prospects and no real idea of what I wanted to do… That was not quite true, since I thought I might become an organ builder.

A year or so earlier I had managed to persuade the Leyton organ-building firm of Robert Spurden Rutt to let me assist at their factory during school holidays. A bus ride from Chingford each morning would get me there in time for an 8.30 a.m. start, and I would help with everything from making the tea to demonstrating assembled organs in their workshop to would-be clients.

Occasionally Mr. Rutt would ferry the possible customer and me to a church where he had built the organ, and I'd demonstrate the various stops in return for a half-a-crown 'fee' – about 12.5p in to-day's currency. The money was very use-ful, and I really believed that a career in organ building might be for me.

My father had other ideas. 'Why don't you get a proper job,' he said, 'work-ing in a bank or an insurance office?' Robin Sims, one of my school friends, had obtained a job at the head office of W.H. Smith & Son Ltd., the stationers and booksellers. 'Come and work here,' he said. I went for an interview and was accepted into the insurance section of their estates department.

Strand House, the head office, was lo-cated in Portugal Street, London WC2, just off Kingsway, and the estates de-partment was on the second floor. From there, the company's shops and wholesale

warehouses were bought and maintained, new premises were designed in the drawing office, and maintenance contracts were sorted out for shop refurbishing and paint-ing. Our small section was responsible for all aspects of insurance on the company's properties – buildings, contents, public liability – as well as the many delivery vans. Situated at various wholesale depots through the country, these vans were responsible for the speedy delivery of newspapers to the WHS shops in the area, and because of the urgency were often involved in accidents, either with other vehicles, or skidding on wet or icy roads in the dead of night as they raced from one shop to the next. My job was to collate the insurance claim-forms that came into our office, make sure that estimates for repair were obtained, and then forward everything on to the insurers.

In our open plan office, I was allocated a desk where I worked under the direction of Mr. John Oliver, who himself worked under the boss of our section, Mr. L.A. Stainton. It was suggested that I should study for the Associateship of the Chartered Insurance Institute (ACII), and I dutifully enrolled for a correspondence course through the Metropolitan College in St. Albans. It was not long before I began to realise that the world of insurance was not really for me, and the exercises and essays were left undone and unposted.

Mr. Oliver (ACII) was genuinely interested in my musical background, and al-though I lost contact with him when I left the firm, he did come and visit me later at

St. Paul's, where I could sense his pride that this young lad he'd taken on and encouraged all those years ago had found his true vocation.

Round the corner from Strand House were a series of patents offices, and in one of these worked Mr. Southgate, an organist from Woodford who played for the daily weekday evening Services at the famous church of St. Martin-in-the-Fields. I had previously met Mr. Southgate at Chingford Old Church where he had been the Organist, and soon I was standing in for him at St. Martin's, on an organ that had been rebuilt by Robert Spurden Rutt.

The evening Services at St. Martin's lasted about 25 minutes and were mostly attended by workers on their way home or visitors to the capital. They usually consisted of two hymns, a reading and some prayers, and at the end I played a short and reflective voluntary. The organ console was situated at the north-east end of the gallery which runs around three sides of the church, and it had stops which lit up in different colours when they were engaged: yellow for the foundation stops, red for the reed stops, and green for the manual couplers. To anyone passing by it must have looked rather like the twinkling coloured lights on the end of Southend-on-Sea Pier.

It was Mr. Oliver who introduced me to the Strand House Choir and their conductor, James Roff. Soon I was playing for some of their rehearsals. James had a fine, natural tenor voice and would demonstrate Henry Purcell's *Soul of the World* at the top of his voice, making it sound more like a Verdi aria than something more delicate written about 200 years earlier. Gradually I became more involved with the choir, and when they were to perform John Stainer's Passiontide meditation *The Crucifixion*, they asked if I'd play the organ for it. We gave performances in St. Francis Church, West Wickham, Kent, where Dick Goldsmith (one of the basses) was a member of the church choir; Holy Trinity Church, Kingsway, London; and also at Hambleden Parish Church, Buckinghamshire. Although a small village, this was a prestigious venue for us since Viscount Hambleden, who lived in nearby Hambleden Court, was the managing director of W.H. Smith & Son and would be coming to the performance.

It was through a member of the Strand House Choir that I took part in two contrasting events during the 1951 Festival of Britain celebrations. The first was a talent competition at the firm's annual sports day at their Wembley sports ground, which I managed to win. The second was much more high profile, and an exciting step into the world of professional music making.

St. John's Church, Waterloo Road, is situated a few yards from the South Bank Festival site, and it was there that a performance of *The Man born to be King*, by Dorothy Sayers, took place. Originally written for broadcast by the BBC in 1941, this was a series of 12 plays now being presented on six evenings in the church, complete with members of the original BBC cast. The incidental choral and organ music had been specially written by Eric Taylor, a former organ scholar at Christ Church, Oxford, and later Professor of Music at Durham University.

I was invited to play the organ, and was handed a heap of newly written manuscripts, mainly choral interspersions to highlight the drama at that moment. The modern and adventurous musical idiom was completely new to me, and I spent many anxious moments both at work and at home trying to decipher the handwritten scores, as well as learning the notes in time for the next performance. Taking place in the mid-evenings, it was a quick dash from work to the church for a short rehearsal, and although there was no

St. John's Church, Waterloo Road

payment, it was such valuable experience, even if it did mean getting back home late at night.

Despite all this music making, it still looked as though I had to be content with a career in insurance. Music would have to remain a hobby. But for how long? Any decision would have to be put on hold since the two years that most young men of my age dreaded were now on the horizon: National Service.

4

National Service
Royal Air Force 1952-1954

In March 1952 an official brown envelope arrived at 85 Beresford Road. Bearing the OHMS[1] crest, it was the notice that I would be required to register for two years National Service, to begin soon after my 18th birthday in May. Sometime after registration there would be interviews and a comprehensive medical at an official central London government building near Russell Square. Whilst there appeared to be some element of choice as to which of the three services one could choose, it was said that of the three, the Royal Navy was the most difficult to get into, the Royal Air Force next, whilst the Army was a last resort for all those who didn't make it into the other two. I opted for the Navy as my first choice, and after that the Royal Air Force.

In late May I went for my medical in London. Many of my friends were doing the same, and all sorts of theories were put forward as to how we might hoodwink the doctors into deciding that we were unfit for military service, the favourites being colour-blindness and flat feet. The doctors, of course, were well prepared for our excuses, and had ways of getting around such deceit. I hadn't got the courage to try to get exemption, and was passed medically fit and assigned to the Royal Air Force as AC2 (Aircraftman 2nd Class) Rose, with the service number 2566832.

On 22nd July, armed with an official travel warrant, I left Beresford Road, caught the train to Liverpool Street and the underground to Euston Station, where I made my way to the train that would stop at Warrington, Lancashire (now Cheshire). There were lots of other people of my age in the compartment, all looking apprehensive. I guessed that they too were bound for the reception centre at RAF Padgate, a camp for basic training, colloquially known as 'square-bashing'.

On arrival at Warrington Station we were herded onto an RAF coach, painted in that shade of blue with which we would become so familiar over the next two years. Already we were getting used to being shouted at and ordered around. Once at Padgate, we were marched to the bedding store where we were issued with sheets, blankets and pillowcases, as well as a knife, fork, spoon, mug, and a metal container

---

1   On *Her* Majesty's Service. Elizabeth had acceded to the throne on 6th February 1952.

known as a mess-tin. From there it was straight to the NAAFI (Navy, Army and Air Force Institute) for a welcome evening meal, during which we were talked to, or rather lectured by a Flight Sergeant, one of the senior ranks amongst the non-commissioned officers. He didn't mince his words. His basic message was obey orders and look smart; if it moves, salute it; if it stands

First stop: RAF Padgate

still, paint it! We never found out if he was joking or not when he said that our tea, which did taste a little unusual, had been laced with bromide to keep our sexual urges at bay.

From there, we were marched to a wooden hut – known as a billet – in which there were up to 20 beds arranged in dormitory-fashion, ten along each wall, with two private rooms at the end in which the corporals-in-charge slept. Outside, under a partially covered walkway, were communal lavatories, wash basins, and showers with little or no hot water. It was going to be a rude awakening for many of us who had come from comfortable and easy lives at home. Each of us had a small locker by the side of our bed, and in order to keep any personal belongings secure we'd need to buy a padlock from the NAAFI. The floor was highly polished linoleum, and we soon got used to the fact that it was better to shuffle along on old pieces of blanket, rather than mark it and then have to polish it again and again at what was known as 'bull night' twice each week.

During the next couple of days we were measured for the RAF uniform, both battledress and formal wear. We were also issued with shirts, a tie, underwear, handkerchiefs and socks, together with a kit for darning them (known as a housewife), and a heavy pair of black lace-up boots, the toe caps of which were dull and matt. By the time we were due to be on the parade ground the toe caps of the boots would need to be shined to a mirror finish, achieved over several days, with hours of buffing with black shoe polish, a cloth and lots of spittle. Next, we collected two small discs on which our service number had been engraved – they were to be worn around our necks at all times, and would help with identification in case of serious injury or death, one of them being indestructible by fire. Finally, we were issued with a large kitbag on which our service number had been stencilled. Having stuffed everything into it, we returned to our billet. Other essentials such as razor blades, black boot polish and brass cleaner would need to be bought at the NAAFI, so it was a good thing that I'd brought what was left of my last week's wages at W.H. Smith & Son Ltd. with me.

The full impact of what was to come was finally brought home when we parcelled up our civilian clothes ready to be sent back home. No-one was looking forward to the endless, and mindless, hours of drill out on the square, and in conversation with the guy in the next bed to me, he said, 'I think I'll try for aircrew and get out of here as quick as possible.' I asked him how I might be able to try. 'Easy,' he said. 'When we go to the education centre tomorrow, simply ask to be put down for aircrew selection, and they'll probably send you to RAF Hornchurch for tests and interview.' He was right. In less than a week's time we were travelling south again, this time in full RAF uniform, *en route* to Hornchurch. Somehow I managed to make a quick diversion home and stay overnight.

Chingford is only 13 miles from Hornchurch, and I got there on Monday morning, just in time for the intelligence and aptitude tests. I must have done reasonably well, since when the results were published, I was on the list of successful candidates. Returning to RAF Padgate, those who were unsuccessful would commence 12 weeks of gruelling square-bashing and hard physical training, whilst we would be sent to Cranwell, where we would be further tested for suitability as pilots, navigators, flight engineers, or air gunners.

Cranwell is a small village, some 15 miles south of the city of Lincoln, and whilst the cream of the career-seeking aircrew talent was housed in a magnificent, classically styled college, we, the National Service 'new boys', were herded into huts similar to those at RAF Padgate, though with better facilities, and with non-commissioned officers who addressed us as 'Mr.' rather than 'you 'orrible little man'. We now wore two white flashes on the lapels of our uniform, and a white disc behind our cap badge indicating that we were officers-in-training.

After two weeks at Cranwell, we were split into smaller groups, ours being moved 15 miles north of Lincoln to RAF Kirton in Lindsey, for what was known as 'grading'. Through that process we would either be selected as a pilot or navigator, and part of it was to be taken up in a Tiger Moth aircraft to see how we took to flying. The Tiger Moth was a two-seater aircraft (known as a biplane) originally built in the 1930s by the de Havilland Aircraft Company. Open to the elements, the passenger or co-pilot would sit behind the pilot. Each of the officer cadets was given a twenty-minute flight by a qualified

instructor, in my case Mr. Drazga, a Polish pilot who had served in the RAF during
the war.

I was terrified of flying. I'd never been happy on the swings or roundabouts when
the visiting funfair had come to Chingford, and the possibility of doing the loop-
the-loop or a spin during the flight was more than I could take. We communicated
through the microphone in the mask attached to our flying helmets, and since I was
then feeling quite sick, he aborted the flight, landing well before the allotted time. In
the following interview with the selection officer, I saw him write LMF on my report
(Low Moral Fibre).

That was it. There was no hope of becoming a pilot. I'd have to train to be a
navigator, though they had yet to find out that mathematics was not my strong
point! Grading completed, we were taken by train to a holding barracks at Bootle,
in Liverpool, and from there we boarded a ship to the
Isle of Man and No. 1 Officer Cadet Training Unit, RAF
Jurby Head, located at the remote north-west corner of
the island.

Here we were scheduled to spend the next six months,
receiving basic training in navigational techniques in daily lectures and classes. Added to this, every officer cadet
was required to keep a day-to-day diary, reflecting not
just personal but also national issues, and this was peri-
odically inspected and marked by the officer in charge of
our billet.

There were also the inevitable drill sessions (although
far fewer than those left behind at Padgate would be enduring), survival exercises and
initiative tests. One of mine consisted of building a raft from old oil drums and planks
of wood and getting a group of fellow officer cadets across a deep lake.

All this time I was nursing a secret: I could not swim – something essential to every
member of aircrew. There had been some swimming and survival-on-water sessions
at Kirton in Lindsey, but somehow I had managed to get out of these. Up to now my
secret had been safe, even though I could well have drowned had my raft not floated!

Christmas came, and we were allowed a week's leave. Before travelling home, I
was walking past one of the billets and heard the most lovely harmonised singing of
Christmas carols. I poked my head round the door to find that they were being sung
by a group of choral scholars who had been pre-elected to Oxford and Cambridge
colleges, where they would be going after National Service. Back in Chingford, I
played the Christmas Services at St. Anne's mission church, and all too soon, leave
came to an end, travelling back to RAF Jurby at the beginning of January 1953.

Navigator training continued in classroom sessions, and a priority was to keep the comprehensive daily diary up to date. Much of my commenting in early 1953 was on the breaking news that the Queen's Coronation, in June of that year, would be televised. Being the very first time this had happened, there was huge fore planning, including maps and diagrams of where cameras and microphones were to be placed in Westminster Abbey. Already it seemed that I had developed a fascination with broadcasting, and especially with sound-balancing. My diary included several drawings of the proposed BBC layouts, gaining high marks from my assessors.

There was little chance to make music, though on a few occasions I did manage to walk to the remote Jurby church and try the organ. Meanwhile, at the camp, there was a talent contest, and with two other officer cadets we formed a small jazz trio to take part. It wasn't really my scene, and besides, there was a superb and natural jazz pianist already on site, though he didn't show any interest in entering. In the end, I played a version of a pop song which I'd turned into a Tchaikovsky concerto, a Mozart sonata, and a Chinese-style rhapsody, and it won the competition.

Final exams came and I failed to make the grade, mainly caused by my lack of application and understanding of some mathematical principles. Even though I'd been pre-measured for the smart new uniform, I would not now be an officer; I would simply revert to being AC2 Rose. We failures, and there were a few of us, were dispatched to RAF Wilmslow in Cheshire, where we would now be subjected to the square-bashing that we'd fought so hard to avoid.

Never an operational airfield, even though there was a Spitfire at the entrance gates, RAF Wilmslow was known as No. 4 School of Recruit Training. It was back to the wooden huts, the endless round of shining and polishing, and drill sessions on the square at what seemed like all hours of the day and night. In one of my few moments of relaxation, I walked past what seemed a huge aircraft hangar, and opening the door, found myself inside the station church. Over in one corner was the console for a two-manual Jardine pipe organ, and it was open. I switched on the blower and started to play hymns, only to be interrupted by the chaplain, who suddenly appeared from nowhere. I began to apologise, but he was more keen to see if I would be available to play for the Sunday Services. In conversation back in his office, I explained that I was rather out of practice and would need to spend some time learning voluntaries etc. Using his squadron leader rank, he instructed the corporal in charge of our billet to release me from square-bashing to assist in his office, whilst also giving me as much time as I needed to practise on the organ. Time at Wilmslow wouldn't be that bad after all.

A few weeks later, we were given our notices of posting, each of us being assigned to a trade. As a result of the time I had spent in the chaplain's office helping with paperwork, I was going to be a clerk, and my posting was to No. 22 FTS (Flying Training

School) Syerston, Nottinghamshire, situated on the A46 road between Newark and Nottingham. My new life was to be spent in the very hub of the station – known as Headquarters – and we clerks would be working in the orderly room. Each of us was given a specific responsibility and title, mine being Leave Clerk. It was to give me a great deal of popularity on the station, not least because I worked out a way whereby some could have more than their leave entitlement, provided they were willing to pay me money for fixing it!

We worked under the direction of long-retired Squadron Leader Sydney Searle. A Yorkshireman with a very broad accent, he was not shy about telling us off publicly: 'Aw Christ, Rose, you've dun (done) it again' could regularly be heard ringing around the office. However, he did help me to progress to LAC (Leading Aircraftman), and finally to SAC (Senior Aircraftman), both useful, not just in status, but also in pay.

It was also here, in the midst of all the daily and boring paperwork, that I would make my very first contact with another aspect of my future career: broadcasting. No. 22 Flying Training School had its own radio station – Radio Syerston – broadcasting on four evenings each week from a small studio at one end of the orderly room. I was working late one evening when two senior airmen, John Ellis and Robert Dougall, came in to open the studio and start broadcasting. Would I like to watch? It was not long before I was a regular visitor, learning how to operate the faders on the control desk and observing the way they used the microphones.

A few months later, John completed his National Service, and I took his place as a presenter at Radio Syerston. After Robert had been discharged, I assumed the responsibility of running it. Most of the output was from 78 rpm records (a mixture of pop and light classical), and there was the occasional talk from an officer or the station chaplain. I was given a budget to buy new records, keeping up with the latest releases, since these were the ones which were the most popular in the twice-weekly request programmes.

The radio station only operated on weekday evenings, which meant that I could now get home nearly every weekend, assuming there was a suitable and affordable way to do so. Sometimes the journey was by coach, sometimes by train, but usually, to save money, by hitch-hiking down the A1 Great North Road that ran through the outskirts of Newark, some six miles away from Syerston. Although we were now allowed to have civilian clothes in our lockers, I soon discovered that you got a lift more easily if you were in uniform. Usually it was in a heavy lorry, which meant a slow journey, often being dumped in the outskirts of London, miles away from Chingford. But at least it hadn't cost me a penny.

St. Anne's was now very different from that dual-purpose corrugated iron mission hall where I'd started playing the harmonium all those years ago. A new architect-designed brick church had been built, and since no space or money was available for a traditional pipe organ, we had a Compton Electrone, the first of the pipeless organs specially designed for churches – the sounds being generated by a weird and wonderful series of tone wheels housed in what looked like an oversized refrigerator. The console was placed under an arch behind the choir seats, the tonal cabinet in the clergy vestry, whilst the two large loudspeakers were concealed in specially built alcoves behind the large dossal (altar curtain).

The new church was consecrated on a Saturday afternoon in May 1953, and I was able to get a week's leave in order to be there to play for the Service. It was a splendid occasion, attended by the Bishop of Chelmsford and many other clergy from the diocese.

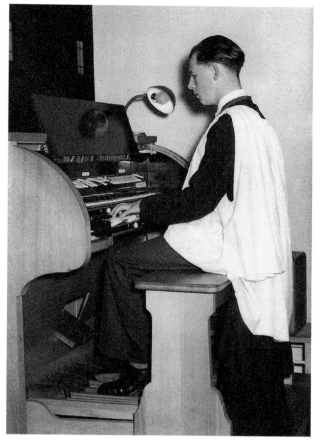

At the Compton console in the new St. Anne's Church, 1953

Now that we had the new church and organ, I was more than keen to get back to Chingford each weekend. Evensong at St. Anne's was at 6.30 p.m. which meant that there was always a frantic rush to get back home after the Service and change back into RAF uniform. It was then a race to the train from Chingford to Liverpool Street, and from there to King's Cross by tube, just in time to catch the midnight train back to Newark. Arriving around 3.00 a.m. on Monday morning, four or five of us would pile into a taxi, knowing that all we'd have in the way of sleep would be two to three hours before we'd be back at work again.

With just a small harmonium in the chapel at Syerston, those weekends at home were the only chance I now had to play a 'proper' organ, though once a week I was able to hear the real thing as a member of a congregation. The imposing and large

15th century church of St. Mary Magdalene stands in the centre of Newark, and each Wednesday evening the choir of boys and men sang a full Choral Evensong.

Wednesday afternoon duties in the orderly room usually finished early, so I was able to catch the bus into Newark, arriving in time to hear some of the choir rehearsal, while standing outside the song school. Directed by E.F.R. Woolley (whose music we would later sing at Guildford Cathedral), this was a really good choir, expertly accompanied on the church's impressive four-manual Willis organ. Little did I realise that the Vicar, the Reverend George Clarkson, and I would meet and work together seven years later when he was appointed as the very first Dean of the new Guildford Cathedral.

This was the weekly pattern of over a year spent at RAF Syerston as I gradually ticked off the days to my official demobilisation in July 1954. One of the perks at the end of National Service was a week's paid leave with a railway warrant to anywhere in the country, and a ticket from there to home. Fascinated by cathedrals and their music, I chose Wells as my destination – the first time I'd ever been there. I stayed at the Ancient Gatehouse Hotel, a rambling Tudor building facing the west front of the cathedral, and when not attending Evensong or visiting other churches, I took a bus to other places, including Downside Abbey, a wonderfully atmospheric building, with its pervading smell of incense as soon as you entered.

At the end of that week it was time to return to civilian life, living at home, and returning to work in the insurance section of the estate department at W.H. Smith & Son Ltd.

How would all that now seem to a 20-year-old, still with a secret longing that one day music might be his whole life?

5

Return to E4
1954-1956

The adjustment from RAF to civvy street was not easy, at work, at church, or at home. Initially, my mother and father seemed very happy that the family were all together again at 85 Beresford Road, though Wendy, now working at Barclays Bank, and Jill (just 13) had outgrown the bedroom they were sharing. I was in the small front bedroom that I had always occupied, and it now felt very cramped. Our mother was working at Richmond House School, mainly as a cook and housekeeper, but sometimes teaching the piano and playing for dancing classes. Our father was now employed as a laboratory technician at Enfield Rolling Mills. In 1950 he had ceased his association with Bishop and Brooke Ltd., and had been driving his lorry doing contract work for Enfield Rolling Mills, situated at Brimsdown, just three miles away from Chingford. The expense of running and maintaining the vehicle had become too much and physically too demanding, and through the manager of the transport department, who was also a keen musician, he had secured a job in the research laboratory.

With the independence I'd gained during those two years in the Royal Air Force, I was not keen on being homebound. I didn't make myself popular, staying out until late into the evening, having been at St. Anne's, or at Bob and Sheila Birchnall's house, which had become a sort of second home. Wendy was dating Malcolm Jennings – they had met at the local church hall whilst she was a girl guide and he a boy scout – and they were married at St. Anne's 18 months later.

I'd been away from work for two years, and all of my duties had been absorbed by the other members of staff in the estate department at W.H. Smith & Son Ltd. Although the law stipulated that they had to take me back, there was little to do apart from the menial tasks I'd first been given when I had started there four years ago. However, it was a job, and it paid a weekly wage of £2.12.6d.

I did manage to make some music, playing a couple of lunchtime concerts both at Strand House and in the company's other large London premises, Bridge House in Lambeth, but time was standing still at work. Perhaps I should look for a job elsewhere?

At church, I'd not been near a choir practice for two years. Bob Birchnall (the Vicar) was still choirmaster for the small mixed choir, totally at ease with the group, and doing the job that one day I hoped I might be able to do. He was very keen to re-form the boys' choir that John Forsdyke had started all those years ago, and asked me to take it on.

There was no shortage of recruits, even if there was a shortage of know-how on my part in how to teach singing, as well as how to control a group of 14 or so boys who, by nature, could be quite unruly. Most of my time in our twice-weekly choir practices was spent in trying to get them to stop talking, so there was little time for singing. It wasn't working, so I planned a few social activities – outings, cricket and football matches – in the hope that they'd see that those were the times to use all that excess energy, rather than in rehearsals. It partially worked, but the real problem was that I was only 20, about six years older than the seniors in the choir, and as far as they were concerned, just another of the lads. In the end they did sing at some of the Services, and one of them, Brian Cook, went on to become an internationally known baritone soloist, under the name of Brian Rayner Cook.

The reality was that I had neither the experience or the understanding of singing to run a boys' choir, and somehow I had to find that, away from St. Anne's, and almost certainly away from Chingford.

St. Anne's Choir, c. 1955. I am the fourth from the left in the back row

Our mixed voice choir was going from strength to strength, and we wanted to have some permanent memento of them. One way to do that would be to make more gramophone records. On a Saturday afternoon in the autumn of 1954 we borrowed High Beach Church (where I had been Organist a few years earlier), hired a mobile recording company, and made three twelve-inch 78 rpm records of anthems, carols and psalms. As with the previous recordings a few years earlier, these were cut straight on to acetate discs, which meant that there was just one copy of each. Passing them around among the choir, it was inevitable that every playing with steel needles would wear away the soft surface and cause background clicks and crackle.

In the meantime, we were invited to sing Evensong in Chelmsford Cathedral, and we also planned a special Advent Service that would include my aunt, uncle, and cousins Pauline and Martin from Watford. The music was J.S. Bach's Cantata 140 – *Sleepers, wake!* – specially written for Advent Sunday, with accompaniment for strings and oboe. Aunt Nell and Pauline would play violin, Uncle George would be on viola, and Martin, later to become principal cellist of the BBC Symphony Orchestra, would make up the quartet. Leo Forsdyke arranged for soprano and baritone soloists from the Royal College of Music, as well as an oboist. It was an ambitious undertaking for a small choir. There was no conductor, and I played the organ continuo. It wasn't perfect, but it was greatly appreciated by a large congregation, as was the Service of Nine Lessons and Carols a few weeks later.

1955 dawned and would be special: in May I would be 21, and several seminal events would point me further towards a possible career in music. Early in 1955 my grandfather died and in his will he left a sum of money to each of his grandchildren. I now had money to spend, and invested it in my first car – a black Ford Prefect. More influential to my future life, I bought the very first model of a domestic tape recorder available on the open market – a Grundig Reporter 500L.

The Grundig Reporter 500L tape recorder, 1955

Complete with a small microphone, I was now in a position not just to make live recordings, but also to record programmes from the radio. In the confined space of my bedroom at Beresford Road, and much to my mother's disgust, I rigged up a small valve radio, a gramophone turntable and pickup, together with the new tape recorder. There was hardly room to get in the door, and I had to gingerly climb over all the equipment to get in and out of bed. Having run a wire from the gramophone pickup to the input socket on the back of the radio, I spent many hours listening again and again to the choir of York Minster singing Charles Villiers Stanford's *Magnificat in B flat*. This was one of the 39 twelve-inch 78 rpm records issued as part of the *Anthology of English Church Music* on the Columbia record label between 1950 and 1954. Leo had acquired each one as they were released and had given me the York record as a Christmas present. A few weeks later we queued up at the music shop in Walthamstow to buy the very first church music long-playing 33 rpm record – the

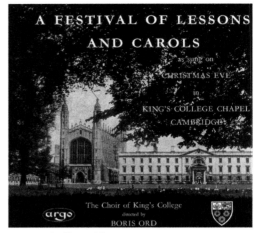

King's College Christmas LP

King's College Cambridge Festival of Nine Lessons and Carols (Argo ZRG 39).

My Grundig tape recorder was advertised as portable, but in truth it was quite heavy. Sometimes I manhandled it the one and half miles or so to St. Anne's, usually to record the organ, but also parts of choir practices and Services. Any recordings were transient since reels of tape were expensive and you simply recorded over what had been there previously. In later life, I wish I had preserved some of the better radio broadcasts from that time.

At church there was much excitement. We were to receive a visit from a Royal School of Church Music commissioner – in those days, one of the benefits available from your affiliation fee. The commissioner was George Guest, the Organist of St. John's College, Cambridge, and on Friday 25th March 1955 he attended our weekly choir practice, after which I drove him the seven miles to his hotel in Forest Gate. It was the first time we had met, and that meeting was to lay the foundation for a long musical and personal friendship that would last well beyond George's retirement from St. John's in 1991. A week or so after his visit to St. Anne's, we received a full report, written by his own hand. It was complimentary – very complimentary.

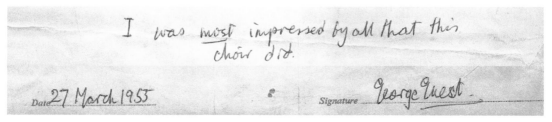

'I was most impressed by all that this choir did.' – George Guest, 27th March 1955

Three months later, soon after I'd celebrated my 21st birthday, the St. Anne's choir made the journey to Cambridge, where, at George's invitation, we sang in the chapel of St. John's College – a rare privilege.

And it was to Cambridge that I returned in December of that year – this time to King's College. First broadcast in 1928, the Festival of Nine Lessons and Carols is world famous, and I had an invitation to be there. This was not just any invitation. It had come from no less a person than King's choirmaster, Boris Ord. An old Monovian who was then lecturing at King's had remembered my keen interest in church music, and somehow had persuaded Boris to write a card allowing me access to the organ loft for the whole of the Service. The large congregation had queued up from early morning to get a seat in the ante chapel, but I was able to walk straight in and present my handwritten card to the chapel clerk who took me up to the organ loft, much to the surprise (and disapproval) of Richard Popplewell, the organ scholar.

It was an inspiring occasion that I will never forget, as I peered over the top of the organ screen, getting the best view and sound of the choir. Somehow, Midnight Eucharist back at St. Anne's, Chingford Hatch, wasn't going to seem quite the same.

Just as 1955 had brought new musical excitements, 1956 was to bring musical and personal change. It may have been hearing radio broadcasts, gramophone records, or King's College Choir in person that set me thinking that it was time to leave my musical roots in Chingford. In the end the decision to leave St. Anne's was made for me, following an ongoing disagreement with Sheila Birchnall, the vicar's wife, over some musical matter over which I felt I ought to have been consulted and have the final say. Bob Birchnall had to support his wife, so I resigned, leaving St. Anne's in May 1956 after ten years as their Organist.

Home life wasn't easy either. My mother and father now seemed to spend most of their time quarrelling, and there was even some disturbing physical violence. Years later, trying to pinpoint the reason for this, I reckon it was frustration on my father's part that he'd not achieved as much as he wished to in his working life. Wendy, now

With my mother and father, May 1955

married, had moved away, and though Jill and I were still living at Beresford Road, I spent as little time there as possible, and began to think of ways in which I might move away and start a new life elsewhere.

In musical terms, the one thing that kept haunting me was my lack of know-how and ability as a singer. If I was to be any sort of choir trainer I'd need to know just what it was like to sing in a choir. Maybe I should try and join one. But where? And how? Again, providence took a hand, and came in the shape of Jeremy Symonds, a visit to Hampstead, and Martindale Sidwell.

6

Hampstead
1956–1957

The outwardly affluent London suburb of Hampstead sits on a hill, north-west of the city. Its tree-lined streets and smart detached houses make it a desirable place for the rich and famous to live. With trendy shops, boutiques, theatre, and a wide variety of public houses, its steep streets and narrow lanes are also a mecca for artists and those seeking a more bohemian lifestyle. Occupying a prominent position at the end of Church Row, with its facing rows of Georgian houses, is the handsome Parish Church of St. John. Built in the 18th century, it was extended and enlarged eastwards a century or so later with the addition of a new chancel and organ.

In 1947 John William Martindale Sidwell was appointed as Organist and Choirmaster and set about building a choir which was to bring Hampstead considerable musical fame. Educated at Wells Cathedral School, where he was a chorister in the Cathedral, Martin (as we knew him) had studied the organ with C.H. Trevor at the Royal Academy of Music, and later returned to Wells as Assistant Organist before his wartime service in the Army. Prior to his move to Hampstead, he had been Organist and Choirmaster at the large 19th century Holy Trinity Church, Leamington Spa, in Warwickshire.

I had first heard the Hampstead choir on one of the 78 rpm recordings they had made for the Parlophone label, and also through their occasional live broadcasts of Choral Evensong on BBC Radio. It struck me that here must be something very special, since the weekly Evensong broadcast usually featured the choirs of our great cathedrals and those collegiate foundations at Cambridge and Oxford that maintained a boys' choir and sang daily Services during term-time.

Hampstead Parish Church

And there my interest in the Hampstead choir might have remained had it not been for a personal contact in early 1956 in Chingford. Jeremy Symonds lived at his family home in The Ridgeway, a mile or so from our house in Beresford Road. We had attended different schools and had only met occasionally at musical functions connected with the local parish church. A student at London University's Slade School of Art, Jeremy was singing tenor in the now famous Hampstead Parish Church Choir. Through a chance meeting, he suggested that I might visit his house and play the piano for him in some of the solo songs he was then studying. It was another of those occasions that was to change my life, for it was Jeremy who suggested that I, too, might like to consider auditioning for the Hampstead choir. 'But I don't sing,' I protested, to which he immediately replied that he would help me start. Would I like to try and sing something to him then and there?

Jeremy's father was organist at a City church in London, and on the piano was a selection of anthems that he used with his choir. One was thrust into my hand and I sight-read the bass part, reasonably well as regards the accuracy of the notes, though with little or no vocal quality or breath control. Jeremy was more than encouraging. He asked if I would like to do some more singing practice at his house, and also if I would be prepared to play the harpsichord continuo in a performance of Heinrich Schütz's *St. Matthew Passion* that he would be conducting in the enclosed cloisters at University College, London.

Needless to say, the answer to both was yes, and he handed me a vocal score of the Passion. Originally written in German for unaccompanied choir, this was a later Victorian edition with accompaniments to the extended recitatives, over which Jeremy had written his version of the English text. Playing the harpsichord was to be a totally new experience to me, though I dared not tell him that!

As the day of the one and only rehearsal drew near, I spent some time at the piano making sure I knew the music well. In the settings of the Passions, the recitatives are sung by a tenor Evangelist, narrating the story of the events leading up to Christ's crucifixion and death. Jeremy's tenor soloist was another of his colleagues in the Hampstead choir, David Johnston, who was later to carve out a distinguished career as a soloist and teacher. Michael Vaile, another member of the Hampstead choir, and then studying at the Bartlett School of Architecture, would be singing the part of Judas.

To accompany these two and to hear them sing was a complete revelation to this young would-be singer. David's full-blooded and declamatory tenor voice carried the story along with the momentum and drama it demanded, whilst Michael displayed the most extraordinary sense of musicianship and delicate vocal quality I had ever heard. It was like being in a musical paradise, and *if* I ever managed to get into the

Hampstead choir, these two would be my singing colleagues. In the midst of such talent I felt very inadequate.

The performance went well, apart from one slightly hilarious moment when a member of the choir singing the part of Pontius Pilate momentarily lost his sense of pitch; setting off four notes higher than printed, he sounded more than somewhat vocally strained and confused, leaving us displaying some inappropriate mirth.

Visits to Jeremy's house became more frequent, and having seen an advertisement in *The Musical Times*, I applied to take a few formal singing lessons in Catford, South London, with W. John Dyer, who was then Organist and Choirmaster at the Royal Naval College in Greenwich.

I had never been to Hampstead Parish Church or heard the choir at work, so Jeremy suggested that I might go with him to a rehearsal they were having for a live broadcast of music by Martin Peerson that they were preparing for the BBC's Third Programme. It was a Saturday afternoon, and mercifully the weather was fine as I perched on a tombstone in the churchyard, adjacent to the choir-room, listening to the highly polished and skilled sounds of the boys and men. And it was there, on that day, that it finally dawned on me that this was something of which I had to be a part.

A few weeks later I wrote my letter of application to Martindale and was surprised to receive a prompt reply inviting me to come to the church to audition the following day.

From MARTINDALE SIDWELL, 10, KIDDERPORE GARDENS, LONDON, N.W.3.   HAM 9210

August 15th, 1956.

Dear Barry Rose,

Thank you for your letter.

Yes, I would like to hear you sing.   If you get this lette in time, please come to the church tomorrow night,(Thursday) at 6.45. Otherwise give me a ring.   I am going away for ten days on Saturday.

With best wishes,

Yours sincerely,

With Jeremy's help I prepared the bass line of a simple anthem and took myself to Hampstead. Martin was seated at the piano in the choir room. I sang my short anthem and he handed me another piece, asking me to sight-sing the bass part. With that nervous vocal tremor that afflicts all singers when their breath control is unsteady, I struggled through to the end, and was more than surprised to hear him say that I had got in. He asked if I could start in two weeks' time, when the choir reconvened after a short summer break. My answer was yes. I didn't even stop to think how I would get to and from Hampstead from Chingford.

The boys had two rehearsals each week, the men joining them in the choir-room for an extended rehearsal each Friday evening. Looking back on it now, the choir was an extraordinary mixture of talent, with an age range of seven to late 40s or early 50s. I was then 22 and the more senior members of the choir seemed very old to me. There were 16 boys, four altos, four tenors and four basses, split on the two sides of the chancel, and known as Decani and Cantoris.

All singers need a technique, and I didn't have one. My vocal range was quite small, especially in the lower notes. I was put on Decani, where my co-bass, Dick Harvey, was an older man with a superbly produced voice, though he was not among the most able in sight-singing. But there may have been some wisdom in Martin's decision to let me into the choir and put me there, since I could read the notes, whilst my colleague, standing right next to me, sang them with great quality and aplomb. We made quite a good team!

My second Friday evening rehearsal in the Hampstead practice-room was not the happiest of experiences. The boys had been away from choir for several weeks over the summer, so Martin decided that the anthem for that Sunday Evensong was not going to overtax them. He chose *My beloved spake*, a verse-anthem by Henry Purcell, with short choruses to include the treble line. Verse-anthems consist of extended solo sections, often for the lower voices, and in this case, it was scored for alto, tenor, baritone and bass soloists. Looking round the room, he asked Michael Vaile to sing the alto, Cyril Ellis the tenor, and Cyril Prestage (who was on the Cantoris side) the

Martindale Sidwell at Hampstead Parish Church organ

bass. His eye then fell upon me, and I was ordered to stand up and sing the baritone part. The tenor and the alto delivered their opening solos with great panache, and then it came to my turn. I simpered the first phrase, nervous and bashful, but at least the notes were right. He stopped the rehearsal and came out with a typical Martin comment: 'My boy,' (most of his comments to all the boys and men began that way), 'what you need is more cornflakes every morning.'

It was a baptism by fire, but somehow I survived. The next 14 months were to teach me everything I know about choir training, showing me that most important and often ignored facet of the choral director's art: *think like a singer*. I could not have wished for a more formative experience, and that, under the direction of one of the country's finest choir trainers.

In addition to the regular practices and Services, there were other duties, including an obligation (at least it seemed like an obligation at the time) to join the rehearsals of the Hampstead Choral Society each Wednesday evening. It was there that I had my first experience of singing larger scale works by Monteverdi, Bach, and some 20th century composers, often challenging in their tonality. The rehearsals were accompanied at the piano by Martin's long-suffering wife, Barbara, a distinguished pianist who taught at the Royal College of Music. We were often taken aback at the way he spoke, or rather shouted at her, drawing some small comfort that we were not the only ones to be on the receiving end of some of his direct and withering comments.

For the church choir there were regular broadcasts, recordings and film soundtracks. But perhaps the icing on the cake was a full-scale Christmas concert in London's Royal Festival Hall on 19th December 1956, at which we sang the four-part arrangement of Benjamin Britten's *A Ceremony of Carols* with harpist, Gwendolen Mason, together with a variety of seasonal carols and anthems. I was even chosen to sing in a quartet. Ralph Downes, the designer of the Festival Hall's Harrison and Harrison organ, also took part in the concert, playing a variety of music, including the *Toccata* from Charles-Marie Widor's Fifth Symphony, later to become well-known through its use at two royal weddings. We had an audience of over 1,400 and the critics were unanimous in their praise:

The Sunday Times,
23rd December 1956

The highlight in a week devoted almost exclusively to " Messiahs " and other seasonal music has been the singing of the Hampstead Parish Church Choir under Martindale Sidwell at a Festival Hall Carol Concert. I doubt if there is a church or cathedral choir in the country to surpass it in tone and discipline.

It has been said that in every singer there lurks a would-be conductor, and I too harboured the dream that one day I might be able to train and conduct a choir as well as Martindale Sidwell. The first step was to find a small group of enthusiastic singers, though in doing so, I didn't take into account how unpopular this would temporarily make me with Martin. There were several in the Hampstead choir who said they would like to explore some of the works that the church choir did not sing. However, these were only the lower parts – altos, tenors and basses. To find a soprano line might be more difficult, though it was partially solved by a change in my personal circumstances: a move away from the family home at Chingford to a shared flat in Golders Green, another north-west London suburb, next door to Hampstead.

The move had come about as a result of a chance conversation in a City of London public house after a concert given by Michael Howard's Renaissance Singers in a nearby church. Michael Vaile had spent a short while singing in Michael Howard's choir at Ely Cathedral and was a member of The Renaissance Singers, and it was through him that I attended the concert. Also in the audience that evening was Bruno Turner, a highly respected musicologist who had prepared some of the editions being sung. In conversation with Bruno, I gathered that he was the Director of Music at St. Edward's Roman Catholic Church in Golders Green and that he lived nearby. More importantly, he was looking for someone to share his flat, and since I was now spending a lot of time at nearby Hampstead, would I be interested?

My answer was yes, and it coincided with a long overdue decision that I should leave W.H. Smith and look elsewhere for a job – though still in insurance. Early in 1957 I was appointed as the Assistant Insurance Manager to Joseph Rank Ltd., whose head office was in Millocrat House, Eastcheap, in the City of London.

At the same time, I left the family home in Chingford, moving into Bruno Turner's downstairs flat at 34 Highcroft Gardens, Golders Green. It was part of the home of more Roses – Mr. and Mrs. – though we were later to find out, after seeing some of the official-looking letters arrive through our door, that they were Mr. and Mrs. Rosenbloom (Golders Green has a large Jewish population and was often irreverently known as Goldberg Greenstein).

Now with an organist in his flat, Bruno invited me to play for some of the weekly Masses at St. Edward's, and it was there that I met several very able sopranos who became the core of the top line of my new mixed-voice choir, The Jacobean Singers. To the sopranos from Bruno's choir I added a few friends from the Chingford area, and to the men from the Hampstead choir who had joined us, some members of the then flourishing choir at St. Alban's Church, Golders Green.

The initial contact with these talented singers had been on a Friday night post-choir practice visit to The Marinella coffee bar opposite Golders Green tube station.

Peter Burrows, one of the St. Alban's choir, had recently joined the Hampstead choir as an alto, and it was at the coffee bar that I first met several members of the St. Alban's choir: Colin Wykes, the Miller brothers (John and Donald), Derek Baker, and Peter Chapman, a talented artist, organist and singer, to whose sister, Madeline, I would later become engaged. They too joined The Jacobean Singers, and our line-up was complete.

Our debut concert was at the Roman Catholic Church of Notre Dame de France, Leicester Square, on 11th December 1957, repeated on the following evening in what was then the London University Church, St. George's Church, Bloomsbury Way.

The centrepiece of the programme was Heinrich Schütz's *The Christmas Story*, an extended oratorio for tenor soloist, organ or harpsichord continuo, choir and orchestra. It was to be a total learning experience for me since I really did not have the first idea how to conduct an orchestra, or even how to use the choir rehearsal time efficiently. But I had a sound in my head and knew what I was hoping to achieve.

The Jacobean Singers rehearsing in St. George's Church, Bloomsbury

Peter Chapman agreed to play the harpsichord continuo, and through the kindness of the Reverend Gordon Phillips, then Priest-in-Charge of St. George's, Bloomsbury, and Anglican Chaplain to the University of London, I was put in contact with Edward Croft-Murray, Keeper of Prints and Drawings at the British Museum. He possessed a collection of valuable harpsichords and he agreed to lend us a two-manual Kirkman for the concert, on condition that we used and paid for an expert firm of pianoforte removers to transport his precious instrument to and from the two churches we were using for the performances.

The soprano arias, representing the angel appearing to the shepherds, and later to Mary and Joseph, were sung by Doreen Harrington, then a member of Bruno's church choir and a first-study singer at the Royal Academy of Music.

The continuing narrative in *The Christmas Story* is sung by a tenor soloist, and this presented a bit of a dilemma since we had two tenors who were keen to sing it – Jeremy Symonds, and David Johnston, who by then had moved on from the Hampstead choir to become a tenor lay vicar at Salisbury Cathedral. The solution was to have the two performances on successive evenings, with different soloists.

I had no idea how to assemble an orchestra, but we were fortunate that Dr. Leslie Russell, the London Schools' Music Adviser, lived in Hampstead and worshipped at the parish church together with his two daughters, Jill and Carole. They, too, joined The Jacobean Singers. Through that contact I was able to find a group of young players who agreed to form the orchestra. We also decided to include some organ solos, and it was Bruno who suggested that we might ask a talented young player, Nicholas Danby, then studying at the Royal College of Music.

The only means of publicity was by printed handbills which we left in various London churches and as many libraries as we could visit. Admission to the concerts would be free since we felt that this was the only way we might attract an audience. Our spirits were somewhat dampened on the first night when a heavy snowfall kept people away. David Money, the music critic from the *Daily Telegraph* did attend, however, and his report (published on the 12th December, 1957) was quite encouraging: 'This was a sincere performance, and there were many moving moments' (see page 51).

Musically speaking, it might have been a success, even if it was a financial disaster, and all the more so after most of the retiring collection had been spent in a celebration after the second performance.

It would be several months before I'd be able to pay off the various bills out of my weekly wage from Joseph Rank, and the small remuneration I was now receiving from my new appointment: Organist and Choirmaster of St. Andrew's Church, Kingsbury.

The Jacobean Singers in relaxed post-concert mode

7

Kingsbury and the Royal Academy of Music
1957–1960

When news of the formation of The Jacobean Singers reached Martindale Sidwell, he was not best pleased that a member of his church choir was using other members to form what he regarded as a vocal splinter group. One evening in October 1957, he took me aside, saying in his usual blunt way that he thought it was time that I moved on to run a church choir of my own, and by doing so, I would find out just how hard it would be to build a group to sing to a high standard.

Whatever his reasoning, it was to push me into the totally unknown field of training boys' voices, and all these years later I look back with gratitude for virtually being forced to do so. The short time I had spent in the Hampstead choir would be priceless to my future career, and in the years that followed, Martin and I were to work closely together again, both through and at the BBC, as well as with his London Bach Orchestra.

With Martindale Sidwell at his retirement party in Hampstead, 1991

One of the places in which to seek an appointment as a church organist and choirmaster is the weekly publication, the *Church Times*. In late September 1957 an advertisement had appeared for an Organist and Choirmaster at St. Andrew's Church, Kingsbury, NW9. Another north-west London suburb, Kingsbury adjoins the Borough of Wembley, famous as the venue for the 1924 Exhibition, its large stadium being the home of international soccer matches and the venue of the 1948 Olympic Games.

Until 1934, St. Andrew's had been a small mediaeval church serving what was then a village community. As the housing development spread to that side of London, the congregation outgrew their small building, and the Diocese of London was faced with a

 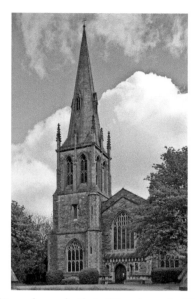

St. Andrew's in its original Wells Street setting (left), and as rebuilt in Kingsbury in 1934 (right)

choice: either build a new church or take the unusual step of relocating one from somewhere else. They chose the latter, and it so happened that a famous London West End church, St. Andrew's, Wells Street, had recently closed. The decision was made to transport it, stone-by-stone, to Kingsbury, and rebuild it on a grassy knoll adjacent to the old church. Described by *The Times* newspaper as 'The world's biggest jigsaw puzzle', every stone was carefully numbered and re-assembled in its right place.

A typical design of the Tractarian (or Oxford) movement, St. Andrew's is elegant and ornate, with a carved alabaster reredos that covers the whole of the east end. Short in length, because of the constricted London site in which it was originally built, the interior is lofty and light, with gothic style arches.

In its heyday it had been famous for its music, with its own choir school and distinguished Organists and Choirmasters, including Joseph Barnby, composer and former Principal of the Guildhall School of Music. The organ, an original Father Willis, had been slightly reduced in size in the move to Kingsbury, and the console was now situated in the west gallery from where it was easy to see the choir in their stalls at the east end.

I took the No. 83 bus from Golders Green to Kingsbury to look at the church and decided that I would apply to be the new Organist and Choirmaster. The present holder of the post was Dennis Harris, and he was due to leave Kingsbury to take up a teaching appointment in Kirby Muxloe, Leicestershire. If I was to be appointed, I would need to begin as soon as possible.

The Vicar was the Reverend Frank Springford, and he immediately responded to my application by asking me to come and see him. A family man, he lived in the adjoining vicarage with his wife and their three children, one of whom (Michael) was in the church choir. It may have been the Hampstead connection that prompted him to offer me the job; the first step in my quest to become an expert choir trainer was now complete. There was the church, the organ and the choir, and all I had to do now was to prove my worth.

Ranging in age from 7 to 13, the boys came from a variety of homes, backgrounds and schools. My predecessor was a skilled teacher, but I had no experience in the psychology of coping with children of that age, and little idea how to keep their attention and interest in rehearsals. It was to be a steep learning curve, with no help other than reading one or two books. I turned to Charles Moody's 1924 book *The Choir Boy in the Making* to find out what sort of vocal exercises I might use to cultivate a good tone and better breath control. In some ways it was useful, but you can't take a choir practice with a book in your hand, so it was more of a case of blind instinct and occasional panic.

The regular weekly schedule was an hour-long boys' rehearsal at 6.30 p.m. on a Tuesday evening, and the same time on Friday evening, with the men of the choir joining them at 7.30. There were few men, and none of them were near the standard of those I'd been singing with in the Hampstead choir, either in voice or ability to read music. It was soon obvious that if we were to make any progress, we would need better singers in the back rows.

Working in the City of London was sure to lead to occasional conflicts in timing, not least in getting to the boys' rehearsals on time. Quite often I would arrive breathless after a sprint from Wembley Park tube station, about a mile away from the church. It was not an ideal situation.

Our Tuesday rehearsals were held in the small choir vestry, where there was a serviceable piano. Soon after I arrived, I acquired a blackboard, painting on the five lines of the treble-clef stave. This was my first attempt to teach boys to read music and understand note values and keys, rather than learning everything off by heart. Using what voice I'd managed to develop whilst at Hampstead, I gradually managed to coax them into making a bigger sound, if a little breathy and 'hooty'.

With the increased confidence and ability in the treble line, it began to dawn on some of the men in the choir that they were not able to match up, musically or vocally. After consulting with Fr. Springford, we decided to close down the men's section, leaving us with a treble line that would sing alone at the Sunday morning Eucharist, and, hopefully, be joined by some of the men of The Jacobean Singers for the 6.30 p.m. Evensong. It was a bold move, and rightly unpopular with some members of the congregation, who resented this outsider dispensing with long-serving tenors and basses. But I think they appreciated the goals at which we were aiming, and gradually began to change their minds.

Several of the boys showed promising musical ability, but perhaps the most talented and instinctive musician among them was Andrew Jackman, whose parents, Bill and Pauline, lived in nearby Mallard Way with their other two sons, Jeremy and Gregory. Bill Jackman was a musician by profession; he played saxophone and clarinet in several of the BBC's light music orchestras, also featuring as a clarinettist in the Beatles' recording of *When I'm Sixty-Four*. Andrew, then a pupil at Preston Manor Grammar School, was already showing that he had inherited some of his father's musical skills. Not a great singer in the higher part of his vocal range, he could already sight-read any new piece I gave the boys, and in doing so, established himself as a leader and future head chorister. He was also a very able recorder player, taking part in The Jacobean Singers' very first performances of Heinrich Schütz's *The Christmas Story*, and being singled out by the *Daily Telegraph* music critic as the 'very small boy' playing the recorder in the alto trio *Let us even go now to Bethlehem* (see left).

I had no doubt that Andrew would end up in the music profession. Despite dropping out of a formal course at Trinity College of Music, he went on to establish himself as a sought-after orchestral and choral arranger and composer, conducting the Royal Philharmonic Orchestra in the hit 1970s albums, *Classic Rock*, and several other classical-style arrangements for cover versions of songs from groups such as the Beach Boys and The Police. Andrew was also to make front-page news in several national newspapers when he used an amateur choir as backing to the Peter Skellern hit record, *You're a Lady*, that reached number three in the charts. Simply described as The Congregation, their inclusion aroused the wrath of Equity, the singers' union, who forcibly

DAVID MONEY
DAILY TELEGRAPH
DEC 12. 1957

"THE CHRISTMAS STORY"

SINCERE PLAYING

Heinrich Schütz, Bach's famous predecessor in Germany, spent much of his life in Italy and came under the influence of such great masters as Monteverdi and Gabrieli. The Jacobean Singers and Orchestra, under Barry Rose last night performed "The Christmas Story," a fine example of his florid writing.

The setting was the Church of Notre Dame de France, Leicester Square. This was a sincere performance, and there were many moving moments, such as "The Shepherds in the Field" for three altos, continuo and two recorders.

One of the recorders was played by a seemingly very small boy. Jeremy Symonds was a sympathetic and dependable Evangelist and Doreen Harrington sang the Angel's part with a good line.   D. M.

expressed the view that professional singers should have been used. As someone once said, any publicity is good publicity, and the continuing row did nothing but generate more sales of the record, whilst the arguments about using amateur singers gradually faded away.

Andrew was to die tragically young. With his wife and two children, he had moved to rural Norfolk, from where he continued to write original compositions and arrange vocal and orchestral parts for recordings. Part of his recreation and inspiration was a daily walk with his dog through the local countryside. One day the dog returned home without Andrew, who was later found dead from a heart attack. Buried with his beloved Arsenal scarf in his coffin, he lies at peace in his home churchyard at Tivetshall St. Margaret.

A year after I arrived in Kingsbury, Andrew's younger brother, Jeremy, joined the choir as a seven-year-old probationer, and it was soon obvious that not only had Jeremy inherited the family's musical genes, but he was also a promising soloist, with a clear voice and keen sense of pitch. Soon he was singing with the choristers, but only for a short while before going to St. Paul's Cathedral as a chorister. In later life, he was the high countertenor in one of the world's most distinguished vocal ensembles, the King's Singers.

Just around the corner in Salmon Street lived the Bennett family and the Squire family. Duncan Bennett was one of the first choristers I recruited to the St. Andrew's choir. Quiet, well-mannered and gifted with a good ear and a clear voice, his parents thought that he ought to try to gain entry to one of the country's more prestigious choirs – New College, Oxford. Despite reaching the last few finalists on the day of the voice trial, he was not successful. However, the experience he was to gain in the Kingsbury choir was to play an important role in his future life, since he went to work for the celebrated organ-building firm of Harrison and Harrison, becoming the sought-after tuner and adviser for many of our best-known cathedral organs.

A few doors away from the Bennetts lived Chris Squire, his house instantly recognisable by his father's black London taxi usually parked outside. Stockily built and intelligent, Chris always gave the impression of being slightly laid back in his approach to singing, though he was a loyal member of the choir, and was later to go on to fame and fortune as bass guitarist in the pop group Yes. We were to meet up in various places after I left Kingsbury – Guildford Cathedral, where he sang in the Service of Consecration in May 1961, also coming down on successive Saturdays to help the fledgling Cathedral choir; and in the mid 1970s (at the height of his fame with Yes) at St. Paul's Cathedral, where, in the dead of night, I recorded a solo organ track in the Cathedral with him and his musical arranger, Andrew Jackman, for his solo album *Fish out of Water*.

These were but a few individuals out of a group of 16, all of whom contributed in their own way to the choir. Christopher Slatter became a most able soloist, and he introduced his school friend, John Bowring, who lived in the same small estate of pre-fabricated houses near the bottom of Salmon Street. Ginger-haired Paul Gerrett was a gregarious and delightfully mischievous personality, whilst Michael O'Farrell was one the quietest and self-effacing amongst the choristers. Graham Burgess lived virtually opposite the church and was probably the naughtiest of all the boys. He found it difficult to behave in church, and it soon became obvious that the new regime in the choir was not for him, and neither did it suit young Michael Springford, the vicar's son, so he also left. Of the other boys in the choir, Robert Matthews came from a family who were regular members of the congregation, and the three Longman boys, Michael, Robert and Roger, all attended the local Fryent School, where the music master, Graeme East, helped us with recruiting until he moved on to be Sub-Organist of Newcastle Cathedral.

With the marked improvement in their singing, I decided to take the boys into central London to join in a Jacobean Singers concert in St. George's Church, Bloomsbury. The programme included Heinrich Schütz's *St. Matthew Passion* and *Missa Dominicalis* for treble voices by Lodovico Viadana. A year or so earlier I'd heard the choristers of Ely Cathedral sing the Viadana Mass under Michael Howard's direction. They'd made it sound easy and mellifluous; we found it much harder. It was a style that was completely foreign to the Kingsbury boys, and since there was no printed version available, Bruno Turner, my flatmate in Golders Green, prepared a performing edition for us.

Kingsbury choristers, 1960. Back row, from left: Frank Greaves, Chris Squire, Andrew Jackman. Front row, from left: Paul Gerrett, John Bowring, Jeremy Jackman

Back at St. Andrew's there was musical encouragement from a distinguished member of the congregation. Leslie Woodgate was director of the BBC Chorus (later to be renamed the BBC Singers) and lived in Wembley Park, about a mile away from the church. From the organ console in the west gallery, I could see him and his wife, Lena, taking more than a casual interest in the musical elements of the Service, and it was not long before I was invited to his house. Unabashed by the gulf of experience and achievement between us, I asked if he would consider acting as guest compere for a concert I was planning in the church. To my surprise, Mr. Woodgate said yes, and in July 1959 he introduced the items in the programme, returning early the next year to direct the choir in another concert.

A few months after the first concert, Leslie invited me to play the whole of Handel's *Messiah* on the organ at Dunstable Priory, Bedfordshire, where he would be directing the BBC's large amateur choir, the BBC Choral Society, in a Christmastide performance in aid of charity. Usually accompanied by orchestra, it took weeks of careful preparation, playing from a special organ reduction that I'd managed to find in a London music shop. There was one rehearsal in the Priory on the day of the concert, which meant playing through the entire work twice in the space of about seven hours, a trial of stamina and concentration on an organ I'd never seen before.

The relationship with Leslie Woodgate was also to bring another chorister to St. Andrew's: his nephew, Leslie East, who would later carve out a distinguished

Choristers of St. Andrew's, Kingsbury, December 1959. Back row, from left: Leonard Greaves, Michael O'Farrell, Duncan Bennett, Michael Longman. Front row, from left: Leslie East, Robert Longman, Paul Bennett, Christopher Slatter

career in music as Director of Music at London's Guildhall School of Music; Head of Choral Publications at Novello and Co., Ltd; and later, in 2013, Chief Executive of the Associated Board of the Royal Schools of Music. In 2016 Leslie was invested with an OBE for his services to music in Middlesex – surely the first and only Kingsbury chorister to be honoured in this way.

A regular member of the back row of the Kingsbury choir on Sunday evenings was Peter Chapman, and it was through that connection that I met his delightful sister, Madeline. Slim, dark haired and vivacious, she was with Peter on one of the Saturday mornings that he and other men from the local St. Alban's Church Choir met for coffee in the Express Dairy cafe in Golders Green. The attraction to Madeline was immediate and magnetic, and I plucked up the courage to ask her for a date. We went to the local cinema, and gradually a close relationship began, which ended up with our official engagement a year or so later.

Peter and Madeline came from a divided family. Their father had left home for another woman and was then living in West Sussex, and that broken family relationship was to have lasting effects on the two children. In Peter's case it manifested itself though anxiety and chronic asthma. Madeline, though outwardly poised, lacked self-confidence, both in her ability and appearance, and often talked of herself as being worthless. Initially, like all engaged couples, we were very close, but the insecurity of the family situation may have been responsible for a cooling-off in the relationship, or it may well have been my fault for not being more understanding of her problems. We drifted apart, she to a job as a waitress in a works canteen, and it broke my heart when I learned she was having a relationship with another man.

A couple of years later, soon after I had moved to Guildford, she reappeared at No. 1 Cathedral Cottage, but by then our close relationship could not be rekindled. She stayed the night, and the next morning returned to Brighton, where she was working as a waitress and living in a hostel under some psychiatric care. A few months later she was found dead, lying peacefully under a tree in a field not far from where her father lived, having taken an overdose of tablets. A tragic waste of the life of a lovely girl, and I still ask myself what, if anything, I could have done to save her.

Among Peter's friends and acquaintances was Felix Aprahamian, the highly knowledgeable and respected music critic of *The Sunday Times* newspaper. Somehow, Peter persuaded Felix to listen to me play the organ at Kingsbury. His initial reaction was not encouraging: 'You need some proper organ lessons,' he said, 'and the man for you is C.H. Trevor at the Royal Academy of Music.' It was now April 1958, and it was obvious that if the boys of the Kingsbury church choir were to make any further progress, I would need to be able to devote more time to them, and that meant more weekday rehearsals after school. With my full-time insurance job in the City, that simply was not possible. I had reached the crossroads, and with Felix Aprahamian's words ringing in my ears, I decided the time had come to leave the world of commerce and hope to get into the Royal Academy of Music.

It was not an easy decision, and it was Ronald Hicks, my boss in the insurance office of Joseph Rank Ltd. who pushed me into making it. I'd given a lunchtime recital at a nearby City church, and he was not pleased when I was late back into the office. 'You need to make up your mind if it's to be insurance or music,' he said. More in a fit of pique than considered reasoning, I simply said 'music…', and on the eve of my 24th birthday, I gave in my notice at Joseph Rank Ltd.

Now without a steady income, how would I live? I had no savings and could not expect any financial support from my parents (who I now saw only very occasionally). One possible way forward was to gain a place at the Royal Academy of Music and then apply for what was then called a County Major Scholarship. That would mean playing to and being interviewed by the Middlesex County Music Adviser, Dr. Donald Hughes.

Without even having Grade 1 in any music examinations, I wrote to the Royal Academy of Music, hoping to be included in their forthcoming entrance examinations; they usually expected Grade 8 standard from their applicants. It turned out I was too late. The entrance exams had already taken place, but they did offer me the opportunity of a special audition.

I prepared a couple of pieces and went and played them on the organ in the Academy's Duke's Hall, where a panel sat half-way back, listening to my efforts. This was followed by an interview with the Principal, Sir Thomas Armstrong, who had previously been Organist at Exeter Cathedral and Christ Church, Oxford. He was very sympathetic to this would-be church musician, pointing out that entrance to the Academy would also mean taking a second study instrument (piano), harmony and counterpoint, as well as attending choir training and aural classes.

A week later I was surprised to receive a letter from the Academy offering me a place from September. Now it was time to audition for the County Award, which, if I was successful, would pay the fees and give me a maintenance grant towards living expenses. Dr. Hughes came to St. Andrew's and I played my 'party-pieces', followed by a short interview, in which he seemed genuinely interested in what I was hoping to achieve with the church choir. Yes, he would offer me a County Award as from September 1958. Until then I'd have to manage without any regular income.

One thing was certain: I could no longer afford to live in Golders Green; on top of the expense, it was a 30-minute journey to and from Kingsbury, as well as the interminable time often spent waiting for buses to arrive. Quite by chance I met Peter Ball, who lived with his parents in Church Lane, Kingsbury, a few yards along from the church. Peter had got to know my cousin Martin, the cellist, and was a great admirer of his playing, so when we met, we had something musical in common. A salesman for the Bulmers cider company, Peter spent much of his days and evenings visiting London restaurants and clubs, though he would often appear in the organ loft at Kingsbury when I was practising. Anxious to cut his parental ties, he suggested that we might share a flat together, and that there was one coming vacant in St. Andrew's Mansions, just around the corner from the church. Realising that I could not afford it, he was very gracious in offering to pay two-thirds of the rent, and with the money saved from travel, and in the hope of more income from playing at weddings and funerals to cover my share, I accepted.

We moved into a well-appointed, furnished flat in the 1930s mock-Tudor block, and being so close to the church gave me the option to increase the number of rehearsals for the Kingsbury choirboys. Now they could attend not just on Tuesday and Friday, but also have the choice between a Wednesday or Thursday post-school rehearsal, and the occasional Saturday morning.

Each of the boys was now rehearsing three or four times a week, and with that timetable we began to make some real musical and vocal progress. By August of the following year, we were able to take on a week's summer residence at St. Paul's Cathedral (our Diocesan Cathedral), singing five Evensongs and two morning Matins. We must have sung to the satisfaction of the clergy, since a few months later, an invitation came for the choir to lead two Carol Services at the Cathedral for the readers of *The Eagle*, a highly popular and best-selling comic at that time. Through another contact we were asked to sing a Christmas concert in the chapel of the Royal Danish Foundation of St. Katharine in London's Regent's Park, and also to sing carols at the annual dinner of the Anglo-Norse Society in one of the City of London's livery halls.

In mid-September 1958, in company with many others, I turned up at the Royal Academy of Music as a new student. The first two days were spent in acclimatisation with the building, and more importantly, meeting the teacher for your designated first study. In the audition interview, following the advice I'd been given by Felix Aprahamian, I'd expressed the hope that I would be able to study with C.H. Trevor, but on the noticeboard allocating the new students, I found that my name was not on his list. I would be with Douglas Hawkridge, a fine player and teacher, but not the one I'd asked for or felt that I needed. Somehow I managed to find Mr. Trevor, and asked if he would be prepared to take me on, and was most relieved when he said yes.

Known as one of the country's finest and most senior organ teachers, C.H. Trevor had previously taught Martindale Sidwell, my choirmaster at Hampstead, and more recently, Simon Preston, who had just taken up the prestigious organ scholarship at King's College, Cambridge. As I was to discover, Mr. Trevor had some startlingly able pupils, including Steuart Bedford, who later went on to become Conductor-in-Residence at the Britten-Pears Foundation at Aldeburgh, and Artistic Director of the Aldeburgh Festival.

With my lack of a real technique it was going to be an uphill struggle to reach a high standard of playing, though I had one thing that none of his present or new pupils could offer: I had passed the BBC audition as a solo organist. In those days the BBC Third Programme broadcast regular organ recitals given by different organists from cathedrals or collegiate chapels. I had written to the BBC in the hope that they might add my name to the long list of those waiting for a formal audition. Quicker than I expected, a letter arrived summoning me to an audition in St. Gabriel's Church, Cricklewood, London, a venue often used by the BBC for its recordings and live broadcasts of sacred music. I was instructed to play two contrasting pieces and would be allowed 15 minutes or so to acquaint myself with the organ before the auditioning panel reconvened to hear me.

I chose the four-movement *Pastorale in F* by J.S. Bach, and a set of variations on the Christmas carol, *Herr Jesus hat ein Gärtchen* (*King Jesus hath a Garden*) by the contemporary Flemish organist and composer, Flor Peeters. Having selected what I thought were suitable sounds, the panel came into the church, where they sat behind a screen, clinking teacups. I never found out who or how many they were, though I guessed that one of them must have been Dr. George Thalben-Ball, the famous Organist of London's Temple Church, and also at that time the BBC's Music Adviser to the Head of Religious Broadcasting.

Two weeks later I received a letter to say that I'd passed the audition, and I'd be hearing from them again. Sure enough, a letter arrived offering me a first broadcast, though not, as I expected, from St. Andrew's, Kingsbury, but from the chapel of Magdalen College, Oxford; they had muddled me up with Dr. Bernard Rose, the Organist and Informator Choristarum (Master of the Choristers) at Magdalen! Much as I would like to have broadcast from Oxford, I rang the BBC to point out the mistake, and a date was arranged for me to record the recital at Kingsbury.

On the day of the recording, the BBC outside broadcast van arrived at St. Andrew's, and the engineers set up their microphones in the church. It was a relief to know that it was a recording rather than a live broadcast – 'Ah,' I thought, 'if I happen to make a mistake, I'll be able to go back and play it again.' Those hopes were quickly dashed. The producer was Alan Giles, and his first words to me were, 'This is as a live broadcast. There will be no re-takes.' Not exactly what a nervous young organist wanted to hear as he mounted the steps to the organ loft to play his very first BBC solo recital. The recording went ahead, and as far as I could tell, it was alright.

Back at the Royal Academy, none of this impressed Mr. Trevor, and rightly so. I had taken one of the larger Bach works to my first lesson, and he immediately suggested that we should go back to the same composer's *Eight Short Preludes and Fugues*, usually a starting point for organists first learning to play Bach. He made the point that by doing so I would learn to play much more accurately with correct note values and articulation – and who was I to argue? Here was the most experienced teacher I could ever hope to find.

Organ lessons were held in the Duke's Hall, and mine was on Monday at 5.00 p.m., the one day of the week there was no rehearsal at Kingsbury. I would arrive in the Hall around 4.45 p.m. and be swept off my feet by the skill of the previous pupil playing some huge work by Reger or Liszt, and there I would sit, waiting to take my turn to play the simplest of the Bach preludes and fugues. But it did me a power of good, and to this day I treasure some tattered copies which still bear Mr. Trevor's neat pencil markings with suggestions for fingering, phrase-breaks etc.

I was not the ideal student at the Academy, in any subject. My knowledge of harmony, though instinctive, was scanty. Lessons with Malcolm McDonald usually involved solving the most basic problems of how to write the simplest four-part chorales without consecutive fifths or octaves. Piano lessons were a nightmare, since it took my teacher Robert Edwards no time at all to discover that I had no real technique. His reaction was immediate; I should get a book of Czerny studies and start at the beginning. The problem was that I had neither the time nor the inclination to practise, and I began to invent all sorts of excuses for missing lessons. Mr. Edwards soon gave up any hope of turning me into a reasonably competent pianist. His frustration was obvious, and it was better for both of us if I didn't attend.

Aural classes were taken by Terence Lovett. A group of us would assemble in one of the Academy's classrooms, where, if possible, I would sit next to Sebastian Forbes, then a fellow student, and later to become Professor of Music at the University of Surrey. Sebastian had been head chorister in the Hampstead choir during my time there and was an extraordinarily gifted musician; his father was Watson Forbes, the viola player in the well-known Aeolian Quartet. Confident and brash, Mr. Lovett

would bounce into the room and bombard us with musical phrases, which we then
had to write down in our manuscript books after a couple of hearings. Sebastian
always got these correct, whilst I struggled to make sense of some of the time signa-
tures and intervals, even if I did have a good sense of pitch and could readily identify
the key. A furtive glance over Sebastian's shoulder would help me on my way, and I
was able to give the impression of being able to keep up, even if I couldn't. On one
memorable occasion, Sebastian wrote down the same example in two different ways,
alleging that on second playing, Mr. Lovett had played it slightly differently. I didn't
know which one to copy, and Terence Lovett was not best pleased that he'd been
found 'rhythmically wanting' by a student!

Then there were the Tuesday morning choir training classes with Dr. Douglas
Hopkins. Among the organists, Dr. Hopkins was a bit of a legend, for all the wrong
reasons. He was well-known for having an attraction to the same sex, and it is alleged
that this had caused his hasty departure from two previous cathedral appointments
– Peterborough and Canterbury. Whatever the truth of the situation, he would think
nothing of taking the hand of the guinea-pig conductor, ostensibly to make sure that
you were conducting three or four in a bar correctly. Some of us were not so sure
it was solely for musical reasons. Intended for first and second study organists, the
class took place in the Duke's Hall and lasted an hour. During that time we usually
looked at two or three contrasting anthems or oratorio choruses, learning something
of their history from Dr. Hopkins. After this, one of us would be invited, or rather
commanded, to conduct it, whilst another was told to accompany it on the organ –
the remainder of the class forming the choir. My lasting impression of the sessions
was being instructed to beat time in a methodical way (probably useful for those of us
who would work with an orchestra later on) and Dr. Hopkins' pungent criticism of
anyone who didn't do that, but tried a more expressive style, hoping to communicate
the meaning of the text.

As the oldest member of the group – most students at the Academy had gone there
straight from school at the age of 18, and I was now 24 – I felt out of place with my
fellow organ students. As we adjourned to the canteen, they would discuss the finer
points of phrasing in Bach's trio sonatas, whilst I usually sat alone, planning that
afternoon's boys' rehearsal in Kingsbury.

For the next 18 months it was a balancing act between being a student at the
Academy and an ever-ambitious choir programme at St. Andrew's. If there were any
conflicts, it was usually Kingsbury that won, though I was always careful to make sure
that I attended my lessons with Mr. Trevor, even if I often turned up with a woefully
unprepared piece. At that point he would delve into his neatly arranged briefcase and
bring out some sight-reading and transposition tests from past ARCO (Associateship

of the Royal College of Organists) examinations. I was adequate at sight-reading, and very inadequate at transposition. Ever patient, he suggested that I ought to persist with the tests and take the ARCO examination next July. That meant learning two prescribed and contrasting new pieces – Buxtehude and Reger – and I was glad to have something new to tackle in the playing, even if I was unconfident about success in the paperwork section of the exam.

My hunch was proved to be correct. I passed the ARCO playing but failed the paperwork by several marks. Mr. Trevor didn't seem surprised or worried. His part, the teaching of the pieces, had been successful. Perhaps I might try again...? Probably not.

Meanwhile, the treble line at Kingsbury was becoming more widely known, and we were now supplying soloists for local concerts, ranging from Benjamin Britten's *St. Nicolas* to the yearly carol concerts in Wembley Town Hall. The boys were also one of the first, if not the very first, to give a concert performance of the newly written *Missa Brevis* by Benjamin Britten. Written in May 1959 for the boys of Westminster Cathedral Choir, it was first sung there on Wednesday 22nd July, and again on the following Saturday morning. Bruno Turner suggested that he and I might go, and we sat in the Cathedral that Saturday morning listening to the electrifying sounds from the choir and George Malcolm's organ playing, with the composer and Peter Pears sitting a few rows in front of us. Just under a year later, some of the Kingsbury boys gave a performance of the complete Mass at the end of a Sunday Evensong, singing from the west gallery of the church, adjacent to the organ console.

Earlier in the year, the boys had also made their debut on the BBC in a series of four pre-recorded segments in the weekly Network Three (later BBC Radio 3) programme *Christian Outlook*. I knew two of the presenters of the programme: the Reverend David Edwards (later to become Provost of Southwark) had been a curate at Hampstead Parish Church during my time in the choir, and Walter MacDonald was the minister at Kingsbury Baptist Church and had heard the boys singing at St. Andrew's. It could have been one or both of them who had recommended us to the producer of *Christian Outlook*.

The brief was to present four short anthems, both in rehearsal and performance, suitable for the top line of any parish or

W·NEWS 7·7·60·
St. Andrew's, Kingsbury

After Evensong on Sunday nine boy members of the choir went up to the organ loft and from there gave what is believed to be the first public performance in a parish church of Benjamin Britten's "Missa Brevis in D," a setting of a Mass for boys' voices. The work was written only last year. It is suitable really for a larger boys' choir, one including boy altos, but considering the limitations the nine from St. Andrew's gave an impressive rendering of the Mass.

The Wembley News, *7th July 1960*

school choir. In late March the BBC would come and record us as we rehearsed in the choir vestry and in the church, also recording a finished performance of each work with organ accompaniment. *Christian Outlook* was a live broadcast from a studio in The Langham, a former hotel opposite Broadcasting House, and on four successive Wednesdays during May I went up there to take part in the programme, providing some basic historical notes about the pieces we were singing, as well as commenting on vocal and technical points that might be of some use to listening choir directors. Apart from Radio Syerston, this was my first experience of live broadcasting as a speaker. My delivery sounded stilted, too carefully read from a prepared script, and lacking in spontaneity.

The four broadcasts, beginning on 4th May, were very well received, and the producer was kind enough to share some of the appreciative letters and comments about them.

And it was those broadcasts that were to play an important part in my musical future...

Network Three

7.0 CHRISTIAN OUTLOOK
Introduced by
the Rev. David Edwards
News Comment: by Mark Gibbs
Christian Aid Week, May 7-14: Janet Lacey, director of the Inter-Church Aid and Refugee Service, speaks of the enterprise of 1,000 local groups taking part this year
Anthems for Treble Voices: four illustrated talks by Barry Rose, with the boys of St. Andrew's Church, Kingsbury, on music within the range of the average church choir. 1—'God liveth still' (*Bach*)
(The last item is recorded)

RADIO TIMES
WEDNESDAY EVENING   MAY 4

8

Kingsbury to Guildford
1960

Peter Ball, my flatmate at Kingsbury, had attended one of the BBC recording sessions in church, sitting quietly in the west gallery reading a newspaper. When we got home, he threw down the *Daily Telegraph* on the sofa, open at the Situations Vacant General column, saying, 'Here, have you seen this?'

'This' is the advertisement from 29th March 1960:

> ORGANIST & CHOIRMASTER required in September for Guildford Cathedral. The post may be combined with that of Director o. Music at the Royal Grammar School.—Details available from The Provost, Castle Gate, Guildford, to whom application should be made.

Of course I hadn't seen it; I never bought a newspaper. 'You should go for it,' he said.

Perhaps this is the moment to explain that then – and now – the usual career path for a cathedral organist is via an organ scholarship at one of the major universities, with formal qualifications such as a BA (Bachelor Arts) or BMus (Bachelor of Music), plus the accepted practical and theoretical diploma examination for organists – the ARCO (Associateship) or FRCO (Fellowship) of the Royal College of Organists. Unfortunately, I had failed the ARCO examination in July of the previous year and since I hadn't been to university, I had none of those professional musical qualifications.

Undaunted, I sent off my letter of application, and was more than surprised to receive a phone call from the Very Reverend Walter Boulton, the Provost of Guildford, asking if I would be free to come to the Royal College of Music for an audition and interview in three weeks' time. Either someone behind the scenes must have mentioned my name to him, or he might have taken notice that the Kingsbury choirboys were about to embark on the series of BBC broadcasts for *Christian Outlook*.

There was little time to prepare something special to play. Easter, with its extra rehearsals and Services was imminent, and I also needed to find three people who would provide me with a reference before the interview day. There were two obvious choices: C.H. Trevor, my organ teacher at the Royal Academy of Music, and Leslie Woodgate, the Director of the BBC Chorus, who had recently conducted the Kingsbury choir at a concert. The only problem was that term had finished at the Academy, so I'd either have to phone or write to Mr. Trevor to ask him, whilst Leslie Woodgate and his wife were in the throes of moving into a flat in central London and I didn't have their address!

The third person ought to have been a priest with whom I had worked, but I really didn't want to alarm Fr. Springford, my vicar at Kingsbury. Instead, I plucked up the courage to write and ask Dr. John Dykes Bower, the Organist of St. Paul's Cathedral, and was more than surprised to receive a handwritten note from him saying that he'd be glad to write a reference.

Having contacted Mr. Trevor and found Leslie Woodgate's London address, the next job was to collect their references and send them off to Walter Boulton a week or so before the interview and audition. Mr. Trevor's covering letter wished me all success, whilst Leslie Woodgate wrote: *'If you don't get the job because of lack of qualifications it won't be your fault. It will simply mean that you* must *add several letters after your name. This may be important for your future career! And I mean this.'*

My first visit to the unfinished Cathedral had been a year earlier when I had accompanied a friend who was learning to drive. At that time the east end of the building was open to visitors, whilst the nave was still under construction. In the short time still available before the interview and audition I needed to go back to Guildford. The building was very much as I remembered it: in the chancel was a grand piano, and there were chairs arranged in the form of choir-stalls. I gathered that the Holy Trinity Pro-Cathedral choir had given a concert there on Good Friday – it would have been good to have heard them.

Buildings can speak to you, and Guildford did. I felt that this was the place, but I also knew it was a long shot. However, as William Cowper had written some 200 years earlier: *God moves in a mysterious way.*

A week later, on Thursday 28th April 1960, wearing the only suit I had and clutching my organ music and a large and heavy Ferrograph tape recorder, I turned up at the Royal College of Music on the back of Peter Chapman's motorbike. The Provost had suggested that I bring the tape recorder, so that the musical advisers could hear what the Kingsbury boys had just recorded for the BBC. The two advisers were both highly distinguished: Sir Ernest Bullock, formerly Organist of Westminster Abbey, and then Director (Principal) of the Royal College of Music; and Dr. H.K. Andrews, the recently retired Organist of New College, Oxford. On arrival at the College, I was directed to a waiting room where there were four other short-listed applicants, all older and more distinguished than me. One of them had been assisting at King's College, Cambridge, while another was known as a composer and musical editor, though I had never thought of him as a practising church musician.

The formal business of the audition began with the organ playing in the College's concert hall. Each of us was given 15 minutes to try out the instrument and choose the stops for our chosen piece. I had decided on the variations by Flor Peeters that I'd learned for my BBC audition. In those days, organs did not have a computer system for programming stop changes, so all of my stop changes between the movements had to be remembered. Having passably negotiated my way through the Flor Peeters, I was presented with a piece of manuscript paper on which was written a hymn tune I'd never seen before – probably specially written for the occasion. I played through it and was then asked to improvise around its melody for the next few minutes: this is the sort of thing any organist has to do in a Service, and not an easy thing for someone who does not have that natural flair. My efforts were musically dull and rather square, somewhat similar to the way one of the lay clerks at Guildford would later laughingly describe my pre- and post-Service improvisations – 'A succession of unrelated chords in varying keys.'

Following the organ playing there was the formal interview in the Director's office, a spacious but rather dark and forbidding room, or so it seemed on this occasion. Seated around a large desk were Sir Ernest, Dr. Andrews, and Walter Boulton, who acted as chairman. It was Walter who piloted the conversation towards my work with the choir at St. Andrew's, Kingsbury, and he asked me to let the panel hear the BBC recordings we had just made. That done, it was over to the two musical advisers.

The post had been advertised with the possibility of combining it with the position of Director of Music at the Royal Grammar School. I made it clear that I was not interested in that – whoever was appointed would need to devote all their time and effort to a choir for the new Cathedral. This did not go down well with Sir Ernest, who said that he could not see why both jobs could not be done side by side. His reaction may have been justified since, at that time, there was no plan for daily sung Services in the new building. I insisted that I was not interested in that part of the job, and anyway, I did not have the relevant teaching qualifications.

Dr. Andrews took a more academic approach. A well-known Palestrina scholar, he presented me with a large piece of manuscript on which was written a motet and asked me how I would conduct it and handle the changes in tempi. Having little idea what he was talking about, I said that I'd contact someone like him and ask their advice. It was not going well, and I had the temerity to point out that no-one had yet raised the matter that in just 12 months, on a date already fixed in May 1961, this new Cathedral would be consecrated, and here we were discussing Palestrina and the Royal Grammar School when we should have been discussing how we were going to found and train a brand-new choir in this very short time span. Walter Boulton quickly brought the interview to an end. We were wasting each other's time. However, he must have had some sympathy with my practical approach since he followed me out of the College, put a friendly hand on my shoulder, and asked me if I would be able to come down to Guildford the following morning.

Despite that invitation I was despondent. I'd blown it – or so I thought. I climbed on to the pillion of Peter Chapman's motorbike and we headed back towards north London, dropping off the tape recorder in Kingsbury, and going on to attend Evensong at St. Alban's Abbey. Here was a musical set-up and tradition of which the new Guildford Cathedral would one day be a part. Or would it?

The following morning, as arranged, I caught the train from Waterloo to Guildford and made my way to the Provost's home in Castle Gate. Not sure what was going to be said, I must have seemed very nervous, but Walter soon put me at ease over coffee and biscuits as he talked about his plans for the new Cathedral. What did I envisage? It was more youthful enthusiasm than considered logic that made me say, 'daily sung Services.'

That must have been a real 'Damascus moment' for him, since his eyes lit up and immediately he said, 'Let's go up to the Cathedral and talk more.' Once there, a new wave of enthusiasm came over me as I talked about the way I might institute the pattern of daily sung Worship with a choir of 16 boys and 12 men. To be honest, it was all 'pie-in-the-sky' since I had no idea how I'd do it, or if there would be the resources, either educationally or financially – or even *if* I could do it.

Back at the Provost's house, we talked more about his vision for the new Cathedral, and just before I left, he offered me the job, which he would confirm in writing as soon as possible. From my later understanding it seemed that he had gone against the advice of his two musical advisers and taken on himself the entire responsibility for the future of the music in the new building. I made my way to the railway station, walking on air. I'd done it – I'd become a cathedral organist, and at the age of 25 I'd be the youngest in the country.

Once off the train at Waterloo I simply had to tell someone. I rang Peter Chapman, who, in a fit of euphoria, rang the *Daily Telegraph* and gave them the news. The following morning, this article appeared in the paper:

> **D. TELE. 30·4·60.**
> Guildford Organist.—Mr. Barry Rose, 45, has been appointed organist and choirmaster for the new Guildford Cathedral.

Apart from being 20 years wrong about my age, it was not a popular move with Walter Boulton, since he had yet to inform the rest of the short-list that a decision had been made. The following day the *Daily Telegraph* published a correction, and I received my promised letter of appointment. It laid out the starting date of 1st September 1960, the salary (£450 per annum), and a final paragraph saying that the appointment would be for a preliminary period of two and a half years, during which I would *'take a suitable musical degree such as Mus. Bac. (Bachelor of Music) or the FRCO (Fellowship of the Royal College of Organists). Then we could review the position, and if agreeable to both of us, we could enter into a five-year contract, which thereafter would be renewable'*. Walter was covering his back, so to speak, since I'm sure that he had anticipated the criticism he would soon receive from the musical fraternity. From my point of view there was no way that I'd be able to achieve a Bachelor of Music or the FRCO in that short period, and anyway, here I was with the responsibility of starting a brand-new musical programme which would take all of my time and energy.

It was now the end of April 1960 and I would need to stay at St. Andrew's, Kingsbury, until the beginning of September since we were committed to singing a week of Services in St. Paul's Cathedral, finishing with Evensong on Saturday 3rd September. I broke the news to Fr. Springford and the boys at Kingsbury as soon as I could, in the hope that they'd not already read it in the press, and I promised that our remaining months together would be much as usual, though at some stage they would meet other people at rehearsals, one of whom would be their future choirmaster.

At the Royal Academy of Music there had obviously been some discussion among the faculty about the forthcoming Guildford appointment, and Mr. Trevor must have told his colleagues that I was on the short-list. The following Tuesday morning I arrived slightly late for the choir training class in the Duke's Hall, and seeing me come in, Douglas Hopkins, who'd obviously not heard the news, shouted, 'That Guildford job's gone, you know,' to which, much to the class's amusement, I was able to shout back, 'I know, I got it!' From then on my attendance at the Academy would be more sporadic, though I was determined to continue with Mr. Trevor for as long as I could. Sir Thomas Armstrong, the Principal, sent me a handwritten letter of congratulation, and later announced that I had been awarded the Frederick Keene Prize for the outstanding organ student of the year – at least my name would now appear on a prize winners' board.

One thing was certain, I'd have to maintain the musical standards at Kingsbury whilst also juggling the demands of forward-planning for the new Guildford choir, even though I would not be in residence there for another four months.

A few days later, after my appointment was announced, I received a phone call from Ralph Woods, the London manager for the Liverpool organ-building firm of Rushworth & Dreaper Ltd. He asked if he could come and see me and talk about the organ for the new Cathedral. I knew little or nothing about the tonal design or internal workings of organs, though when we met, I pretended that I did. Armed with a huge sheaf of papers and drawings, Ralph turned up in the organ loft at Kingsbury, and there we sat while he explained the plans for the new instrument.

In my conversations with Walter Boulton, he had mentioned the possibility of acquiring an organ from another church but had not given any details. It seems that Walter had somehow heard about the Coulthurst Trust, based in Gargrave, Yorkshire, and that with the help of the Trust, there might be a chance to acquire a Harrison and Harrison organ from a redundant Baptist Church in Shipley, Yorkshire. This must have seemed like manna from heaven to Walter, since he was then wrestling with a suggested plan to put a Miller electronic organ into the new Cathedral, with loudspeakers placed in the four corners of the north and south galleries. I never found out the reasoning behind this, apart from the fact that the Cathedral Council were adamant that there was no money available for a traditional pipe organ.

Somehow Walter had made contact with Mrs. Jessie Coulthurst, the widow of the founder of the Coulthurst Trust, and it turned out that as a girl she had attended the large and spacious Rosse Street Baptist Chapel in Shipley. In early 1960 the congregation had relocated to their nearby Sunday school premises in New Kirkgate, and the building in Rosse Street was scheduled for demolition. Jessie Coulthurst was anxious to save the chapel's Harrison and Harrison organ, and through the Coulthurst Trust, had offered to pay for its installation in the new Guildford Cathedral.

The first thing was to find an organ builder who could a) safely remove the instrument in time, and b) have the space to store it. Rushworth and Dreaper had been established organ builders since the 1840s, with large premises and workshops in Great George Street, Liverpool, and they had agreed to dismantle and store the Shipley organ. The initial plan for Guildford was to install the organ in the Cathedral's north transept gallery, exactly as it had originally been in the chapel at Shipley. There was nowhere else to put it, and what seemed to me to be an afterthought on the part of Edward Maufe, the Cathedral architect, was not his fault at all. His original pre-war drawings and plans had shown canopied choir-stalls in the chancel, above which would be situated the pipes of the organ. Post-war austerity and the pressing need to finish the shell of the building had meant severe economies in furnishing. The stalls for the choir would now be much simpler, whilst all plans for an organ in that part of the building were shelved.

Ralph Woods had already made some detailed plans. It was going to take the best part of a year to refurbish parts of the Shipley instrument, make a lot of new pipework, season timber, and to complete the installation in time for the Consecration. He fully understood my concern that there was no way that the organist could play from the north transept gallery away from, and out of sight of most of the choir. We would need a detached console. But where to put it? That proposal and decision would have to wait until I was actually in residence at Guildford.

Our meetings at Kingsbury became more frequent, and gradually we altered the list of stops, adding more and more new ones at considerable expense. Walter Boulton must have formed a real friendship with Jessie Coulthurst, since everything new that we suggested was agreed, including the detached console.

The planning of the organ was now in safe professional hands, and my own thoughts were turning to the promise I'd made to Walter Boulton, that there would be daily sung Worship at the new Cathedral. Who would sing it, and how would we find adequate rehearsal time? There would need to be a daily choir practice, not the once or twice a week that was the current Guildford Pro-Cathedral choir's timetable. And from where would we find choristers who could fulfil that daily timetable? The long-established cathedrals either had their own choir or cathedral school, though there were a few exceptions among the more 'modern' foundations who used boys from the locality. I found out that the closest school to the new Cathedral was Park Barn, but that was a secondary school where the pupils joined at the age of 11 – far too old for choristers to start. Walter told me that there had originally been a plan for a choir school at Guildford. Evidently, the Earl of Onslow, the donor of Stag Hill as the site for the new Cathedral, had also offered nearby Stoke Park Mansion for use as the Cathedral's choir school. The plan never came to fruition, and the mansion was demolished in the early 1960s to make way for Guildford College.

Where should I begin? I asked Walter's advice and he suggested that I approach one of the local preparatory schools. There were four in the area: one at Ripley, six miles north of Guildford; one at Shackleford, six miles south; and two in the more immediate locality – Boxgrove and Lanesborough. If we were to link up with any of these, we would have to come up with a way of getting the boys to and from the Cathedral. Walter pointed out that the idea might not be so warmly received at Lanesborough, since a link had been tried a few years earlier when John Alldis, then the school's music master, had set up a new boys' choir with a view to them singing at Christ Church, where he was the Organist and Choirmaster, and later, at the new Cathedral. 'Nevertheless,' Walter said, 'I will give you an introduction if you'd like to try.'

I weighed up the various options. Both Ripley Court and Aldro (in Shackleford) were boarding schools, and that meant we would have a county or country-wide catchment area for the choristers. Boxgrove School was situated in Guildford and was also a boarding school. It seemed to be the ideal solution, and I was about to make contact with them when someone told me that Christopher Corke, the current music master at Lanesborough School, had been a chorister at St. Paul's Cathedral, and was keen to meet me.

Although hesitant about working with a day school, I went to meet Christopher, and was encouraged by his enthusiasm about creating a link with the Cathedral. He introduced me to Stuart Swayne, the Headmaster. Stuart was enthusiastic about the possibility of establishing a link, though his one firm condition was that all the boys for the new choir should be chosen from those already within the school. If the arrangement proved to be successful, then he might consider bringing boys into the school specifically as Cathedral choristers. He would let us have daily rehearsals in the lunchtime activities period (12.15 to 1.00 p.m.), and these could begin when I arrived in September.

The Consecration was now less than a year away, and if we were to start those daily rehearsals I'd need to choose the boys now, during the summer term. The school had two choirs – senior and

Lanesborough School, 1960

junior – and we needed a wide age range across the first 16 choristers, so that the time of leaving (at the age of 13) would be staggered. Christopher produced a list of possible names from the two choirs. There were 16 on the list, with an age range of 8 to 11, and he arranged for me to hear each one of them sing. There were some promising voices, though no more than two of them had any experience of singing in church, and certainly no idea of the demands involved in becoming a Cathedral chorister.

Armed with a list of parents' addresses and phone numbers, it was now up to me to make contact and try to persuade them to let their son join the new choir. Given the demands of up to seven rehearsals, and up to eight sung Services each week, that might not be easy. However, we had a sort of trump card which would appeal to typical Surrey parents from what was often called the 'gin and Jag(uar) belt': by this time next year their son would have sung for the Queen! Another selling point might have been my promise of a financial scholarship, though as yet I had no authority to offer this, as was curtly pointed out to me in a formal letter from the Chapter Clerk. I made three or four early evening journeys to the Guildford area, often relying on one prospective choir parent to ferry me to the next.

Having seen them all and, hopefully, sold them the benefits of becoming a Cathedral chorister, I was able to concentrate on the Kingsbury choir again, and spend the rest of the summer preparing the boys for our week-long August residence at St. Paul's Cathedral. Getting to St. Paul's each day involved a walk to Wembley Park station, a Metropolitan line train to Baker Street, and a change of train to get us to Farringdon underground station. This would be the daily pattern for what would be my very last week with the St. Andrew's choir, and I chose a very ambitious music list for St. Paul's, culminating with Samuel Wesley's long and exacting unaccompanied eight-part setting of *In exitu Israel* as the anthem at Evensong on our very last day.

In addition to singing the Services at St. Paul's, the BBC offered us a recording on one of the evenings in St. Gabriel's Church, Cricklewood. That would mean a really late night for the boys, since we'd have to make the recording after singing Evensong – there was no other time available. All the repertoire was well known, and I assembled the best of the altos, tenors and basses who were helping us at St. Paul's. Solos were sung by Michael Vaile, Peter Burrows and Peter Chapman (altos); Ian Partridge, Cyril Ellis and Christopher Scott (tenors); and John Miller and Colin Wykes (basses). There was no conductor, and I accompanied on the organ. The recording would be transmitted sometime in the future, and in the end, either by design or accident, it was scheduled to be broadcast on the very same day as the Consecration of Guildford Cathedral, nine months later.

At St. Paul's, the strain of travel, coupled with the ambitious repertoire and the late-night BBC recording, began to show – not least since we also had to sing Saturday morning Matins on our very last day. The psalm for that evening has 51 verses, and with that and the double choir setting of the *Magnificat and Nunc Dimittis in F (Collegium Regale)* by Charles Wood, the boys were really tired by the time we reached the Samuel Wesley anthem. It was not our best – it went sharp, but at least we'd literally ended on a high note.

SATURDAY, SEPTEMBER 3. *Mattins and Evensong by the choir of St. Andrew, Kingsbury.*
† 8.0 A.M.   Holy Communion.
10.0 A.M.   Mattins. Responses. *Smith.* Te Deum and Jubilate. *Travers* in F.
             Anthem. My beloved spake. *Hadley.*
4.0 P.M.   Evensong. Responses. *Byrd.* Magnificat and Nunc Dimittis. *Wood* in F.
             Anthem. In exitu Israel. *Wesley.* Hymn No. 230 (*A. & M.*).

St. Paul's Cathedral music list, 3ʳᵈ September 1960

That evening there was a farewell party in the church hall at Kingsbury at which I was presented with a commemorative pewter mug, inscribed with the names of each of the choristers.

All that now remained was for the boys to sing my last Sunday Services in St. Andrew's, and the farewells as I left the church for the very last time. The following week the choir would be in the hands of my successor, Philip Cooper.

It was time to head to Guildford, with some excitement, but also much trepidation.

9

Into the Unknown
Guildford 1960–1961

Aside from my summer visits to the first chorister parents, all I so far knew about Guildford was that it was 25 miles south of London and that you could get there by train from London's Waterloo Station or on the number 715 Green Line coach from Oxford Circus.

I was due to arrive on Monday 5th September 1960, but where would I live? Accommodation had never been discussed or offered, so I contacted Walter Boulton about it. Apart from two houses at the foot of the steps leading up to the south side, and already occupied, the new Cathedral had just one other property: a brand-new house in nearby St. John's Road, designated for future occupation by the custodian of the new Cathedral, yet to be appointed. Somehow Walter managed to persuade the Cathedral Council (or more likely, had taken the decision on his own) that I could live there until it was needed sometime early in 1961. It would solve the immediate problem, and 32 St. John's Road would be mine for the foreseeable future.

The house was totally unfurnished – bare floorboards in every room. I had a few small pieces of furniture, and these were brought down from Kingsbury with the rest of my belongings by Colin Wykes, one of The Jacobean Singers. It was time to find some more furniture, and that meant finding some money. A visit to Lloyds Bank found a sympathetic ear from the manager who arranged for a loan, most of which I immediately spent in a local furnishing shop. At least there would be a bed, table and chairs, and just the one carpet. Colin, ever the practical handyman, was able to connect a second-hand cooker we had managed to acquire. It was all very spartan, but at least it was a roof over my head.

Now I had to meet the choristers at Holy Trinity Pro-Cathedral, a spacious Georgian building at the top of Guildford High Street. The first practice was a mixture of elation and disappointment. There were no more than 10 boys, and they lacked the enthusiasm of the 16 I'd left behind at St. Andrew's. But there were some really pleasing voices, including two or three very able soloists.

Weekday sung Services at the Pro-Cathedral were Evensong on Friday and Saturday, and on Sunday there was a congregational Eucharist followed by Cathedral Matins, with Evensong at 6.30 p.m. Choir practices for the boys were late afternoon on Tuesday, and on Friday before and after Evensong. The six lay clerks arrived just in time to sing the Friday Evensong, and stayed on afterwards to rehearse for Sunday, the boys also remaining for part of that time. Evensong on Saturday was reserved for visiting choirs from the diocese, and I would usually be there to welcome them and sort out any practical

Holy Trinity Pro-Cathedral, Guildford

details, sometimes playing the organ whilst their own organist conducted them from the choir-stalls.

Having trawled the previous term's music lists, I erred on the side of caution, scheduling pieces that the Cathedral choir already knew. There was no one to direct them in Services, and I, as the organist, sat several feet away with my back to them, the only contact being through a mirror which only showed the backs of the men on the nearest side of the choir. In addition to the six paid lay clerks, a few other men joined them for the full practice after the Friday Evensong and sang on Sundays. The lay clerks were mixed in age and ability. They were all older than me, and perhaps rightly, were somewhat suspicious of this young man who had been drafted in without any consultation with them. One of them, Fielden Buckley, had been the solo boy chorister in the famous choir at London's Temple Church in the 1920s and was now Assistant Headmaster of the Royal Grammar School. He often appeared supercilious and rather sullen, which made me wonder if he was upset that I'd not taken the job at the school and that its link with the Cathedral had been broken.

As the weeks went by, the men and I established some musical rapport, and I began to assess who might be able, and also have the time, to sing at the new Cathedral. There were two or three who could form the nucleus of the new back row. Gordon Anderson, one of the altos, could have been a professional; equally at home as a tenor or alto, he had a real singer's technique. Ron Smith (bass) and Walter Waghorn (alto) were schoolteachers, and both were keen to be part of the new choir. Ron had a pleasant baritone voice, albeit with a slight tremor, whilst Walter was what I'd call an old-fashioned alto, making a rather hooty sound.

Among the supernumerary men, Roger Moffatt was a music teacher at a local comprehensive school and would later become the first (unpaid) Assistant Organist, whilst baritone James Vine was a naturally talented jazz pianist. Two or three ex-choristers had also joined the back row for Sunday Services as they found their 'new' voices. Bass Lionel Fawcett became an opera singer, whilst another, Nigel O'Dwyer, sang in the new Cathedral choir before going on to Magdalen College, Oxford, as a bass academical clerk (choral scholar), and later being ordained. The only problem that I could see was how to say no to anyone who really didn't have the vocal or musical ability to sing at the new Cathedral. It was a problem that I never really solved, and we did end up with some enthusiastic singers in the new choir who should not have been there, but whose heart, if not their voice, was in the right place.

This then was the current Guildford Cathedral Choir which, for the next eight months, I would run in conjunction with the new one. True to his word, Stuart Swayne, the Headmaster of Lanesborough School, had arranged for the 16 boys I'd already chosen to rehearse at lunchtime each day of the week, apart from Wednesday. The venue was a prefabricated hut behind one of the school's main buildings, occupied each morning by the very youngest boys in the school, until they left for their lunch at 12.15 p.m. – the time we were due to start our rehearsal. The building was also used as a makeshift gymnasium, so it was a case of quickly moving all the chairs and gym equipment, wheeling out the piano, and getting benches and music ready for the choir practice. There was no time to waste.

Those first few rehearsals should have been recorded for posterity. It was the first time I'd been faced with a group of real beginners, and this was the choir that in 34 weeks' time would be leading the singing at the Consecration of England's newest Cathedral. It was a hesitant and somewhat unrewarding start – the sound they made was nowhere near the vocal output of the boys of the Pro-Cathedral choir, and unlike a choir already in existence, there were no leaders to look up to and try to emulate. The way to start was to practise simple hymns and do them well. The school didn't have a morning assembly, so hymns were not part of the boys' background. If they were to learn to sing with any understanding of the text and liturgical language, hymns would make an ideal start.

Singing is closely allied to confidence, and initially it was in short supply. After a few weeks the new boys were able to sing The Lord's Prayer on one note without going more than a semitone flat... We were making some progress.

I'd been fortunate that John Boulton, the Provost's son, had offered me the use of his car whilst he was away at university. It was a godsend, since St. John's Road and Lanesborough School were all of two miles apart, and getting there for the daily rehearsals involved a lot of walking, as well as a bus journey. However, old cars are not always reliable, and more than once it broke down at a crucial time, leaving me to stagger on to rehearsal laden with hymnbooks and psalters.

Life at the house had also changed. One evening there was a knock at the door, and there was Colin Wykes, suitcase in hand, having quit his job in the City of London. He had come to make a new life in Guildford; could he use one of the spare bedrooms? Having been on my own since I'd arrived, it was a joy to have some company, and also to have such a useful handyman in residence. It wasn't long before the house had a much more homely feel. Until he got a job, Colin had the time and the expertise to do all the jobs I'd never got around to doing – carpets and rugs were properly installed and light shades and curtain-rails fitted.

Meanwhile, the musical timetable at Holy Trinity Pro-Cathedral was suddenly turned upside down. In November 1960 the Bishop of Guildford died, and his funeral, a major diocesan event, was scheduled for a weekday morning. Having said that there was no way we could get the Holy Trinity Pro-Cathedral choir together for the occasion, someone suggested that perhaps the new Cathedral choir might sing at it. I said that they were nowhere ready to appear in public, let alone able to learn all the special music that would be required. In the end we did manage to get a few of the boys and men from the Pro-Cathedral choir, and they were augmented by a quartet from The Jacobean Singers. It was a long and dignified Service, in which the Sequence (the English plainsong version of the *Dies irae, Dies illa*) was beautifully sung by visiting tenor, Ian Partridge.

Back at Lanesborough we had progressed to psalmody, the daily staple diet of every cathedral chorister. The language was completely new to them, and much of the time in our rehearsals now began to be taken up with reading through the psalms appointed for each evening of the month. For any member of staff passing by, it must have been strange to see the choir in rehearsal but not hear a note of music being sung. There must also have been occasions when they were probably more surprised to hear the most accomplished singing coming out of the hut so early on; sometimes I took a tape-recorder to rehearsals and played the boys the best of the English cathedral choirs, giving them a vocal yardstick at which to aim. Possible boredom in rehearsals was somewhat alleviated by learning a few tuneful carols – the new choir was to make its first public appearance at the school concert in December.

I felt that I should follow the Provost's suggestion and see if boys who did not attend Lanesborough could have the opportunity to sing in the new Cathedral. With that in mind, in November 1960 we advertised an audition in the local papers for The Town Boys' Choir. Well over 25 boys applied. Auditions were held in the choir vestry at Holy Trinity, and by the end of these, 16 boys had been chosen. The plan was that they would sing the Friday Evensong and the Sunday evening Service in the new building, and have Saturday morning rehearsals in Holy Trinity, to begin immediately. Progress was quicker than with the Lanesborough group since a number of the boys already had the experience of singing in their local church choir. Attendance was not always one hundred percent, and the one vital thing we had not considered carefully enough was how and when we could find the time to rehearse once the new Cathedral was in operation. In the end, that problem would be impossible to solve, but in the meantime, we continued to work together on a weekly basis, with a promise that four boys from the group would be chosen to sing in the Service of Consecration.

There was also the big decision to be made about the siting of the detached console for the organ. The architect Sir Edward Maufe, his assistant Mr. Layfield, Ralph Woods and I met at the Cathedral. There was nowhere for the console at floor level, and after a lot of discussion and persuasion, Sir Edward agreed that a gallery could be built at the apex of the westernmost arch of the chancel. This would involve turning the already completed east end of the building back into a building site, whilst heavy steel girders were inserted between the pillars to bear the considerable weight. And we'd not quite finished our planning. On the assumption that architects delight in symmetry, Ralph and I suggested that another gallery should be built in the arch immediately opposite the console. Sir Edward agreed, which was just as well since we had already come up with a tonal scheme for a small division of the organ just above the choir's heads. We had given it the working title of the Positive Organ, a term usually used for a choir or small 'fixed' organ.

During the next few weeks I made a couple of visits to Liverpool, where James Rushworth, the firm's managing director introduced me to several key craftsmen at the organ works. I was able to hear some of the stops in the voicing shop, as well as see the skeleton of the new console which they had just started to build.

In early December 1960 the appointment of the first Precentor for the new Cathedral was announced. The Reverend Eric Ware was then Vicar of Blackheath and Chilworth,

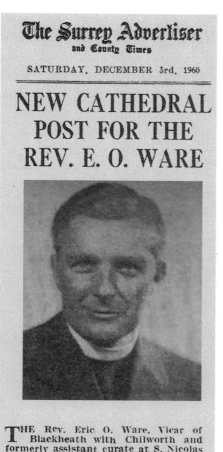

The Surrey Advertiser
and County Times

SATURDAY, DECEMBER 3rd, 1960

NEW CATHEDRAL POST FOR THE REV. E. O. WARE

THE Rev. Eric O. Ware, Vicar of Blackheath with Chilworth and formerly assistant curate at S. Nicolas Church, Guildford, will be the Precentor of the new Guildford Cathedral.

This appointment has been made by the Provost and Chapter of the Cathedral and is the first to be announced.

It takes effect from May 1st, 1961.

a few miles from Guildford, and an accomplished singer. Walter Boulton had long promised Eric the appointment; Eric had sung the priest's part in all the Diocesan Choirs Festivals for many years, and his warm and well-produced baritone voice was well known throughout the diocese. As yet there were no new Cathedral statutes, and therefore no official designation of the number of clergy or the titles they would hold. Walter was assuming that, as Dean of the new Cathedral, his appointments would automatically be confirmed, and he knew that not just the planned daily sung Offices, but the many special Services, would require the expertise of a musical priest who could also mastermind the ceremonial for these occasions. 'There's no money to pay you at the moment,' he told Eric, 'but the diocese has agreed you can continue as Vicar of Blackheath and remain there in the vicarage until a house can be built in the new Cathedral Close.'

Christmas arrived, and the Lanesborough choristers sang their carols at the school concert in Merrow Village Hall. It was still a small, untutored sound, but at least they'd had their first taste of public performance as a choir. At the Pro-Cathedral we sang all the usual Services, including Midnight Eucharist on Christmas Eve with over 500 communicants, and a festal Matins on Christmas Day morning.

Everyone in the choir went off to their homes for their family gatherings, and Colin and I returned to the house at St. John's Road for muted celebrations, though later in the evening I was invited to the Provost's house in Castle Gate. The whole of the Boulton family were there and we spent a hilarious evening playing charades.

Having gathered that Colin and I had not been able to get home to our families, Eric and his wife Esmé invited us over to Blackheath vicarage on Boxing Day. There we met Hilary and Elizabeth (their two daughters), and their son Nicolas, who had recently left Wells Cathedral School and was now at Guildford School of Art on a photography course. That afternoon, relaxing on the sofa, was to shape the whole of my future personal life, since their attractive and delightful younger daughter, Elizabeth (Buffie), would become my wife five years later.

Our first meeting, Boxing Day afternoon, 1960.

After a very short break, the Pro-Cathedral choir sang a post-Christmas Festival of Nine Lessons and Carols on Sunday 1st January 1961, and so began a momentous year in Guildford's history.

I had hoped that January would be a quiet month and allow me to get back to work with the new choristers at Lanesborough. It was not to be. On 18th January the appointment of the Very Reverend George Reindorp as the new Bishop of Guildford was announced, and that meant a large-scale Enthronement Service would take place in the Pro-Cathedral before the opening of the new building in May. George was the charismatic and popular Provost of Southwark Cathedral, and had once described the traditional episcopal dress of gaiters and breeches as 'absurdly archaic uniform'. Now he would have to wear them.

Coupled with the planning of the Enthronement Service were regular meetings of a small committee to plan the details of the Consecration of the new Cathedral. I was spared the longer sessions about protocol, servers, sidesmen, and invitees from the diocese and county, and was given *carte blanche* to make the musical arrangements for both Services, though I did realise that the new Bishop would want to have some input over the music for his enthronement.

For the Consecration, Walter Boulton was most anxious to see my choice of hymns (he would have the final say) and suggested that I contact the Royal Military School of Music at Kneller Hall to see if they would agree to their fanfare trumpeters taking part. I sent a handwritten letter and promptly received an official reply from their Director of Music, Lieutenant Colonel Basil Brown, inviting me there for lunch. Kneller Hall is a fine 17th century mansion in the Middlesex enclave of Whitton, and in true military style, everything there was done with precise efficiency and formality. Lt. Col. Brown was a most gracious host, and at lunch he introduced me to Trevor Sharpe, the Bandmaster. Although Trevor held a captain's rank, he was known as Mr. Sharpe. He was most enthusiastic about the trumpeters' participation in the Consecration – what would I like them to play? He reeled off a list of composers who had written fanfares, but sensing that I knew none of them, he immediately arranged for the trumpeters to assemble and play some. The sound was amazing, and we settled on an opening fanfare by Arthur Bliss; the brass parts in the Vaughan Williams 1953 arrangement of The Old 100th – *All people that on earth do dwell*; Arthur Bliss's recently written interludes between the verses of *Christ is made the sure foundation* (specially composed for Princess Margaret's wedding the year before); and lastly, a new brass arrangement of the last verse of the final hymn, *Praise, my soul, the King of Heaven*, which he (Trevor Sharpe) would score to fit in with the descant by Albert Tysoe that we were planning to use. This would, we hoped, make a grand musical finale to the Service.

Now was the time to think about an organist for the great occasion. Simon Preston had also been a student of C.H. Trevor at the Royal Academy of Music, though we had never met, since he had taken up the organ scholarship to King's College, Cambridge, in September 1958, just as I arrived at the Academy. His skill as a soloist and accompanist was already legendary, so I thought I'd aim for the top and see if Simon could play for the Consecration, even though it was during term-time at Cambridge. I wrote to David Willcocks, the Director of Music at King's, and received a handwritten reply, saying that he would be pleased for Simon to play. This would mean Simon being in Guildford for two or three days before, giving him time to get to know the organ and practise his voluntaries, but more importantly for us, to accompany the final rehearsals.

Great occasions such as these demand special choir music – but what? I spent a long time trying to find something appropriate for the choir to sing as the royal, ecclesiastical, and legal processions moved up the length of the nave at the start of the Service. One obvious choice was Hubert Parry's great anthem, *I was glad*, regularly used on great ceremonial occasions. But we wanted our Service to be different, and felt that there should be something more reflective between the loud opening fanfare and the first congregational hymn.

I turned to the psalms, and chose three that seemed very appropriate – 121 (*I will lift up mine eyes unto the hills*), 122 (*I was glad when they said unto me*), and 84 (*O how amiable are thy dwellings*). Psalm 121 would be sung to a beautiful chant by Michael Bishop, an architect who was singing alto in the church choir at St. Laurence, Catford, and The Jacobean Singers. I had already written a chant for Psalm 122 at St. Andrew's, Kingsbury, and that would follow on nicely from Michael's chant. Having two chants that would be unknown not just to the congregation, but also to everyone listening and watching via the BBC, it was time to be traditional with the chant to Psalm 84, so we turned to good old Henry Smart for something that many people would have heard before.

With the opening now planned, there remained a few verses from Psalm 43 to be sung at a later stage in the Service; the Litany, sung by the Precentor and choir to the traditional setting by Thomas Tallis; and a short unaccompanied anthem at the consecration of the high altar: *Sacerdotes Domini* (Then did the priests make offerings at the altar) by William Byrd. The only problem with the Byrd was that, in the final rehearsals, it was found to be too short, so we had to take it a lot slower than we would usually have sung it.

That was it, apart from the procession at the end of the Service, when the Bishop of Guildford and the royal party would leave the Cathedral. We would need more choir music at this point, and it had to be the right length, celebratory, and yet not take anything away from the impact of the final hymn – *Praise, my soul, the King of Heaven.* The piece that immediately came to mind was John Mundy's verse-anthem, *Sing joyfully unto God our strength.* No-one at Guildford knew it or had even heard of it, and eyebrows were raised in the steering committee as to whether it was suitable. I had sung it in a broadcast Choral Evensong at Hampstead a few years earlier, and since then it had become a favourite with the Kingsbury choir. Scored for bass solo, choir and organ, it is an ebullient and rhythmic setting of Psalm 81, and I knew from my Hampstead days that it would sound really well and sonorous if the solo parts were sung by all the tenors and basses rather than just the one solo voice. I couldn't find a recording of it anywhere, so I played it to the Provost on the Holy Trinity organ, and immediately he approved.

Everything was settled and sent off to the printers. Now I had to teach the chosen pieces to the new choristers, and I was sure that would be possible in the time that was available before the big day. Coupled with all that learning, the new choristers needed to get used to the order and formality of Evensong – an Office that they would be singing up to six times a week as from the day after the Consecration. There was no way we could do this in the hut in which we rehearsed at Lanesborough, so I arranged for them to come to the new Cathedral on a couple of dark evenings in February 1961, to sing through an Evensong as though it were the real thing.

It was then that the reality hit home that we had to find a way to transport the choristers from the school to the Cathedral, not only for these two occasions, but also every day they would sing Evensong after 17th May. Walter Boulton must have had a word with the treasurer of the New Cathedral Fund, since I was instructed to visit Grays, the local Hillman and Commer agent, to arrange the purchase of a minibus. There was not enough money for the model with comfortable upholstered seats, so we ended up with the basic version with wooden slats, in the Cathedral's adopted colour – dark blue.

The crypt chapel was still being used as a local parish church, and in it was a harmonium to accompany the singing. I re-arranged the chairs at the front of the chapel to face each other, simulating choir-stalls, taught the boys how to process (albeit in this very confined space), and they entered the chapel in formal procession to sing through Evensong. There were no choir robes and no congregation. It was all very simple – plainsong responses, a short psalm, the Magnificat and Nunc Dimittis sung to Anglican chants (we had yet to learn a setting of the canticles), a short anthem, and a final hymn. I read the lessons from the harmonium and also sang the priest's part in the responses, as well as taking the intercessions after the anthem. At the end of the 'Service' they processed out, met their parents who were waiting upstairs, and were whisked off home to do their prep – this would be the timetable they would keep on four weekday evenings from May 18th onwards. Next day, at the lunchtime rehearsal, I went through all the positives and not-so-positives from the evening before, saying that we needed to do it again in the great spaces of the Cathedral itself – and there they would have to be really confident!

The following week they came up to the Cathedral again for their very first experience of singing in the new building. I arranged rows of chairs facing each other in the still unfurnished chancel, and wheeled out the grand piano into the centre, on which I would accompany our trial Evensong.

February 1961 in the unfinished chancel. Boys – from the left: Paul Williams, Andrew Imrie, Richard Rusbridger, Mark Bryant, Paul de St. Croix, Jeremy Evans, and David Gurney

Eric Ware, our new Precentor, sang the responses, read the lessons, and took the intercessions. The large corrugated iron screen separating the nave from the crossing had yet to be removed, but even so, this was a vast space in which these inexperienced boys were singing.

To say it was dispiriting is a real understatement. When you walk into a tall ecclesiastical building, there is an expectation that the sound will reverberate around.

Here at Guildford, this was not so, and was intentionally not so. Sir Edward Maufe, the architect, had engaged the services of Hope Bagenal, a distinguished figure in the world of acoustic engineering. Mr. Bagenal had 'designed' the acoustics of London's Royal Festival Hall and had stipulated that the whole of the ceiling vault, from end to end of the Cathedral, should be covered with a deep layer of wool-like soft absorbent acoustic plaster. It was that, coupled with the lack of any other reflective surfaces, that produced the effect of deadening the sound of any music. As one of the boys in the choir remarked, 'It's just like singing into blotting paper.'

He was right, and though the singing that evening proved that this group of new choristers had learned something, they had neither the technique or the confidence to project any sound further than a few feet – and this in a building which would have the nearest member of the congregation seated at least 20 feet away. Bearing in mind that distance, and the positioning of the organ pipes in the north transept gallery – a sort of sound barrier between choir and congregation – I had anticipated the problem of audibility, and soon after my appointment had requested a meeting in the Cathedral with Sir Edward, his assistant Mr. Layfield, and Mr. Bagenal to discuss the problems we would face. Mr. Bagenal was not at all helpful, saying, 'The brass will sound well...' – as if we had brass every day, rather than on the isolated 'great' occasion. When I pointed out the problems of the sound of the choir projecting into the nave, his reply was to point to the south gallery, saying, 'Well, you must move the choir to some place like that until you find the right position for them.' It was a total unawareness of the fact that our position would be fixed in the chancel, in the choir-stalls that were about to be installed. I knew there was no way forward and it was best to end the meeting there and then.

There was now increasing publicity about the new Cathedral. An article published in the local paper early in March highlighted the music for the Consecration and the plans for daily sung Services, including the link to Lanesborough School. In my initial recruiting visits, I had promised the parents that there would be choral scholarships for their boys as from September 1961. The scholarship details were included in the article, and a week or so later I received a curt and formal letter from John Brown, the Chapter Clerk, saying that Chapter were dismayed to learn that I had made this financial commitment without any reference or request to them. There was little possibility of my promises being honoured.

This was not our first correspondence. One evening, early in February, there had been a knock at the door of the house in St. John's Road where Colin and I were living. The visitor was Mr. William Taft, who announced to us that he had just accepted the post of Custodian of the new Cathedral and would be moving into the house in three weeks' time. I had immediately written to John Brown saying that if there

was no alternative accommodation available, I would have
no option other than to resign
immediately and return to my
parents' home in Chingford
– and this, just a few weeks
before the Enthronement
of the new Bishop and the
Consecration of the new
Cathedral. His reply, in typical legal terminology, had
been short and not very promising, but either he had contacted Walter Boulton about

No. 1 Cathedral Cottage, with the Cathedral tower under construction in the background

the situation or Walter had somehow found out, since after Evensong that Friday,
Walter asked me into the clergy vestry. I feared a dressing-down, but instead, Walter
put his hand on my shoulder saying, 'There's a house in Ridgemount at the foot of the
Cathedral steps which is now empty, and if you'd like that, you can move in at any
time.' In doing this, an important precedent was established that accommodation for
the Organist would be provided from now on.

With the cooker tied on to a borrowed trailer, and laden with other bits of furniture, Colin and I gradually moved into No. 1 Cathedral Cottage at the end of February
1961. And more by default than design, it was to become the official residence of the
Organist until 1968, when a new house was built in Cathedral Close.

Back at Lanesborough, we were gradually learning and polishing the music for
the Consecration – this was to be one of the most rehearsed Services ever! However,
our routine was suddenly interrupted by the news that the Enthronement of the new
Bishop, in Holy Trinity Pro-Cathedral, was to be televised live by ITV.

Would I arrange for the new choristers to sing at the Service, and perhaps some of the men of the new choir as well? In my desire to get the new boys' choir up and running, I'd not forgotten that we would also need an expert back row of singers, and that they would need to commit themselves to several Services each week.

The first lay clerk to be appointed was John Barrow. A superb baritone, John already had a link with Guildford in that he had married the daughter of Sir Roy Pinsent, whose family had a connection with the house next to Walter Boulton in Castle Gate. Walter suggested that I contact John, and I arranged to meet and audition him in the flat in Bayswater Road, London, where he and his wife Rosemary were then living. A student of Henry Cummings, John had the finest baritone voice I had ever heard, full and rich with a superb technique. I gathered that he and Rosemary would soon be moving to Churt, a small village near Hindhead, Surrey, about 15 miles from Guildford, and that John would be available to sing in the choir for the Consecration and on a regular basis after that.

David Gibbs was a former chorister of Southwark Cathedral, and had been one of the three Pickled Boys who sang in the first London performance of Benjamin Britten's cantata, *St. Nicolas*, conducted by the composer himself. Now a tenor and teaching English at Tillingbourne School, it was his colleague, Roger Moffatt, who suggested that he come and sing to me. David's version, which I'm sure is true, is that I thrust a copy into his hand and said, 'Here, sing this', after which I immediately signed him up for the new choir.

Both David and John agreed to join the choir for the Bishop's Enthronement on Wednesday 12th April, five weeks before the Consecration of the new Cathedral. From a musical point of view it was to prove an ideal dry run for the Consecration, since the Enthronement would also have trumpets (this time from the Central Band of the Royal Air Force), microphones, television cameras and lighting, and a large congregation to lead in the hymns. Apart from Psalm 122, none of the chosen music for the Consecration was considered suitable, so we settled on Charles Villiers Stanford's setting of *O for a closer walk with God* as the choir anthem.

On the early afternoon of the Enthronement, and wearing cassocks, ruffs and surplices, some borrowed from local churches, all the new Lanesborough choristers assembled at Holy Trinity to join with the Pro-Cathedral choristers and a large group of altos, tenors and basses for a quick rehearsal and balance test. That done, everyone squashed into the choir vestry to await the start of the live television transmission at 3.00 p.m. Luckily, I had Roger Moffatt to play the voluntaries before the Service, so was able to supervise and assemble the procession in the right order. Everything went well, and the new choristers now had a foretaste of what was to come just five weeks later.

In the new building, the corrugated screen that had separated the nave from the crossing and chancel had been removed. Now we could see the impressive length of the empty nave and finally assess the acoustics. As I feared, Hope Bagenal had done his worst! With the entire vault covered with absorbent acoustic plaster, there was little or no reverberation. We spent an evening in the empty building with two singers – Roger Moffatt and Colin Wykes – recording sounds at differing pitches and from different distances. It was a such a disappointment. It was indeed like singing into blotting paper and there was nothing we could do about it. I had tried to dissuade them...[1]

The priority now was the installation of the new Cathedral organ in time for the Consecration. Lorry loads of pipes and woodwork began to arrive, and the only place to store everything was on the floor of the crossing. The whole area was roped off to any visitors, though many of them still took a keen interest in what was going on. Rushworth & Dreaper sent down a team from Liverpool who were working all day every day, and sometimes through the nights as well. The new and heavy console was hoisted up with block and tackle and gently lowered into its recently finished gallery. Access to it at that time was by workmen's ladders, but a few days later a specially made wooden ladder arrived and was fitted. I now had access to the organ loft, though the steps were narrow and dangerous to negotiate by anyone wearing a cassock and carrying music. Below was a hard stone floor – one slip and you'd either be seriously injured or even killed.

Early in April, BBC television sent a film crew for an item in *Children's Newsreel*, and by then I was able to play something from the newly installed console, as well as stand in the crossing holding a selection of different sized pipes.

Officials from the Lord Chamberlain's office began regular visits, mainly to talk about protocol, seating etc. for the royal party on the great day. With just over three weeks to go, the whole of Guildford was shaken by a seismic announcement in the press that Walter Boulton, the Provost, would not be Dean of the new Cathedral.

A move that we had all anticipated as a formality would not now happen. At Holy Trinity Pro-Cathedral, with its parochial status, Walter had been appointed by the then Bishop of Guildford, Henry Montgomery-Campbell, but the new Cathedral would have new Statutes, in which the Dean would be a Crown appointment – a person recommended by the Ecclesiastical Commissioners. Some months earlier, at the request of the Mother's Union, Walter had written a book on marriage in which

---

1   In 2016-17, 55 years after the Consecration, all the acoustic plaster was removed on grounds of health and safety since it was found to contain asbestos. The result has been a bloom to the sound and a reverberation period that I longed for all those years ago.

he expressed views over divorce that were not in line with the church's teachings at that time. There had been considerable furore after several reviews pointed these out, and the book was hastily withdrawn from publication, triggering extensive comments about it in both the ecclesiastical and national press.

It may have been coincidence that the head of the Mother's Union was Rosamond Fisher, wife of Geoffrey Fisher, the Archbishop of Canterbury. However, as the Archbishop said in a later BBC radio interview, 'I

THE SURREY ADVERTISER AND COUNTY TIMES

SATURDAY APRIL 22 1961

PROVOST NOT TO BE DEAN
He has resigned from office and living

THE Very Rev. Walter Boulton, Provost of Guildford and Rector of Holy Trinity with St. Mary, Guildford, since 1952, is not to be Dean of Guildford after the consecration of the cathedral on May 17th. The following statement was issued this week by the provost:—

"The Very Rev. Walter Boulton has resigned the offices of Provost of Guildford and Rector of Holy Trinity with St. Mary's, Guildford, with effect from May 18th, 1961. He has resigned in order to allow the new constitution to come into effect, and the Bishop of Guildford has accepted his resignation.

"The Crown has intimated that it will not nominate the provost to be Dean of Guildford.

was, of course, consulted about the appointment, and think the Crown's decision fully justified.' At a stroke, the Church had deprived Walter the fulfilment of his ten years' work in bringing the Cathedral from an unfinished shell to its Consecration, and now, the very first day of its new life would be his last.

I was stunned, for this was the man who had stuck his neck out and appointed an unknown and unqualified parish church organist to lead the music at the new Cathedral. And here we now were, 25 days before the Consecration without a leader, and with just three members of staff – the Precentor, the Dean's Verger, and me – to set in motion the pattern of Worship in the new building. The controversy over the non-appointment was to rage on for several weeks, both in the press and on the radio and television. How difficult that must have been for Walter Boulton I cannot begin to

From the Daily Express, *early May 1961*

imagine. Not only did he have to oversee and attend the Consecration on what would be his very last day in charge, but also, on the day before the Consecration, read in the national press the news of the appointment of someone else as the first Dean of Guildford. The Church had given Walter a final slap in the face. Since the Dean was not due to take up office until September, surely 'they' could have waited until after the Consecration to make the announcement?

Despite my disappointment on Walter's behalf, I had to focus on the planning for the big day. The BBC had already sent sound and lighting technicians, as well as Antony Craxton, the producer for the day. Tall, elegant and beautifully spoken, Antony was the second son of the distinguished piano accompanist and teacher Harold Craxton. He had joined the BBC in 1941 as a junior programme engineer, and had moved on to television in 1951, where he pioneered many live outside broadcasts of concerts and several national events. It was heartening to talk with someone who understood music and would be ultimately responsible for what came out of both the radio and television sets on 17th May. Our friendship was to stand us in good stead years later when Antony was in charge

Daily Telegraph and Morning Post,

Tuesday, May 16, 1961

A BISHOP TO BE DEAN OF GUILDFORD

DAILY TELEGRAPH REPORTER

THE QUEEN has approved the appointment of the Rt. Rev. G. W. Clarkson, Suffragan Bishop of Pontefract, as Dean of Guildford.

Bishop Clarkson is 63, four years older than the Very Rev. Walter Boulton, the present Provost of Guildford, who has been passed over for the appointment.

Mr. Boulton's appointment as Provost ends on Thursday, the day after the new Guildford cathedral is consecrated.

THE RT. REV.
G. W. CLARKSON

of the television coverage of HM The Queen's Silver Jubilee Service at St. Paul's Cathedral in June 1977.

The chancel of the new building had now been furnished with choir-stalls. Made of limed oak, they looked rather like ecclesiastical park benches and must have been such a disappointment to Sir Edward Maufe, whose original pre-war plans had been for ornate and canopied stalls, similar to those in Chester Cathedral and Downside Abbey. More importantly, from a musical point of view, they were very far apart, and the spaces behind them were open, which would mean that what little sound the new choristers would make would be lost in the north and south aisles. If only we could have something reflective, to help throw the sound out towards the nave. I suggested that it might be possible to have glass screens from the back of the stalls to the springing line of each arch, and maybe they could have similar engravings on the glass to match those on the west doors by John Hutton. At least the glass would reflect the sound from one side of the choir to the other and prevent it from dissipating into the aisles. I was firmly told that there was no money available. Like so many things, it was put on the back burner and later forgotten.

One saving grace was that both the front and back rows of the choir-stalls could accommodate more singers than we would usually have at daily or Sunday Services, and that meant that I could plan for an enlarged choir to sing at the Consecration. As far as the boys were concerned, what we needed was experience. That would come from the leading trebles in the Holy Trinity Pro-Cathedral choir, as well as six of the boys I had left behind at St. Andrew's Church, Kingsbury. With them, the 16 new Lanesborough choristers and four of the The Town Boys' Choir that I had promised would sing at the Consecration, we now had a front row of 16 boys each side. We would need to balance that sound with some extra men.

As of right, the six lay clerks of the Pro-Cathedral choir would be singing, and so would the men I had already appointed to the new choir – John Barrow, David Gibbs and Colin Wykes. To them I added some members of The Jacobean Singers – altos Michael Vaile and Peter Chapman, tenors Cyril Ellis, Ian Partridge and Christopher Scott – and bass Cyril Prestage from Hampstead Parish Church.

The line-up was nearly complete, though we also invited two more altos – Grayston Burgess from Westminster Abbey, and Charles Cleall, a former member of the Westminster choir who was due to take over from me as Organist and Choirmaster at Holy Trinity when it reverted to being a parish church on 18th May.

We arranged for the six boys from Kingsbury to come and stay in Guildford from Sunday night, 14th May, billeting them with families of the new Lanesborough choristers. There was no way that we would have enough of the new cerise-coloured cassocks to fit them, but these were the days before colour television, so only those in the Cathedral would see the front row in choir robes of different colours. Designed by Lady Maufe, the new cassocks had been made of a specially woven material with a cut-away at the front to expose a white cravat that everyone would wear. The mothers of the new choristers altered the Kingsbury boys' black cassocks to look the same, and we had just enough spare men's cassocks and surplices to fit everyone.

In the two days before the Consecration there were full rehearsals. Simon Preston had also arrived on the Sunday evening, and spent a considerable amount of time alone in the building, getting to know the organ. Not all of the guest singers were able to attend rehearsals, and the first time we would sing together as the complete choir would be on the morning of the day itself. As far as the music was concerned, the choir was ready, not just for Guildford's greatest day, but also a red-letter day in England's history – the Consecration of the very first Cathedral to be built on a new site in the Southern Province since the Middle Ages.

The night before the Consecration, the Bishop of Guildford hosted a dinner party at his home, Willow Grange, to which I was invited. Later in the evening, he and I made our way back to the Cathedral for a live BBC television broadcast hosted by Richard Dimbleby. Antony Craxton, the producer, asked for some organ music to open the programme, and I played part of the *Toccata* specially written for me ten days before by a young composer, John White. As well as being a celebration of the new building, it was a poignant occasion for Walter Boulton, who gave a memorable and dignified interview about his non-appointment as Dean of the new Cathedral. Tomorrow would be a big day – my first official one in the new building, and his last.

It was time for a good sleep.

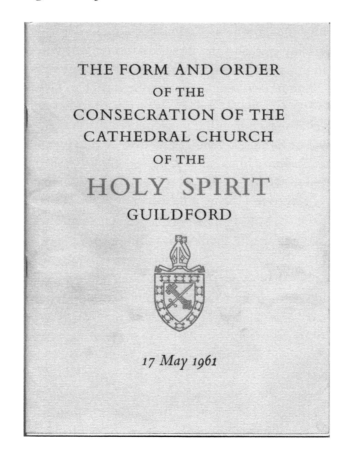

10

Consecration – Concern – and Change
Guildford 1961–1965

T he great day was here, and I hadn't slept well the night before. Keeping me awake were such mundane but salient thoughts as: what would happen if one of the boys was taken ill in the Service, or what if one or more needed to go to the toilet? You can prepare for most things but not for those kinds of emergencies!

At 11.00 a.m. the complete choir assembled in their places and we ran through all the Service music, much to the delight of the BBC sound technicians, who were able to do a final check on their microphone balances without any of the ambient noises they'd had to endure in previous rehearsals. We left the Cathedral around 12.30, the men going off in different directions to find some lunch, whilst the boys were picked up by their parents. Simon Preston and I went back to No. 1 Cathedral Cottage along with some of the visiting singers.

By 2.30 p.m. the huge congregation was almost complete; Simon was playing his pre-Service voluntaries; the 12 brass players had taken their places in the north organ gallery; and two Rushworth & Dreaper technicians were inside the organ in case there were any problems. The choir had re-assembled in the crypt, and I had carefully double-checked that every boy had been to the toilet.

17th May 1961 – outside No. 1 Cathedral Cottage, waiting for the Consecration to start. John Barrow (left), Grayston Burgess (pointing), and Ian Partridge (hidden) in conversation

This was it.

At 2.40 p.m. we processed into the chancel. It was jammed. Aside from visiting Bishops, Deans and Provosts of the Cathedrals in the Southern Province, every incumbent from the diocese was also seated there, a few feet away beyond the choir-stalls – yet more absorption to the already unresponsive acoustic! There was no time to worry, the civic processions had started, followed by the other visiting dignitaries.

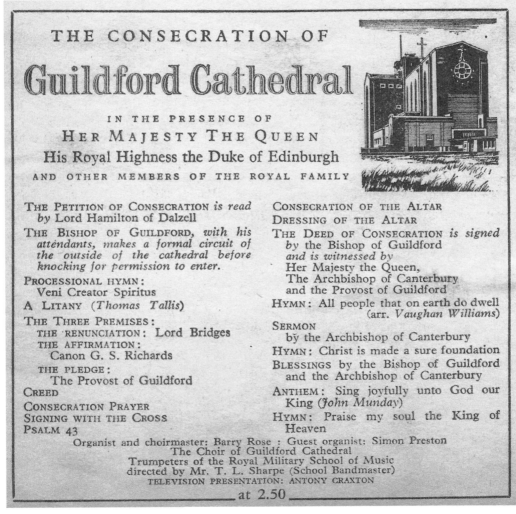

THE CONSECRATION OF
Guildford Cathedral

IN THE PRESENCE OF
HER MAJESTY THE QUEEN
His Royal Highness the Duke of Edinburgh
AND OTHER MEMBERS OF THE ROYAL FAMILY

THE PETITION OF CONSECRATION *is read by* Lord Hamilton of Dalzell

THE BISHOP OF GUILDFORD, *with his attendants, makes a formal circuit of the outside of the cathedral before knocking for permission to enter.*

PROCESSIONAL HYMN:
  Veni Creator Spiritus

A LITANY (*Thomas Tallis*)

THE THREE PREMISES:
  THE RENUNCIATION: Lord Bridges
  THE AFFIRMATION:
    Canon G. S. Richards
  THE PLEDGE:
    The Provost of Guildford

CREED

CONSECRATION PRAYER
SIGNING WITH THE CROSS
PSALM 43

CONSECRATION OF THE ALTAR
DRESSING OF THE ALTAR
THE DEED OF CONSECRATION *is signed by* the Bishop of Guildford
  and is witnessed by
  Her Majesty the Queen,
  The Archbishop of Canterbury
  and the Provost of Guildford

HYMN: All people that on earth do dwell
  (arr. *Vaughan Williams*)

SERMON
  by the Archbishop of Canterbury

HYMN: Christ is made a sure foundation

BLESSINGS by the Bishop of Guildford
  and the Archbishop of Canterbury

ANTHEM: Sing joyfully unto God our King (*John Munday*)

HYMN: Praise my soul the King of Heaven

Organist and choirmaster: Barry Rose : Guest organist: Simon Preston
The Choir of Guildford Cathedral
Trumpeters of the Royal Military School of Music
directed by Mr. T. L. Sharpe (School Bandmaster)
TELEVISION PRESENTATION: ANTONY CRAXTON
___ at 2.50 ___

17th May 1961, from the Radio Times

At 3.00 p.m. precisely, everyone stood, and Lord Hamilton of Dalziell formally petitioned the Bishop of Guildford to consecrate the new Cathedral.

The fanfare of trumpets rang out and we started to sing the first of the three psalms, during which the Queen, the Duke of Edinburgh, Princess Margaret and her husband, Anthony Armstrong-Jones, made their way up the nave preceded by the procession-al cross, the architect, the Archbishop of Canterbury and the Provost. Would our timings be right? These things cannot be rehearsed to the last second, but everything worked as we had planned.

An hour and a half later, the first part of the Cathedral's Consecration was over. Everyone breathed a sigh of relief. It was now time to say thank you and farewell to the visiting singers and Simon Preston. Tomorrow morning the Consecration would be completed with a Solemn Eucharist.

The royal party, together with the great-and-the-good who had attended the Service, made their way to a reception in a marquee on the green at the east end of the Cathedral. I wasn't invited, so Colin and I went back to No. 1 Cathedral Cottage. Later in the evening we'd be able to watch a shortened version of the Service on BBC television, as well as listen to a Home Service broadcast of some of the high-lights. And whether by design or coinci-dence, the BBC Third Programme would also be broadcasting the programme of English Church Music that the choir of St. Andrew's, Kingsbury, had recorded the previous August.

There was no food left in the cottage, so Colin and I made our way into Guildford to the Abbot's Kitchen. That title might conjure up a rather smart restaurant in a

The Third

9.40
ENGLISH
CHURCH MUSIC
Choir of St. Andrew's Church
Kingsbury
Conducted by Barry Rose
Almighty God, who by thy son
....*Gibbons*
O Lord, make thy servant Elizabeth
....*Byrd*
Out of the deep....................*Morley*
Civitas sancti tui; Sacerdotes
Domini..*Byrd*
Great Lord of Lords............*Gibbons*
From St. Gabriel's Church,
Cricklewood, London
BBC recording

The Radio Times, *17ᵗʰ May 1961*

historic building, but in truth it was a greasy-spoon cafe up the back stairs of an un-pretentious shop in North Street. Open until 10.00 p.m., we were regular customers and well known by the waitress who did the late evening shift. She addressed everyone as 'dear' and today was no exception:

'Had a good day, dear?' she asked.

'Well yes, actually, we have,' I said, 'We've consecrated the first Cathedral on a new site in the Southern Province since the Middle Ages.'

'Nice, dear... do you want fried bread or toast with your egg and chips?'

We knew we were back in the real world – as we were also to find out when musi-cal reality hit hard the next day.

The morning of Thursday 18th May dawned. We were famous. The national press was full of reports and pictures of 'Guildford's great day'.

The Queen leads 2,000 worshippers in consecration service

THE PILGRIMS TO THE CATHEDRAL ON THE HILL
Guildford's great day

The Daily Mirror, *Thursday 18th May 1961*

There was no time to bask in any of that reflected glory. This morning at 11.00 a.m. would see the second, and probably the most important, part of the Consecration, as described in yesterday's Order of Service: *'This Service of Consecration to set apart the building for the worship of Almighty God will be consummated tomorrow, Thursday 18th May at 11 o'clock, when the Consecrating Bishop will celebrate the first Eucharist in the Cathedral Church at the High Altar.'*

In musical terms it would be the start of the stark realisation of just how much work I still needed to do to have a 'real' cathedral choir. This morning, the singing would be led by the 16 boys of the new choir plus the six Kingsbury boys who had specially stayed on to help. The back row was made up of the lay clerks from Holy Trinity, some of whom would be retiring today, and the few lay clerks for the new choir that I'd so far been able to appoint. I would play the organ and there would be no conductor.

It was not good, at least compared to yesterday's singing. Inevitably there was some sense of anti-climax, and with the nave full of robed clergy – all the diocesan incumbents, curates and lay readers – the sound was weak and timid; it probably didn't carry very far beyond the first few rows of the nave. Reality had hit hard, and we also had the challenge of singing Evensong that same day, starting as we meant to go on. From now on I would not just be Organist and Choirmaster, but also unpaid bus driver, ferrying the boys from Lanesborough School to the Cathedral, and driving several of them home after each Service.

To maintain a pattern of daily sung Evensongs, we were going to need at least eight men, and if possible, twelve. A few weeks before the Consecration I had auditioned and accepted some extra singers: Barry Brett (tenor) was a teacher and a member of Guildford Baptist Church, and Gerald Durrant, a printer by profession, was the son of the Organist and Choirmaster at local St. Saviour's Church and had a fine alto voice. Two more came from further afield: baritone John Burrows-Watson and tenor Herbert Elms were both members of the Weybridge-based Ripieno Choir. Together with Ron Smith, Gordon Anderson, Roger Moffatt and Walter Waghorn from Holy Trinity Choir, they would join John Barrow, Colin Wykes, David Gibbs and Eric Ware (our Precentor) as the back row. Not all of them would be able to sing every day, so as far as the men were concerned, I had to accept that the new musical foundation at Guildford Cathedral would set off on a rota basis.

I had also made the decision that from the very outset we would sing the psalms appointed for the day[1] and this priority was to take most of our focus and time, not just in the boys' practices but also in the full rehearsals each day before Evensong. While all other cathedral choirs would sing the Magnificat and Nunc Dimittis to an extended setting, the boys at Guildford were not yet able to do so, so each day we would sing them to Anglican chant (in the same way as the psalms). Described on the printed music list as Set A, Set B, Set C, Set D etc., I wrote out the chants by hand in a manuscript book for each of the men, and the boys realised which chant they should sing when it was played over on the organ. For the more experienced singers in the back row, there was no way it could be described as a musically challenging start, and was probably frustrating. But it was a start, and more importantly, it was establishing a routine that would remain virtually unaltered during the next 13 years.

All choirs need a music library, and we had to begin from scratch. I negotiated with Charles Cleall, the new Organist and Choirmaster of what was now Holy Trinity Parish Church, and secured several settings of the Magnificat and Nunc Dimittis,

WEDNESDAY 17	3.0	IN THE PRESENCE OF HER MAJESTY THE QUEEN AND H.R.H. THE DUKE OF EDINBURGH. THE CONSECRATION OF THE CATHEDRAL CHURCH BY THE LORD BISHOP OF GUILDFORD. PREACHER: HIS GRACE THE LORD ARCHBISHOP OF CANTERBURY.	
THURSDAY 18	11.0	THE FIRST SUNG EUCHARIST, celebrated by THE LORD BISHOP OF GUILDFORD. *Darke* in F. Creed and Gloria—*Merbecke.* At the Communion: Hymn 398, 418 (tune E.H. 315 (ii)). Hymns: Introit 382; Gradual 231; Offertory 257; Post-Communion 399 (2nd tune), 379. Preacher: The Lord Bishop of Guildford. Organ Voluntary: Prelude and Fugue in F minor—*J. S. Bach*	
	5.30	Evensong. Psalms: 93 and 94. Ferial Responses Office Hymn: 247. Magnificat and Nunc Dimittis: Set A. Anthem: God omnipotent reigneth—*Charles Wood* Hymn: 258. Organ Voluntary: Toccata—*Eugene Gigout*	
	8.0	Service of Thanksgiving for the Consecration of the New Cathedral. GUILDFORD DEANERY.	

Extract from the Cathedral's very first Service list, May 1961

---

1   In the Book of Common Prayer, the 150 psalms are divided into the mornings and evenings of each day of the month.

officially the property of Guildford Cathedral Choir. Learning these would keep the Lanesborough boys busy for months to come. Their colleagues – the senior choristers who had been with me at Holy Trinity – already knew most of them and would give a useful lead when they were first sung. The new choir had already learned a few anthems, and in addition to the copies from Holy Trinity, we had the nucleus of a library from Trinity College, Cambridge. The College had recently disbanded its boys' choir, and through the good offices of George Guest, I was offered the chance to choose any volumes from the Trinity choir library that might be useful to us in Guildford. Help also came from another source – St. Paul's Cathedral – who were disposing of some of their old bound volumes of 16th and 17th century anthems and settings. Cyril Taylor, their choir librarian and alto vicar choral, arranged to have them and some spare St. Paul's Cathedral psalters sent down to us.

With any choir, rehearsal time is vital, and whilst we had a set 50 minutes on four weekday lunchtimes at Lanesborough School, there were already problems in finding sufficient time to work with The Town Boys' Choir. The initial plan had been for them to provide the top line at Friday Evensong and the Sunday evening Service each week, but the only time we could get them all together for rehearsal was after school on Friday and the occasional Saturday morning. It was not going to work. A few of the boys in that group were already experienced, having sung in their local church choirs for several years, and in the end we decided to co-opt them into the main choir.

But it was to the leadership of the boys from the Holy Trinity Pro-Cathedral choir that we owed most: Christopher Barnett (the first head chorister), Richard Fawcett, Richard Banks, Paul Barnett, Richard Down and Alan Bowley. With just a short amount of post-school practice each day, they were the ones who could be relied upon to give the vocal lead for what was still a very inexperienced group from Lanesborough.

Meanwhile, we decided to cast the net wider in the search for altos, tenors and basses. One way of doing this was to advertise in *The Musical Times*, and I decided to make the advert more eye-catching than the usual wording:

MUSICAL TIMES

APRIL 1961

GUILDFORD NEW CATHEDRAL

There are vacancies for ALTO and TENOR Lay-Clerks at the Cathedral of the Holy Spirit, Guildford, which will be consecrated on 17 May 1961.

Although it is planned to sing six Evensongs per week (5.30 pm), the number of male-voices at each service may vary according to personal commitments, and the organist will be pleased to give full information to anyone who could be available for one or two services each week.

Remuneration will be relatively small, and the music not over-ambitious at first, but we do have a most beautiful new building, a fine 4-manual Rushworth & Dreaper organ and two new boys' choirs.

The Lay-Clerks need not necessarily reside in or around Guildford, since there is an excellent 40 minute train-service from Waterloo.

For anyone considering coming to live and work in Guildford there are in the locality many school-teaching posts available in most subjects.

Please write to, or phone: Barry Rose, No 1 Cathedral Cottage, Ridgemount, Guildford, Surrey. Telephone: Guildford 66507.

The only person to express interest was Roger Lowman, then a second year undergraduate and choral scholar at The Queen's College, Oxford. We met at the Cathedral, and it was a fortuitous meeting. Roger joined us on 10th June 1961, just three weeks after the Consecration, and was to become the real anchor and father-figure of the choir, staying for ten years before moving on to teach at King Alfred's College, Winchester, as well as singing with and sometimes directing Winchester Cathedral Choir.

The only way we were going to attract any talent from a distance would be by offering a place to live, and the Cathedral had no means to do that. One solution was to offer accommodation in No. 1 Cathedral Cottage, and when he wasn't required to be in college or staying at his home near Maidenhead, Roger slept in the small third bedroom, travelling to and from Oxford in an old 1934 Morris 10/4 that I'd recently bought. Roger also masterminded the choice and preparation of our first psalm chants, as well as suggesting repertoire, much of which was new to me.

The Morris 10/4 outside No. 1 Cathedral Cottage, with the blue Cathedral bus in the foreground

Although the organ was being played for all the Services, it had not yet been featured as a solo instrument. I asked Dr. Francis Jackson, Organist and Director of Music at York Minster, if he would give the opening recital. On 5th July 1961, just seven weeks after the Consecration, he played to a large audience, several of whom made the perilous ascent to the organ loft afterwards to view the console.

In those early weeks, it became clear that I needed someone to play the organ whilst I directed the choir. One occasion brought that sharply into focus – a Sunday morning Matins when I played the two preparatory octaves to introduce the *Jubilate in B flat* by Charles Villiers Stanford, only to be greeted by silence from the choir. It took two or three more stabs at the introduction before anyone started singing…

Letters were now appearing in the local press saying that those sitting in the nave could not hear the choir above the organ. This was not unexpected or unjustified – there was no room for the congregation to sit anywhere other than the nave, and in the chancel there were those open arches and no reflective surfaces anywhere. As yet we didn't have the Positive organ, and the main organ in the north transept gallery was a sound barrier to audibility. I knew there would be more chance of getting the sound across if I could stand in the middle of the chancel and direct the choir as they faced towards the nave, rather than singing straight across the stalls to each other.

Three months later, in September 1961, that was possible. Guildford Cathedral had its first official sub-organist. Gordon Mackie had just graduated from Cambridge University where he had been organ scholar at Clare College, and was doing his teaching-practice at nearby Tillingbourne School. Roger Moffatt, former temporary Assistant Organist, was also teaching music there, and he persuaded Gordon to make contact. As we started the new choir year in September, I could now direct the choir each day, with Gordon playing the organ.

We also had a Dean. Bishop George Clarkson, whose appointment had been announced in May, was formally installed on 9th September at a Diocesan Service attended by a large congregation. He was the first resident of the new Cathedral Close, sharing the recently finished Deanery with his sister, Dora Braithwaite. Very much of the 'old school', relationships between us were formal – he was Mr. Dean, and I was simply 'the Organist'. But here at last was a leader who was not just encouraging, but also totally supportive of what we were hoping to achieve with the Cathedral's music.

Both the Dean and Gordon Mackie's arrival coincided with a special musical milestone: our first broadcast of Choral Evensong.

It would be the first time that many people would hear the new choir, and the music was carefully chosen to showcase the vocal talent we had. Christopher Barnett and Richard Fawcett were the experienced treble soloists in the canticles, whilst the John Travers anthem featured Gordon Anderson as the declamatory tenor soloist

Radio Times *billing for the first broadcast Evensong – 18th October 1961*

at the opening, and John Barrow singing with him in duet, as well as the florid and demanding solo aria, *Let the heavens rejoice.*

A month later the boys sang to a discerning London audience when they were featured in a high-profile concert of Robert Fayrfax's Christmastide *'Tecum Principium' Mass* in St. George's Church, Bloomsbury, London.

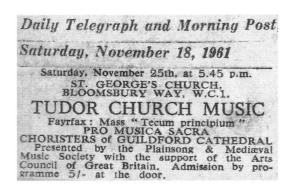

It was a busy time. I had also been playing an organ recital at St. Mary Abbots church in Kensington. Sponsored by the Organ Music Society, the unusual programme included Sigfrid Karg-Elert's *Third Symphonic Canzona* for organ, violin and upper-voice choir, the first time it had been heard for the past 30 years, as well as the first London performance of John White's *Toccata* that he had written for the Guildford organ a few months earlier.

November 1961 was to bring another alto to the choir, by a roundabout route. Having heard the recent broadcast, Michael Barry had tagged along with a Mothers' Union outing from his local church in Barnes. At that time he was singing with the choir at HM Chapel Royal, Hampton Court, and was due to go up to St. John's College, Cambridge, the following September as a choral scholar. I was working down in the crypt and Roger Lowman had gone up to the organ loft to collect some chant books, only to find Michael standing at the foot of the ladder. 'Are you a singer?' asked Roger. 'Yes,' said Michael, and having explained that he was an alto, he was immediately whisked down to the practice room and presented with the alto duet from the Nunc Dimittis of the *Tomkins Fifth Service*, which he sang with Roger.

The following Saturday he was back at Guildford, this time singing with the choir in Evensong. We were all so impressed by Michael and hoped to persuade him to come and join us on a more regular basis, at least until he went up to Cambridge. With his commitment to the Chapel Royal, and living so far away, that was not going to be immediately possible, but the seeds had been sown for what would turn out to be a lifelong association with the Cathedral and its choir, ending up with his Presidency of the Cathedral Choir Association prior to his untimely death in 2016.

A few weeks later, on Christmas Eve, Michael was back again as one of the extra singers in the back row of the choir at the Cathedral's first Midnight Mass, televised by ITV. It didn't finish until well after 1.00 a.m., and I had to drive Michael back to London, since he was required to sing at Hampton Court Chapel on Christmas morning. It was cold and very frosty and there was no proper heating in the Cathedral minibus, which meant that for most of the journey we had to keep stopping to scrape off accumulated ice from the inside and outside of the windscreen. It was well after 3.00 a.m. when I ultimately got back to Guildford; less than six hours sleep before the next choir practice for the Christmas morning Service.

Michael joined the choir at the start of 1962, moving into No. 1 Cathedral Cottage until he was due to take up his alto choral scholarship to St. John's in September. Having already been at university in Durham where he had failed his finals, he would not be eligible for another grant towards his fees and maintenance. We managed to get him a teaching post at George Abbot School. Although it was paid at a lowly unqualified teacher's rate, it was the possibility of staying on there, as well as the worry over money for Cambridge, that led him to write to George Guest to withdraw from St. John's. I also wrote an apologetic letter to George, to which he replied that he felt 'sixty percent anger and forty percent sympathy.' Michael needed some form of transport, so we arranged for him to start driving the Cathedral minibus, which meant that he was now able to relieve me from collecting the boys from school and driving them home after Services.

With up to four residents, life at No. 1 Cathedral Cottage was exciting and usually chaotic. It was a cold winter, and we had no central heating. The only way of keeping warm was through open fires in two of the rooms and leaving the gas cooker on in the kitchen, which would at least take the chill off the dining room. When we ran out of coal for the fires, we hit upon what we thought was an ingenious plan: Colin and I would create logs out of the chairs that had once been congregational seats when the crypt chapel (now the choir practice room) had been used for Services. These were stacked in various places in the crypt, and one of us could often be seen going up to the Cathedral under cover of darkness and returning with two or three chairs. We chopped them up for the living room fire. When questioned about their disappearance by Alfred White, the Dean's Verger, we looked surprised and feigned innocence.

January 1962 was also to bring us a large and much needed financial windfall to help the day-to-day running expenses of the men of the choir. Official lay clerkships, funded by the Cathedral, had not yet been established, and to have some means of paying the men I opened a music fund account at the bank. We found a large collecting box, put it at the back of the nave, labelled FOR THE MUSIC, and I had the only key. The thousands of visitors who came to the Cathedral following the Consecration had been very generous, but now, in the long winter months, visitor numbers had dwindled and there was precious little money coming in.

Sir Edwin Herbert, who lived nearby, was a director of Associated-Rediffusion who were part-sponsoring the Hallé Orchestra and its conductor, Sir John Barbirolli.

*The Hallé Orchestra rehearsing in Guildford
Cathedral, 18th January 1962*

Sir Edwin graciously offered us two concerts by the Hallé and Sir John, with the entire proceeds going towards the maintenance of the men of the choir. The first concert took place on Thursday 18th January 1962, and it was our job to arrange the publicity and tickets and get them ready for sale. The occasion is forever etched in my mind. A thousand tickets had been printed, and we sat in the living room of No. 1 Cathedral Cottage numbering and lettering each one to correspond to the nave seating plan. Since there would be limited visibility from the cheapest seats in the side aisles, we thought we should make that clear on the tickets. We bought a John Bull printing outfit, stamping those tickets 'Unreserved – little or no visibility'. At least we thought we had, until someone pointed out that that they actually read '*Unreseved* – little or no *visiblity*.' It was too late to change them, and despite a cold January evening, we had a fully sold-out and exciting concert from which the music fund benefited by more than £2,000.

That extra money now gave me the chance to aim for 12 men to sing each day. In the absence of any more suitable singers from the locality, I contacted Cyril Taylor, the alto and choir librarian at St. Paul's Cathedral, and we came to an arrangement whereby he would find a tenor and bass from St. Paul's to join him at Guildford on two days each week. It was going to be expensive since we'd have to pay a fee which would more than cover the cost of their deputy at St. Paul's, as well as their return train fares. Cyril found us the best – Robert Tear (tenor), and either John Shirley-Quirk or John Huw Davies as the bass, and this arrangement was to continue for much of the following year. Cyril made the most of his visits: in the train on the way down to Guildford he would pre-order a meal of kippers (smoked herrings), and on the return journey – the train having gone on to Portsmouth Harbour before returning to London via Guildford – Cyril would board it after Evensong to find his kippers ready cooked and waiting for him.

But our aim was to have enough lay clerks of our own, and it was Roger Lowman who would be instrumental in bringing two more to sing with the choir – tenor Robert Hammersley and baritone Robert Wilson.

Robert Hammersley had been a chorister at King's College, Cambridge, under Boris Ord, and had gone on to The King's School, Canterbury, as a music scholar. A prodigiously talented pianist, he had played George Gershwin's *Rhapsody in Blue* with orchestra in the school's prestigious King's Week concerts. We were singing John Stainer's *The Crucifixion* on Good Friday 1962, and Robert, waiting to go up to Magdalen College, Oxford, as an academical clerk, was persuaded to come and join us for the day. It was to be the start of a nine-year stay for Robert, who, having gone up to Oxford as planned, failed his preliminary exams, and returned to Guildford eight months later as another resident of No. 1 Cathedral Cottage. What a coup for the choir this was. Robert is one of the most instinctive and gifted musicians I have ever had the privilege to meet. Everything he sight-read sounded as though he had known it all his life, and his musical influence soon spread among his colleagues as well as to the impressionable front row.

Around the same time, he was joined by alto Michael Vaile, with whom I'd been singing in the Hampstead Parish Church choir six years ago. Michael's parental home was in Surrey, and we persuaded him to sing with us as often as he could.

The combination of Robert and Michael was to be pivotal to the choir's success in the years to come, and for me it was a musical dream come true. Either of them

Robert Hammersley (left) playing the piano at our house in Guildford, c. 1969. Michael Vaile (right), with Roger Lowman in the background, c. 1970

could be quite lethal in reducing the whole of the Cantoris side of the choir into fits of laughter, sometimes in Services, and both were such perceptive musicians that any slight error by others was immediately played upon, even to the extent of imitating the miscreant. On one occasion the whole of Cantoris virtually stopped singing as Michael spoonerised verse 5 of Psalm 108 in the middle of Evensong ('Set up thyself, O God…'). In another Evensong he would create the same chaos in the opening line of the hymn 'Praise, my soul, the King of Heaven'.

Gradually we were building a complete team of back row singers of my choice, most of whom were prepared to sing on a daily basis. Having that continuity and experience not only encouraged the trebles, but also gave the new choir an extra sense of musical cohesion that we'd not so far been able to achieve. It was also helped by the installation of the Positive section of the organ in February 1962. Now with something right above the heads of the choir, they could not only hear the organ whilst they were singing, but they could also be heard in the nave since less of the main organ could now be used. We were beginning to sound more like a real cathedral choir. Tenor David Gibbs, who would sing with the choir for the next 40 years, put it like this:

> *The psalms were perhaps the first to move from routine competence to daily beauty. In these instants (they can be numbered on the fingers of one hand) the words and music assumed a life of their own and carried the performers into what can only be described as total shared consciousness in which individual identity vanished. We were part of something where, in defiance of mathematics, the whole greatly exceeded the sum of its parts. We had become a Cathedral choir.*[2]

One of my plans was to let the new choristers see and hear other cathedral choirs in action. Before the Consecration I had taken them to Chichester and Salisbury Cathedrals for Evensong, and now we were going to sing Evensong in Salisbury Cathedral. I had played a recital in Salisbury in August 1961, and when talking with Christopher Dearnley, the Cathedral Organist, we'd discussed the possibility of the Guildford choir singing there. He offered us a date on a Saturday in February 1962, though, because of work being carried out on the organ, we would be singing in the lady chapel rather than the open spaces of the quire. With just a small chamber organ to accompany the Service, the three psalms for the day would need to be sung unaccompanied – a real challenge since it would be the first time we had done this. Everything went well, and a year or so later we were able to return the favour and invite the Salisbury choir to sing a Saturday Evensong at Guildford.

---

2   From *The Beat is Irrelevant* by Simon Carpenter, 1996.

```
SATURDAY    10  |  5.15   EVENSONG
                         (Sung by the choir of Guildford Cathedral)
                         Byrd Responses      Psalms 53, 54, 55
                         Daniel Purcell   in   E minor
                         Anthem: The Blessed Son of God
                                                    Vaughan Williams
```

Detail from the Salisbury Cathedral music list, February 1962

In May 1962 Gordon Mackie announced that he would be leaving. EMI Records had offered him a part-time contract as repetiteur with international opera star, Maria Callas. It had gone so well that Maria offered Gordon a permanent job. A month before he left, we changed places. Gordon conducted the choir and a large congregation in a live BBC television transmission, and I played the organ. *Songs of Praise* had started in October the previous year, and this was their first visit to a cathedral. We were pleased to welcome back Antony Craxton as producer, and also Simon Preston, now Sub-Organist of Westminster Abbey, to introduce the hymns. There was one choir item, in which the featured soloist was Michael Vaile, singing Orlando Gibbons' setting of *Great Lord of Lords*.

In our search for a new sub-organist, it was Peter Hall who came up with the answer. Peter had sung with Michael Barry at Hampton Court, and was due to take up a tenor choral scholarship at King's College, Cambridge, later in the year. In the meantime, he came down to Guildford on several Saturdays to sing in Evensong, and in conversation he mentioned Peter Moorse, who he knew from his choir in South London. Would I like him to ask Peter to contact me? I said yes, and a month later Peter Moorse was appointed as Sub-Organist at Guildford, bringing a wealth of experience as an organist and choir trainer. Amazingly inventive in his pre- and post-Service improvisations, Peter soon discovered sounds on the organ we never knew existed, and as we processed in and out we'd often hear Messaien-style variations on the anthem or the setting – impressive to the musicians, if not always to the clergy.

It was Peter who started the first group of Guildford probationers, with boys from the immediate locality as well as some from Lanesborough School. As far as I was concerned, all the present Lanesborough choristers were still probationers since they were in their first year of singing Services, though I was well aware that next summer (1963) some of them would be taking the Common Entrance exam and leaving the school and the choir. Peter's first group of probationers included two or three that we would like at Lanesborough, and since, by then, the new Dean had confirmed the scholarships I'd publicised two years ago, we could now offer the parents an initial thirty-three percent scholarship if their boys would join the school in September.

Summer of 1962 was special – the first of two trips to Switzerland, and our second live broadcast of Choral Evensong. The Swiss visit was planned around an invitation to sing Evensong and a recital at the English church in Geneva. All the boys and lay clerks agreed to come, the boys travelling in the Cathedral minibus, and me and several of the men bringing our cars. The adults stayed in hotels, and the boys stayed in youth hostels at (or near) the venues. It was a last-minute scramble to confirm the bookings, since Michael Barry had inadvertently folded the reservation cards the wrong way round and all were returned to Cathedral Cottage instead of reaching their destinations. We left the day after the BBC broadcast, singing first in the French Jura village of Montfleur, then to Geneva, Bern and Basle, returning to Guildford eight days later for a well-earned summer break.

As we assembled for the new term in September 1962, the first choristers from outside the school joined Lanesborough, establishing, with the headmaster's agreement, a precedent for the future. They were welcome arrivals, since three of the original choristers had now left the choir, and we were due to lose three or more at the end of the academic year. We'd also said farewell to some of the Holy Trinity boys, including Christopher Barnett, the first head chorister. I had co-opted replacements from the now defunct Town Boys' Choir, so the front row still numbered around 20.

A chance enquiry led to the appointment of a tenor lay clerk from Eton College. John Bilton had written to enquire about possible deputy work. He explained that it would fit in with his daily commitment at Eton since their Evensong was early in the afternoon, and he could get a train to Guildford in time for our choir practice. It was a useful arrangement for both of us, though it ceased soon after Robert Hammersley started singing on a regular basis. We also appointed former Holy Trinity chorister, Nigel O'Dwyer, to join the bass line, together with Bill Tilden from Cookham, and part-time alto Peter Driver, who, when he was not singing, was representing England as a long-distance runner. At weekends the back row was also augmented by alto Peter Chapman from London, and also tenor Gordon Anderson.

The weather hit hard at the start of 1963. Known as 'the big freeze', January 1963 remains the coldest month in the U.K. since 1814. With heavy snow and icy roads, access to the Cathedral by the usual route was impossible. We managed to sing some Services by delivering the boys to the foot of the cleared steps on the south side of the Cathedral, even if getting up and down them was still quite dangerous.

The real worry concerned another concert by Sir John Barbirolli and the Hallé Orchestra, scheduled for late January, and sponsored once again by Associated-Rediffusion. In the end, the snow was cleared from the access hill to the Cathedral, and we had another superb concert with a near-capacity audience, the music fund benefitting by nearly £2,000.

The first official Guildford Cathedral Choir photograph, 6ᵗʰ January 1963

Throughout the next two terms the boys steadily improved, learning new repertoire more quickly and singing the statutory parts of the Services with more assurance. It was just after Easter that Clifford Mould first came to Guildford. A chorister with Robert Hammersley at King's College, Cambridge, Clifford was singing tenor with Ely Cathedral Choir. Robert persuaded him to come and audition at Guildford, to fill the vacancy for a permanent tenor lay clerk on Decani. My memory of the audition is still clear since I was not quite sure who was auditioning who! Clifford produced a handwritten manuscript copy of a 17ᵗʰ century lute-song and asked if I would transpose it up a minor third. There was little time to listen to his singing as I struggled to work out which chord came next, but as soon as he opened his mouth to sing, I knew that here was a voice we simply had to have. We arranged that Clifford would join us in September as yet another resident of No. 1 Cathedral Cottage, whilst at the same time, he would go to the Royal Academy of Music as a first study singer.

Meanwhile in July we said farewell to three Lanesborough boys, each having gained a music scholarship to their next school, as well as the senior and more experienced boys from Holy Trinity. September would seem like a new start again.

And that's how it turned out. At Lanesborough, with the seniors gone, the boys' sound was weak, breathy, and lacking in confidence. Their lack of confidence transmitted itself to me, to the extent that I nearly couldn't face turning up to one choir practice. I approached the Dean and Precentor to see if we might lose sung Evensong on Mondays. Their wise counsel was that if we did, it would not be possible to reinstate it. It was time to look in the mirror and see what I needed to do to improve things. Perhaps more emphasis on vocal technique and a little less ambitious repertoire, giving the boys more time to learn simpler things thoroughly?

July 1963: The first Lanesborough choristers to win music scholarships – Robin Knight, Jeremy Evans, and Stewart Aylward

It worked, and by the middle of 1964 we were able to accept an invitation from the composer Alan Ridout to give the first performance of a short cantata, *Moses and the Red Sea*. Scored for solo baritone, choir, and piano duet, it was commissioned by the BBC for a television programme called *The Artist in Society*. To record it we travelled to the studios in London, and the programme was transmitted on 20th August, during the choir's summer break. It was the first time I was interviewed on television, an unnerving experience when I had no idea what the questions might be.

In mid-1964 I made my first recording as a solo organist. Spotting an untapped niche in the souvenir market, producer

7.30

THE ARTIST IN SOCIETY

Three programmes which set out to examine different aspects of the role played by the artist in society during a thousand years of European civilisation

3: The Modern World

Introduced by
Ronald Fletcher
Professor of Sociology,
University of York
Contributors include:
Anthony Burgess
on
THE NOVELIST TODAY
with the recorded voices of
JANETTE RICHER, DREW RUSSELL
TONY BRONTE, JOHN WOODNUTT
*
Alan Ridout
on
COMPOSING TO COMMISSION
with
Members of the
GUILDFORD CATHEDRAL CHOIR
Choir-Master, BARRY ROSE
and
DONALD FRANCKE (baritone)
NOEL CLARKE (piano)

Radio Times *billing for Tuesday 20th August 1964*

Norman Austin and recording engineer John Timperley set up Ryemuse records to make 7-inch EP records for sale at cathedral shops. They had started at Christchurch Priory in Dorset, and Guildford was to be their first cathedral recording. I played four pieces, ranging from Bach to Parry, and it was quickly available for sale on the Cathedral bookstall. To this day I'm not sure who benefitted from the sales – I didn't, but it was useful to be 'out there' in the world of recordings as an organist.

The back row of the choir was now more settled. Colin Wykes had moved on and Robert (Bob) Wilson had taken his place as a lay clerk, having already sung with the choir several times whilst he was a choral scholar at The Queen's College, Oxford.

Out of the blue there was an unexpected offer for the choir to record for the most famous of all the record labels: EMI producer Brian Culverhouse must have been to an Evensong to hear the choir, and no-one was more surprised than I when he rang up to see if we would make a record for the HMV label. At first I thought it was one of the lay clerks playing a practical joke, but once convinced that the offer was genuine, my excitement was tempered when he announced that it would be John Henry Maunder's much-derided Lenten cantata, *Olivet to Calvary*.

But here was a golden opportunity to bring this new cathedral choir to a wider audience, and once I'd persuaded a sceptical group of lay clerks, we agreed to make the recording later in the term. EMI would engage the tenor and baritone soloists, and we would provide a soloist for the part of Pontius Pilate. I'd recently made contact with Terence Clifford, a former bass choral scholar from St. John's College, Cambridge, who had moved into the area, and realised that his rich baritone timbre would match the professional soloists, Frederick Harvey and John Mitchinson. The boys, now much more assured, learned the music quickly, and Peter Moorse provided the most colourful organ accompaniment, never putting a finger (or foot) wrong during the various takes.

Recording took place on three evenings during November and December 1964 and the disc was released in March 1965. To celebrate the launch, EMI hosted a reception at their headquarters in central London, including a complete playing of the finished record. Favourably reviewed in *Gramophone* magazine the following month, the choir was described as 'ineffably smooth'. *Olivet to Calvary* was to stay in the catalogue for over 50 years and was the first of five records that we would make with producer Brian Culverhouse.

My personal life was soon to change for ever. For the past three years I'd been courting Elizabeth (Buffie), the Precentor's daughter, and late in 1964 had plucked up courage to ask her to marry me. Since our first meeting on Boxing Day 1960, she had finished the course at Guildford School of Art, been to secretarial college, and was now working in central London. Her father was very much in favour of the union, whilst her mother was not so keen, saying that marrying someone who worked for the church would mean that we would never have any money! Regardless, we got engaged, and planned our wedding to take place in the Cathedral on 21st April 1965, just three days after Easter. As husband and wife we would live in No. 1 Cathedral Cottage, and that would mean an exodus for the lay clerks who were still there. Choir life and No. 1 Cathedral Cottage were about to change.

1965 – Marriage and more recording

Much of the early part of 1965 was taken up with plans for our wedding. Since the Cathedral does not have parochial status, we needed to go through the lengthy process of getting an Archbishop's Licence. Choosing the music proved much easier, and I asked Simon Preston if he would come and play us out with the *Final* from Louis Vierne's First Symphony that he had played at the end of the Consecration four years earlier. Peter Moorse would accompany the choir, who would sing Psalms 127 and 128 as Buffie entered the Cathedral on her father's arm. Having the wedding in what was officially the start of the choir's post-Easter holiday meant that we issued an invitation to sing, rather than making it an official duty. All the boys were there, and a large number of present and former lay clerks. I had arranged that Robert Hammersley would conduct the choir, but he was delayed, so I took the choir practice

myself until he arrived just in time for the Service. A lady visitor asked me for whose wedding I was rehearsing, and she looked rather shocked when I said, 'Mine!'

Sir Edward Maufe, the architect of the Cathedral, offered us a converted oast house on his East Sussex estate for our honeymoon, and we stayed there for a few days before going on to the town of Rye, where we splashed out all the money we had on a romantic dinner and a night in The Mermaid Hotel. The next day Buffie drew out the very last of her savings in her Post Office book so we could eat – fish and chips out of a newspaper.

Back at the Cathedral I needed to find a replacement for Peter Moorse. After four years, Peter had decided to leave. I could sense that although he had enjoyed his time with us, he was getting restless and wanted to run his own choir again. That opportunity came when he was offered, and accepted, the post of Organist and Choirmaster at Maidstone Parish Church as from the beginning of May.

His successor was Gavin Williams, a fourth-year student at the Royal Academy of Music, studying organ with C.H. Trevor as well as orchestral conducting. Gavin lived at his parents' home in Haslemere, not far from Guildford, and started as soon as the choir re-assembled after the Easter break. He made his first recording with the choir a month or so later when they made a 7-inch EP for the Ryemuse label.

At the same time, tenor Rowland Sidwell joined us. Rowland was a member of the Tilford Bach Choir and had been singing with them at a Cathedral concert when he'd first heard the choir at Evensong. He came for an audition, which he says I had quite forgotten about and answered the front door in my pyjamas! Whatever the truth of that situation, here was a beautiful, natural tenor voice, and though his sight-reading skills couldn't match Robert and Clifford, his full-throated singing could probably surpass them. Another one with an infectious sense of fun, Rowland soon became an integral part of the choir, and in later life made the leap into the world of opera, with starring roles for English National Opera and Glyndebourne.

John Barrow was now making his way as a professional singer and had to be absent from a number of Services. We needed another bass, and in conjunction with Lanesborough, I advertised the post. We appointed Phillip Mindenhall to start in September. EMI had asked us to contribute to the forthcoming recordings of the *Treasury of English Church Music*, and with our outstanding soloists, Brian Culverhouse and I agreed that we should take on Volume Three – mainly verse-anthems for solo voices, two of which would be accompanied by a string ensemble. I primed Phillip Mindenhall about being one of the soloists and gave him an advance copy of Henry Purcell's anthem, *I will give thanks unto the Lord*. At the first sing-through the other soloists thought he was sight-reading and were most impressed.

The completed volumes of music would not be ready in time for the recording sessions in October, so Blandford Press, the publishers, sent down proof copies of all the music on single sheets. I knew this could (and probably would) cause all sorts of problems in keeping them in order or being dropped at crucial moments. There was only one answer: Buffie got out her new sewing machine, and after a lot of work, we ended up with complete copies of each piece neatly sewn together.

The full choir recordings showed up a few weaknesses and a lack of experience in the boys, especially in the long unaccompanied *O clap your hands together* by Maurice Greene, in which the treble line is divided throughout. Gavin and I each conducted one item with the string ensemble, and we also changed places, each playing one of the longer anthems with organ accompaniment.

One of the three evenings was devoted to recording the main soloists – Michael Vaile, Robert Hammersley and John Barrow. It was John who would later receive further offers from EMI, other recording companies, and the BBC, following his accomplished display of technique and delivery in the long florid aria, *Let the heavens rejoice*, in John Travers' *Ascribe unto the Lord*.

October 1965: recording The Treasury of English Church Music, *with soloists (seated) Robert Hammersley, Michael Vaile and John Barrow. Gavin Williams is conducting and I am playing the chamber organ continuo*

Christmas 1965 saw an important milestone in the Cathedral's schedule of Services. On Christmas Day at 4.00 p.m. we sang our first Service of Nine Lessons and Carols. Not many people will come, we thought, but as we went to the west end to start the processional hymn, we were more than surprised to find the Cathedral full, even in the west gallery. The success of that afternoon meant that we'd have to do it all again next year, and it established a pattern that still continues more than 50 years on.

11

Fame – But Not Fortune
Guildford 1966-1970

Fame? Well yes, if you count taking the name and the sound of Guildford Cathedral into not just hundreds, not just thousands, but tens of thousands of homes. Our first appearance to a wider listening audience was at the beginning of 1966, with two broadcasts in the same week. Wednesday 16th February was a live broadcast of Choral Evensong on the BBC Home Service, and two days later the choir was featured on BBC Network Three in John Betjeman's series, *Britain's Cathedrals and their Music*. Produced by Sebastian Forbes, who I had known as a chorister at Hampstead Parish Church and a fellow student at the Royal Academy of Music, Gavin Williams and I shared the conducting and playing.

Just four weeks later, and now in the penitential season of Lent, we had to think about Christmas! EMI producer, Brian Culverhouse, asked us to record the Ralph Vaughan Williams *Fantasia on Christmas Carols*, together with a selection of other carols which would fill one side of an LP. The other side was to be the very first English recording of Victor Hely-Hutchinson's *Carol Symphony*. In four movements and scored for full symphony orchestra, the only extant recording had been on a Dutch label many years earlier.

It would be my first experience of conducting an orchestra of that size, and they would be reading off parts that were handwritten, as was my full score. The Pro Arte Orchestra consisted of the best players from the London orchestras, led by the former concert master (leader) of the Philharmonia Orchestra, Max Salpeter. I needed a quick crash course in conducting, and found out that Maurice Miles, professor of conducting at the Royal Academy of Music, lived in a village only a few miles from Guildford. I rang him and he offered to take me through the score, giving many helpful hints and guidance about stick technique.

The orchestral sessions took place on a March afternoon and evening, and it was very much a learning experience for both the orchestra and me. None of them knew the work, so it was a case of learning and rehearsing each movement and then recording it. By the end of the evening we had completed all four movements, and Brian Culverhouse was happy with the result.

March 1966, listening to a playback of the Hely-Hutchinson Carol Symphony. On the left is the orchestra leader, Max Salpeter. Brian Culverhouse, the producer, is standing behind with the score under his arm, and next to him is viola player Stephen Shingles.

The next evening was the turn of the choir. The *Fantasia on Christmas Carols* featured our own bass soloist, John Barrow, and was accompanied by string ensemble, tubular bells and organ. In three more choir and organ carols, solos were sung by Robert Hammersley and Clifford Mould. The final item was a last-minute addition – Peter Warlock's unaccompanied *Bethlehem Down* – new to the boys at their lunchtime rehearsal that day, and to the men when they arrived that evening.

Our recent *Treasury of English Church Music* recording for HMV was issued in June and the reviews were quite complimentary. The always perceptive, and often critical, Kenneth Long wrote in *Records and Recording*:

The singing throughout is outstanding. On the showing of this disc, Guildford Cathedral Choir must take its place amongst the finest in the land. They have a first-rate choral technique, good tone, clear diction, a feeling for phrasing and a real sense of varying styles. This is one of the best church music records to come my way for some time.

There was no time to rest on our laurels. In the height of summer we had to start thinking about Christmas again, this time for the more 'popular' market.

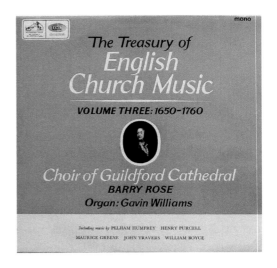

mono

The Treasury of
English
Church Music

VOLUME THREE: 1650–1760

Choir of Guildford Cathedral
BARRY ROSE
Organ: Gavin Williams

Including music by PELHAM HUMFREY   HENRY PURCELL
MAURICE GREENE   JOHN TRAVERS   WILLIAM BOYCE

EMI and the publisher Paul Hamlyn had recently launched the 12/6d budget Music for Pleasure label, and this was to be their first classical music record. Brian Culverhouse, the producer, asked us to sing 12 of the most popular traditional Christmas carols. With one eye on copyright, he said that no published arrangements could be used, but we were welcome to make some of our own, though there wouldn't be royalties either for them or any sales of the record. If anyone was going to get rich through this record it wasn't going to be us. Roger Lowman, Clifford Mould and I set to work on a few arrangements, handing out the manuscript copies at each of the two recording sessions. The weather was hot, and it was somewhat incongruous to see everyone standing on the steps of the chancel, perspiring and in shirtsleeves, trying to bring some real feeling into *See, amid the winter's snow*. There was one memorable moment when organist Gavin Williams decided to decorate the last verse of *The First Nowell*, only to be told over the talkback, 'Thank you, Mr. Williams, but please could we have just the 12/6d (traditional) harmonies?'

None of us, including Brian Culverhouse and his colleagues, had any idea just how successful that record would be. Issued in late November, it was soon selling in tens of thousands, reaching the pop charts, and some years later earning not just a Gold but a Platinum disc as well for nearly one million copies sold!

We wondered if the Vaughan Williams and Hely-Hutchinson record would be as well received when it was released in November. Before that could happen, and at the request of EMI, I had written to the local paper to ask if any reader had a top-quality

Gavin Williams, Brian Culverhouse and me holding our Platinum and Silver Discs outside Guildford Cathedral, 1991

photograph of the Cathedral surrounded by snow. Luckily one professional quality transparency was submitted, and it was duly used as the cover illustration.

We need not have worried about the reviews. Geoffrey Cuming, writing in *Records and Recording*, reflected the comments in all of the other reviews:

> *What a sumptuous, warmly welcoming acoustic the (HMV) engineers have given us. The sheer sound of this record is thrilling, especially in the stereo. The balance between soloist, choir, organ and the orchestra is indeed beyond praise, and the sense of triumph which flows from the glad sequence of music is exhilarating.*

The record had obviously made quite an impact at the BBC since they gave it a special featured playing on Christmas Day morning.

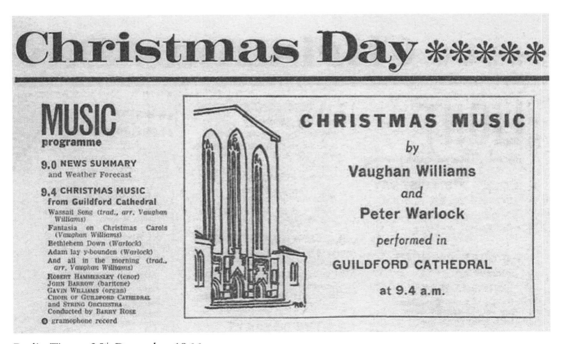

Radio Times, *25th December 1966*

1967: New (ad)ventures

1966 had put Guildford Cathedral Choir firmly on the musical map. Where, we wondered, would 1967 take us?

In June we were sorry to say goodbye to John Barrow. The first lay clerk I had appointed, John was now much in demand as a soloist, and had been offered an overseas tour by the British Council. It was going to be hard to find someone to replace him.

Following on from the success of recent EMI releases, I suggested that one item we should record as soon as possible should be the *Miserere* (Psalm 51) by Gregorio Allegri. Usually sung in the English translation, there was already an Argo recording of it by the choir of King's College, Cambridge, in which the soloist was Roy Goodman. At Guildford we also had a superb treble soloist: John Dexter could manage those top Cs without any problem, and I was very anxious to get his voice on record quickly – he was nearing 13 and due to leave the choir in July. EMI said they couldn't make any commitment at that moment, saying that it might well be a project for the future.

It was at that point that we made the decision to form our own record company, Guild Records, and make the recording ourselves.[1] We began by recording three 7-inch EPs in July, and the Allegri was recorded later in the year as part of a 12-inch LP of Passiontide music. One of the singers on the very first Guild EP was alto Christopher Helyer, who had only joined the choir a few days before – a real baptism by fire.

Soon after we made the recordings, I took the choir on a unique tour – at least unique to us. Whilst this new cathedral choir may now have taken its place alongside some of the choirs of the older foundations, all that the present choristers knew was the one modern building in which they sang each day. I explored the possibility of taking them and the lay clerks to some of our more venerable cathedrals and wrote to the Deans and Organists of Lincoln and Peterborough to test their reactions. The replies were very positive, and both cathedrals said that they would welcome us to sing Services in late July after their own choirs had stopped singing for the summer. More in hope than anything else, I also wrote to David Willcocks at King's College, Cambridge, to see if there was any way that we might be allowed to sing something in the chapel – just one piece would be such a thrill for the choir. Knowing that King's did not usually have visiting choirs to sing Services, I was all the more surprised when David replied with an invitation for the choir to sing Evensong in the chapel on Sunday, 30th July. What an honour for us. It also tied in nicely with the King's choir timetable, since they were due to give their annual concert at Holy Trinity Church, Stratford-upon-Avon that same afternoon.

---

1   Full details can be found in 'Guild Records', page 282.

We now had the framework of a tour, and to it we added Skegness Parish Church, where George Clarkson, our Dean, had formerly been Rector. Finally, to start the tour, I negotiated with the one cathedral that was younger than us (by a year) – Coventry – singing Evensong completely unaccompanied, since Joseph Poole, their rather officious Precentor, had decreed that only their organist would be allowed to play. Everywhere we went the choir's singing was greatly appreciated, especially at Lincoln, where the Dean presented us with a signed photograph of the Cathedral as a thank you after we had sung a 7.30 a.m. Saint's Day Eucharist.

We saved King's College, Cambridge, for the last day, and since we were to sing in that legendary acoustic, I arranged for a Saturday morning rehearsal in the reverberant acoustics of the lady chapel of Ely Cathedral. On the following afternoon we made a little bit of Guildford history as we rehearsed and sang Evensong in the world-famous chapel at King's College. For two of our lay clerks this was a special and highly charged occasion; Robert Hammersley and Clifford Mould were back in the choir-stalls in which they had spent so many years singing treble. Attended by the usual large congregation, the choir sang their hearts out in what to them, and me, was a unique space in which to lead the Worship.

The choristers arriving at King's College Chapel, Cambridge, Sunday 30th July 1967

Our first UK tour had been a great success. Had we set a pattern for years to come?

Back in Guildford, there was excitement for the boys when they were asked to sing at London's Royal Albert Hall. In October of each year, the Church of England Children's Society held an annual rally at the hall, and we were asked to provide a musical interlude of about 15 to 20 minutes. That huge space, and an audience of several thousand, must have seemed very daunting to 20 small boys standing on the stage, but their singing obviously impressed the organisers, and we were immediately asked back to sing next year.

Singing in the Royal Albert Hall

1968: Moving and travelling

Buffie and I had lived in No. 1 Cathedral Cottage for nearly three years, and now, in 1968, we were to move into a new house being built for us. Cathedral Close was gradually being extended from three to six houses, and No. 5 was designated as the Organist's official residence. Built into the hillside, and much more spacious than Cathedral Cottage, the new house would be on three different levels, with a large purpose-built music room and a double garage for our car and the Cathedral minibus. We couldn't wait to move in, and every so often we would nip along the road to check on progress, even though we knew it wouldn't be ready until August.

February saw us giving two performances of the Fauré Requiem. The first was in the chapel of Wellington College, at the invitation of the newly appointed Director of Music. Jared Armstrong had recently moved to Wellington from Cranleigh School and was keen for his chapel choir to hear us sing. I drove the choristers there in the Cathedral minibus, but since many of their parents were in the audience, they took the boys home, leaving me to drive back to Guildford in the empty bus. It was a very cold night, and the roads were icy. On one of the country lanes I put my foot on the brake quite sharply. The empty bus spun round and round, and it seemed that my whole life flashed before my eyes – was it going to overturn, and was I going to die?

Still a building site! Buffie checking out the unfinished drains for No. 5 Cathedral Close

Somehow it came to rest on the edge of a deep ditch. I'd been spared, and very shaken, I completed the rest of the journey at a sedate 20 mph or so.

The second Fauré Requiem was at Dover College in their 12th century chapel, formerly the Guest House of the Priory of St. Martin. Leo Forsdyke, Director of Music at the College, had helped and encouraged me during my school days, and we had renewed contact when he brought his choir to sing an Evensong in Guildford Cathedral. Now we were returning the compliment, and spent part of the weekend at the College, singing a concert on Saturday evening and joining with their choir for the Sunday morning Service.

Bishop George Clarkson, our Dean, retired in May. He had come to Guildford seven years ago in a time of turbulence and upset about the non-appointment of Walter Boulton as Dean. With dignity and compassion he had healed those wounds and brought the new Cathedral to life. An ardent supporter of the music, we could only hope that his successor would be the same.

When I started the choir, the back row was, of necessity, run on a rota basis. Now in 1968, and with the Dean's support, we could have a more permanent team of really able singers. At Evensong each weekday there were usually up to 12 men, and this year we would welcome Richard Barnes, a bass choral scholar from King's College, Cambridge, to replace John Barrow, and alto David Burrowes, previously singing in Edinburgh. Bass Colin McKenna also joined us to sing at the weekends.

In June I made an organ LP for the Philips Fourfront label. Recorded over three successive evenings, the programme included some of Mozart's organ music, and two pieces with vocal contributions: Nicolas de Grigny's variations on *A solis ortus cardine* used the tenors and basses of the Cathedral choir singing the plainsong verses between the organ movements, whilst Sigfrid Karg-Elert's *Third Symphonic Canzona* had a distant choir of upper voices, sung by members of the choir of Guildford County School for Girls, together with our own altos.

If we were to tour again in the summer, I'd need to find suitable venues. It was Michael Barry who suggested the north of England, and having arranged to sing Services in Durham Cathedral and York Minster, I also contacted Jessie Coulthurst, the donor of the Guildford organ, to see if she would like us to sing at her local church. The answer was yes, so we added Gargrave Parish Church to the schedule, as well as Linton-in-Craven church where Mrs. Coulthurst had recently financed the refurbishment of the church organ. We sang two Evensongs in Durham, two in York Minster, and a Sunday afternoon Evensong and recital in Gargrave. Whilst I helped to look after the boys for the evening, the lay clerks went on to sing Evensong in Linton-in-Craven, directed by Roger Lowman, who, because of the already crowded church, had to take choir practice in the churchyard.

Open air rehearsal. Roger Lowman and the lay clerks, Sunday 29th July 1968

Our new Dean was to be Anthony (Tony) Cyprian Bridge, Vicar of Christ Church, Lancaster Gate, London. What would he be like to work with? I soon found out when I rang him up to ask his permission for the choir to make another EMI recording in December. 'You don't need to ask me,' he said, 'you run the bloody choir, do what you bloody well like.' (He became well-known for his regular use of expletives, both in and out of the Cathedral.) Hurrah, I thought, now here's a(nother) man who tells it like it is! Tony was installed in October and would stay at Guildford for the next 18 years.

It might have been the success of the earlier carol record that brought Brian Culverhouse and his EMI recording team back to the Cathedral in early December. Were Music for Pleasure hoping for another best-seller, and was that why they'd chosen John Stainer's *The Crucifixion* for us to record? Passiontide in mid-Advent? Another challenge for us. Brian had engaged soloists David Hughes (tenor) and John Lawrenson (baritone), and we supplied two other soloists of our own – Terence Clifford and Phillip Mindenhall. Gavin Williams played the organ, and the choir sang at two of the sessions, the third being for the soloists alone.

Leaving the Cathedral after one of the sessions, Robert Hammersley jumped into his car and drove off at speed, not noticing a huge pile of leaves that had recently been swept up. One side of his car hit these, turning the vehicle on its side. After we'd rescued him, we thought we'd better take him to be checked up at the Accident & Emergency Department of the local hospital. Once there, we rang Christine, his wife, to tell her what happened to Robert, only to be greeted by 'Is the car alright?'

On Christmas Day, for the very first time, we were able to host a post-Nine Lessons and Carols party in our new home at No. 5 Cathedral Close, after which it was time for a good sleep and a welcome break.

1969: New music – new words

The basis of any varied musical diet is to explore compositions from across the centuries, rather than concentrating on just one period. It may have been because of our recordings that I'd landed myself with a Victorian/Edwardian tag – J.H. Maunder's *Olivet to Calvary* (1904); Christmas carols by John Goss and other Victorian composers; and now, John Stainer's *The Crucifixion* (1887). Although settings and anthems from previous centuries were in the choir's repertoire, so far they had not sung a great deal of 20th century music. They and I were ready for a change and a challenge, and this year was to see two contrasting works specially written for us.

But before all that, two more LPs of the choir were to become available – the Music for Pleasure record of *The Crucifixion,* and Guild Records' first LP, *Music for Passiontide*. Both were released and reviewed around the same time in March. All the reviews of the Stainer were positive:

This is certainly a good performance – very good. – Audio & Record Review

The performance is admirable. Barry Rose directs his choir with much skill. – Records & Recording

And the forecast from one of the reviewers that *The Crucifixion* would sell in the tens of thousands came true. Twenty-three years later it was awarded a Silver Disc for over 100,000 sales, and it remained in the catalogue for another 25 years or so.

It was time to focus on newer music, and we decided to turn our attention to un-recorded 20th century repertoire – something which might give Guild Records a distinctive voice in this niche area of the classical record market. I had sent one of the first Guild EPs to the composer Alan Ridout, since it included his first set of *Sacred Songs for Treble voices.* Alan offered to write another set for the Guildford choristers, and between us we chose texts associated with the Holy Spirit, appropriate for

The Cathedral Church of the Holy Spirit. In April he delivered the score, and we gave the first performance at a concert in Kingsclere Church, Hampshire, on 12th May. Two weeks later, on Whit Sunday (our Patronal Feast), the boys sang the songs at Evensong in place of the sermon, with Alan introducing his own composition.

Meanwhile, we had ambitious plans for the Diocesan Choirs Festivals. Although these weren't due to take place until October, the music booklet needed to be printed and available to the parish choirs well before the summer break. Ian Freeegard was a regular member of the weekday Evensong congregation. He taught English at Cranleigh Junior School, and had offered to write the words for a new Harvest-tide anthem.

His text needed striking music to match it, and that came from Derek Bourgeois, who at that time was doing his teaching-practice at Cranleigh Senior School. His brilliant but demanding score would nearly defeat the combined parish choirs at the Diocesan Choirs Festivals, but it was ideal for the Cathedral choir and our plans for the recorded 20th century anthology.

The recording sessions took place in late June and early July, and with all these pieces now in the repertoire we could include them in the concerts and Services on our forthcoming tour. Yes, it was that time of year again, and staying in the U.K., we'd be going southwards and westwards. Through an invitation following a couple of organ recitals I'd given in Freshwater Parish Church on the Isle of Wight, we spent the opening weekend there, singing a Saturday evening concert and a Sunday morning Service. It was a relaxing start, even allowing time for everyone to relax on the beach in the sunshine. Our next stop was in Bruton, Somerset, where we sang

Rehearsing in Llandaff Cathedral, 30th July 1969

Meeting Princess Margaret at the Royal Albert Hall

Sunday Evensong and a short recital in the parish church. From there we went on to Wells, singing Evensong in the Cathedral, and a concert the following evening in the beautiful church of St. Mary Redcliffe in Bristol. The tour finished in Cardiff, with Evensong in Llandaff Cathedral.

For the third time the boys were invited to sing at the Royal Albert Hall. By now we were used to the occasion, the huge audience, and the space we had to fill with sound, and it was an extra thrill for some of the choristers and myself to be presented to the guest of honour, Princess Margaret (see previous page).

1970: Home and away

1970 began and ended with the BBC.

Just 13 days after Christmas there was a live broadcast of Choral Evensong. School term was not due to start for another week, so the Service was sung by the lay clerks, including two new members singing their very first Service. Taking the place of Phillip Mindenhall, baritone Simon Deller had joined us from Ripon Cathedral, and alto Adrian Culshaw was replacing David Burrowes. Both Simon and Adrian had been appointed to teaching posts at Lanesborough School, where Simon would later become headmaster. The broadcast, on 7th January, featured no less than six different soloists in a programme of music that covered three centuries, with Gavin Williams and me playing an organ duet for the sung excerpts from *The Christmas Story* by Heinrich Schütz.

A month later the choir went abroad – at least that's what several of the boys were telling their parents. We'd had an invitation to sing on the Isle of Jersey, a self-governing dependency of the U.K., just 14 miles off the coast of France. On a Friday evening in February the choir flew there for a hectic weekend. In the space of just 72 hours, they sang a two-hour concert, Evensong in St. Helier Parish Church, and two schools' concerts on the Monday, the second being chosen for its proximity to the airport so that we could make a last-minute dash for the plane home.

Soon afterwards I had to think about finding a new sub-organist. Gavin Williams had been offered a teaching post in the music department of The King's School, Rochester, and was due to take up the appointment in September. We would need to find his replacement quickly.

4.0
Choral Evensong
from Guildford Cathedral
(men's voices)
Introit: I said to the man who stood at the gate of the year (*Sir William Harris*)
Responses (*Thomas Tallis*)
Psalm 97
Lessons: Isaiah 43, vv 1-13; 1 Thessalonians 5, vv 12-28
Canticles (*Sumsion in G*)
Anthem: from The Christmas Story (*Heinrich Schütz*)
As with gladness men of old (A and M Rev 79)
Organist and Master of the Choristers BARRY ROSE
Sub Organist GAVIN WILLIAMS

The Radio Times, *7th January 1970*

Return from Jersey: Richard Barnes and Michael Vaile (seated) at Southampton airport, 9th February 1970, with chorister Mark Purkiss looking on

A rare meeting of Guildford Cathedral Sub-Organists. From the left: Peter Moorse (1962-65), Gavin Williams (1965-70), and Anthony Froggatt (1970-77)

After audition and interview in early May, we appointed Anthony Froggatt, former organ scholar at Emmanuel College, Cambridge. A pupil of Brian Runnett, Tony's first appearance with the choir was as guest organist on our tour in July, and he was to stay at Guildford for the next seven years.

Our previous tours had taken us north, south and west. This year we were going east. Our first stop was Chingford Parish Church, where I'd had my very first organ lessons. From there we travelled to Bury St. Edmunds to give a concert in the old and new Cathedral. 'Old and new' since the original mediaeval building was in the throes of a major extension, not yet finished. Despite the builders' clutter and an all-pervading smell of wood preservative (causing several of the choir to complain), we sang a full-scale concert in both parts of the building. The next evening we gave a concert in Norwich Cathedral, and then it was time to head to Cambridge.

David Willcocks again invited us to sing the Sunday Evensong in King's College Chapel whilst the College choir was giving its annual concert in Stratford-upon-Avon. Just before our rehearsal, we discovered that the King's choral scholars had picked up the wrong wicker hamper and taken all our boys' robes, rather than their own. A hasty fitting session saw us singing our final Evensong of the year in the King's choir cassocks and surplices. And what a thrill it was to sing *Stanford in A* and E.W. Naylor's *Vox dicentis* in that wonderful space and acoustic (see overleaf).

Back in Guildford I had an unexpected phone call from John Poole. As the conductor of the BBC Choral Society, John was enquiring if it might be possible to bring them to sing a concert in the Cathedral in November. It would be a live broadcast,

Rehearsing in King's College Chapel, Cambridge, Sunday 26ᵗʰ July 1970

including the Requiem by Maurice Duruflé. Would I like to play the organ part? The answer was yes, and having checked the Cathedral diary, everything was confirmed. The boys took part in the concert, and that evening was to lead to my appointment to the BBC as their Music Adviser to the Head of Religious Broadcasting.

The BBC had also contacted Dean Tony Bridge about the possibility of a broadcast on Christmas Day morning. 'Could we do it?' he asked. 'Yes,' I replied, 'provided that we excuse the boys from singing Midnight Mass on Christmas Eve.'

1970 ended in the same way as it had begun – with a live broadcast. Seven days later I started my job at the BBC – a new challenge that was to last for the next 19 years, and something that would need to dovetail with my continuing work at Guildford Cathedral (and later at St. Paul's, Canterbury and St. Albans).

How would that work out in practice, and what new challenges would I face as a new member of staff of the world's oldest national broadcaster?

12

Broadcasting – A New Challenge
The BBC 1971–1990

A pillar of the British Establishment, the BBC (British Broadcasting Corporation) is known and respected around the world for the high quality of its radio and television programmes. Since 1933 there had been a Music Adviser to the Head of Religious Broadcasting, the first holder being Sir Henry Walford Davies, former Organist and Choirmaster at London's Temple Church, and already a regular broadcaster with his popular series, *Talking about Music.* Aside from directing the music at some of the six weekday morning broadcasts of the Daily Service, there were no specified duties for the Music Adviser, though he was always on call to advise on anything musical connected with the output of the department, often composing and arranging music at very short notice. On Sir Henry's death in 1941, the mantle had passed to his successor at the Temple Church, Dr. George Thalben-Ball.

One of the most distinguished organists in the country, GTB, as he was known, had achieved international fame as a choir trainer through his late 1920s recordings with Ernest Lough, one of his senior choristers at the Temple Church. Young Master Lough's recordings of Mendelssohn's *Hear my prayer* (and its following *O for the wings of a dove*) were to sell by the million, later making it the first church music recording ever to be awarded a Platinum disc.

When GTB took on the BBC post, Britain was at war, and whilst the Corporation strove to maintain most of its regular broadcasts, for safety's sake, many of them were moved to venues away from London. The Religious Broadcasting Department was now in the town of Bedford, some 55 miles north of the capital, and it was from there, in the lady chapel of St. Paul's Church, that the Daily Service continued to be broadcast live through those dark days in the country's history.

As they had done in London, an octet of singers drawn from the BBC's own professional choir, the BBC Chorus, assembled in the chapel each weekday morning, ready to rehearse with GTB. The Service consisted of a short introit composed by GTB, two hymns, a short psalm, a scripture reading and some topical prayers, and at 10.15 a.m. it was broadcast live to the nation. The music was sung unaccompanied, and the presenter sat at a desk a few feet away from the singers.

Another of GTB's duties was to perform improvised musical links from one pro-gramme to another, and the mood of these depended on what was to follow. If it was a bulletin with grave news, GTB would play something in a minor key, whilst a major key would be a clue that there was to be good news in the opening headlines.

After the war, the Religious Broadcasting Department returned to London, where it re-located to offices in what had formerly been the Langham Hotel, immediately opposite Broadcasting House, the Corporation's iconic headquarters. GTB continued his duties as the Music Adviser, remaining in post until late 1968, by which time he was 72 – well past the Corporation's official retirement age.

George Thalben-Ball directing the music in a post-war studio broadcast of the Daily Service

Early in 1970, John Poole, then Assistant Conductor of the BBC Chorus and con-ductor of the Corporation's amateur chorus, the BBC Choral Society, had contacted me to see if it might be possible for the Choral Society to broadcast a concert from Guildford Cathedral. John and I had first met back in 1958 when he was Organist and Choirmaster at St. George's Church, Bloomsbury Way, London, then the London University Church, where he ran a choir of undergraduates drawn from the univer-sity's various colleges spread in and around the capital. The University Chaplain, Prebendary Gordon Phillips, had kindly allowed me to use the church for the first concerts with the newly founded Jacobean Singers, and as a result of that, he had asked if there was any way that I could bring my choir from St. Andrew's, Kingsbury, to sing Evensong on some Sunday after-noons. John had been a welcoming host, as well as playing the organ for us on some occasions.

This unexpected 1970 contact was a renewal of our past musical friend-ship, and I persuaded the Dean that we should host the concert on Saturday 24th October, to be broadcast live on BBC Radio 3. The programme would include Franz Josef Haydn's *Te Deum in C*, and Maurice Duruflé's Requiem in the version for strings, in which I agreed to play the organ part.

As the date of the concert drew near, John came down to Guildford to check out all the practical details. It was then

GUILDFORD CATHEDRAL
(by kind permission of The Dean and Chapter)
Saturday 24th October 1970 7.30pm

BBC Radio 3 in association with the Haydn-Mozart Society presents:

JACK ROTHSTEIN (VIOLIN)
BBC CHORAL SOCIETY
LONDON MOZART PLAYERS
(Leader, Robert Masters)
CONDUCTOR: **JOHN POOLE**
Barry Rose (Organ)

HAYDN: TE DEUM IN C MAJOR (1800)
MOZART: VIOLIN CONCERTO No 5 in A MAJOR (K 219)

Interval

DURUFLÉ: REQUIEM

Admission by programme, obtainable from
The Vergers, Guildford Cathedral and Harveys of Guildford

17/6d   12/6d   7/6d   5/0d

that I suggested that he might like to use the boys of the Cathedral choir in a few excerpts in the Duruflé, and that they could sing these ranged along the front of the north organ gallery, high above the choir and orchestra – a sort of angelic choir. After some hesitation, John agreed, and I set about teaching them the parts they would sing in the *Offertorium*, the *Libera me*, as well as the opening of the *In paradisum*.

I asked Roger Lowman, one of the founder members of the new Cathedral choir, if he would direct them in the concert – and much to my relief he accepted. The concert went well, and John seemed to be most impressed with the contribution from the Guildford choristers. In conversation afterwards, he mentioned that the Religious

Broadcasting Department still had a vacancy for a Musical Adviser since no-one had yet been appointed to succeed George Thalben-Ball. Would I like him to men-tion my name? 'Yes please,' I said, and thought no more about it until, about two weeks later, I had a phone call from the Reverend John Lang, then Head of Religious Programmes, Radio (known as HRPR), inviting me to join him in London for lunch.

We met at the Gay Hussar, a popular Hungarian res-taurant in Greek Street, and the occasion is forever etched

The Reverend John Lang – later to become Dean of Lichfield

in my mind. For my starter I had ordered wild cherry soup, which arrived stone cold (as it should have been), and I nearly sent it back with the complaint that they had forgotten to heat it! Mercifully I didn't, and by the end of the lunch, John Lang had offered me the part-time post of Music Adviser to the Head of Religious Broadcasting, subject to a formal interview and suitably acceptable contractual terms – and all that had been due to John Poole's recommendation after hearing the Guildford boys singing in the Duruflé Requiem.

A few weeks later, following a further interview with Penry Jones, the Head of Religious Broadcasting, all the formalities were completed, and it was agreed that I would start on the 1st January 1971. I would be only the third Music Adviser to the Corporation's Head of Religious Broadcasting, in direct succession to Henry Walford Davies and George Thalben-Ball – a post that would be discontinued after I left 19 years later.

My first official BBC duty was on Wednesday 6th January 1971, playing the organ in a live morning broadcast of an Epiphany Choral Eucharist in St. James' Church, Piccadilly, a prominent London landmark where, a few years earlier, I had heard the Ely Cathedral choristers in concert. The music in this service was provided by the professional BBC Chorus, conducted by John Poole. Unusually, they were to be joined by a small jazz group since the setting of the Mass was by the well-known jazz saxophonist, John Dankworth, who, coincidentally, had also been a pupil at Sir George Monoux Grammar School in Walthamstow, though several years ahead of me. Mr. (later Sir John) Dankworth was in church that morning for the pre-Service rehearsal and balance-test, and though he was encouraging, I was still nervous, in the knowledge that each of the singers was sizing me up and waiting to see how this young and inexperienced successor to the great George Thalben-Ball would cope with live broadcasting.

After the Service, I walked over to my shared office on the second floor of The Langham, and sat there wondering what to do next. The decision was made for me when there was a knock at the door and in walked K-B – the

With George Thalben-Ball at the console of the organ in the concert hall, BBC Broadcasting House, London

Reverend Prebendary W.D. Kennedy-Bell, Reader (Associate Priest) of the Temple Church, founder and conductor of the St. Martin's Singers, and long-serving BBC employee as Organiser of Religious Broadcasting Overseas, known around the department by the acronym ORBO. Spending his time between two BBC premises – Bush House and the Langham – K-B was also the editor and chief London producer of the weekly live broadcast of Choral Evensong. We had met over the past nine years when the Cathedral choir at Guildford had taken part in the series. His welcome was warm, and he asked if I would like to meet the other members of the department, starting with his loyal and long-serving secretary, Beryl, and the department's organiser, Doris English, who held all the purse strings for programme budgets, travel and hospitality. Senior producer, the Reverend Hubert Hoskins, was responsible for several Worship programmes as well as the weekly Sunday night Epilogue and Compline broadcasts, on which he and I were to work closely over the next two decades. Nearer my age was the Reverend Colin Semper, also from Guildford, where he had been curate at Holy Trinity Church (formerly the Pro-Cathedral), and another colleague of his from Guildford, the Reverend Roy Trevivian.

Colin would become HRPR (Head of Religious Programmes, Radio), going on from there to be Provost of Coventry, and later, Residentiary Canon at Westminster Abbey, until ill-health forced his early retirement. Roy Trevivian was less conventional, and had been the charismatic priest-in-charge of a small church on the Park Barn housing estate in Guildford. Known for his colourful and outspoken language, he brought that charisma to the many programmes he produced for Radio 2, though his heavy drinking and dogmatic style with his colleagues were to be his downfall at the BBC, and his life ended a few years later after a severe stroke.

A year or so after I started, John Lang was promoted to be Head of Religious Broadcasting (HRB), his place being taken by the Reverend Michael Mayne, a former parish priest from the Diocese of St. Albans, who, like myself, had little previous experience of broadcasting. Michael was to run the radio unit of the department for the next seven years, going on to become vicar of the University Church in Cambridge, and from there to be Dean of Westminster Abbey.

There were other ordained members of the department, including Father Patrick McEnroe, the Roman Catholic Assistant to the Head of Religious Broadcasting, who also held the position of parish priest at a Roman Catholic church in nearby Kensington. Each member of the department was required to be a presenter on the Daily Service, which was broadcast live each weekday morning, usually from the church of All Souls, Langham Place, next door to Broadcasting House.

The longest continuous radio programme anywhere in the world, the history of the Daily Service stretches back as far as January 1928 when it was first broadcast from

All Souls Church, Langham Place, London. Broadcasting House is the white building on the left

a BBC studio in Savoy Hill, London. After the Corporation moved into the newly built Broadcasting House in 1932, a special chapel studio was set aside for the use of the Religious Broadcasting Department. Sometimes broadcast from there, and sometimes from All Souls Church, the music was led by eight singers from what was then the BBC Wireless Chorus, who were often required to wear morning dress.

Now, nearly 40 years later, my contribution to the Daily Service broadcasts would begin. Every weekday morning, eight members of the BBC Chorus – two sopranos, two contraltos, two tenors and two basses – still led the singing in the Service, deputed through a weekly duty rota prepared by chorus manager, Stanley Pine. That first morning in All Souls Church there was no-one to help or advise me, so at 9.40 a.m. I was left to rehearse two hymns, a psalm and an introit with the singers. The sight-reading skills of this group were legendary. Someone once said that if ink had been shaken from a pen on to some manuscript paper and covered it with blobs, the BBC Chorus would sing it without any problem.

There were no worries about getting the notes right on the first sing-through, though there was now the option of having unison verses rather than harmony all the time, since I would also be playing the organ. No-one had done this since GTB had retired more than two years previously. I got the impression that the singers weren't used to rehearsing in any detail, whilst some didn't see the need to rehearse at all. We reached a slight balance problem in the psalm where the tenors and basses were reciting on the same note in the chant. I stopped the rehearsal, and as politely as I could, pointed out that unless they sang that note a little more quietly, they could overbalance that of the sopranos and altos – to which the immediate retort from a rather sullen and senior elderly bass was 'I'm singing *my* line.'

It was not going to be easy, and the first thing that struck me on that and successive mornings was that most of the singers seemed to have been chosen for their vocal ability rather than choral expertise. Many of them had been, and indeed sometimes were, more at home on the operatic stage rather than in this liturgical context, and perhaps that was not surprising since they had been appointed by their present director, Peter Gellhorn. Formerly on the music staff at the Royal Opera House and Glyndebourne, Peter had come to the BBC following Leslie Woodgate's death in May 1961, and as I was told, had hardly, if ever, worked on the Daily Service. Although I was directing members of his choir, we were never to meet – he retired a year later in 1972, returning to Glyndebourne and the world of opera.

Whilst that first morning of directing the Daily Service may have been a baptism by fire, gradually as the weeks and months went by, the members of the Chorus (later to be re-named the BBC Singers) and I began to forge a musical and personal relationship which, in turn, changed the sound and the attitude from being just an irksome professional duty to something in which they actually enjoyed taking part. A number of famous musicians of the future were to join the group, including composers Judith Bingham and Bob Chilcott, singers Sarah Connolly and Brindley Sherratt, and choral directors Harry Christophers and Stephen Jackson. Over the years we also had help from several distinguished choral conductors, among them Martindale Sidwell, Simon Joly, Kerry Woodward, and Nicholas Cleobury, and the choir now had a new manager, Geoffrey Mitchell, also an expert singer and choral director.

Eight BBC Singers take part in each service. At the back are director Barry Rose (right) and assistant Nicholas Cleobury; front right is manager Geoffrey Mitchell

From the Radio Times *– March 1980. Singers (from L to R): Veronica Lucas, Jennifer Adams (soprano), Marion Dodd and Catherine Denley (alto), David Fieldsend and Andrew King (tenor), Jeremy White and Jonathan Robarts (bass)*

It was at the Daily Service that I linked up again with John Poole. He, too, was on the rota of musical directors for the Service, and often we would work together, John directing the choir and me playing the organ. The presenter sat at a table close to the singers and was usually in the church for most of our rehearsal. Each had their own style, and since there was no complete run-through, all the starts of the musical items were either cued from the script or started by a hand signal. We learned to listen closely to the announcement of the last hymn since there was often the possibility of a verse being omitted if speech or music had slightly over-run.

The Service always began with music – a short introit from a published collection, *Laudate Dominum*, composed by George Thalben-Ball. The red light would flash, during which the announcer in the continuity suite in Broadcasting House would be speaking, and I would play a quiet organ chord just before our balance engineer, in the basement studio in All Souls Church, faded us up. Usually that went without a hitch, though I'm told there was one occasion when the steady red light failed to function, and the voice of one of the sopranos was broadcast to the nation telling her colleague that it was time to put away her knitting.

Security in those early days was an occasional problem, and there was always the possibility that anyone could walk into the church, either to take part in the Worship or to disturb it – on one occasion a protestor had grabbed the presenter's microphone. In the end it was decided that a BBC commissionaire would be on duty at the church door each morning during the transmission.

Situated on busy Regent Street, we were also subject to the ambient noise of car hooters in the usual traffic jams, as well as any nearby construction work. One memorable week saw roadworks just outside the church, and throughout the pre-transmission rehearsal we could hardly hear ourselves for the noise of pneumatic drills. In the end the balance engineer ran outside to ask the workmen if they could take a break for 15 minutes whilst the broadcast took place, though for that and successive mornings the Corporation had to pay for their coffee and late breakfasts.

Directing the music at the Daily Service was to be a continuing pattern for three or four mornings each week, and to be there in good time I had to catch a train from Guildford at around 8.15 a.m. Because of the deadline of a 12.15 p.m. choir practice at Lanesborough School on four weekdays, I needed to leave the car either at home or near the station, ready laden with the music for the rehearsal. As soon as the red light went off at 10.30 a.m. I would race down Regent Street, into Oxford Circus underground station and down to the Bakerloo line. If I was lucky I'd catch the 10.50 a.m. train from Waterloo Station, reaching Guildford in good time to set up the music at Lanesborough for choir practice, though sometimes it was the later 11.20 a.m. train, which meant a breathless last-minute arrival, just in time for the 12.15 p.m. start.

With no sung Evensong at Guildford, each Wednesday was a full day devoted to the BBC. After the Daily Service I would make my way to the office to find various notes on my desk about musical items that would be needed for the department's future programmes. These ranged from instrumental and choral items for the weekly Sunday late-night Epilogue to specially arranged and composed signature-tunes. I also began to write detailed reports about the singing on each Wednesday's live broadcast of Choral Evensong which were passed on to the regional producers, not always meeting with their approval. The weekly broadcast was allocated on a regional basis; at that time the Religious Broadcasting Department had full-time employees in Bristol, Birmingham, Manchester, Glasgow, Cardiff and Belfast. I felt that the standard of some of the chosen choirs was sometimes not worthy of the programme, but the allocated regional slots were jealously guarded, at least for the time being.

Prebendary Kennedy-Bell (ORBO) was due to retire from the BBC in two years' time, and John Lang suggested that I should start to take over the editorship of the Choral Evensong programme, and also act as producer from the cathedrals covered by the London area, including the collegiate chapels of Oxford and Cambridge. This would involve selection of venues in and around south-east England as well as bringing some subtle pressure to bear on the regional choices, usually through first-hand or reliably reported knowledge of which choirs were of an acceptable standard. As I pointed out to my regional colleagues, Choral Evensong was now on Radio 3, the BBC's flagship music channel, and sandwiched between the very best of live or recorded orchestral music. We needed to match those musical standards.

There was no formal training to be a producer, though I was able to shadow K-B on some of the Choral Evensong broadcasts he had produced. Now, in 1973, it was over to me, and for the first time I would meet my cathedral organist colleagues wearing a different hat. How would they react to another church musician making suggestions about the way their choir sang? Reactions were mixed, ranging from deeply suspicious at first to 'Please tell that bass on Cantoris that he's singing flat. I've been telling him that for years to no avail, but he'll take notice of you.'

Dealing with cathedral clergy was quite another matter. Deans and Canons were not used to advice on how they should read the lessons and take the prayers; broadcasting usually requires a more intimate style of delivery rather than the vocal projection needed to fill a huge building. Often appearing just 15 minutes or less before the live broadcast, reaction ranged from willing cooperation to 'I've been reading this way for the past forty years and have no intention of changing it just for you.'

As with all live musical broadcasts, the sound that the listeners hear is created by skilled technicians who place the microphones and operate the complicated mixing-desks. The art of the producer is to oversee every practical detail whilst working in tandem with the sound engineers to transmit the right broadcast sound and take it into the listeners' homes.

On the day of the broadcast, the BBC van would arrive at the venue sometime during the morning. Cables were run into the cathedral, microphones tested, and by the time the choir arrived in the early afternoon for the balance test, we would be ready to listen and work on the sound balancing. My hands were not on the faders of the control-desk that created the balance, but on many occasions, I persuaded the engineers to

A BBC mobile studio in which we would sit to broadcast Choral Evensong

go into the cathedral to make a small microphone adjustment, and whilst they were gone, I would adjust the faders to the balance I felt was right. Luckily, it usually stayed that way when they returned.

To a practising cathedral musician, it was fascinating to see and hear my colleagues at work with their own choirs. Some used the balance-test to polish repertoire they had already rehearsed, whilst others used it as a learning session. When there were long psalms, I'd tell them that it was not necessary to sing every verse in the balance-test unless they wanted to, so there was never a complete run-through for timing purposes, and often it was more by luck than judgement that we finished on time.

Radio 3 was used to being flexible over timings, though not always, and especially on one occasion at Winchester Cathedral: that day I was being shadowed by Robin Hicks, then Controller of BBC West of England (and son of Ronald Hicks, my former boss at Joseph Rank Ltd.). By now I was working at St. Paul's and had to leave the transmission early to get the train back to London for a special event at the Cathedral. Robin said he would take over the last 15 minutes. In the middle of a long anthem it was obvious there was going to be a six or seven minute over-run, and in the usual way, one of the engineers got on the line to the continuity suite in Broadcasting House to let them know, only to be greeted with 'Sorry, we'll have to fade you out.' Unfazed by this, Robin grabbed the phone. Finding out that it was the continuity announcer's very first duty day, and explaining who he was, Robin added that 'Radio 3 *never* fades out music,' and if there was any comeback, he would be personally responsible to the Controller of Radio 3. The Evensong stayed on air until it finished.

It was always my ethos that the listener should feel as though they were walking into Evensong, as the organ played under the opening continuity announcement from

London; and leave the cathedral during the organ voluntary at the end, which in those days was usually faded out, and a very useful buffer if any other part of the service had over-run. The start of the broadcast was signalled by a red light, placed where everyone could see it. The choir had already processed in and were sitting in the stalls. As the opening announcement was made from Broadcasting House, the red light would flash, operated by the balance-engineer in the BBC van, and inside the cathedral the choir would stand. There would be a slight pause, the red light would come on steady once continuity had faded up the atmosphere of the cathedral, and the broadcast would begin. This usually worked, though there were a few instances when it did not. One memorable occasion was at Canterbury Cathedral where the BBC van was parked in the Close, just outside the south transept:

As usual the organ was playing quietly while the red light was flashed during the opening announcement from London. In the van we were linked to the flashing light and could also see that it was on a steady red for the transmission to begin. At that point the organ usually stopped, and the choir started the introit. Not today – at one minute past four the organ was still playing, and I suggested to the engineers that the red light might not be working inside the Cathedral. 'Not possible,' they said, 'if it's on here in the van, it must be on in there.' Still the organ played on, and in the Cathedral they may have been thinking that the previous broadcast had over-run and that they would be starting a little late. Obviously the red light was not on in there, and I needed to tell them that we were now on the air. Just down the path from the van was the door into the south transept, and during the balance test we'd been in and out of it to adjust microphones. I ran down the path and found it was now locked. The only way to get in would be via the west porch. I sprinted as fast as I could, only to be confronted by a verger who snapped, 'You can't come in here, there's a broadcast going on.' Having persuaded him that I was the producer, I took off my shoes, and running the whole length of the nave, up the steps into the quire, tapped choir director Allan Wicks on the shoulder, whispering as softly as I could, 'We're on the air... please can you start?'

The same thing also happened a year or so later at Norwich Cathedral when Martin How was directing the RSCM Summer Course choir. In the extant recording of that Service you can hear the whispered conversation, with Martin saying 'Is it on? – OK'.

Back in London, John Poole and I had also linked up for some Choral Evensong broadcasts with the BBC Chorus (shortly to be renamed the BBC Singers), the first being in October 1971 from St. Gabriel's Church, Cricklewood. John directed the choir and I played the organ. A year later we did a similar broadcast, this time in St. Augustine's Church, Kilburn, in a Service that included a world premiere of a new anthem by William Mathias, specially written for the BBC.

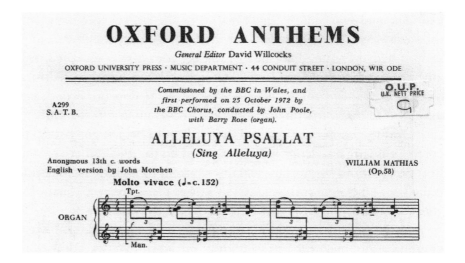

Title page of the anthem for the broadcast of Choral Evensong, 25th October 1972

John had just become the director of the Chorus, and this time the producer of the programme was one of my colleagues from the Religious Broadcasting Department. I remember the afternoon well. My closing organ voluntary was the *Toccata* from the *Toccata, Fugue and Hymn on 'Ave Maris stella'* by Flor Peeters, and I'd carefully calculated that even if we finished the rest of the Service a bit early, the length of the *Toccata* (which I knew well) would be more than sufficient until we went off air. Imagine my horror when I reached the end to find that the red light was still on. I started to read my way through the *Fugue*, and as the music got more complicated so the mistakes started to creep in. Now in a state of panic, I heard the sound of uncontrollable laughter from the vestry below – we'd been off the air for at least five minutes, and they'd purposely left the red light on!

The whole of the department had now moved from the Langham Hotel to the second floor of Broadcasting House, and there I had my own office, complete with the piano that had been passed on from Henry Walford Davies and George Thalben-Ball. It was probably on this venerable instrument that HWD and GTB had written some of their hymn tunes for the BBC's own hymn book. Now, in 1980, I was a member of a small committee working on the preparation of a supplement – *Broadcast Praise*. As with my two predecessors, I was asked to contribute some new tunes – five in all, one of which was appropriately named *Langham Place*.

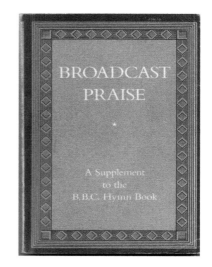

Published in 1981 and publicised by an hour-long Radio 4 programme, it soon came into regular use.

In addition to the Daily Service and Choral Evensong duties, I was also closely involved in the weekly broadcast of the Epilogue, in which the BBC Singers usually took part. On two or three days each quarter we would assemble at a London church and record a whole variety of items that I'd slotted into previously submitted scripts. The music ranged from part-songs to negro spirituals, and even nursery rhymes to opera and oratorio choruses. Each item had to dovetail into the later recorded speech, and when I wasn't accompanying on the piano or organ, John would often invite me to conduct the Singers. If it wasn't possible to find suitable music to match the speech, I was expected to write something, setting solo songs from Shakespeare to Siegfried Sassoon, usually with just the melody written out on a scrap of manuscript paper for the chosen soloist from the Singers.

And then there were the signature tunes for various series of programmes being made by different members of the department – such as *Sweet Songs of Zion*, *Priestland's Progress*, *The Good Book*, *The Case against God*, and *Ten to Ten*, the short-lived Saturday evening meditation on Radio 4. As with all signature tunes, the music needed to match the mood of the programme, and since there was usually no specific budget for music, I was lucky that we were able to use players from the BBC Concert Orchestra and the BBC Symphony Orchestra rather than having to pay freelance musicians. Usually small-scale in orchestration, the compositions ranged from Gerald Priestland whistling his own theme for *Priestland's Progress*, accompanied by violin, flute, trombone, cello and bass, to a shofar player and just me on the piano with radiophonic effects for *The Good Book*. John Poole and I played a piano duet of a chorale as the signature tune for one series of Epilogues, whilst another series gave me the chance to link up with my cousin Martin, then principal cellist of the Symphony Orchestra, in a piano and cello arrangement of the hymn-tune *Ellers* by E.J. Hopkins.

Perhaps the most high-profile original composition was the setting of the Corporation's motto, *Nation shall speak peace unto nation*. 1982 was the BBC's 60th Anniversary, and a celebratory Service took place in St. Paul's Cathedral, where I was then Master of the Choir. Produced by my colleague Chris Rees, it was he who suggested the setting, to be sung by the BBC Singers and the Cathedral choir. In a Service of great musical splendour, in which the BBC Symphony Orchestra was also taking part, the anthem provided a reflective moment following the Archbishop of Canterbury's sermon, during which he quoted the BBC motto. Attended by HM The Queen and the Duke of Edinburgh, it was a great occasion both for the Corporation and St. Paul's, and it was highlighted in the *Daily Telegraph* the next day:

> ## Majestic birthday party for the BBC
>
> ### By RICHARD LAST, TV Staff
>
> NO ONE actually uttered the words "sixty glorious years" when the BBC celebrated its diamond jubilee with all the pomp and pageantry that St Paul's Cathedral could muster yesterday. But they hung, pregnantly unspoken, in the air.

An invitation came from Ian McIntyre, controller of Radio 3, to attend their monthly planning meetings – the first time anyone from Religious Broadcasting had done this – and there I was able to talk about the plans for Choral Evensong which, for a short while, had been increased to two broadcasts each week. Ian had graduated from St. John's College, Cambridge, from where we were now broadcasting the annual Ash Wednesday Choral Evensong, and the St. John's connection may have been in his mind when he suggested to Colin Semper (then HRPR) that we ought to broadcast their Advent Carol Service. As the designated producer of the programme, I was asked to negotiate with the College through the Dean, and Dr. George Guest, the Director of Music, who at that time was also my son's choirmaster.

We arranged the first live broadcast for 6.00 p.m. on Advent Sunday 1981, with a full-scale balance-test and rehearsal on the morning before. From talking with other choir parents, I gathered that the chapel would be completely jammed for the Service, with congregation sitting in every nook and cranny, even in the apsidal east end sanctuary of the chapel, and I guessed how much this would deaden the acoustic. For the choir it would be like singing into blotting paper, though somehow, for the listeners at home, we would need to convey the usual ambience of the chapel. Our skilled engineers were equal to the task. During the long Saturday morning rehearsal, they programmed a reverberation unit in our mobile studio to replicate what we were hearing in the way of ambience and acoustic. The parents were right: on Sunday evening the chapel was over-full and the warm acoustic we'd experienced the day before had completely disappeared. At the start of the transmission the engineers threw the switch on the reverberation unit and the real sound of St. John's chapel was broadcast to the nation. This Service is now a broadcast tradition, and as I write, is about to celebrate its 40th consecutive year.

A few yards down the road from St. John's is King's College, with its famous chapel and choir. Known throughout the world, their annual Service of Nine Lessons and Carols had been broadcast every year since 1928, with just one exception, 1930.

Although I had been an avid listener since boyhood, I'd only been there on one occasion, when Boris Ord had let me into the organ loft (see page 37). At the BBC I was never quite sure who had been responsible as producer over those years, but now, in 1989, I was asked if I'd like to do it. In accepting, I decided to experiment with the traditional opening moments, and having persuaded a slightly hesitant Stephen Cleobury, the Director of Music, we asked Brian Kay, then working with Radio 3, if he would come and introduce the Service from under the organ loft. The reasoning behind this was to do with the level of comparative volumes at the opening – the announcer in the continuity suite in London usually sounds loud and very present, whilst the beginning of the Service is a boy soloist singing the first verse of *Once in Royal David's City* from the back of the antechapel. As a listener, I had found the contrast between the two volumes quite disturbing, and it always took several seconds for my ear to adjust to what was happening in the building. I asked Brian to say a few quiet words about the history of the Service right at the very start of the broadcast, standing under the arch of the organ screen, with quiet organ music in the background, in the hope that this would allow the listener time to adjust to the new ambience. I think it worked, though it was never done again.

Although I still held the (officially) part-time BBC post, my circumstances had twice changed – we had moved to Canterbury at the beginning of 1985, and in September 1988 to St. Albans Cathedral, where I'd become Master of the Music. Times had also changed for the Religious Broadcast department, though it was still split into two sections – radio and television, and it was with television that I was now also working, with the new BBC 2 four-programme series called *Close Harmony*. I always felt that using this title might not attract many would-be viewers. Clever though it was, with its musical allusion to a Cathedral CLOSE, to the average viewer the usual meaning of close harmony conjured up images of pop-groups singing notes closely clustered together.

As a television presenter I was not a natural and had no training or advice how to speak directly to the camera. There was no autocue, so every spoken link was apparently impromptu, though there had to be a basic form of script to allow for retakes and camera cutaway shots. Sometimes I was moving around the interior of the building, sometimes walking the cloisters, and occasionally sitting at the organ and playing it.

The first programme was filmed in Canterbury Cathedral and given a lot of pre-publicity in a specially written article for the *Radio Times* (overleaf). The second programme was at Christ Church, Oxford, and from my point of view it was much better. I was now more confident about the filming process, and the opening shot, with me standing on one of the roofs of the College looking windswept, was

22-28 MARCH 1986

A chorus of approval

*Music and history come together in
'Close Harmony', a new series taking a conducted tour of
the English choral tradition. Meredith Oakes writes*

**Close Harmony
Good Friday
4.20 BBC2**

BARRY ROSE tells a good Canterbury tale. Like the one about Thomas à Becket, murdered in the cathedral in 1170. 'It's lovely to go into a building and say, "Look, can you imagine that night in December 800 years ago…"'

In **Close Harmony** he explores the way such buildings as Canterbury and their music go together. For one of Britain's leading cathedral choirmasters the role of TV presenter is something of a new departure, even if he once measured his audience in millions when he conducted the choir of St Paul's at the royal wedding of the Prince of Wales and Lady Diana.

That was before a much publicised showdown with the authorities at St Paul's. It is said they didn't like his sharp tongue, his resistance to financial cuts, his success in finding alternative finance from commercial recordings (the heavenly choir came down to earth as the Frog Chorus on Paul McCartney's hit single and in *The Snowman* and the music for *Tinker, Tailor, Soldier, Spy*) or his general unwillingness to compromise on quality. He doesn't talk about that, except to say: 'The more formal the building, like St Paul's, the less it lends itself to the "clap your hands" stuff.'

Now Rose is master of choirs at King's School,

Praising God: Barry Rose at Canterbury

Canterbury, which makes the cathedral, 'the mother church of everywhere in England', doubly appropriate as the first place visited in this occasional series. 'The Canterbury programme is filmed in six or seven different places,' says Rose. 'One minute I'm in the organ loft, the next I'm down in the nave by Orlando Gibbons's monument, the next by Becket's martyrdom spot.'

As for the music, he says: 'Many carols were written after Becket's martyrdom, so we're using one of those; there's a *Te Deum* written by Vaughan Williams for the enthronement of an archbishop in 1928; a motet by Thomas Tallis, who was a lay clerk at Canterbury; and a verse anthem by the later Tudor composer Orlando Gibbons.

'Gibbons was director of music at the Chapel Royal,' adds Rose, 'and he was in Canterbury when he had a fit of apoplexy and died as he came out of the cathedral. Then we come right up to date with Alan Ridout, who has lived in Canterbury for the last 20 years and whose window faces the cathedral as he writes his music – much of it for Dr Allan Wicks and his choir at the cathedral.'

Publicity for 'Close Harmony' in the
Radio Times, *March 1986*

eye-catchingly panoramic. Nobody was more surprised than I when, in the middle of a take, a window below me was thrown open and a voice said, 'Whatever are you doing up there, sir?' It was Barry Holden, a former chorister at St. Paul's Cathedral and now an undergraduate. Barry would later go on to become a vice-president at the Universal Music Group. Transmitted on Whit Sunday 1986, the Christ Church choir, with Stephen Darlington, their recently appointed Director, sang a wide range of music, from John Taverner to William Walton, using various parts of the Cathedral as well as the stairs to the College Hall.

From Oxford we went to Worcester Cathedral for an Advent programme, and then lastly to King's College, Cambridge, where, as with Donald Hunt at Worcester, we were able to film Stephen Cleobury working with the boy choristers.

The weekly television programme *Songs of Praise* also called on my services, and not just as a musician! For two separate programmes I wrote 'hymn-like' words to the signature-tune for EastEnders, and also to *I do like to be beside the seaside* for a special programme from the Tower Ballroom, Blackpool. Perhaps the most exciting and demanding occasion was a whole day's filming in Salisbury Cathedral, conducting and keeping the attention of nearly one thousand schoolchildren – a wonderful sound I still remember nearly forty years on.

The radio team had been moved again, this time to Yalding House, just off Great Portland Street, the home of the BBC Music producers and the music library. I was one of the lucky ones with a separate office, necessary because I would often be playing the piano. David Winter was now head of the department, and there were many new faces and new programme ideas. I was not sure if some of them realised the value of the core output of the department – Worship – and sometimes there seemed to be a lack of support or willingness to fight for that strand of our output. This resulted in the loss of the Saturday morning Daily Service and the late Sunday evening Epilogues and Complines. Choral Evensong, the department's flagship Worship programme, was not really valued or understood by some of the new arrivals, typified by a remark from the Reverend Stephen Oliver in a staff meeting, when he said that 'Choral Evensong can be produced by a monkey holding a stop-watch.'

It was about then that I decided maybe the time had come to take stock and reconsider my place in the department. The enthusiasm was still there, though making enough time to be in the office and availability for production duties was becoming more difficult. I had enjoyed the most wonderful support across the years from a series of personal assistants – Caroline, Sarah-Jane, Marion and others. Without their efficiency and diplomacy there was no way I could have managed the demands of schedules, meetings, travel, and seemingly endless paperwork. Help had also been at hand with the appointment of Stephen Shipley. Stephen had joined the BBC in 1975 as a studio manager, and he'd started working on religious programmes in 1981 whilst taking a part-time ordination course in the Chelmsford Diocese. We would often travel to Choral Evensong venues together (I used to introduce him as my trainee!), and it was a programme he would later take over and run with great distinction from

1995 until his retirement in 2019. We were also now getting back-up from James Whitbourn, an accomplished church musician, and it was James who would take over my duties, albeit without the title of Music Adviser, when, in 1990, I decided to leave the BBC. It was an opportune time to go since there was already talk about the whole of the department moving to new premises in Manchester, some 200 miles north-west of London, which they did four years later.

It wasn't quite the end of my connection with the Daily Service. Having left the Corporation as the third and last of the Music Advisers to the Head of Religious Broadcasting, David Winter offered me a short-term contract in an advisory capacity, with one weekly duty of directing the music at the Daily Service. There had been a 'new broom' there as well. The form of the Service was no longer tied to the previous format, and whilst there were still two hymns, there was now an anthem whose text would relate to the biblical reading it would follow. The long-standing arrangement with the BBC Singers had also ceased, and a new auditioned freelance choir, the Daily Service Singers, had taken their place each day, apart from Wednesdays. It was Wednesday when I would direct the music, not just with eight of the BBC Singers, but the whole group of 24.

Another recent innovation was a producer, usually one of the newer members of staff who was not very experienced and often over-zealous. This was sure to rankle with the Singers, who really didn't need the 40 or so minutes allocated to the pre-Service rehearsal, and the shouted comments from the basement control-room of 'I can't hear the words' usually resulted in even less diction. It didn't worry me – I'd worked with the Singers for the past 19 years and knew that once the red light went on they would be the consummate professionals and give of their absolute best, believers or not.

A tribute to their expertise and musicality was the Wednesday morning when we arrived for rehearsal to find no music on their seats. The time ticked by and everyone seemed quite resigned to the fact that the standby tape would have to be broadcast. Five minutes before the scheduled start, the church door burst open and a breathless librarian rushed in with piles of music. He'd overslept. As he distributed the two hymns and copies of Samuel Sebastian Wesley's six-part anthem, *Cast me not away from Thy presence*, I asked the Singers, 'Do we go for it?' 'Yes,' they all said, and a few minutes later, live on air, they gave the most accomplished and moving performance of an anthem that at least seventy-five percent of them had never seen before.

I would miss those Wednesday mornings, though I did spend some time working with the Daily Service Singers up in the north-west, live broadcasting the Services from Emmanuel Church, Didsbury – a happy association which was to last for another ten years.

In April 1990, a month after I had officially left the BBC, the Corporation hosted a farewell dinner for Buffie and myself. Attended by many friends from different departments, we were presented with a bound autograph book into which many distinguished church musicians and BBC colleagues had written personal messages. All of those are still treasured, but one I treasure most is from the Very Reverend John Lang, now Dean of Lichfield, who, 20 years before on John Poole's recommendation, had given me the honour of succeeding Henry Walford Davies and George Thalben-Ball:

'Barry – I remember how awful it was having to tell George Thalben-Ball he must retire (12 years over the proper age) and what a pleasure it was appointing you to succeed him. I never did a better thing! With good wishes, John.'

13

Ten Years On – Two Roses Plus One
Guildford 1971–1974

I n January 1971 I had taken up my BBC appointment, travelling to and from London on up to three mornings each week. At the Cathedral we celebrated the tenth anniversary of the Consecration with a concert attended by a large and appreciative audience.

But it was family matters that took pride of place in our lives at this time. For a little while, Buffie and I had been hoping to have a child, but that had not happened. We made enquiries of the Church of England Children's Society about the possibility of adoption, and after detailed interviews with them, we were accepted as future parents. In mid-June I was away in Jersey when Buffie had a phone call saying that there was a new-born boy who had been matched to us. Could we be ready in two weeks' time to meet his foster-parents and take him home with us? It seemed as though it was meant to be, especially as he had been born on our wedding anniversary. Buffie stopped working at the College of Law the Friday before, and just four days later on the following Tuesday, we became parents, driving down to Hampshire and returning home with Timothy Peter Rose. It was 29th June, St. Peter's Day, and we gave Tim his middle name in honour of that special day. From now on, life at No. 5 Cathedral Close would be very different.

Buffie with Tim, July 1971

The Cathedral choir had been offered two broadcast Evensongs on successive weeks, and I was able to arrange for the second of these to take place whilst we were away on tour. This year, it was the north-west of England, starting with a concert in St. Matthew's Church, Bolton, Lancashire, going on from there to Cartmel Priory where we sang an evening concert as well as the Choral Evensong broadcast the following afternoon. The next day we sang Evensong in Chester Cathedral, and lastly, a concert in the recently consecrated Roman Catholic Cathedral in Liverpool. Known locally as 'Paddy's Wigwam', the interior is a huge, circular open space with the altar in the centre. In the concert we sang from the choir-stalls, in front of the central altar, and for the Allegri *Miserere,* the ethereal-sounding solo quartet of Simon Davis, Mark Blatchly, Adrian Culshaw and Richard Barnes were in one of the small galleries high above the audience.

In September we welcomed tenors Robert Gibbs, Peter Young and Grayston Ives (known to his friends as Bill). Robert had come straight from Tonbridge School, whilst Peter had been a choral scholar at Jesus College, Cambridge. Bill Ives had been doing his teaching-practice at nearby Cranleigh School and took the place of Robert Hammersley, who was about to return to Magdalen College, Oxford, to finish his degree. Not just a wonderful singer (he was to become the tenor in the King's Singers), Bill was also a gifted composer, and over the five years he sang at the Cathedral, he wrote several pieces for the choir, one of which, *Listen, sweet dove*, is regularly sung in churches and cathedrals around the world.

1972: Sadness – and happiness

The Reverend Eric Ware, my father-in-law and the Cathedral's first Precentor, passed away on Friday 5th May 1972. He had gone into hospital for an operation, and had developed complications. Although we knew it was serious, we were not prepared for the tragic news, and Evensong that day had more than a special poignancy. The last verse of Psalm 27, sung that evening, seemed to be a most appropriate summary of Eric's life: 'O tarry thou the Lord's leisure: be strong and he shall comfort thy heart, and put thou thy trust in the Lord.'

It is impossible to quantify Eric's contribution to the Cathedral in words. It was he who ordered and organised the Worship and ceremonial from the very beginning, as well as being the regular bass Cantoris 2 in every sung Service. His memory lives on with a carved inscription on the pillar adjacent to the stall that he occupied for nearly 11 years, as well as the choir-stall lighting

The Eric Ware memorial candles, 1972

(originally for candles with glass shades), designed and manufactured by Rowland Sidwell and his colleagues at the Delta Thermal Technology factory in Andover.

Eric and his wife Esmé had been looking forward to their retirement, and with that in view, had purchased a single-storey house in the coastal village of East Wittering, West Sussex. At the end of a quiet cul-de-sac, and less than five minutes from the beach, it was an ideal hideaway. In view of Eric's ongoing illness, Esmé decided that she would remain close to her children back in Surrey, and this gave us our first opportunity to become house

Our West Sussex hideaway

owners, buying the Wittering property and taking possession of it later that summer. Over the next few years it would be a lifeline for Buffie and the children, providing a welcome escape from the hustle and bustle of London.

I was especially sad that Eric would not be able to be at Addington Palace in June. George Guest and I were receiving a Fellowship from the Royal School of Church Music, and we were both to be invested at their Addington Palace headquarters on 30th June. It was a special and unexpected honour, mine having been awarded on the personal recommendation of Dr. Gerald Knight, the Director of the RSCM.

Also in June, the lay clerks gave a concert in the prestigious Bath Festival. The venue was the cloisters of 13th century Lacock Abbey, Wiltshire, and the programme was built around Gregorian chant and mediaeval polyphony. We were to process around the cloisters, stopping to sing at various points, with the audience sitting on chairs in the central grass reservation. At least that was the plan, until the rain started an hour or so before the concert. All the chairs were quickly moved into the cloister walks, and we had to squeeze

FRSCM – June 1973

by everyone, while singing in a long candlelit single-file procession. It was impossible to keep everything together, and the evening was quickly renamed 'La Cockup!'

In July it was time for another tour, and as some of the boys put it, we were going 'abroad' again. Jersey choir-conductor Arthur Lobb, and Mel Davidson, the Music Adviser to the Education Committee, had worked out a plan for the choir to spend most of a week on the island singing concerts and Services, including a live broadcast on BBC Radio 3. This time we even had our own plane. A chartered aircraft, complete with our own stewardesses, flew us from Gatwick to Jersey on Saturday 15th July.

The following afternoon, on St. Helier's Day (the island's Patron Saint), there was a Festal Evensong in the town-centre St. Helier's Church. On Monday afternoon and Tuesday morning we sang to several hundred schoolchildren at two schools' concerts, and on Tuesday evening gave another concert in the large and spacious Roman Catholic church of St. Thomas.

Our broadcast Evensong the following day remains unique in the annals of the programme. The BBC had sent a mobile studio on the ferry service from Weymouth, and it was parked outside St. Simon's Church when we arrived early on Wednesday afternoon for the balance-test and transmission. Missing were the senior sound engineer, the producer, and the vicar of the church. Fog at the airport meant that no planes could land or take off. The engineer and the producer were planning to fly in from Bristol, whilst the priest had been visiting the neighbouring isle of Guernsey and was stranded there.

Everything was ready; cables had been run into the church and the microphones had been tested. A message came through from BBC Bristol that we should abort the broadcast and they would play a standby recording instead. As the BBC's editor of the programme, I was able to override that suggestion, and decided that we would go ahead with what can best be described as a 'do-it-yourself' broadcast. Two of the lay clerks read the lessons and another took the prayers. I spent much of the time in the mobile studio creating the broadcast balance, whilst Roger Lowman, another of the lay clerks, directed the choir. I was able to get into the church to conduct the unaccompanied responses and anthem, and the broadcast went ahead as planned.

That same evening, the lay clerks sang a late-night concert of mediaeval music in St. John's Church, and on Friday morning the whole party assembled at the airport to catch our plane back to Gatwick. We were disappointed – the fog was still persisting, so everyone had to return to their hosts until we were able to get away on Saturday afternoon. It was not an easy journey for Buffie and young Tim (then just 14 months old), but we all made it back in time to be on duty in the Cathedral the next morning.

Three days later we were again broadcasting Choral Evensong – this time from the Cathedral, and it was another Service with a difference. Now without Eric Ware, we needed to find someone to officiate, and on that afternoon Prebendary W.D. Kennedy-Bell was not only the BBC's producer but also our precentor. It was probably the most ambitious broadcast repertoire we had ever attempted: the Michael Tippett setting of the canticles for St. John's College, Cambridge, and the recently written setting of *O be joyful in the Lord* by Grayston Ives as the anthem.

The very same evening, Buffie and I, together with her brother and a group of ten lay clerks really did go abroad, setting off for the Gordes region of France. The French record label Harmonia Mundi had asked us to sing two concerts of Gregorian chant in the Abbaye of Notre-Dame de Sénanque. Travelling overnight by boat-train, we arrived in Avignon, found a church with a suitable acoustic for our rehearsals, and stayed in nearby Forcalquier, where Simon Deller's father (Alfred) had a holiday home. Situated amongst lavender fields in a wonderful rural setting, the

Abbaye Notre-Dame de Sénanque

Abbey church was an inspiring building and acoustic in which to make music. Both concerts had capacity audiences, and on the second night they were so enthusiastic that choir and audience moved into the cloisters where we sang a few polyphonic items as encores.

More singers joined the back row of the choir in September, including alto Simon Hill, tenors John New and Julian Coward, and bass John Alley. Both Simon and John New would later move to London – Simon to St. Paul's Cathedral as a vicar choral, and John New to Westminster Abbey as a lay vicar. Already a freelance orchestral player, Julian Coward became second flute in the Royal Philharmonic Orchestra, whilst John Alley, a former chorister at Westminster Abbey, had a career as a highly acclaimed pianist, playing with most of the major London orchestras.

1973: An eventful May, and a happy November

May 1973 would turn out to be a month like no other – musically and personally. Early in the month, the boys of the Cathedral choir made their first excursion into the world of lighter music. At the Decca Record Company's West London studios, they recorded the backing for May Brahe's famous song, *Bless this house*, in a new version sung by Diana Coupland, the star of the television series of the same name.

On Saturday 19th May we welcomed the Friends of Cathedral Music – a day that set in motion a chain of events that would change my life for ever.[1]

Just two days later we sang the opening concert of the Guildford Festival. In a programme of music that spanned the Church's year, the organisers of the Festival had commissioned a new piece from Grayston Ives – a setting of *Let all the world in every corner sing*. It was a large-scale work, with adventurous vocal writing and a challenging organ part, and we spent many hours learning it. In a somewhat fraught rehearsal, one of the lay clerks complained that he couldn't understand what I was conducting. The immediate answer from one of his colleagues has since been oft-quoted: 'The beat is irrelevant.[2] Just watch his face and body-language.'

The concert, and Bill's piece in particular, went well, but there was no time to relax. We had to think about another recording – this time for Woolworths! Brian Culverhouse, producer of our EMI recordings, was also making recordings for the Contour label, on sale in all Woolworths' U.K. stores. Would we be prepared to sing items from Handel's *Messiah*? After checking with Anthony Froggatt, who would have to play all the accompaniments on the organ, I said yes, and on two evenings in June we recorded some of the best-known choruses, ending up with the *Hallelujah Chorus*, *Worthy is the Lamb*, and the *Amen Chorus*. Among the soloists engaged by EMI we were delighted to welcome back John Barrow (bass), and to work with tenor superstar of the future, Anthony Rolfe Johnson, making his very first commercial recording (on the sleeve he is simply described as Anthony Johnson).

Towards the end of July we were off again on tour, although not very far this time – a mere 30 miles! The two venues were in West Sussex – Boxgrove Priory and the Roman Catholic Cathedral of Our Lady and Saint Philip Howard in the town of Arundel. At Boxgrove we sang an evening concert, returning there a couple of days later to make some carol recordings for the publishing firm of Novello. In Arundel Cathedral we also sang an evening concert and broadcast the Office of Vespers the next afternoon. After a short break, the lay clerks recorded the Office of Compline for the BBC while the boys enjoyed an evening by the sea.

At the start of the autumn term William Kendall joined us as a tenor lay clerk, and a month later, the choir was doing more recording. This time it was back to the lighter side of music, at the invitation of former Kingsbury chorister, Andrew Pryce Jackman, musical director for Peter Skellern. Trained as a classical pianist at London's Guildhall School of Music, Peter had made a pop single called *You're a lady*. Reaching No. 3 in the charts, it set him on a solo career in a lighter musical style. The item which

---

1   See page 153.
2   The title of Simon Carpenter's 1996 book about the early history of Guildford Cathedral Choir.

we sang was a crossover, in the style of a ballad juxtaposed against the well-known hymn – *The day Thou gavest, Lord, is ended*. Entitled *Hymn Song*, it remained one of Peter's favourite recordings until his late Ordination in 2016 and death in February 2017.

In November, the boys travelled to London for a live broadcast of Benjamin Britten's *A Boy was born*. The venue was St. John's Smith Square concert hall, where they and the BBC Singers were conducted by John Poole.

Meanwhile, Buffie and I had received the happiest of news. Contacted by the Church of England Children's Society, they told us that we had been matched to a baby girl, born in mid-November, and would we like to become her parents? The answer was an enthusiastic yes. Tim would now have a sister, and in the second week of December we brought Julia Elizabeth Rose home to No. 5 Cathedral Close.

December 1973 – Tim, Buffie and baby Julia

With two children, our last Christmas in Guildford would now be even more special. Next year would be very different – in the centre of the City of London.

14

Guildford to St. Paul's
1973-1974

On Saturday 19th May 1973, the Friends of Cathedral Music visited Guildford. Founded in 1954 by the Reverend Ronald Sibthorp, a Minor Canon (junior clergy staff) at Truro Cathedral, the Friends had been instrumental in providing some initial financial support to Guildford's music back in 1961 when the Cathedral had been consecrated. Mainly brought about through the influence of John Gurney Smith, their Guildford diocesan representative, his frequent letters to the local paper, *The Surrey Advertiser*, exhorted readers to give money to support the Cathedral choir, whilst inviting them to join the Friends of Cathedral Music. We gathered that Dr. Gurney Smith was a consultant at The Royal Earlsfield, a mental hospital near Redhill. Unkempt in appearance, he would often appear at Evensong in a food-stained suit; either he was an extremely messy eater, or else some of his patients had been throwing food in his direction.

That day in May 1973 must have gladdened his heart. The choir that he and the Friends of Cathedral Music had helped to fund 11 years ago was now widely known in musical circles, and today the Friends were coming to Guildford for their Annual General Meeting and a celebratory lunch at the Civic Hall, after which they would attend Evensong. Together with some of the lay clerks, I was a guest at the lunch, also attended by some civic dignitaries, including the Mayor and Mayoress. There must have been around one hundred of the Friends present, including their Chairman, Christopher Dearnley, Organist of St. Paul's Cathedral, and after the usual speeches I managed to slip away to the Cathedral in time to take the boys' practice.

Evensong went well. We sang the psalms for the 19th Evening, a setting of the Magnificat and Nunc Dimittis by the contemporary composer and former Organist of St. John's College, Cambridge, Robin Orr, and as an anthem, the setting of the Jubilate written for us a year earlier by Grayston Ives, then a tenor lay clerk in the choir. At the end of the Service the choir sang a short recital from the chancel steps.

It had been a long day, and rather than make our customary visit to the pub, we went home. During the evening the phone rang. It was Christopher Dearnley saying thank you for such a successful day, and especially for the singing of the choir. He then said something rather strange, the meaning of which would later become all too clear: 'I bet you couldn't get psalm singing like that in St. Paul's.' I replied something to the effect of 'I don't see why not', and from there the conversation turned to my possible interest in a move to London. Dr. Harry Gabb, the long-serving Sub-Organist at St. Paul's, was due to retire in a few months' time, and that would be the position I would be filling. I said I'd need to think about it and discuss it with Buffie.

After getting over the initial shock, two attractions became clear. Firstly, the regular weekday morning commitment to the BBC Daily Service would be so much easier if we lived in London. Secondly, I had now run the Guildford choir for nearly 14 years, and in my heart I could sense that both they and I might now be ready for a new and different challenge. It would certainly be very different for me since I would be playing the organ a lot more than before; I had never accompanied many of the standard or larger works in the cathedral repertoire, having had a succession of highly capable assistant organists at Guildford to do just that.

The so-called audition process at St. Paul's was simply a formality to make it seem above-board to the other candidates (and especially to Christopher Herrick, then third organist at St. Paul's, who had shown interest in succeeding Dr. Gabb). Christopher Dearnley and I met in London a few times and we talked about the part I would play at St. Paul's. Even then, it seemed that there would be some role in training the boy choristers, a fact later confirmed by Martin Sullivan, Dean of the Cathedral, in his autobiography.

The deliberations of the Cathedral's governing body, the Dean and Chapter, though minuted, are kept secret so I was never to discover if it was true, or otherwise, that Christopher had been taken to task by them over the musical and vocal standards of the choir – both boys and men. In 1968 he had gone to St. Paul's from Salisbury Cathedral, where he had been Organist and Master of the Choristers, a move I think both he and his family were to regret. They had been very happy in Salisbury, but London and St. Paul's were extremely different, both from the point of view of family living, and also in terms of the way the Cathedral hierarchy behaved towards their employees. Christopher was not the first choice as Organist. The post had been offered to Allan Wicks, the charismatic Organist at Canterbury Cathedral, but he had turned it down. Allan had rung me that very day to say that he'd told the Dean and Chapter of St. Paul's to offer it to me, saying, 'They won't, because you are not sufficiently academically qualified,' adding, 'as if that matters.'

But now, five years later, here was an invitation to go to St. Paul's, albeit as Sub-Organist. At the same time, I was giving advice to the Dean and Canons at St. George's Chapel, Windsor, over the appointment of a new Director of Music. There might have been a possibility of going there, but I had already made the commitment to St. Paul's and advised them that the man they really needed was Christopher Robinson at Worcester Cathedral. They offered it to Christopher, and to my delight he accepted.

My so-called audition at St. Paul's in November 1973 consisted of taking the full choir for part of a Wednesday afternoon rehearsal in the crypt rehearsal room, and as arranged between Christopher and myself, accompanying the *Magnificat in G* by Charles Villiers Stanford, a piece I usually played in Evensong at Guildford. There was a certain irony in that Christopher Herrick is a far more capable organist than I, yet he was given the slower-moving Nunc Dimittis whilst I played the faster Magnificat. According to one of the vicars choral (the men of the choir), I endeared myself to them in the choir practice, though not to the boys, by threatening to confiscate one boy's watch if he looked at it once more during the rehearsal.

Three weeks later my appointment was confirmed in writing, though we had yet to sort out a final salary, and more importantly, suitable accommodation for Buffie, me and our growing family. The starting date at St. Paul's was to be September 1974, and I needed to tell the members of the Guildford Cathedral choir before they heard about it from some other source. At that time the Guildford choristers were preparing the boys' parts in Benjamin Britten's *A Boy was born* for a concert in Oxford, to be conducted by Robert Hammersley, formerly a lay clerk in the Guildford choir. I thought I'd wait until that concert was over and then send a letter home with the boys, also telling the men of the choir at the same time.

Those plans were scuppered when I contracted a nasty dose of flu, as did most of the choir. We had to cancel the visit to Oxford, and from my sick bed in Guildford, I wrote a letter to each of the parents and lay clerks telling them of the appointment to St. Paul's, asking them now to forget all about it, since it would be at least seven months before we left.

Despite all the recent illness and cancelled rehearsals, the choir excelled themselves, especially at the Christmas Day afternoon Service of Nine Lessons and Carols. The whole Service was recorded by my brother-in-law, Nicolas (Nick) Ware, and items from it were later used on CDs charting the growth of the Cathedral's music.

The following term my job was advertised, and short-listed candidates, chosen by Dean Tony Bridge and the new Precentor, Canon Bob Gibbin, came for audition and interview. By Easter, Philip Moore, then Assistant Organist of Canterbury Cathedral, had been offered the post and would take over in September.

My last Services in Guildford Cathedral were in July 1974, just over 14 years after I had been appointed. On Wednesday 24th we broadcast Choral Evensong. At the end of the Service the choir sang the *Te Deum in G* by Ralph Vaughan Williams, preceded by some appropriate and personal prayers led by the Dean. The following day, I directed the Cathedral choir for the very last time in an Evensong to which we had issued an open invitation to former lay clerks to come and join us. It was an emotional yet happy occasion, and several past members of the choir turned up to sing, heavily outnumbering the boys, who easily managed to hold their own both vocally and musically. The canticles were sung to the *Collegium Regale* setting by Herbert Howells, with Bill Ives singing the solo in the Nunc Dimittis most beautifully.

Adrian Culshaw conducting the choir in the farewell song, 25th July 1974

After the Service there were photographs on the steps of the Cathedral where the choir sang Arthur Sullivan's *The Long Day Closes*. The choir parents hosted a farewell party in the refectory, then a wooden hut opposite the site where the present refectory now stands. There were several speeches, together with the presentation of a cheque, a Wedgwood commemorative plate bearing an engraving of St. Paul's Cathedral, and an engraved silver platter to Buffie.

We returned to No. 5 Cathedral Close, exhausted but happy, though the following evening we were at yet another farewell: this time, a dinner hosted by lay clerks past and present, at the Clavadel Hotel in Aldersey Road, a few yards from Lanesborough School. Naturally, it was expected that I would make a speech, and rather than have the usual formal reminiscences and thanks (though they had to be one part of the evening), Rowland Sidwell, Nick, and I, came up with the idea of a sound montage which would take a less-than-serious look at several members of the choir, and life at Guildford Cathedral in general. The previous week, the three of us had spent nearly all night in the Cathedral, putting together a tape which included Rowland imitating the Dean, the Precentor, several lay clerks, the Dean's Verger, and especially the

Sub-Organist, Tony Froggatt, with his supposed thoughts while playing the choir into Evensong. Tony was absent-mindedly musing as to how the Service was to start – was it to be the responses by William Smith, William Byrd, Richard Ayleward, or plain-song? The alarming switches of key as he explored all options provoked howls of laughter from the assembled company. The recording became known as the Guildford Farewell Tape, and several of those who were parodied that evening were later given a copy – after I had safely left the area!

∼

On the last Sunday in July I went to St. Paul's for the Sung Eucharist, at which Franz Josef Haydn's *Nelson Mass* was being sung with orchestral accompaniment. Known as The July Masses, these had been innovated by Christopher Dearnley shortly after his arrival in 1968, and each year, during the Sundays in July, they attracted huge congregations. The performance that morning was somewhat lack-lustre, probably due to the fact that it was the last day of a long term for both the boys and men. Most unconvincing was the use of a small group of boy choristers to sing the col-oratura-style solo part for soprano. To put it bluntly, they were nowhere 'near it' in matters of vocal technique or musical understanding, and the result was more than slightly embarrassing. I resolved that if ever I was given the responsibility of conduct-ing that Mass at the Cathedral, I would use an accomplished soprano soloist.

A few weeks earlier, Buffie and I had been up to St. Paul's to look at the accommo-dation that had been promised us in Amen Court. To say that we were disappointed is a real understatement. The Cathedral clergy, known as the Dean and Chapter, consists of the Dean and four Canons, and they live in some elegant houses in a small private enclave, known as Amen Court, about 200 yards from the west front of the Cathedral. On one side are three spacious period houses. In No. 3 was Canon Douglas Webster, the Precentor, and his colleague/partner the Reverend Peter Lillingston. They occupied the whole of the house, apart from the basement which was let to Andrew Giles, an alto vicar choral. Canon John Collins lived in No. 2, whilst No. 1 was occupied by the Chancellor, Canon Harold Wilson. On the north side of the court is a row of later Victorian houses, one of which, No. 4, was already divided into two flats. No. 5 was the official Organist's residence, whilst the remainder were occupied by two minor canons, Samuel Cutt and Michael Moxon, with Sam Woodhouse, the Archdeacon of London, living at No. 8, the house adjacent to the east end entrance arch.

We had also been promised accommodation in the Court – the first time they had done this, since Harry Gabb, my predecessor, had held a part-time post at the Cathedral and lived a train journey away in Surrey. As Precentor, Douglas Webster was nominally in charge of the Cathedral's music and musicians, and had arranged for

us to see our accommodation. It turned
out to be an upstairs flat just inside the
archway into Amen Court, reached by
two long flights of stone stairs – totally
unsuitable for any family, and especially the two small children we would be
bringing with us. We made it very clear
that we could not accept that offer, and
were then told to go to No. 4, at the
far end of the Court adjacent to the old
Newgate prison wall, ring the upper of
two bells, and look around the upstairs
flat. That might be far more suited to
our needs.

*The entrance to No. 4 Amen Court with the
old Newgate Prison wall on the left*

To our surprise the door was opened
by one of the Minor Canons, who said
that he had only just been told why we
were there. Even more of a shock to his system was the fact that we might be moving
into his flat a few weeks later. The poor man, whose name was Peter Lynn, was under-
standably brusque, and from the way he emotionally described the contents of certain
rooms, we gathered that his marriage had recently broken up. Approached through
a large communal hall, the flat was up one flight of stairs. The living room was large,
light and airy, with a handsome plaster frieze just below ceiling height. The spacious
kitchen, complete with dining area, and the study were on the same level, as was a
toilet with the highest ceiling we have ever seen in such a room! Upstairs were two
bedrooms, a bathroom, a utility room, and an airless storeroom with a sloping ceiling,
and up yet another flight of stairs was what could serve as a third bedroom. With a
promise that we would be moved should anything more suitable become vacant, we
accepted the offer of living upstairs at No. 4.

There was now a problem over the timing of our move, since we were due to vacate No. 5 Cathedral Close, Guildford, for the arrival of my successor Philip Moore,
his wife and children. Our flat in Amen Court would not be ready until mid to late
September, by which time I would already have been working at the Cathedral for two
to three weeks. The Precentor agreed that St. Paul's would pay for our furniture to go
into storage for a month or so, and I would move into a nearby hotel at their expense,
whilst Buffie and the children would stay in Wittering.

15

From Sub-Organist to Master of the Choir
St. Paul's 1974–1977

At the beginning of September 1974 I moved to a hotel in London, leaving Buffie, Tim and Julia in Wittering.

My first Service at St. Pauls was Matins on Tuesday 3rd. There were 18 vicars choral (the men of the choir), and apart from Wednesday Evensong and three Sunday Services, they worked on a rota basis, so that 12 of them (or their deputies) appeared for each of the other Services. They sang at Evensong on Tuesday to Sunday, and at 10.00 a.m. Matins on Tuesday, Thursday, Saturday and Sunday, as well as at the 11.00 a.m. Sung Eucharist on Sunday. Rehearsals were minimal – five minutes or so before weekday Matins, and if they were all on time, about 20 minutes before weekday Evensongs. There was no rehearsal on Sunday morning, and the only way to sort out any musical points was to write a note for each side of the choir and leave them to pass it down the row during the sermon at Matins, which wasn't much help if we had needed to re-arrange anything before that point in the Service!

Ninety percent of the repertoire was new to me, which meant spending a lot of time at the Cathedral organ, usually after the building had closed for the day. Often I'd be there well into the small hours of the morning, with only Doug, the night watchman, for company as he made his regular patrols of the building. We got on very well, and he usually invited me for welcome cups of tea in his hut at the foot of the Chapter House steps.

The vicars choral vestry was in the crypt, and after putting on their vestments, they'd either appear in the rehearsal room (also part of the crypt) or in the Dean's aisle, ready to process into the Service. If I was playing the organ, the first time I would see them was when they reached the choir-stalls, and then it was only possible to get a clear view of the Decani (Dean's) side of the choir by opening the shutters, in the form of dummy organ pipes, in the north case of the organ where the console was then situated.[1] You could just see the Cantoris row (the side of the Cantor or Precentor)

---

1   In the 1977 rebuild, a new north choir division was installed in that space, and a new console was placed on the top of the stalls on the south side of the quire.

immediately below the console if you
leaned out of the opening, but that was
frowned upon, since it meant that a disembodied head was visible to members
of the congregation in the dome and the
quire.

The first thing that struck me was the
lack of camaraderie among the vicars
choral – some didn't even speak to each
other. Nigel Beavan started on the same
day as me, and we became close friends
throughout my ten years there, as in the
end did the rest of them.

The solos in the Services were pre-al-
located by a system called 'verse-weeks',
and since there were three altos, three
tenors and three basses on each side
of the choir, these were deputed on the

Nigel Beavan and Cyril Taylor (choir librarian)

weekly sheet by Cantoris (or Decani) I, II, or III – I being the longest serving member
of the choir in each part, II the next longest serving, and III the newest and most junior. It was not the best system, since certain voices don't suit certain pieces. Some of
the voices of the more senior members were well past their best, and though they may
still have been useful in choir, singing solos could sometimes be an embarrassment,
both to them and the listeners. Those who realised had the grace to pass their solos
on to their colleagues, but some persisted in trying to sing things that were now well
beyond their capabilities.

Just before the boys returned from their summer break, we were able to move into
the upper flat in No. 4 Amen Court and were back together as a family. The appropriately named Sue Dean, the Dean's secretary, lived downstairs with her companion
and successor, Marion Harris. Both were most gracious and welcoming to the new
occupants of the flat above, even though we would often be coming and going past
their sitting-room to gain access to our half of the house.

The first thing to become clear to any occupant on our side of Amen Court was
the 'them and us' factor. Compared with the informality of living and working at
Guildford Cathedral, this was a rude awakening. 'Them' – the Residentiary Canons
living in the grander 17th century houses – were afforded all the privileges imaginable,
a typical example being the provision of furnishings for the kitchens. As described to
us, the Canons would be supplied with unlimited 'white goods' – refrigerator, freezer,

dishwasher etc. – while 'us', the lesser mortals on the north side of the Court, would be entitled to just one.

That example was typical of how the Dean and Chapter looked upon their junior clergy and lay employees, communication often being by a note thrust through the letterbox, either with a command or the vague opening sentence, 'It has been agreed that...' We were not used to being treated like that, and it was something that would rankle and come to a head ten years later, reminding me of a conversation I'd had with Albert Dudley, one of the vergers, soon after I'd arrived, when he said, 'What's a nice fellow like you doing in a place like this?'

A week later, on a Saturday evening, I met the boy choristers. They had just re-turned to the choir school after the long summer break, and not only was there a new sub-organist, but also a new headmaster – a big change in their lives and routine. Derek Sutton had come from Salisbury Cathedral where he had been Assistant Headmaster of the Cathedral School, as well as a tenor lay clerk during Christopher Dearnley's time as Organist. The previous headmaster at St. Paul's, Canon John Llewellyn, had a reputation of having ruled the school with a rod of iron, and it soon became obvious that Derek's approach was to be more relaxed and more reliant on self-discipline, rather than an imposed harsh regime. To some of the boys this was unsettling. They were used to having every waking moment thoroughly organised, and it was not the easiest time for either Derek or me, getting to know, encourage and teach a group of 38 boys, some of whom were nearing adolescence, and not taking kindly to two new interlopers in their cloistered lives. I suppose it was inevitable that there would be problems, and some of the senior boys, unable to cope with the changes, left the choir and school during our first few months there.

The official duties of the Sub-Organist included taking the eight new probationer choristers for practices, as well as all the choristers once or twice a week, and directing them and the vicars choral in the sung Services on those days. I knew that Christopher wanted me to work with the boys a lot more than that, and he offered to play the organ on a much more regular basis so that I could direct the choir.

Although nothing official had been written about taking over the choir, the Dean and Chapter's intentions over my appointment were later revealed in Dean Martin Sullivan's 1975 autobiography, *Watch how you go*, where he writes about my ap-pointment as Sub-Organist: 'He will take over the training of the boys'.

Running a choir is like looking in a mirror, and what they do is an exact reflection of you – your approach, your personality, your body-language, the way you speak to them, and even your mannerisms. It had seemed to some that Christopher Dearnley was not happy or confident when working with the boys and needed help – hence his informal approach to me after attending that Evensong in Guildford Cathedral in

May 1973. Now, here at St. Paul's over a year later, I was faced with the long-term challenge of creating a new sound for the boys, together with a new enthusiasm for what they were singing – and all this to be built into their demanding daily routine of schoolwork, sports, instrumental practice, rehearsals and Services.

It was not going to be easy, and especially since much of the repertoire was new to me. There was no lack of efficiency in being able to sing the notes, and there were a *lot* of those to get through each week, but beyond that, there seemed to be little emotional or facial involvement in the singing, and certainly not much understanding of the meaning of the text, or any enjoyment of the music. It was going to be a steep mountain to climb, but we had to start somewhere. I began by asking for volunteers to sing single phrases in rehearsals, and then commending those who sang musically and with some obvious understanding of what they were singing, in the hope that others would copy what they were doing. That method was to pinpoint a few able and very competent would-be soloists. It seems somewhat invidious to mention names, but it was to be a very formative time in the choir's life, greatly helped by John Bowen (who went on to become a tenor choral scholar at King's College, Cambridge), Craig McLeish (later a versatile freelance singer and conductor) and Robert Eaton, who tragically lost his life on 11th September 2001 in the attacks on the World Trade Center in New York.

Continuation of my work for the BBC had been part of the understanding and acceptance in my appointment to St. Paul's, though in later years there were to be inevitable clashes when both the Cathedral and the BBC required my presence on the same day. Getting to the Daily Service at All Souls' Langham Place dovetailed nicely with the boys' morning rehearsals in the choir school. From there it was a short walk to St. Paul's tube station and the Central Line train to Oxford Circus – a much easier and shorter journey than I had previously faced to and from Guildford.

As editor of the weekly Wednesday afternoon Choral Evensong programme, part of my duties was to act as producer for the venues in the London area, as well as occasionally standing in for my BBC colleagues in the West, Midlands and North regions. This took me away from St. Paul's on those days – and Wednesday was the 'big' day for the Cathedral choir, since that was the afternoon when all 18 vicars choral were required to be present. Apart from all 18 forming the back row at Evensong, they also rehearsed for an hour and a half with the boys, not just working towards that day's music, but looking ahead to Sunday morning – a slightly pointless exercise, since many of the 18 regulars could well be away on a Sunday, sending in a deputy.

Despite a schedule of 12 choral Services each week, the Dean and Chapter only employed two musicians – Christopher and me. Neither of us had any secretarial help, each having to type his own letters, schedules and memoranda. Although we lived next door to each other in Amen Court, we did not often mix socially, though in the first year we had a regular weekly post-Evensong meeting to work out who would do what over the following seven days. It was at one of those early meetings that Christopher suggested that we might choose the music term and term about, and in the summer of 1975, I was given the opportunity to put my own stamp on the choir's repertoire, choosing the music from April to July.

Meanwhile, we had worked out a timetable whereby each of us could be free of Cathedral duties on two days each week – mine being Monday and Tuesday, and his, Thursday and Friday. This arrangement worked well since part of the Sub-Organist's duty was to give a short 40-minute organ recital every Friday in term time. The origins of this stemmed from the days when the full Cathedral choir sang The Litany at that time every Friday. When it was discontinued, Chapter decided that there should be some music instead – and as they say, the lot fell upon the Sub-Organist.

By the end of the first term I had virtually run out of repertoire, and I hit upon a solution which would save me having to learn lots of new pieces. I wrote to the Principals of the Royal College of Music, the Royal Academy of Music, and the Guildhall School of Music, asking if they had any organ students who would value the experience of playing a concert on the St. Paul's Cathedral organ. It was not long before I was able to fill all the Friday dates with visiting players. In theory that freed up Thursday evening and part of Friday, though it didn't work out like that. Someone (i.e. me) had to be at the Cathedral on Thursday evening to welcome the visiting recitalist, let him or her into the organ loft and arrange a time to let them out. Added to that, there needed to be someone (i.e. me) to introduce the recitalist on Friday lunchtime and entertain them for lunch or a drink after the recital. But at least I didn't have to do the playing.

Christopher was in charge of Monday Evensong, sung by the boys alone, and Tuesday with a choir of boys and 12 of the vicars choral (or their deputies). Until the 1950s, cathedral choirs were not conducted at Evensong – the Cathedral organist simply sat at the console and accompanied the Service, though this had changed when Michael Howard was appointed to Ely Cathedral in 1953, and Stanley Vann to Peterborough in the same year. Both Michael and Stanley were responsible for raising the standard of daily choral Worship in our cathedrals by directing their choirs at Evensong and having their assistant play the organ. In Michael's case, he was only at Ely for five years, but Stanley continued at Peterborough until 1977, setting the standards for most other cathedral choirs in the land.

If we were to raise the musical standards at the Cathedral, that was what we needed at St. Paul's. But – with just two musicians on the staff to cover the 12 choral Services each week – how?

1975: Settling in

The improvement in the choir's singing at Services in which both Christopher and I were involved was obvious, and I think that was the spur to Christopher thinking about how we might get some help with accompaniments on the days when we were on duty alone, or when one of us had to be away. As far as they were concerned, the Dean and Chapter had already improved the musical set-up at the Cathedral by appointing another resident musician for the first time, and there was no way they were going to be persuaded to employ a third one, even on a part-time basis.

There was no easy or immediate answer of any permanency, but in late October 1974, soon after the end of my first half-term, Christopher had made a temporary arrangement that would lay the foundations for the post of organ scholar, now an accepted part of the Cathedral's musical set-up.[2]

Stephen Barber was studying organ with Nicholas Danby at the nearby Guildhall School of Music. A gifted, self-effacing musician, Stephen had graduated from St. John's College, Cambridge, and had been awarded a bursary to the Guildhall by one of the City's ancient livery companies, The Merchant Taylors, who had recently acquired a splendid rebuilt Renatus Harris organ for their Great Hall in Threadneedle Street. Christopher approached Stephen about the opportunity to play occasionally at St. Paul's, and so began a relationship which lasted for the next two and a half years, with Stephen playing for some statutory Services and several special occasions.

In the meantime, I had contacted John Dexter, a former chorister at Guildford (1962-67) who, in September 1974, was just beginning his final year as organ scholar at Jesus College, Oxford. His father, then an executive at the Bank of England, had been a chorister at St. Paul's in the early 1920s, with such luminaries as the conductor Sir Charles Groves, and comedian Jimmy Edwards. Knowing that John was already an accomplished organist and would know my musical style, I rang Jesus College and left a message for him, asking if he would come and play at St. Paul's for one of the weekday Evensongs I was directing. It was the beginning of several similar visits, and gradually we hatched a plan whereby John might be able to help on a more permanent basis. He was due to leave Oxford in summer 1975, coming to London to take up a post-graduate place at the Royal College of Music. That could dovetail nicely with helping out at St. Paul's and playing on the days when neither Christopher or Stephen Barber were available.

---

2   In 2021, as I write, the musical staff consists of a Director of Music, a Cathedral Organist, a Sub-Organist, a fully funded Organ Scholar and an organ outreach Fellow – together with a PA to the Director of Music and a dedicated music office.

The Dexter family's previous connection with St. Paul's was to prove very useful, since John had an aunt who had known the current Precentor at the Cathedral, Canon Douglas Webster, whilst he was working as a missionary in India – and it was the Precentor who would need to know about and sanction any arrangement with John, even though the Cathedral would not be paying him anything. If he was going to live in Amen Court, a room would have to be found, and rent would have to be paid. (It was an open secret that some of the Canons of St. Paul's boosted their already comfortable income by letting out rooms in their large grace-and-favour houses on the south side of the Court.)

Canon Harold Wilson, the Cathedral Chancellor, was living at No. 1. Sharing his name with the current (and unpopular) Prime Minister, he was widely known as Harold Wilson, not Iscariot – an oblique reference to the 22nd verse of the 14th chapter of the Gospel according to St. John – *Judas, not Iscariot...* A blunt-speaking Yorkshireman, Harold had been the inspirational Principal of Salisbury Theological College, moving to St. Paul's as Canon Chancellor in 1973, though his tenure was cut short when he died on All Souls Day 1975. Always ready to speak his mind, both in and out of Chapter meetings, a typical example from Harold was after a rather second-rate performance of the choral version of Josef Haydn's *Seven Last Words from the Cross* on Good Friday 1975. Standing on the steps at the west front of the Cathedral, and surrounded by the outgoing congregation, he loudly exclaimed, 'It's a bloody good thing that Jesus didn't say more than bloody seven last words, otherwise we would've been in there all bloody night.'

As far as the Cathedral musicians were concerned, the advantage was that Harold was a bachelor and had spare rooms in the upper floors of his large house. One of these was occupied by Jonathan Alder, an alto vicar choral who had come to St. Paul's from Cambridge, where he had been singing with the choir of King's College. An accomplished pianist, Jonathan was already beginning to carve out a career as an accompanist and repetiteur, and having the top floor to himself, was none too pleased to learn that another musician (John Dexter) was to move into his 'kingdom'. In the end, the arrangements were finalised, and John became resident at No. 1 Amen Court for the next two years, not just accompanying the Cathedral Services, but also directing the choir on many occasions. He and Jonathan formed a close friendship, which was mutually beneficial to both, since John was able to gain experience by playing for several rehearsals that Jonathan could not manage.

Even with an extra pair of musical hands, there were still times when Christopher was not on duty and I had a BBC commitment that would leave just John in charge of Evensong. We had now got used to having two people on duty at most Services, and although John and Stephen Barber did not actually work together at St. Paul's, it was a happy coincidence that three years later, Stephen became John's assistant organist after John had been appointed as Organist and Master of the Choristers at St. Patrick's Cathedral, Dublin; Stephen's audition taking place in the crypt of St. Paul's. Future organ scholars would include Mark Blatchly (later organ scholar at Christ Church, Oxford, Assistant Organist of Gloucester Cathedral, and Organist and Master of the Choristers at St. Edmundsbury Cathedral); Ian Richards; Simon Lole (a former St. Paul's chorister who went on to become Organist of Sheffield and Salisbury Cathedrals); Ian Sadler (also a former chorister); Rosemary Field; and Roger Sayer, who became Organist and Choirmaster at Rochester Cathedral and at London's Temple Church.

Just two years after I arrived, the choir made its first recording for Guild Records – *Music for a Great Cathedral* – featuring composers who had been associated with St. Paul's across the centuries. It may seem strange that such a prestigious venue and its choir would feature on what was then the country's smallest and least-known record label, but no major record company had shown any interest in the St. Paul's choir for the past few years. Nick Ware and I were still running Guild Records as a part-time hobby, and up until then, had persuaded everyone who had recorded for us – choirs, organists, and soloists – to do it for no other reward than having a recording of themselves available on the open market. At St. Paul's it was going to be different, and expensive. We would have to face up to paying professional session-fees to 18 men out of our own pockets. We didn't make any such formal arrangement to use the Cathedral with either the Registrar or the Dean and Chapter, thus avoiding paying any facilities fee. Christopher Dearnley and producer John Dexter graciously agreed to take part without any payment. The boys also would not be paid, but the majority would have their first and valuable experience of taking part in recording sessions in the Cathedral – something they would get used to over the next few years. For three evenings in May 1976, we borrowed the Cathedral, giving monetary backhanders to Bill Box, the resident electrician, and Bob Harvey, the Clerk of Works. Without them we would not have had any lighting or quiet in the building after it had been closed for the night.

In the following weeks, Nick edited the tapes, Martin Palmer designed the sleeve, and EMI were persuaded to replicate the discs for us. *Music for a Great Cathedral* was ready for sale. The critics were quite kind. Stanley Webb in *Gramophone* wrote:

Barry Rose has a touch of magic as a choir trainer, and he and Christopher Dearnley have formed a fruitful partnership since he moved up from Guildford Cathedral. The component parts of the choir blend well, and there are two excellent groups of solo singers.

By now, up to 16 of the probationers that I had trained had become full choristers, and a more musical sound and understanding of the text was beginning to emerge. Although it was not yet the sound I was seeking, I now felt more comfortable with a choir that was beginning to become my own, both in terms of commitment and delivery. More and more, Christopher began handing over the choral duties and responsibilities, including the musical direction of the Festival of the Sons of the Clergy – a prestigious event held in May of each year, in which two other cathedral choirs were invited to take part.

It was also around this time that the major rebuilding of the organ commenced. Noel Mander and I had formed a friendship during my time at Guildford, when he had financed a Guild Records 7-inch EP on which I played one of his Hoxne model organs, then installed in the generous acoustics of Farnborough Abbey. We had later followed that up with a second promotional EP, made at his factory in Bethnal Green, on which he spoke about, and I demonstrated, some of the smaller organs he had built, as well as a few historic instruments from his own personal collection. Now, at St. Paul's, the major work would include a new north choir division, to be installed in the area occupied by the present console; a new west end division including Royal Trumpets *en chamade*; and a new detached console, to be placed on top of the stalls on the south side of the quire. All the planning and detailed arrangements had been made by Christopher, who was keenly aware that the deadline for finishing the work had to be early 1977, since the Queen's Silver Jubilee Service was scheduled to take place in June.

Noel Mander had agreed that different divisions of the organ would remain useable during the rebuild, though as a precaution, the Cathedral's Willis-on-wheels organ was put in place just below the chancel railings on the north side, where it would remain for several months for use if and when needed.

Maurice Bevan, then Senior Vicar Choral, asked if I would accompany him in the *Six Bible Songs* by Charles Villiers Stanford, and could I persuade Nick Ware to record them for him as a personal keepsake? Maurice had joined the Cathedral choir as a baritone back in 1948. Now in his 60s, he was still a most elegant and musical singer. A man of few words, he had defined the choir's motto that I later adopted when, after a tenor deputy at Evensong had sung the Gibbons *Short Service* Magnificat as though it was an aria from a Verdi opera, Maurice leaned over during the Second Lesson and whispered, 'You know, it's not enough to make a noise.'[3]

We recorded the songs over three evenings during October 1976, though it was by no means easy for me, since only the Great, Solo, Pedal and Dome divisions of

---

3   Later translated into Latin: *Strepitum facere non sufficit.*

the organ were operative – there was no Swell or Choir. Over the next few weeks, Nick and I did the editing, and gave Maurice a cassette of the finished product. His response was very enthusiastic, and it was then that he suggested that perhaps Guild Records might like to issue it as an LP, since it would be the very first complete commercial recording of all six songs. We said that we'd be very happy to do so, but we would also need to include the six short hymn-like anthems that follow each of the songs, which would mean another recording session as soon as possible. Scored for SATB choir and organ, each of the short anthems is based around a well-known hymn tune or chorale, to which Stanford added his own accompaniments, usually quoting from the preceding song. If we were to record these, we couldn't do it officially since it would involve the expense of more recording fees for the men. Maurice suggested that we get a group of friends together to sing the alto, tenor, and bass parts, and I said that I would ask Derek Sutton, the headmaster of the choir school, if I could 'borrow' a small group of choristers for that evening. John Dexter agreed to play the accompaniments and I would direct the choir, which we would call The Barry Rose Singers.

Everything was arranged, and I set to work teaching the six anthems to a small group of Senior and Intermediate choristers (known as First and Second desks). On the day of the recording, I received a phone-call from the headmaster to say that the Sacrist had decided that he wanted most of that group for an extra Confirmation class that evening, and could I manage with a group of junior boys plus two or three of the seniors who had already been confirmed? There was no option but to go ahead, and with a most able back row of musical friends, mainly from the Guildford choir, but also including Maurice and Nigel Beavan, we managed to get all six songs recorded. It was not the boys' sound that I had envisaged or wanted, and our next challenge was to edit the songs as seamlessly as we could into Maurice's master tape. That done, the record was released on the Guild label in March 1977 to favourable reviews. The *Gramophone* critic welcomed it with a summing-up that '*soloist, choir and accompanists have achieved total accord and given an admirable performance.*'

1977 – Royalty, recording, and role-change

St. Paul's has long been the venue for Jubilee celebrations of the monarch's accession to the throne, and 1977 would see one of those occasions – the Silver Jubilee of Queen Elizabeth II. Planning for the Service on 7th June had been underway for several months, and with special festive music in mind, we took the opportunity to make another LP on the Guild label, calling it *Royal Music from St. Paul's*. The recording sessions took place on three evenings in February 1977 with John Dexter, then organ scholar, as producer. By tradition, Jubilee Services always include a setting of the

Te Deum, and both Christopher and I opted for Benjamin Britten's setting in C major – a choice later vetoed by Buckingham Palace. Added to that we recorded choral music from the 1953 Coronation Service, together with other items with royal connections. As well as the choir and the now newly rebuilt organ, we also arranged for the trumpeters of the Royal Military School of Music to join us in one of the sessions, where they were conducted by Lieutenant Colonel Trevor Sharpe OBE (with whom I had worked at the Consecration of Guildford Cathedral). They recorded fanfares and accompanied the choir in Parry's *I was glad*; the Vaughan Williams Coronation setting of *All people that on earth do dwell*; *Praise, my soul, the King of Heaven,* as arranged by Trevor for the Guildford Consecration; and Gordon Jacob's arrangement of *The National Anthem.*

The challenge of placing the singers and brass fell to Nick Ware who was making the recording, and in the end the choir stood on the steps around the quire railings, facing west, whilst the brass were placed half-way down the great space under the

dome, facing east – each with their own conductor. In that reverberant acoustic, audibility in loud music was always going to be a challenge, and it was all the more difficult for the organist at the new console, quite a distance away from the rest of the musicians. Christopher and I shared the playing and directing the choir, and the LP was issued well before June in a handsome double sleeve, bearing the official Silver Jubilee crest on the cover.

Another LP was to follow soon after. In July 1977 Nick and I were back in the Cathedral with Christopher, making the very first recording of the newly rebuilt organ. Featuring works by Walter Alcock, César Franck, Niels Gade, Carl Nielsen, and Jean Sibelius, it was issued later in the year and was well received by the critics – *Hi-Fi News* of December 1977 hailing it as '*a well-produced and important disc. The result must rank as the best recording made in this difficult building to date.*'

On this occasion we were able to pay Christopher a token fee and an ongoing royalty, though Nick and I were still well out-of-pocket from the Royal Music recording. Luckily, sales of the records on the Cathedral bookstall at the back of the nave were very brisk, and by the end of the year we had virtually recovered our outlay. For some

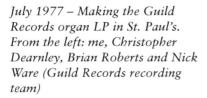

July 1977 – Making the Guild Records organ LP in St. Paul's. From the left: me, Christopher Dearnley, Brian Roberts and Nick Ware (Guild Records recording team)

reason, the Chapter of St. Paul's got the idea that Guild Records was making money at their expense, so we resolved that on a future occasion when we recorded the choir, we would ask them to invest in the costs with a possible return of capital and, hopefully, a later profit once the disc had been issued.

In all these projects, Christopher and I needed to work closely together, though there were now some growing differences between us. Perhaps it was understandable that the news of my move to St. Pauls as Sub-Organist had been greeted with some incredulity. What might have been foremost in some peoples' thinking was how the relationship between two people, both of whom had held the No. 1 post at different cathedrals, might work out in practice when they were together in the same building. In our first informal conversations about the possibility of my coming to St. Paul's, Christopher kept alluding to the word 'loyalty', which made me think that his previous organists, or maybe some of the vicars choral, had not been too complimentary about his work with the choir. Certainly, the vicars choral I knew, who sometimes sang as ad-hoc members of the BBC Singers, were somewhat scathing about the vocal standard of the boys and were not afraid to say so. That may have been why they had helped persuade Christopher, or the Chapter, that I should be appointed.

It would also be true to say that Christopher and I had differing personalities and that our approach to music and its performance was different – his being the more soundly academic, and mine too often based on musical instinct rather than acquired knowledge. There was nothing wrong in that, though it could, and did, lead to differences of opinion about interpretation, not least over tempi and phrasing. If there was a crack appearing in our relationship, it had appeared quite early, less than two years after my appointment.

The last Friday in April 1976 happened to fall on the 30th day of the month – for which the psalms appointed are the last four of the 150, all in celebratory mode. The on-going custom at St. Paul's, and in some other cathedrals, was to have Evensong totally unaccompanied each Friday, choir and clergy processing in and out in complete silence. (I'm told that at one Friday Evensong a member of the congregation turned to the person next to him loudly remarking 'Oh, I see that the organist hasn't turned up today.') As the duty musician that day, I decided otherwise, and played the organ at the start of the Service, accompanied the psalms, and played a celebratory final voluntary. Christopher heard about this, and immediately sent me a note reminding me that the Service should have been without the organ, to which I replied in detail that I was 'in charge' that day, and as such, expected to make my own decisions. I did add:

> I hope we can agree to leave the other to make his own decisions regarding the Services he directs, and if I am to continue to take full responsibility for Thursday, Friday, and Saturday, I also expect to decide how the music is sung. However, if you want to take these decisions yourself, then I shall quite understand, and suggest that you take back the responsibility for each day by being there to direct the music yourself, and I will make myself available to accompany, as required. I see no compromise here – as I am sure you probably don't – and look forward to hearing your decision.

Although this might seem too forthright, it was necessary to re-establish at this early stage that ours was, as Christopher had wanted, an equal partnership, rather than the usual organist and assistant arrangement.

There was no response to what I had written, so we carried on, Christopher taking responsibility for Monday and Tuesday, me for Thursday and Friday, and both of us switching between directing or playing on Wednesday, Saturday and Sunday. That arrangement continued until 1977 when the Organist's official residence, No. 5 Amen Court, was to play a crucial part in the official re-designation of the musical responsibilities between the two of us. This was the year in which Dean Martin Sullivan was due to retire. He would officiate at the Queen's Silver Jubilee Service on 7th June, and step down at the end of December, vacating the Deanery a few weeks later. A thorough examination of the Grade 1 listed building, in Deans Court on the other side of Ludgate Hill, had revealed that a great deal of remedial and restoration work would be needed before the new Dean could occupy it.

For whatever reason, the Dean and Chapter decided that they could not possibly justify the considerable expense, and, through their lawyers, arranged to lease it to an American Bank on condition that they carried out the necessary work. That meant there was nowhere for the new Dean to live. Alan Webster, the new Dean, would be moving from the Deanery at Norwich Cathedral and would expect comparable accommodation here at St. Paul's. All the houses in Amen Court were occupied – the Canons on one side, and the Minor Canons and Organists on the other. It seemed an impossible problem for the Dean and Chapter to solve.

But Christopher had a trump-card. He and his wife Bridget had recently acquired a handsome seafront house in the Essex town of Dovercourt, some 80 miles from London, and wanted to move their family there. This might have been the decisive factor in Christopher suggesting to me that the time had come for me to take over as Director of Music, and to the Chapter, (either before, or at the same time) that should they agree to his plan, he would vacate No. 5 Amen Court in time for the new Dean's arrival, and instead, occupy a *pied-a-terre* in 8b, the smaller upstairs flat at the opposite end of Amen Court that we had been sent to view a few years earlier.

In effect, what Christopher was suggesting was a ratification of what was already happening. At his request, I had gradually taken on more responsibility for rehearsing and directing the choristers, as well as training the eight probationers. In June 1977 he drew up a formal document which set out two distinct posts – he to continue as Organist, and me as the new Director of Music – laying out the responsibilities for each of us in considerable detail. It was duly presented to the Chapter, and to this day I am not sure if Christopher was invited to attend their meetings – I certainly wasn't.

It might have been because of the Statutes (which specified that *there shall be a Cathedral Organist* – and nothing else in musical terms) that the suggested post of Director of Music was rejected, or it might have been for other reasons. Instead, the Chapter created the post of Master of the Choir, with the added information that I would be free to continue with my work at the BBC (which was already accepted by them when we moved to St. Paul's), and that the new appointment, starting at the beginning of December, would be ratified by Dean Sullivan. At the Queen's Silver Jubilee Service, we pre-empted that new arrangement by sharing the musical direction, Christopher conducting the choir for the first half with me accompanying, and vice-versa for the second half.

Although not ready in time for the February LP recording of Royal Music, each of us had been asked to compose special music to be included in the Service, and, as it turned out, each of us would conduct the other's composition. Christopher wrote a reflective four-part unaccompanied setting of a text used in the Coronation – *Let thy hand be strengthened* – to be sung after the Blessing. My contribution was a new setting of Psalm 121, and although I didn't realise it at the time, it would be subject to scrutiny by someone at Buckingham Palace. I'd completely forgotten about the deadline for submitting it, and a phone call from the Lord Chamberlain's office came as a shock since I'd not even thought about what to write. In a fit of panic, I asked Buffie to take Tim and Julia out so that I could have a couple of hours peace and quiet, by which time the setting was complete and the finished manuscript was ready.

Since I was to play the first half of the Service, that would include Her Majesty's procession from the west door to the front of the dome, at which point we would sing the Vaughan Williams arrangement of *All people that on earth do dwell*. Improvisation was never my strong point, and certainly not on a great state occasion such as this. I searched the organ repertoire but couldn't find anything suitable, so I rang Bill Ives to see if he could help. I explained that we'd need a grand Elgarian-style piece, beginning in E flat (the key in which the State Trumpets would play the opening fanfare) and ending on the dominant chord of G major, so that we could go straight into the Vaughan Williams setting. A couple of weeks later, his manuscript arrived, headed *Jubilee Piece*, and after some initial preparation I was able to persuade Buffie to come and process up and down in the Cathedral so that I could work out timings, and assess whether or not I'd need to include any repeats at the actual Service. Now completed in its original key and named *Intrada*, it has been published and is often played at great occasions and in concerts and recitals.

Every organist has nightmare moments, and I could well have had a traumatic one in the Jubilee Service. I was playing the organ part in Hubert Parry's *I was glad,* and for this special occasion we included the *Vivat Regina* section, usually reserved for the Coronation. That required chords on the full organ, followed by the quiet and reflective *O pray for the peace of Jerusalem.* At that point I put my hand on to the fourth manual of the organ to play a quiet solo on the clarinet stop only to see Alan Parish, who was turning pages, push in a stop-knob a millisecond before I started. I'd inadvertently left the Tuba stop on!

Just before Dean Martin Sullivan retired in December 1977, the details of our new posts were published in the *Church Times*:

MUSICAL CHANGES AT ST. PAUL'S

THE extension of musical activities at St. Paul's Cathedral has necessitated a division of responsibilities between the organist and the sub-organist.

Mr. Christopher Dearnley will continue as Organist, while the Sub-Organist, Mr. Barry Rose, will take up the new post of Master of the Choir. The direction of the Cathedral music will be in their joint charge.

I was now responsible for all decisions concerning the men and boys, and Christopher, as Organist, was responsible for everything connected with the organ, including the provision of organ scholars, all organ concerts and, hopefully, securing a more permanent arrangement of help by a third musician. Although outwardly a promotion for me, the lack of the title of Director of Music was to cause major problems in the next seven years, culminating in a decision by the Dean and Chapter to reverse our initial agreement.

As the new Master of the Choir, one of the first decisions I made was about the July Masses. I had never been happy with the boys attempting to sing the florid coloratura soprano solos in Haydn's *Nelson Mass* – always sung on the last Sunday of the choir year – so for the first time, in July 1977, I invited a soprano soloist to take part. Julie Kennard was then a member of the BBC Singers and she and I had formed a close relationship through some concerts we'd done together, as well as a recording of the Schumann song-cycle *Frauenliebe und Leben* in nearby St. Martin's, Ludgate Hill. She sang the Haydn quite beautifully, and the change from not using the boys was especially appreciated by the vicars choral. They seemed genuinely pleased about my new appointment, though Owen Grundy, one of the basses, did take me aside saying, 'If I were you, I wouldn't be in too much of a hurry to make changes – give it six months or so.' Owen was the long-serving bass on Cantoris, and it took me a while to discover why, in verse 20 of Psalm 136, all the men on Decani would formally bow to Cantoris when it was being sung in Evensong. They later explained that instead of *Og the king of Basan,* he was known to them as *OG* (Owen Grundy) *the king of Bass Can.*

With the rebuild of the organ now completed, Christopher arranged a series of evening recitals starting in October 1977. He suggested that the home team should play the first one, and John Dexter, then in Dublin, returned to take part, playing the opening on the west end trumpets, featuring a fanfare specially composed for the occasion by James Ellis. I followed on, highlighting the new north choir division with a four-movement Maurice Greene voluntary, Herbert Howells' *Master Tallis's Testament*, and *Introduction, Passacaglia and Fugue* by Brian Brockless, Organist at nearby St. Bartholomew's Church, Smithfield. Christopher played the second half of the evening, featuring some of the works he had recently recorded for the new Guild Records LP, and we were able to sell copies at the end of the recital.

16

New Duties – New Decisions
St. Paul's 1978-1979

At the beginning of 1978 the Dearnley family left Amen Court to make their permanent residence in Dovercourt, giving the Chapter time to prepare the temporary Deanery at No. 5 for Dean-elect, Alan Webster. Christopher and I had already reversed our timetables, enabling me to direct the weekly boys-only Evensong on Monday. He would usually leave London after, or sometimes during, Sunday Evensong, returning in time to play for the full rehearsal and Evensong on Wednesday afternoon. I was now released from all Thursday duties (men's voices) and the Friday lunchtime recital arrangements, as well as Evensong on that day. Saturday would remain a joint duty day, as would Sunday.

In addition to the statutory and special Services, there were regular requests for the boys to take part in recordings, broadcasts and television appearances. Some of these had gone through the official process of discussion and approval by the Chapter, but others needed a decision on the spur of the moment and there simply wasn't the time to go through the usual protocols. Soon after I'd arrived we'd been asked to do the backing for a cover version of the Beach Boys' famous song *God only knows*. Organised and musically arranged by Andrew Pryce Jackman, an ex-chorister of mine from St. Andrew's Church, Kingsbury, this (in mid-1975) would be the first of many trips the boys would make to a recording studio, usually on a Saturday evening in their free time. Later recordings would see them working with Rick Wakeman (the album *White Rock*); Elton John (the album *Jump Up*); Paul McCartney (the film *Rupert and the Frog Song*); and a Christmas single, *Run with the Fox*, with Chris Squire and Alan White. There were also radio appearances with Monty Modlyn on LBC Radio, and Bishop Bill Westwood on BBC Radio 2 on Christmas Day morning 1983, as well as television appearances with Roy Castle, Val Doonican, Perry Como, and a host of celebrities in an award-winning BBC *Arena* programme about the song *My Way*.

Several soloists also featured in recordings, television, radio and film, including Paul Phoenix (Geoffrey Burgon's *Nunc Dimittis* for the *Tinker, Tailor, Soldier, Spy* BBC television series, and the ITV television advert *This is the Age of the Train*); Peter Auty (the original recording of *We're walking in the air* from *The Snowman*, a cover version of *Walking on the Moon* by The Police, and also *This is the Age of the Train*); Mark Higgins (an upbeat version of *O for the wings of a dove*); Charles Mindenhall (the film *The Dresser* and the David Essex LP *Mutiny*); Matthew Vine (*Camille the seal* from the *Captain Beaky* album and *Silent Night* with Val Doonican on BBC television); Jeremy Vine (the BBC Radio 4 series *The Lord of the Rings*); and Benjamin Revill (the closing music to the final episode of the *Blackadder II* series on BBC television, a 1983 BBC Radio 4 play *Solo Boy,* and also *This is the Age of the Train*).

On the more 'serious' side, the boys provided the ripieno choir for the new recording of Bach's *St. Matthew Passion* with the Bach Choir and Sir David Willcocks; Vaughan Williams' opera *Hugh the Drover*, conducted by former St. Paul's chorister, Sir Charles Groves; incidental music by Stephen Oliver (another former St. Paul's chorister) for the Royal Shakespeare Company's production of *Nicholas Nickleby*; and live broadcasts with the BBC Singers and John Poole of Kurt Weill's *Recordare* and Benjamin Britten's *A Boy was born.*

These were just a few of the outside engagements involving the boys, but both they and I knew that we were at St. Paul's for the one overriding priority – singing the Cathedral Services well – and anything else had to slot in around that commitment. None of these outside activities would have been possible without the co-operation of Derek Sutton, the headmaster.

Derek and I worked closely together, and he was already used to the boys going to other places to sing; for several years, Christopher had been taking a group to the BBC once a week during term-time, where they were the resident choir in the BBC Schools programme, *Singing Together*. As far as I was concerned, taking 16 or more boys out of school on a Saturday evening could well have been a convenience for the headmaster and the other residential staff – fewer boys to supervise in their leisure time – though ultimately the headmaster was responsible for their well-being and safety.

At a recording studio in a busy and sometimes sleazy part of London, the boys would be handed a manuscript copy of their part. In the space of an hour or so, they'd sing through it a couple of times and then record it, often wearing headphones while singing to a backing-track. A typical example was the backing for Harry Nilsson's

Derek Sutton, with Buffie and me, at a Choir School reception

Harry Nilsson with St. Paul's Cathedral choristers at the May 1977 recording session for his song All I think about is you

single *All I think about is you*, with accompaniment by string players from the major London orchestras.

After the sessions we'd visit the nearest fish and chip shop, followed by a race to the nearest tube station and back to St. Paul's on the Central Line. By then it was getting late, so chips were eaten on the train and the wrappings hurriedly disposed of before the boys arrived back at the choir school to find matron busy pacing up and down, looking at her watch and muttering about how this was too late when they had a big day coming up on Sunday.

A new organ scholar had also arrived at the start of September 1977. Former Guildford chorister, Mark Blatchly, joined us straight from Charterhouse School, moving into the basement of No. 1 Amen Court, now occupied by Canon Douglas Webster and the Reverend Peter Lillingston. Although he was not receiving anything from the Cathedral, Mark had to pay £10 a week for his room, and was regularly threatened with eviction for being so untidy!

It wasn't long before Mark was accompanying the Cathedral choir on a regular basis – good practice for something he'd have to do daily the following term; Christopher was taking a three-month sabbatical and that meant that all 12 weekly choral Services had to be covered by 17-year-old Mark and myself. It was an exhausting challenge for both of us, not least since it would involve the whole of Holy Week and Easter, including the annual performance of the Bach *St. John Passion*, as well as another LP recording for Guild Records. Mark coped brilliantly, receiving a signed photograph from the vicars choral in appreciation.

The main work in the recording was the *Mass in G* by Franz Schubert, accompanied by the London Bach Orchestra. This time we moved the recording position away from the dome, placing the choir and orchestra up in front of the high altar where we could get a more intimate and focused sound.

There was space on the record for other pieces. We moved the choir back to the dome area and Mark accompanied Charles Villiers Stanford's *Te Deum in B flat*. A week or so later, Christopher came back for one evening to accompany the large-scale *Hear my Words, ye people* by Hubert Parry. We were also able to include the two

pieces that Christopher and I had specially written for last year's Silver Jubilee Service – his setting of *Let Thy hand be strengthened* and my through-composed version of Psalm 121. The record was issued in a handsome double sleeve, and a real coup for us was the cover illustration – Canaletto's 1740 painting of the River Thames and city from the terrace of Somerset House (with St. Paul's on the skyline). Owned by Lord Vestey, who had an office in nearby Smithfield where it was then hanging, he gave us permission to take and use our own photograph, the only condition being an acknowledgement of ownership on the reverse side of the sleeve.

It was also in early 1978 that I had received a phone call in my BBC office from one of my colleagues, Peter Armstrong. Another of John Lang's appointments, Peter had joined the Religious Broadcasting Department at the same time as me in 1971. Initially working in radio, he had moved on to television and was instrumental in creating the Sunday night series *Everyman*. 'I've got an idea for a documentary about St. Paul's Cathedral Choir,' he said. 'Can we meet and discuss?' As we talked, it became clear that this was going to be a major project to be filmed across several months, showing the lives of St. Paul's choristers, both in the Cathedral, as well as in school at work and play. With the title *Paul's Children*, it was scheduled for a prime transmission spot on BBC 1 on the Sunday evening before Christmas. Naturally, this would need the Chapter's permission since film crews would be in and out of the Cathedral and school for several months. They agreed, and filming began in June around the time of the Friends of St. Paul's Festival, at which the choristers were featured singing for Her Majesty Queen Elizabeth The Queen Mother, the Friends' Patron, in Stationers Hall. Further filming took place at Sports Day in July, at the voice trial in October, and during November when the boys recorded Christmas carols in the Cathedral. There were also sessions at classes in school, and even in the dining hall and dormitories.

May 1978 also saw the biggest cathedral choir ever, singing for the 300th Anniversary of the granting of the Royal Charter to the Corporation of the Sons of the Clergy. The Festival takes place in St. Paul's each year, and a recent innovation had been the inclusion of two visiting cathedral choirs. This year was to make history. Every U.K. cathedral and collegiate foundation had been invited to send three trebles, one alto, one tenor, and one bass to take part. Aside from being a logistical nightmare over accommodation (mercifully handled by the Corporation of the Sons of the Clergy), we needed to organise space and seating for up to 175 trebles and around 120 men, all turning up on the day in time for just the one afternoon rehearsal.

A choir of this size and expertise needs something special by way of accompaniment. I contacted Sir David Willcocks, now Director of the Royal College of Music, and he agreed that their orchestra could take part, accompanying the *Magnificat and Nunc Dimittis in A* by Charles Villiers Stanford (originally composed for the Festival in 1880), Herbert Howells' own orchestration of his *Collegium Regale Te Deum*, and Hubert Parry's *Hear my words, ye people*. Orchestral parts were readily available for the Stanford and the Howells, but no-one seemed to know if there were any for the Parry and where they might be. I contacted Richard Barnes, who had been singing in the Guildford choir, to see if he would orchestrate it for the occasion. He agreed, and a week or so before the Festival, a neatly hand-written full score and orchestral parts were delivered, just in time for the one rehearsal I was able to have with the orchestra at the Royal College. I asked Sir David if he would conduct the Howells *Te Deum*, so all I needed to rehearse was the Stanford and the Parry. Both idioms were unknown to most of the orchestra. It was hard work, but on the day they provided that extra dimension to the sound, and it (mostly) held together.

To celebrate the 300th Anniversary of the granting of its Royal Charter
The Sons of the Clergy—the oldest Clergy Charity—Invite you to an

HISTORIC CHORAL SERVICE

at
St. Paul's Cathedral

on
Tuesday 16th May, at 5.30 p.m.

Music to include *Stanford's Evening Service in A*
Parry's Anthem "Hear my words ye People"
Herbert Howells' Te Deum "Collegium Regale"

will be sung by a massed choir drawn from Cathedrals and University Colleges throughout the United Kingdom and the Chapel Royal, Hampton Court Palace

Director of Music **Barry Rose**, Master of the Choir St. Paul's Cathedral

The Symphony Orchestra of the Royal College of Music, Director Sir David Willcocks and the Trumpeters of the Royal Military School of Music will take part

H.R.H. Princess Alexandra will be present

The Archbishop of Canterbury and the Lord Mayor of London
will by custom attend the Service in State

PREACHER: *THE BISHOP OF LONDON*

Admission by ticket only, available from
The Corporation of the Sons of the Clergy, 1 Dean Trench St., Westminster London, SW1P 3HB
Telephone   01-799 3696 & 01-222 5887

There was one memorable practical matter to solve just before the Service began. I was sitting quietly in the Dean's vestry, contemplating the task ahead, when there was a knock at the door. Two St. Paul's choristers were standing there, and I assumed they were going to tell me that it was time to process. Not so. 'They've run out of paper in the boys' toilets,' they said, and this just 20 minutes before the start of the Service. Having ascertained that there was no hope of finding a verger or any member of the works staff to help, I grabbed Rowland Sidwell, who was singing with us that day, and with cassocks flying, the two of us ran through the crypt and up into Paternoster Square where there was a Lipton's supermarket. Barging our way through the waiting queues, we gathered heaps of toilet rolls, paid for them, and raced back to the crypt, throwing them over the doors of the occupied cubicles. Ten minutes later, everyone was safely in their processional places, and the Service began.

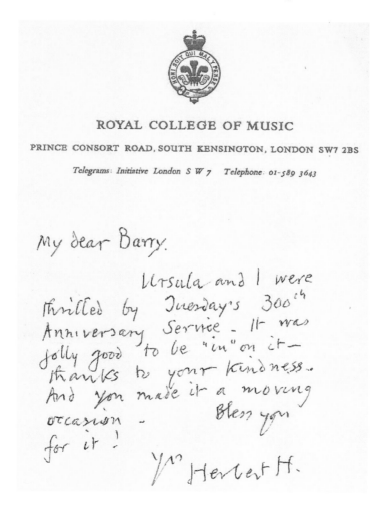

ROYAL COLLEGE OF MUSIC

PRINCE CONSORT ROAD, SOUTH KENSINGTON, LONDON SW7 2BS

Telegrams: Initiative London S W 7   Telephone: 01-589 3643

My dear Barry,

Ursula and I were thrilled by Tuesday's 300th Anniversary Service. It was jolly good to be "in" on it — thanks to your kindness. And you made it a moving occasion — Bless you for it!

Yrs Herbert H.

Now back from his sabbatical, Christopher was working hard to persuade the Chapter of the need for a third organist. We both hoped that this might become a reality through a joint arrangement between Southwark Cathedral and St. Paul's – Southwark offering accommodation and St. Paul's paying a small stipend. Harry Bramma, the Organist at Southwark Cathedral, had already started the process by approaching John Scott, organ scholar of St. John's College, Cambridge. I'd first met John around the same time when I was producing Choral Evensong from St. John's. In one of the two broadcasts on successive weeks, George Guest, the Director of Music, was ill, and I'd arrived in the chapel to find John conducting the choir. He had written to me after the broadcasts saying that if the joint arrangement could be made, he'd be very keen to play at both Southwark and St. Paul's. Buffie and I made an appointment to visit St. John's to talk about Tim, our son, becoming a chorister there. John was due to show us around that day, so I said I'd talk to him about it.

John Scott, Buffie, and Tim at St. John's College, Cambridge, summer 1978

A few weeks later, Christopher and Harry Bramma formalised the arrangement, and in September 1978 John started at St. Paul's, a move which would lead him to be Sub-Organist (1984-1990) and then Organist and Director of Music for 14 years.

In early November we completed the final stages of the filming of *Paul's Children*, and the 50-minute programme was first shown on BBC 1 on Sunday evening, 17th December. *Radio Times* featured a full colour photo of the boys on the front cover

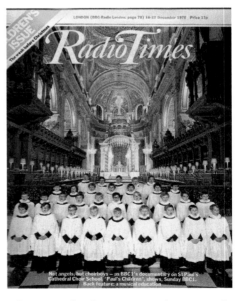

The St. Paul's choristers on the cover of the Radio Times, *December 1978*

as well as a four-page article about them. Much of the programme focussed on eleven-year-old Paul Phoenix, though other soloists and instrumentalists were featured.

Three days after the showing of *Paul's Children* we were again featured on the BBC, this time with the full choir broadcasting Choral Evensong on BBC Radio 3. It was the first such broadcast during my four years at the Cathedral. As the BBC's editor of programme, I got the impression that the Dean and Chapter were slightly irked by the fact that they had to negotiate with me over the practical and contractual details when they were more used to dictating these. From my point of view, I was used to being the producer, and on this occasion I had to leave the sound balancing and production to one of my colleagues, trusting that the sound they broadcast would have not only clarity but also the spaciousness of the building.

After all that media exposure this year, 1979 would seem normal. Or would it?

1979: Boyce, Burgon – and boarding school

1979 normal? – no chance! The year had scarcely begun when two offers arrived from the BBC, and they could not have been more different. One was sure to gain Chapter's approbation whilst the other would not – probably best not to mention that one.

1979 was the bicentenary of the death of former chorister and composer, William Boyce, who lies buried in the crypt of St. Paul's, and the invitation was for one of four celebratory programmes commissioned by BBC Radio 3 to include music by Boyce and his contemporaries. We settled on two works by Boyce, an anthem by former Organist of St. Paul's, Maurice Greene, and an organ concerto by Thomas Arne, with Christopher Dearnley as soloist, the recording to be made in February and broadcast a couple of months later. The centrepiece of the programme would be Boyce's oratorio-style setting of *Lord, Thou hast been our refuge*, in which we'd be accompanied by the London Bach Orchestra, using the recently published edition by Maurice Bevan, our senior vicar choral.

Before all that, I thought about and accepted the other slightly more controversial invitation: a full-length BBC documentary about the song *My Way* for the *Arena* series of programmes. Alan Yentob, the producer, was very keen that we should take part and sing the song in a hymn-like way. I set to and arranged it for Jeremy Carpenter and Paul Phoenix, the two soloists in our Boyce radio programme, together with choir and organ accompaniment.

There was no way Chapter would have considered letting us record it in the Cathedral. On a cold February evening, having sung Evensong and eaten their supper, the boys came across the road to the church of St. Anne and St. Agnes in Gresham Street, where they were filmed virtually sight-reading their way through the arrangement, written on scraps of manuscript paper. It wasn't the best singing we had ever done: the church was freezing cold and the organ was far too small to help with any real support or musical expression. However, the BBC seemed very satisfied, and the following week I did an interview to camera about the song, filmed in one of the practice-rooms in the choir school.

A month later the completed programme was screened on BBC 2. I'd not seen it before the transmission, and apart from the headmaster, no-one else at the Cathedral knew anything about it. In the programme we were sandwiched between distinguished, and some slightly more questionable, pop company; from Frank Sinatra, Elvis Presley, Shirley Bassey, David Bowie, and Paul Anka, to Sid Vicious and the Sex Pistols. As I'd remembered, the singing wasn't our best, but I needn't have worried. The next day, the *Daily Mail* television critic hailed the inclusion of the boys as a master stroke, and it wasn't long before my phone started ringing with offers from music agents and record companies for us to make a single of our version of *My Way*. Of all the offers, the one that interested me most came from a small independent record company, Different Records. Lynton Guest, the owner, came to see me and we talked about a 45 rpm single, a follow-up disc, and a possible later link-up with a major label for a full LP to include a mixture of church and popular music.

With the continuing interest in the *Arena* programme, we needed to record *My Way* as quickly as possible, this time in the Cathedral. I expanded the arrangement to include three trumpets in the last verse, and John Scott agreed to accompany us on the Cathedral organ. We made a private financial arrangement with the Clerk of Works and Bill Box, the resident electrician, and the recording was made one evening in March, the boys singing from the quire steps, and the three trumpeters playing from the west end of the dome. The finished disc was released within ten days, and with it a lot of publicity in the national press.

Daily Mail, Friday, April 6, 1979

Doing it their way

THESE are the boys who could be the most unusual pop stars yet.

They are the choristers of St Paul's Cathedral — and their recording of My Way, released yesterday, is expected to leap into the charts.

The record, featuring solos by Paul Phoenix and Jeremy Carter, already is a double first: the first secular recording made in the cathedral and the first time an unbroken treble voice has been used on a commercial recording for 50 years.

The BBC 2 Arena programme featuring the two 11-year-old boys and the rest of choir created so much interest that the record was rushed out in time for Easter. Royalties will go to the cathedral.

Aside from getting Jeremy Carpenter's name wrong, this was the first time anyone on the senior Cathedral staff would learn about our new venture, and I hoped they would be pleased that the Cathedral was to benefit from the sales of the disc. As a result of the recording, we were invited to appear on some television programmes, including *Record Breakers* with Roy Castle. To take part in *Pebble Mill at One*, we made an early morning trip up the M1 to the BBC studios in Birmingham, and there was even a trip to Holland, where the producers of a Dutch television gameshow paid to fly us over, just to sing the one song. All of this was fitted around schoolwork and singing the Cathedral Services, where we had a special excitement for our Monday boys-only Evensong: a new Magnificat and Nunc Dimittis specially written for us. Mark Blatchly, now at Oxford University as organ scholar at Christ Church, had written his new setting as a thank you for the time he had spent at St. Paul's. Its world premiere was at Evensong on Monday 12th March (1979), with John Scott playing the organ, and the composer in the congregation.

Around the same time, I had been contacted by another composer, Geoffrey Burgon, about a closing signature tune he had just composed for the forthcoming BBC 2 television adaptation of John le Carré's novel *Tinker, Tailor, Soldier, Spy*. Although we had never met, Geoffrey and I shared a Guildford connection: he had been at Pewley Grammar School where he had been taught English by my mother-in-law. From there he had gone on to the Guildhall School of Music to study trumpet, but, with encouragement from Peter Wishart, had become much more interested in composition. Now at the age of 38, he was writing his first music for television, and in a stroke of genius and lateral thinking, he had come up with the idea of a setting of the Nunc Dimittis as the closing credits for each programme rolled across a picture of Oxford's Radcliffe Camera.

Geoffrey turned up with a rough outline of the Nunc Dimittis, and after Evensong I introduced him to Paul Phoenix. Geoffrey sat at the piano and Paul sang to him. A few days later he was back with the completed work, and in the Cathedral practice room he got out his trumpet, I played the piano and Paul sang it. A month later, at the tail-end of the Easter holidays, Paul and I went to the BBC television music studio at Lime Grove where he made the finished recording.

The series was first aired in September of that year, and the closing music was an instant hit. We needed to record it for an EP as quickly as possible – this time in the Cathedral – and again, Different Records issued the disc, which also included a rhythmic arrangement of *I'd like to teach the world to sing* on the B-side. It wasn't long before the record was in the pop charts, and a month or so later, Geoffrey was given a prestigious Ivor Novello Award, thoughtfully taking Paul with him to receive it at the awards ceremony.

In September our family life changed. Earlier in the year, Tim had auditioned for the choir of St. John's College, Cambridge, and had been accepted. Now at the age of eight, he would be leaving home to become a boarder at St. John's College School. I was more thrilled about it than Buffie. From my point of view, he would be singing in what, in my opinion, was the best church choir in the world (yes, even including King's College), whilst Buffie was none too keen for her young son to be sent away from home.

Tim seemed quite happy about it all and would spend the next five years at the school. I would see him occasionally when I visited the College on behalf of the BBC, and Buffie and Julia (and later,

In his smart new uniform, Tim leaving Amen Court, September 1979

Nicola) were able to visit at weekends whilst I was on duty at St. Paul's.

There were changes in the Cathedral clergy, both at senior and junior level. Evan Pilkington, a delightful and saintly priest from Bristol Cathedral, became Chancellor, bringing a much-needed calming presence in the Cathedral and amongst his senior clergy colleagues. One of 36 chaplains to the Queen, short in stature but big in heart, on special occasions Evan stood out from the crowd in his scarlet cassock.

A newly appointed Minor Canon was now occupying the lower flat at No. 4 Amen Court. For several months before his arrival, the house had been turned into a building site whilst it was re-configured into two distinct halves, each with its own front door. During that time we'd had to cope with dirt and dust everywhere, and the only access to and from our part of the house was by climbing planks up to and through windows – not very convenient or healthy for a family with young children.

Richard Fenwick had come from Rochester Cathedral, replacing the Reverend Samuel Cutt who had been appointed to a Canonry at Wells Cathedral. An accomplished and qualified musician, Richard brought an electronic organ with him, and his wife Jane played the harp – the sound of both instruments clearly travelling up the chimney breast into our living room and bedroom.

Meanwhile, Dean Alan Webster, still living next to us in Amen Court, was making his presence felt at the Cathedral by seeking to introduce changes to the liturgy. His plan to introduce some informality and modern language into the Worship immediately put him at loggerheads with Canon John Collins, the longest serving member of the Cathedral Chapter. As John so rightly said, 'People come to hear the old prayers properly done and the best of English church music. You can't get away with stunts – the building won't let you.'

It was not an easy time. At Norwich, Alan had been able to make the final decisions about such things, whilst at St. Paul's he was *primus inter pares* (first among equals), meaning that he could be outvoted by the other Canons. Relationships quickly deteriorated, resulting in one unseemly public row in the Cathedral, when John Collins said to Alan, 'Don't be such an ass.' Alan immediately lost his temper, threatening to report him to Buckingham Palace. But John was equal to the situation, simply saying, 'But I like asses.' All this had a bearing on a remark I'd previously heard Alan make: 'I must have more power', and the souring of relationships between the Dean and the Canons was to continue until his retirement in 1987, by which time there had been more than one concerted effort by his colleagues on Chapter to remove him from office.

The musical excitements of Boyce, Burgon and *My Way* now well past, I was more than surprised to get a phone call from the USA asking if a representative of the American Guild of Organists could come over and see me. E. Lyle Hagert was Organist of Gethsemane Church, Minneapolis, and a member of the board which was organising the AGO National Convention to take place in Minneapolis and neighbouring St. Paul the following year in June 1980.

They would very much like St. Paul's Cathedral Choir to be in residence for the week to sing concerts, Services and workshops. Might this be possible? I discussed it with Christopher and the vicars choral, who all seemed very keen, and once I was sure there would be no cost to the Cathedral, I forwarded the proposal to Canon Douglas Webster, the Precentor, so that he could take it to a Chapter meeting.

St. Paul's choir had last been to the USA back in 1953, an extended tour lasting for two months. Our visit would be for two weeks, with Air Canada offering partial sponsorship if we would agree to go on from Minneapolis to give concerts in Toronto, Ottawa and Montreal. The AGO would deal with Air Canada over the fares and contribute to the daily subsistence allowance to be paid to the vicars choral. In order to be absolutely sure that the trip wasn't going to cost the Cathedral one penny, Nick Ware (my partner in Guild Records) and I worked out that we could also help with the daily allowances if we could ship LPs over there in bulk to be sold at the Convention. In Chapter there were obviously some in-depth discussions about finance and the choir being away from the Cathedral for two weeks during June. In the end they agreed, and I was able to announce the trip at a choir school Speech Day.

Before venturing across the Atlantic, I thought it would be good to take the choristers on a shorter trip abroad; well, not quite abroad, but to the Isle of Jersey. Over the years I'd built up many musical connections on the island, and especially with Mel Davidson, the Music Adviser to the Education Department. Mel was keen that we should not just sing Services and a public concert, but also give a concert for schools. In the space of the first three days of our half-term break, we managed to fit all of these in, one highlight being a completely sold-out concert in the 1,450-seat Wesley Grove Methodist Church.

The St. Paul's choristers' sold-out concert at Wesley Grove Methodist Church, Jersey, 31st October 1979

After the half-term break, there was another excitement: a full-scale concert in the Queen Elizabeth Hall on 26th November. The choir had previously sung there in 1970, performing either unaccompanied or with the organ. This time we were being joined by the London Bach Orchestra in a programme including the William Boyce *Lord, Thou hast been our refuge* and Thomas Arne's organ concerto, both of which had featured in our earlier BBC recording, as well as a work we were planning to record early next term, Franz Josef Haydn's *Nelson Mass*. Underwritten by the Chapter, some of whom did attend the concert, it was a memorable evening in which the choir, soloists and orchestra sang and played beautifully. The only minor hiccup – or worse than a hiccup – was at the very end of the concert, when one of the choristers could no longer keep his supper inside him and deposited the whole lot on the walkway to the stage, just as the soloists were trying to return to take another bow!

Back at St. Paul's, with what passed for normality, there would be a huge amount of detailed pre-planning to be done for our USA visit, but aside from that, I hoped that 1980 might be a little less frantic than this year.

17

Home and Away
St Paul's 1980-1983

We were now into 1980, and as well as planning the forthcoming USA trip, there was the small matter of another recording. This was to be Guild Records' biggest and most expensive project so far: Franz Josef Haydn's *Nelson Mass*, featuring the Cathedral choir and soloists, a guest soprano soloist, 30 members of the London Bach Orchestra, and a portable Hoxne chamber organ hired from Noel Mander. Adding to that expense, we also engaged Brian Culverhouse, producer of all our EMI records at Guildford, as guest producer. The final budget was an eye-watering amount of around £10,000, and this was the opportunity to ask the Dean and Chapter if they'd like to invest half the cost. Their answer was a firm no, even though there had been pointed comments from some of the clergy, who thought that Guild Records might be making money out of the Cathedral through sales of previous discs. In fact, nothing was further from the truth – we had yet to break even on those we'd already made, and we knew it would be many years before we'd recover the costs of this one.

Through Charles Shears, the Registrar, I negotiated for the use of the Cathedral on three evenings during early February, agreeing a facilities fee, as well as overtime for a verger, the duty electrician, and the Clerk of the Works. Nick, who would be making the recording, was currently involved in a mammoth musical project being filmed around the world to celebrate the forthcoming launch of Channel 4. Entitled *Music in Time*, it was to be presented by James Galway, and when Nick mentioned that he was making our Haydn recording, the producer said that he'd like to film the opening session for inclusion in one of the programmes. Although this would mean bringing extra lighting and technicians into the Cathedral, they would take the sound feed from Nick's recording balance and would not want footage of any rehearsal – just a straight take of one of the movements. I chose the *Benedictus*, which starts with a long orchestral introduction, followed by the four soloists, Julie Kennard (soprano), Ashley Stafford (countertenor), Alan Green (tenor), and Maurice Bevan (bass), and then the choir. To achieve the best possible visual effect for television, we arranged for the entire dome area to be cleared of chairs, and I was slightly taken aback when

Brian Culverhouse (rightly) decided that the choir should be well detached from the orchestra, though the only way I'd be able to hear any sort of balance between them would be to conduct wearing earphones.

Nearly all the three hours of that first evening session were spent on just the one movement, with various stops and starts for new camera angles and adjustments to the lighting. It may have thrown our planned recording schedule into confusion, but at least the fee that the film company were offering would go a little way towards recouping our huge financial outlay.

The recording was completed on time, but already there was another one to consider – not so expensive for us, but more time-consuming. Following on from the two 45 rpm Different Records singles that the boys had made, there was an offer from a major pop-record company to market a complete LP of a mixture of sacred and secular music. K-tel were well known for their cover versions of popular songs, and with their television advertising and cheap pricing of the discs, they achieved huge sales. Nick and I worked out a programme with Paul Phoenix as our featured soloist, singing in the Cathedral with organ accompaniment, and with piano and orchestra at Decca Recording Studios in West Hampstead.

We started as soon as the Haydn recording was over. Paul came over to the Cathedral on a couple of evenings, and with John Scott sharing the accompanying, we managed to record several items, even though we weren't sure how many, if any, would be considered suitable for the new LP. The following Sunday evening, Paul and I went to the Decca Studios in West Hampstead to record some songs with piano accompaniment. The technicians were very helpful, and on condition that I didn't say a word to anyone, they let me use Vladimir Ashkenazy's piano which was there for a recording he was due to make the following week. By the end of the evening, we'd recorded another three items.

For the orchestral tracks, I approached Bill Ives and Mark Blatchly to see if they'd be willing to make some special arrangements for us. Bill came up with a lovely arrangement of *Try to remember* for soloist, choir and strings, whilst Mark's memorably individual

In full flight: Paul Phoenix (centre) in choir practice. On the left is young Peter Auty, who would later be soloist in We're walking in the air *for the television film* The Snowman.

contributions included *Cockles and Mussels, Morning has broken* and *Silent Night*. A week or so later I was back in the Decca studios to record the orchestra on to multi-track, the boys' parts to be added later. To do this, they stayed at school for three days after Easter, completing the recordings at Decca studios on Easter Monday morning, and a couple more items with the orchestra in the Cathedral that same evening. Two days later, they were live broadcasting Choral Evensong with the men, after which it was time for a short holiday before next term's excitements.

I left the editing of the *Nelson Mass* to Brian Culverhouse but was able to sit in at Decca studios as Nick did the final mix-down of the multi-track recordings. We, Guild Records, would try to get our *Nelson Mass* ready by the beginning of June and send copies to be sold in the USA, whilst Different Records took the finished boys' tracks to negotiate with K-tel, who would ultimately decide which items to include on their LP.

Now there were other pressing matters to deal with. Our USA trip was getting near, and the final details had yet to be sorted. At their meeting in March, the Dean and Chapter had again discussed the trip. We had asked Canon Douglas Webster, the Precentor, to come with us, but he had declined. Chapter decided that the Reverend Michael Moxon, one of the Minor Canons, would take his place 'to represent the Dean and Chapter'.

Despite already having assured the Chapter that the trip would not cost the Cathedral one penny, they sent me a formal letter asking to see full details of the financial arrangements we were making. I didn't (and couldn't) answer since we had yet to finalise the fees for the men. Unlike the Dean and Canons, I still had no secretarial help whatsoever and had to type my own letters and schedules. All this had to fit around the 12 sung Services in the Cathedral each week, my ever-increasing duties at the BBC, and what little family life we could have together.

High on the list of priorities for the USA was insurance for the whole party; a meeting with the 18 men of the choir to agree a fee that they would accept each day; and arrangements for the export of hundreds of LPs and cassettes which could be sold at the various venues and help to provide a daily subsistence allowance for each of the adults, as well as pocket-money for the boys.

The insurance was easy, having found a reliable broker. At the meeting with the men of the choir I needed to get their permission for two concerts to be recorded and live broadcast on National Public Radio. The original proposal had been for just the one opening concert, but that was already over-subscribed, with the 3,500 tickets so far distributed nowhere near enough to meet the demand. The organisers asked for an extra concert, in another venue, and that too would be broadcast. It was a positive meeting, even if at one stage there was a throwback to the long-standing animosity between some of the vicars choral that I'd found when I'd first arrived six years ago. As chairman, I presented the apologies for absence, saying, 'Alan Green can't be here today since he's not feeling well.' Up spoke long-serving bass, Geoffrey Shaw. 'Nothing trivial, I hope,' he retorted, to which I immediately replied, 'Do I minute that…?' They reached an agreed *per diem* fee, plus a small daily subsistence which, if there was a shortfall in the budget, would be made up from sales of our records at the Convention.

As ever, Cathedral Services remained the overriding priority. Among the upcoming special events was a Service of Thanksgiving in Celebration of Queen Elizabeth The Queen Mother's 80th birthday, scheduled for the second week of July. This was more than special to us since the Queen Mother was the loyal Patron of the Friends of St. Paul's and always attended their annual Friends' Day. We'd need to finish the planning before we left for the USA, and although the Service would be televised and broadcast, in musical terms it would not be on such a grand scale as her daughter's Silver Jubilee three years earlier.

Choristers with HM Queen Elizabeth The Queen Mother at a later Friends' Day reception

A month before we were due to leave for America, everything seemed to be going smoothly, until our plans were suddenly thrown into disarray. Christopher Dearnley withdrew from the tour, citing lack of consultation and 'representation of his status'. In our working relationship we often passed like ships-in-the-night, each busily concentrating on his own particular duty-days, and often not meeting until after we'd both been at a Service. As requested, I had submitted a draft programme to the American Guild of Organists for the opening concert of the Convention. Allowing space for two organ solos in the first half, I had pencilled in one of these as a suggestion, to fit in with the period and mood of the sung music either side of it. Christopher had caught sight of the draft and rightly took exception to the fact that so far, he'd not been consulted.

We had a meeting in his Amen Court apartment, in which we both aired some strong opinions about the way the joint appointment was working. I tried to explain that this was primarily a choral concert, that the invitation had been to the choir, and although he would be on the trip as the Organist of St. Paul's Cathedral (described that way in all the pre-publicity and Convention brochure), on this occasion he was there primarily as the choir's accompanist. That did not go down at all well, and a day or so later I received a note from him confirming his withdrawal.

Perhaps I should have been less forthright at our meeting. It was no time for self-recrimination – I needed to find someone to play. There were two options: John Scott, or someone already working in the USA. I talked to John about it. He was keen, and this would be his first trip to the USA. We'd need to negotiate his absence from Southwark Cathedral, and he'd fly out on the night before the concert, arriving in Minneapolis the next morning – very little time to get acquainted with the organ, but if anyone could cope with that situation, John certainly could. Meantime, the Chapter had heard of Christopher's withdrawal, and though they said nothing officially at the time, I sensed that the matter might be brought up later – and it was.

On Saturday 14th June, just before we set off in the coach to Gatwick airport, Dean Alan Webster made his way to where I was sitting, and instead of the usual *bon voyage*, he simply reminded me that Michael Moxon would be 'in charge' – though 'in charge' of what I still wasn't sure. What a marked contrast in approach and attitude to the saintly Canon Evan Pilkington who, two days earlier had delivered this card, written with his own hand:

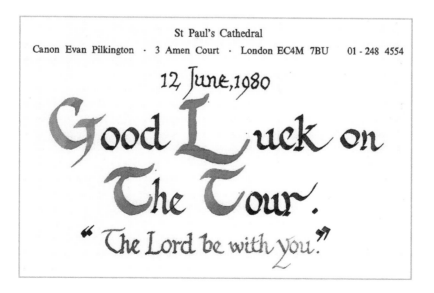

St Paul's Cathedral
Canon Evan Pilkington · 3 Amen Court · London EC4M 7BU   01 - 248 4554

12 June, 1980

Good Luck on The Tour.

"The Lord be with you."

Northwest Orient airlines had recently started a service between London and Minneapolis and we were on one of their inaugural flights in a new 747 jumbo jet. Some 40,000 feet above the Atlantic Ocean, the St. Paul's Cathedral choristers entertained the passengers in both the main and business class cabins with Mendelssohn's *Lift thine eyes* – a first for them, and certainly a first for us.

For the next six days we were based in Minneapolis, the boys staying with hosts, whilst the men, John Scott, the headmaster, the school matron, and I were in the same hotel. Our two concerts were both received with standing ovations for several minutes – a humbling experience from over 5,000 USA church musicians to this group of 30 boys and 18 men. The choir was on stunning form, and it was such a joy, both musically and socially, to have the same 18 men in residence all week.

In addition to the concerts, we sang two Evensongs and two Matins, one with a 7.30 a.m. rehearsal for an 8.15 a.m. start, as well as providing the sung illustrations for a workshop about the Te Deum. On our last morning we sang Matins at a later time, after which everyone piled into a coach to go to the airport. Courtesy of Air Canada, a plane took us to Detroit where we were met and ferried the thirteen miles to Christ Church, Grosse Pointe, singing a concert that same evening.

En route to Detroit, 20ᵗʰ June 1980

The following morning, we crossed the border into Windsor, Canada, and boarded the train to take us to Toronto. The 225-mile journey was scheduled to take around four hours, but because the locomotive hauling the train broke down, we didn't get into Toronto until late afternoon; just enough time to have the briefest of rehearsals in St. Paul's Church, Bloor Street, for our evening concert.

The next morning, John Scott flew on to Ottawa, and the rest of us made the six-hour train journey. Once there, we rehearsed in the large Roman Catholic Basilica of Notre Dame, giving an evening concert a few hours later to a large and appreciative audience.

The last day of the tour involved a shorter train journey to Montreal and a final concert in the Gothic-revival

John Scott at Toronto station, 21ˢᵗ June 1980

Basilica of St. Patrick. It was a very tight timetable, since the concert started at 6.00 p.m. and the plane back to England was due to leave Mirabel Airport at 9.00 p.m. Air Canada collected all the luggage as we arrived at Montreal Central Station and they whisked it off to the airport. They also arranged for a coach to be standing by at the end of the concert to get the choir to the plane in time. By now we were all tired, but it didn't show in a demanding programme, opening with E.W. Naylor's *Vox dicentis*, and ending with Bernard Rose's *Feast Song for St. Cecilia*. The *Montreal Gazette* music critic was most impressed, giving us a glowing review with this heading:

St. Paul's choir music is angelic

The audience would not stop applauding, even after two encores. They were still clapping as we headed to the exit, the coach, and the airport. It was there that I said farewell to the choir, since I was flying on to Houston to direct an RSCM summer school. The boys would now go home for a few days, and we'd link up again when I returned to the U.K. a week later.

It was not a happy return. No sooner had I got back to No. 4 Amen Court than I found a couple of notes pushed through the letterbox, one accusing me of putting the Organist in a position where he felt he could not go on the tour, and the other demanding a full financial statement within the next seven days. At the very outset, both Christopher and I had accepted that we would only be paid a nominal fee, and only then if there was anything left in the budget. In the end, we paid John Scott a suitable professional fee, and I received a fraction of that to cover my expenses. I submitted the figures to Chapter and heard no more, though I hoped that Michael Moxon would have told them what good musical ambassadors we'd been, taking the name and sound of St. Paul's Cathedral to the USA and Canada. Rather than showing any appreciation, I suspect it was from that moment that the Dean (and possibly other members of the Chapter) started working out a plan whereby my responsibilities would be curbed, and my status would change. That would become publicly clear at a certain big event the following year...

For now, we had to focus our efforts on the Queen Mother's 80th birthday Service and make it the grand and special occasion that St. Paul's always manages so well. Security on these occasions is rightly raised to the highest level, and I was to fall foul of that – purely through my own fault. On the morning of the Service (15th July), I made my way over to the Cathedral to take the pre-Service choir practice. I'd forgotten my pass, and despite telling the two security officers who I was (and them sarcastically replying that they were Sherlock Holmes and Dr. Watson), there was no way I was going to get in. A quick sprint home, and grabbing the pass, I got to the choir room just in time, but breathless. Never again!

The long summer break couldn't come soon enough for the choir, and me. The USA-Canada trip had taken a great deal out of us (more than I realised), and learning and singing the July Masses was more of a challenge than in previous years.

≈

Just after we started again in September, I had a letter from the Royal British Legion, to see if the boys could sing at their November Festivals of Remembrance in the Royal Albert Hall. There were three Festivals, one on Friday evening, and two on Saturday, afternoon and evening. It was the Saturday evening that was always attended by the Queen and other members of the Royal Family. We would be the first item in the programme, and since the boys were the youngest performers, we could leave once we'd sung, rather than staying to take part in the Act of Worship at the very end.

Having got the Chapter's permission, I needed to find something to sing. There was nothing suitable in the choir library, so I contacted Mark Blatchly at Oxford to see if he could help. We talked about possible texts and decided to explore Laurence Binyon's poem *For the Fallen*, the fourth verse of which is always read out at the end of the Festivals of Remembrance: *They shall grow not old, as we that are left grow old*. I left the idea with Mark, suggesting that if he was able to write something, could he do it (as I'd previously asked of Grayston Ives for his *Jubilee Piece*) 'in an Elgarian style'? A couple of weeks later, his setting of *For the Fallen* arrived at Amen Court. Scored for three-part upper voices and organ, the final refrain of *They shall grow not old* dovetails with a lone trumpeter playing the instantly recognisable start of *The Last Post*. It was a winner, though a verse too long for the time limit we'd been given for our slot. We set to and learned a shortened version, giving its first performance in the Royal Albert Hall on Friday 7th November 1980. The Saturday evening Festival is always televised with a delayed transmission, so we were able to watch it after we'd all returned to St. Paul's. The boys were to sing it again at the 1981 and 1982 Festivals.

At the Cathedral, I'd been thinking of possible ways to solve a musical problem that had been bugging me since Christopher and I had assumed our new roles – Tuesday Evensong. This was the one day when there was no staff organist available to play; Christopher was not on duty, and John Scott was playing for Evensong at Southwark. No organ scholars had lived-in since Mark Blatchly left us two years ago. The present scholar was very much part-time, and not necessarily available or experienced enough to play every week. We made a few ad-hoc arrangements with other organists I knew, but more often than not, I had ended up playing. Talking with Jonathan Rennert, the Organist of St. Michael's Church, Cornhill, he mentioned Andrew Lucas, then in his final year as a student at the Royal College of Music, and it was on Jonathan's recommendation that I invited Andrew to meet me. He came to a Monday Evensong early in December, and when everyone had left the building, I asked him to play the Magnificat from *Stanford in G*. It was excellent, and the next day he played it at Evensong. So began an 18-year association with St. Paul's, which would end up with Andrew being Assistant Director of Music between 1990 and 1998. The Chapter had made it clear that they were not willing to pay anything more towards the music, so for each Service he played, I paid him out of my own pocket.

The last part of the year put the emphasis firmly back in the world of lighter music – not necessarily popular or approved of by the Dean and Chapter, or my colleague, Christopher Dearnley, though it gave the boys the opportunity to meet and work with one of the icons of the pop world – Paul McCartney.

Paul had written a song called *We all stand together*, and it had been arranged and orchestrated by George Martin for a forthcoming animated film, *Rupert and the Frog Song*. I had a phone call to see if some of the boys could take part in it – imitating frogs! After Evensong and supper on Monday 3rd November, I took a group of them to Air Studios, above Top Shop at Oxford Circus, where, with the King's Singers, they

With Paul McCartney, recording We all stand together *(photo by Linda McCartney)*

recorded their part in the song with Paul conducting. The session over-ran, and rather than leave the headmaster wondering where we were, I asked Paul if he would ring the school to explain. It's not every headmaster who has picked up the phone to hear 'It's Paul McCartney speaking…' The completed film was released in 1984 and none of us had any idea that the single of the song would reach No. 3 in the pop charts.

November also saw the release of our K-tel recording. Using the one-word title, *Rejoice*, they'd chosen 12 of the 20 tracks we'd recorded, including all those with orchestral accompaniment. Paul Phoenix was featured as soloist in nine of the items and also had his photo on the reverse of the sleeve. *My Way* was there, as well as Geoffrey Burgon's *Nunc Dimittis*, and they'd also included items to attract Christmastide buyers – *Silent Night* and *The Little Road to Bethlehem* – excerpts from both those tracks being regularly played in television adverts.

K-tel obviously knew their market; the sales quickly passed 100,000, and a few months later we (the choir school and I) were awarded Gold Discs:

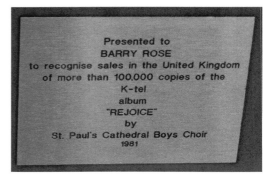

The Gold Disc plaque for the St. Paul's choristers' album Rejoice

1980 had certainly put the choir very much in the public eye at home and abroad. Nothing could match up to that – or so I thought…

1981: Happy surprises – and skulduggery

1981 would spring two surprises – one at the Cathedral, and one at home.

On Tuesday 3rd March I was sitting at home having lunch with Buffie and listening to the one o'clock news on BBC Radio 4. The opening headlines announced that Prince Charles and the Lady Diana Spencer would be married in St. Paul's Cathedral on 29ᵗʰ July. I nearly choked on what I was eating. Royal Weddings don't take place in St. Paul's – they are always in Westminster Abbey. They must have got it wrong. No, they were right. It was to be St. Paul's, as confirmed in the *Evening Standard* newspaper I bought that afternoon:

Charles to marry at St. Paul's

PRINCE CHARLES and Lady Diana Spencer will marry on Wednesday, July 29 at St Paul's Cathedral, Buckingham Palace announced today.

Evening Standard, *Tuesday 3ʳᵈ March 1981*

In no time at all the Cathedral was besieged by press reporters and photographers, all wanting a story and pictures for tomorrow's papers. Choir practice for Evensong that day was more like a circus, with photographers taking shots from all angles, and that continued throughout Evensong, even though they'd been instructed not to do so.

From now on our time wouldn't be our own, and a week or so later, I had another even more exciting and personal surprise – Buffie was pregnant – we would have a new addition to our family in November. For both of us, this was totally unexpected, and the very best of surprises. Both Tim (9) and Julia (7) were excited by the news, if initially crestfallen when, because of Buffie's morning sickness, we had to cancel a planned post-Easter holiday to the Canary Islands at the very last minute.

November would be very special. But for now, I needed to think about 29ᵗʰ July. In any church wedding, music plays a part. In a Royal Wedding, music plays a special part. Prince Charles had been an undergraduate at Trinity College, Cambridge, where he had met Sir David Willcocks, and sung under his direction in CUMS (Cambridge University Musical Society), so it seemed natural that he would turn to Sir David for musical advice. As Prince of Wales, there was also to be a Welsh connection, with a new anthem – a setting of Psalm 67, as appointed for the Marriage Service in the *Book of Common Prayer* – to be written by Dr. William Mathias, then Professor of Music at University of Wales, Bangor.

As the Cathedral's Master of the Choir, I presumed that I also might be part of the detailed music planning. That was not to be, and it soon became clear that as far as they were able, the Chapter, or more likely Dean Alan Webster, would make sure I played no part, informing me that Sir David Willcocks and Christopher Dearnley would now be in overall charge of the music. Sir David would conduct Kiri Te Kanawa, the Bach Choir, and a chamber orchestra in the north transept during the signing of the Registers, though he would not play any role in the actual Service itself. I made an appointment to go and see him at the Royal College of Music. Rather than being helpful, he was somewhat dictatorial, even to the point of informing me that there would be no descants in any of the hymns – though why, and on whose authority, he would not say.

These occasions always seem to bring out the worst in some people; colleagues with whom one usually has a perfectly good and informal working relationship suddenly start appearing with clipboards and being officious. One thing was certain: on the day itself, we'd all do what we did on any other day in the Cathedral – I would conduct the choir and Christopher would play the organ. The manuscript copies of William Mathias' anthem arrived, and on our duty days, both Christopher and I spent time on it in the boys' choir practices. By the third week of July, they knew it well, and I invited Dr. Mathias to come to the choir school and hear it in rehearsal.

Meanwhile, the culprit (if that's the right word) in excluding me from any of the musical details for the day had become clear. It was, as I suspected, the Dean. In his monthly *Paul's Post*, signed by himself, he published the information that would be given to the national press. It was to be the beginning of the end of the post of Master of the Choir, and this is an exact photocopy of what he wrote:

```
On this occasion Sir David Willcocks, Director of the Royal College of Music, assists
Christopher Dearnley, the Cathedral Organist.   The Cathedral Choir, the Choir of the
Chapel Royal, the London Bach Choir and the augmented Covent Garden Orchestra are
combining to lead the singing of the congregation as well as the anthems, some specially
composed for the occasion.   The soprano soloist, Kiri Te Kanawa, will sing during the
signing of the register, just before the bride and bridegroom process from the altar to
the street outside down that great royal carpet, all 160 yards of it!
```

Somewhat dispirited, but undaunted, I continued to work as hard as I could with the choir, including conducting the four July Orchestral Masses, the last of which was just three days before the Wedding. The following morning the full choir assembled in the Cathedral and we had our first proper run through of all the music.

There was also negative publicity about the choir, on two fronts. The first was highlighting the cuts the Chapter had decided to make amongst the men (the vicars choral), reducing their number from 18 to 12 just after the Wedding. Together with the vicars choral, I had made myself more unpopular with the Dean and Chapter by speaking out against it, and the press were having a field-day with stories and opinions from those who would be victims of the cuts.

Then there was more negative publicity on the subject of fees for the Royal Wedding. All sorts of imaginary figures had been quoted in the press, including a payment of £500 to each of the boys. The reality was that Buckingham Palace would pay the same scale of Special Service fees as anyone else – £1 to each of the boys, £12 to each of the men, and £24 each to Christopher and myself. Yes, that amount would become greater as television channels opted to broadcast the Wedding, but that was something negotiated through the Registrar, who usually dealt with all financial matters.

Away from the Cathedral, the Rose family was getting some positive pre-wedding publicity through our daughter Julia. She and a group of school friends had written to Lady Diana to ask if they might be bridesmaids, and the *Daily Mail* had run an article about it, featuring a photo of Julia.

A HOST OF 'HUMBLE SUBJECTS' WRITE TO THE PALACE

Dear Lady Diana . . .

We all love you very much and please could we be bridesmaids?

Story by STUART COLLIER
Pictures by CLIVE LIMPKIN

THERE'S hardly a little girl in the land who doesn't want to be bridesmaid to Lady Diana Spencer.

Letters are flooding into Buckingham Palace from young hopefuls . . . and from boys volunteering to be pageboys.

A Buckingham Palace spokesman said: 'Prince Charles and Lady Diana have been very touched by the many charming requests.' And the Palace has been kept busy writing to tell the volunteers 'in as kind a words as we can' that all the bridesmaids and pageboys have been chosen.

JULIA ROSE
'Daddy can't wait'

Julia Rose—'I'm 7½,' she wrote to the Queen—had her own special reason for waiting a royal appointment at St Paul's.

Her letter said: 'My daddy is going to conduct the choir for Lady Diana and Prince Charles so please can I go to the wedding?' she asked to no avail.

She also revealed a few home truths after putting pen to paper. Her father, Master of the St Paul's Choir Mr Barry Rose, 'says he can't wait for the wedding. He just wants to see Lady Diana,' said Julia.

Then out of the blue she added: 'My mummy is going to have another baby in six months.'

I decided to make my own musical decisions for the choir, and a week or so before the Service, I wrote a descant to the first hymn, *Christ is made the sure foundation*, sending the original manuscript to Buckingham Palace as my wedding gift and receiving a most appreciative letter of thanks in return. The boys didn't sing it in any of the rehearsals, but saved it until the Service itself, where it soared over the top of the vast congregation and the other assembled musicians in the north transept.

The William Mathias anthem went well, with Christopher playing the demanding and exposed organ part with great panache. Standing on one side of the choir to conduct, rather than in the centre where I usually stood, I got carried away at one of the climaxes and with a grand gesture, knocked a shade off one of the choir-stall lamps. It hurtled through the air and was neatly caught by Michael Moxon, the Sacrist, who was in the nearest clergy stall. As I write this, nearly forty years on, it's usually the one thing that people remember when they talk about the 1981 Royal Wedding. I usually reply with what we were told at the time – that despite the loss of the lampshade, this was (and might still be) the world's largest audience ever for a musical premiere – over 700 million people listening and watching worldwide.

After the Service, Buffie and I made our way back to Amen Court where a communal post-wedding open air party was taking place. We couldn't stay long, since the BBC then whisked me, some choristers, and the headmaster off to Television Centre for another party and a live de-briefing on air. Arriving home late in the afternoon, I found this thoughtful telegram on the doormat:

With Buffie in Amen Court – post Royal Wedding

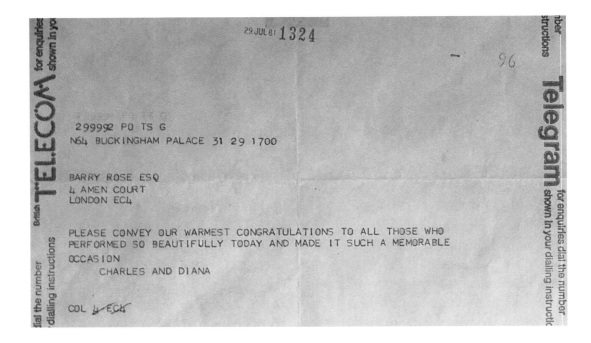

It had all been worth it. Despite the unpleasantness and clergy machinations, on the day we had done what we usually did – I conducted the choir, and Christopher played the organ. It was time for a holiday and, having been lent a chalet in the Canton of Valais, Switzerland, we were able to forget work and St. Paul's and have a relaxed family fortnight together.

For the boys, this was probably their shortest summer break ever. Returning to school at the very beginning of September, two days later, they, the men, and I were thrust into two evening sessions for a new gramophone record. There had already been a concerted move to prevent Guild Records from making any further recordings in the Cathedral, and the Chapter and the Registrar had teamed up with Associated Dairies Ltd. (ASDA), accepting their sponsorship of an LP record of *Music for the Royal Occasion,* the title carefully chosen whilst the Royal Wedding was still in everyone's memory. It's not every choir that can make a commercial recording immediately after returning from their summer holiday, but the sessions were fixed, and we had to get on with it. Hopefully the sponsors had paid a handsome sum to the Cathedral for the privilege of recording in St. Paul's.

The reduction in the back row of the choir had now taken effect and with it the loss of sung Matins on Tuesday and Thursday. Now there were just 12 vicars choral and six extra men, known as Permanent Deputies, only joining us on Sundays and special occasions.

There were also changes afoot among the senior clergy. Long-serving Canon John Collins was about to retire, as was Canon Evan Pilkington. Around the same time, Canon Douglas Webster would step down as Precentor, that role being taken by Bishop Kenneth Woollcombe when he arrived in November 1981.

The boys were again asked to sing Mark Blatchly's setting of *For the Fallen* at the November Festivals of Remembrance at the Royal Albert Hall, with Mark, now Sub-Organist of Gloucester Cathedral, playing for us.

Six days later, in the midst of Julia's 8th birthday party, Buffie suddenly announced that she needed to go round the corner to St. Bartholomew's Hospital – our long-awaited baby was on the way! Two hours into the following morning, Nicola Jane Rose was born, and although Tim was away at school, Julia and I were able to visit Nicola and Buffie later in the morning to celebrate. Our family was now complete, and I was able to take some time off from Cathedral duties to get used to being a new father again.

Buffie and Nicola Jane Rose

Later in the month, and for the first time since I had arrived at St. Paul's, I had to be away for the whole of the Advent Sunday weekend. It was an official BBC duty, as producer of the first broadcast of the Advent Carol Service from the chapel of St. John's College, Cambridge. On my return, there were negative comments about my absence on such an important day. I pointed out that the Chapter had publicly agreed to my BBC duties continuing when they created the post of Master of the Choir, though these were later used as 'absences without permission'.

Nearer Christmas, the choir had an invitation to appear on the BBC 2 television channel in *The Russell Harty Christmas Show*. Before becoming a television personality, Russell had been a teacher at Giggleswick School in North Yorkshire, where he was used to sacred music in chapel. I asked Frank Harvey, the Archdeacon of London, for permission to do it, and he agreed. A live transmission, we sang the Henry Walford Davies arrangement of *The Holly and the Ivy* after which Russell did an informal interview with several of the choristers. A few eyebrows might have been raised back at St. Paul's when we were immediately followed by the anarchic comedian Kenny Everett who arrived wearing cassock, surplice and ruff, light-heartedly pointing towards the St. Paul's choir and referring to us as 'them persons'. With a large viewing audience, St. Paul's had again ended the year very much in the public eye.

1982-83: Falklands, BBC, and darkening horizons

1982 began uneasily. Already I could sense that the Chapter, or at least the Dean, wanted to make musical changes at the Cathedral. Perhaps now was the time to look elsewhere? There's nothing like being ambitious: in March I thought I'd test the water by applying for the Director of Music vacancy at King's College, Cambridge. Having sent in my application, I received the standard rejection letter from the Provost, which ended, '*We are having to make our choice between a considerable number of very strongly qualified candidates*'. Maybe I should have persisted with the ARCO after all!

A few weeks later, on 2nd April, Argentina invaded the Falkland Islands. Prime Minister Margaret Thatcher was quick to act and a ten-week war was fought, with many casualties on both sides. Argentina surrendered on 14th June, and in keeping with a long-established custom, a celebratory Victory Service was planned to take place in St. Paul's on 12th July. Drawn up by the Dean, the Service was more than controversial, especially to Mrs. Thatcher, with its description of 'cessation of hostilities' rather than 'victory'. The Dean had also planned to include the Lord's Prayer in Spanish, but he was overruled. Televised and broadcast by the BBC, as the Service proceeded we could see increasing looks of disapproval, and not just from the Prime Minister. With all that controversy going on in the background, this time, unlike the Royal Wedding, I was left to do my job without any interference.

The same was true, up to a point, two weeks later, when the BBC celebrated its 60th Anniversary with a special Service in the Cathedral, attended by the Queen and the Duke of Edinburgh. Working at both the BBC and the Cathedral, I was properly consulted over the musical items that would be sung by the two choirs I regularly conducted – the Cathedral choir and the BBC Singers. Former St. Paul's chorister Sir Charles Groves would conduct the BBC Symphony Orchestra, and we would have the brass section playing in a specially commissioned anthem by Michael Berkeley. An extended setting of George Herbert's poem *Easter (Rise, heart, thy Lord is risen)*, it included a lyrical central section to be sung by the Cathedral choristers alone.

My commissioned setting of the BBC motto, *Nation shall speak peace unto nation*, was set for the two choirs answering one another, though its exclusion from the *Radio Times* billing (even omitting my name) again aroused my suspicions that the Dean and Chapter were intent on writing me out of the musical establishment at the Cathedral. That view was confirmed when I read the credits at the end, where Christopher Dearnley was now described as 'Cathedral Organist and Master of the Music'. Somebody had invented the title of *Master of the Music* for a reason, and it could only have come from the Chapter, or more likely, the Dean himself. It was another sign of the way they would formally proceed a year or so later.

With the BBC microphones installed for the Service, it seemed a good time to negotiate for a recording of Evensong to be made the following day, for later transmission in August. I suggested to Christopher that John Scott might be allowed to play for us on this occasion, and he readily agreed, the Service including Sir Edward Elgar's extended anthem *Give unto the Lord*, originally written for the 1914 Sons of Clergy Festival at the Cathedral.

Out of the blue, I was contacted by composer Howard Blake about a song for a television film, to be shown on Channel 4 over Christmas. Could he come and discuss it? The film was *The Snowman* and the song *We're walking in the air*. Howard had already recorded it with a treble soloist but wanted to have a second version from one of our choristers. I arranged for Peter Auty to sing to him, and Howard immediately decided that he'd like Peter's voice on the film. Peter made the recording in a central London studio, singing to a pre-recorded orchestral backing track. So successful was the song that Peter has a Gold disc for well over 100,000 sales, and a later recording by Aled Jones reached No. 5 in the charts.

After we returned from summer break, Canon Graham Routledge was installed as Chancellor. A lawyer and late ordinand, he was closely involved in the proposed re-drawing of contracts for Christopher, me, and the vicars choral. From first sight of a draft, I could already see that the end result would be unsatisfactory. Was it time to think about moving to another cathedral?

Again, the boys sang Mark Blatchly's *For the Fallen* for the Royal British Legion Festivals of Remembrance, but this time they also had the extra Saturday morning duty of singing for the new Lord Mayor of London when his procession stopped at the Cathedral for the Dean's blessing.

Advent passed with the annual performance of Handel's *Messiah*, after which Buffie threw a dinner party for my parents, some of the soloists, and Jürgen Hess, leader of the London Bach Orchestra. It was cut rather short when there was a scratching noise, and our cat, usually very domesticated, had decided to defecate on the lino just below the kitchen dining-area where we were sitting! Not the best end to a musical evening, at which my mother was loudly heard to exclaim in front of the assembled company, 'All that money I wasted on your piano lessons'.

Four days before Christmas, Russell Harty again invited us to be part of his live BBC 2 television Christmas show. I made a special arrangement of *Mary's Boy Child*, featuring two treble soloists, the full choir, and five of the choristers playing instruments (two flutes, two trumpets and one cello) as well as a tubular bell part for Russell. It was enthusiastically received, and this year we stayed on to lead the audience carols at the end of the show.

Early in 1983, during the unsettling negotiations over a new contract, I spotted an advertisement for a new Organist at Bristol Cathedral. Realising that any move would need to dovetail with my BBC appointment, I discussed transferring my office from London to Broadcasting House in Bristol. Having got agreement, I applied for the post at the Cathedral, and in mid-February was short-listed. The process consisted of a communal lunch at the Deanery and a formal interview, after which I was offered the chance to try the Cathedral organ, but didn't, since I needed to get back to London.

Two days later the phone rang, and the Precentor of Bristol Cathedral offered me the post. I replied that I would need to think about it. There was the children's schooling to consider, and how possible it might be to continue to take part in the broadcast Daily Services in London. Over and above all that, we would need somewhere to live, and near the Cathedral. All that Bristol had offered was a vague promise of 'a flat somewhere', and it was because of that lack of clarity that I said no. It would be true to say that there was a certain disappointment at St. Paul's that I'd turned it down – acceptance could have solved all the future contractual wrangling that would occupy too much of their and my time over the next year or so.

Christopher and I continued to work together, though in a personal letter in September, he intimated that the spirit of our agreement over joint responsibility that we had agreed in 1977 was now heading for reversal by the Dean and Chapter.

A pointer to their latest attitude came in early December. Malcolm Hicks, father of one of our senior choristers, asked if his son Christopher could be the treble soloist in a BBC carol concert in which he was playing the organ. Derek Sutton (the head-master) and I both recommended it to the Chapter, who replied no. At the same time, Paul McCartney had again approached us to see if we could supply a treble soloist to sing on the soundtrack of his film *Give my regards to Broad Street*, the recording to be made ten days before Christmas when the choristers had a lot of free time, schoolwork having finished for the term. Again, I thought of Christopher Hicks. To get a quick decision from a member of Chapter, both Derek Sutton and I approached the Canon-in-Residence, Graham Routledge, for permission. Seeing him in the clergy vestry after Evensong, he peremptorily dismissed us with a flat refusal to consider or discuss it.

Once more, the Chapter were flexing their muscles. Undaunted, I rang St. John's College School, Cambridge, and Dr. George Guest, to see if our Tim might be available – the College choir was due to leave for Holland in two days' time, but this could dovetail with Tim coming up to London, doing the recording, and linking up with them at Heathrow Airport. The answer was an enthusiastic yes, and I met Tim at Liverpool Street station where we took a taxi, in which I asked him if he'd ever heard *Eleanor Rigby*, one of the songs in the film. Twenty minutes later we were in Air Studios in Oxford Street with Linda and Paul McCartney and George Martin. Although Tim's voice was breaking and he was about to stop singing treble, he sang the chosen excerpts very professionally and gratefully accepted the offered £150 fee that could have gone to St. Paul's...

I wasn't going to let the matter rest, and a few days after we'd made the recording I hand-wrote a letter to Canon Routledge accusing him of being '*brusque and border-ing on being positively rude to two long-serving employees of the Dean and Chapter, both in highly responsible positions, and both supposedly expert at their jobs*'. I add-ed, '*Whether or not you chose to accept our advice is not the issue, but your manner of listening made me think that it was all a bit of a nuisance for you and too much trouble*'. At the end of the letter, I added that the recording had been successfully made since others had been a lot more helpful than St. Paul's. Canon Routledge ob-viously took exception to what I had written. The letter, in its opened envelope, was thrust back through our letterbox.

Next year was not going to be easy. Over the post-Christmas break, it might be a good thing to see if I could learn anything from George Orwell's *1984* novel...

18

Shades of George Orwell?
St. Paul's 1984

The negotiations over a new contract were to occupy a lot of time in 1984, and the very beginning of the year showed a further hardening in the relationship between the Chapter and myself.

In October 1982, having completed eight years at St. Pauls, I had written to the Precentor to enquire about a possible sabbatical during summer term of the following year. The reply came back that Chapter could not accede to my request *'because it has not accepted the principle of staff sabbaticals'*. I pointed out that this was at odds with a 1978 letter I held on file in which the Registrar had written to me *'...during Christopher's sabbatical...'* At the end of 1983 I thought I'd try again, only to receive a formal reply in January 1984 that *'Chapter has* not *accepted the principle that members of the cathedral staff are entitled to sabbatical leave, and therefore declined to accede to your request.'*

Meanwhile, the terms of the new draft contract were becoming more worrying. The crux was the re-designation of Christopher's title from Organist to Organist and Director of Music, thus placing him in overall charge of the Cathedral's music. This would create the vertical structure that Christopher had already forecast in his letter last year, and a paper clarifying the proposed changes was ringing alarm bells for me. Now in the hands of the Dean and Chapter's legal advisers, in the background was Dean Alan Webster and his dislike of what he had once called 'a two-headed monster' when it came to dealing with musical matters. Two-headed it may have been, but that was the agreement Christopher and I had worked out way back in 1977 before Alan Webster had arrived, and the Chapter's following public announcement that *'the Cathedral music will be in their* joint *charge'*. Although nothing had been said, I could also sense some unhappiness on Christopher's part that he was no longer making decisions about the choir.

If I signed the new contract we would move from the structure in the 1977 document prepared for Chapter when creating the new posts (shown in the top panel in the following diagram) to a new structure that was the basis of the new contracts we were being asked to sign (shown in the bottom panel).

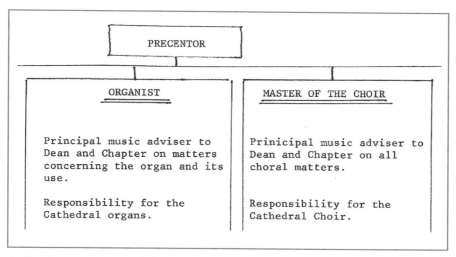

St. Paul's music responsibilities as set out in 1977...

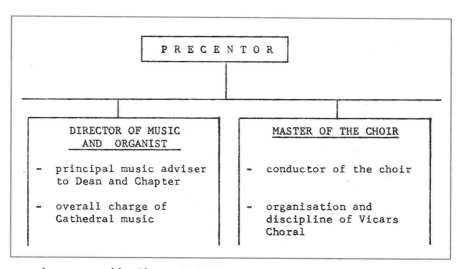

... and as proposed by Chapter in 1984

There was no way I could sign any contract that formalised an arrangement whereby the decision-making about choral matters passed from my hands and I would simply be left as the conductor of the choir. In practical terms, the Director of Music is the person standing in front of the choir each day, and that was even true when John Scott directed the choir and I accompanied – he was the Director of Music for that time. We were heading for an impasse, though, as professionals, everything would outwardly continue as normal, including a rather special recording.

Philips Records had approached the Registrar with a proposal that the Cathedral choir should link up with Dame Kiri Te Kanawa and the English Chamber Orchestra – the recording to be made in All Saints Church, Tooting Graveney, sometime during June. Dame Kiri had been the soloist at the Royal Wedding in 1981, and her *Let the bright Seraphim* solo from that day would be one of the items on the new record.

Before that, May turned out to be memorable – in all the wrong ways. There had been some whispers among the parents that all was not well in the choir school regarding two of the resident masters, with alleged bullying and inappropriate approaches towards their sons. I decided to try and find out if this was true. One day after Evensong, I assembled 20 of the Intermediate and Junior boys in the darkened crypt and formed them into a large circle in which I stood in the centre. I closed my eyes and asked them to switch places with each other so I wouldn't know who was standing where. Asking them to disguise their voices, I posed the direct question – 'Has anyone, at any time, in school been molesting you in a nasty way?' Back came several replies of 'yes'. The parents' suspicions had been confirmed and the only way I could raise it in any official capacity was to write a letter to the Precentor. His reply was quite dismissive. I was told that it was none of my business and that he would report me to Chapter. In later years, John Scott also heard and acted on the same allegations, receiving the same response. In 2002, 2008 and 2009, both masters were jailed on separate counts of indecent assault, and one or more of the victims later received a compensatory payment.

Meanwhile, there had been more pressure on me to sign the new contract, including a visit by David Faull, the Chapter Clerk, to my BBC office. We couldn't come to any agreement, and it was quickly followed by a letter from him, asking me to meet the Dean and Chapter to 'discuss the question of your employment and the terms of your contract'. At the end of our monthly music meeting on 17th May, Bishop Woollcombe, the Precentor, handed me a further letter with the comment, 'I'm afraid this is grievous news, and if I were you, I would blow a gasket.'

The letter contained seven specific points that had led the Dean and Chapter to 'consider with you the termination of your employment at St. Paul's Cathedral.' Their points included: 'Absences from the Cathedral without permission'; 'Arranging for choristers to make recordings without the prior consent of the Dean and Chapter'; and 'Failure to work in co-operation with the Organist.' The letter added, '*Discussions relating to your contract have led the Dean and Chapter to the view that it is not possible to meet your requirements or to accommodate your methods of working, which are incompatible with the needs of the Cathedral as governed by the statutes.*' I had no idea what that last comment about 'the needs of the Cathedral' and 'the statutes' was meant to signify. The Cathedral was there for Worship, and as far as I was concerned, every member of the choir was putting their heart and soul into every Service they sang.

Put in plain English, the Chapter were saying, 'We don't like the way you run the Cathedral choir.' Obviously there had been a vote in one of their meetings, and as often happens in these cases, despite their differences, the clergy closed ranks to present a united front. With the help of Jonathan Hunt, father of one of the choristers, I managed to engage a solicitor to be with me at the Chapter meeting the following week – two days before my 50th birthday. It was short and very formal. There was no point in attempting to discuss, explain or refute any of the points in the letter. The Chapter were adamant that we needed to come to some arrangement whereby I would leave St. Paul's at the end of the current term, in just ten weeks' time. The Dean had got his way.

They recognised that there would be financial implications in my departure, and, probably in the hope of ensuring a 'quiet' exit, they also agreed to meet all my legal fees. It seemed that there were two options: refuse to resign, risking possible dismissal and an inevitable and very public employment tribunal for wrongful dismissal, or simply accept that the management didn't want me to stay. I shared the letter and outcome of the meeting with Buffie, who was rightly indignant, though maybe not surprised that someone who had worked so hard for the Cathedral for the past ten years was being treated like this. But this was St. Paul's…

What would we do next, and where would we go? There were our children to consider; Tim, now 13, and due to move on from St. John's College School; Julia, age ten, would change school in a year or so; and though we had our own small house in Wittering, and I had the part-time BBC job, I would still need to find work elsewhere.

Celebrations for my 50th birthday on 24th May could have been overshadowed by the circumstances. In the end we went ahead with a party at No. 4 Amen Court, whilst at the BBC I was lured to a staff meeting where, in the presence of the whole of

the Religious Broadcasting Department, the day was brightened when I was accosted and 'entertained' by a scantily clad young lady strippagram!

Aside from working out the exact terms of my departure, I discussed the situation with the vicars choral and

A real surprise at the BBC Religious Broadcasting Department staff-meeting on my 50th birthday

several close friends, and in the end it was left to me to tell the boys before the news broke. I was quite open with them, explaining how one left a job, as later reported in the national press:

Mr Rose declined to comment, beyond saying: "It is true that I am leaving St Paul's. Some people are saying that it is sad that no one has asked me to reconsider."

However, according to parents of pupils at St Paul's, Mr Rose was given little choice. He is reported to have told his choir that there were three reasons for leaving a job: retirement, another job, or being forced to leave. He added that he was too young to retire and he had no job to go to, so it was for the third reason he was leaving.

The Daily Telegraph,
Saturday 1ˢᵗ July 1984

Around the same time, we were making the recording with Dame Kiri Te Kanawa and the English Chamber Orchestra, and we needed to put all thoughts of everything else out of our minds. I visited Dame Kiri at her home, playing the piano for her in the repertoire we'd be recording so that I would know her tempi and other musical points before we got to the first session. The record company sent a car to collect me from Amen Court, and we did the first session with just Kiri and the orchestra. The choir sang in the sessions on the following two evenings and everyone, soloist, orchestra, choir and producer, seemed happy with the results, the record being scheduled for release in October. A couple of months later, just after I'd left St. Paul's, I got a message saying that Dame Kiri would like to re-record *Let the bright seraphim*. At that time, I was on the staff at the Canford Summer School of Music, and had to get a train up to London, where they had re-assembled the orchestra and recording equipment in All Saints, Tooting Graveney, just to record this one item. What it is to be a famous singer and have all that influence!

The news of my departure from St. Paul's was now public, as were some of the details of the disagreements with the Chapter.

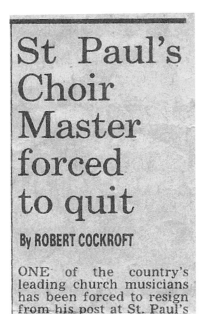

St Paul's Choir Master forced to quit

By ROBERT COCKROFT

ONE of the country's leading church musicians has been forced to resign from his post at St. Paul's Cathedral, London.

Behind the scenes, Andrew Pryce Jackman, former Kingsbury chorister and now a choir parent of Henry, was writing to the musical great-and-good, seeking their support for a petition for my reinstatement. There were also letters to the Bishop of London, the Archbishop of Canterbury, and even the Queen Mother, though in my heart of hearts I knew that nothing was going to change the Chapter's decision. I had a post-resignation conversation with Christopher Dearnley, in which I pointed out that with my departure, the Chapter would now expect him to take back the daily running of the choir. His response was that he would get the new sub-organist to do that. In the end he was instructed to do it himself, though that arrangement was short-lived, and John Scott, the new Sub-Organist, was deputed to take over the choir training, under Christopher's direction – not a happy arrangement, either for John or the choristers.

As well as the recording with Kiri Te Kanawa, my last few weeks at the Cathedral saw us broadcasting Choral Evensong on the Eve of the Ascension – the next time they broadcast I would be at the Cathedral wearing a different hat, as the BBC's producer.

We were now also into the final detailed legal negotiations, including the agreed wording of a testimonial, which, as it turned out, I would not need. Among the many contacts following the news of my impending departure, was a phone call from Canon Peter Pilkington, Headmaster of The King's School, Canterbury. Might I be interested in joining the staff there to work with the school choirs? Paul Neville, the school's director of music, had visited us at the choir school a year or so earlier in the hope of persuading some of the choristers to apply for music scholarships at King's.

It might have been he who had suggested my name to the headmaster, though it was more likely to have been Alan Ridout, who was also on the music staff at the school. Unassuming and greatly underrated as a composer, Alan had been associated with Canterbury for many years, initially writing a great deal of music for the Cathedral choristers and their director, Allan Wicks, and later teaching composition and advanced harmony to O- and A-level students at The King's School.

We arranged that Buffie and I would visit Canterbury soon after I finished at the Cathedral, but now there were the four July Masses to prepare and conduct, as well as all the usual daily Services right up to my very last Evensong on Sunday 29th July. Tongue-in-cheek, I submitted the choices of canticles and anthems for my last week, quite expecting them to be thrown back in my face. They weren't, so we had a week of *There is no Rose* anthems (see overleaf)!

On Sunday 29th July there was a larger than usual congregation at Evensong, and as we processed in I caught sight of some of my cathedral organist colleagues, including Simon Preston from Westminster Abbey. It was so good to have their support that afternoon. At the end of the Service there was an embarrassing moment in

JULY 1984

THE FIFTH SUNDAY AFTER TRINITY   22 JULY   Decani 2
07.30   Mattins (*said*)   Psalm 76
08.00   Holy Communion
11.00   Holy Communion "Coronation" Mass in C (K317)   *W. A. Mozart*
            Communion Motet Jesu, joy of man's desiring *J. S. Bach*
            Introit 697 (EH)
            Hymns 375, 329, 400 (AMR), 318 (EH)
            Preacher: The Reverend Canon Evan Pilkington, Canon Emeritus of St. Paul's
15.15   Evensong   Psalm 102. 1-12   *Rose* Responses
            Magnificat and Nunc dimittis: *Darke* in F
            Anthem: For lo, I raise up   *Charles Villiers Stanford*
            Hymns 221, 26, 169 (AMR)
            Preacher: The Venerable F. W. Harvey, Archdeacon of London, Canon in Residence

MONDAY   23 JULY
07.30   Mattins
08.00 & 12.30   Holy Communion   Psalms 114, 115
17.00   Evensong (*boys' voices*)
            John Wood in G
            Anthem: There is no rose *Britten*

TUESDAY   24 JULY   ST. MARY MAGDALENE
·07.30   Mattins
08.00 & 12.30   Holy Communion
17.00   Evensong and short sermon   Psalm 63
            S. S. Wesley in F
            Anthem: There is no rose *Ronald Corp*
            Preacher: Prebendary H. A. H. Moore, Vicar of St. Stephen, Gloucester Road
            Hymn 556 (AMR)

WEDNESDAY   25 JULY   ST. JAMES THE APOSTLE
07.30   Mattins and Litany
08.00 & 12.30   Holy Communion
17.00   Evensong and short sermon   Psalm 94
            Howells The St. Paul's Service
            Anthem: Give unto the Lord *Elgar*
            Preacher: Prebendary D. E. Barnes, Vicar of St. Peter's, Belsize Park
            Hymn 557 (AMR)

THURSDAY   26 JULY   ST. ANNE, MOTHER OF THE B.V. MARY
07.30   Mattins
08.00 & 12.30   Holy Communion
17.00   Evensong (*men's voices*)   Psalm 119. 145-176
            Plainsong (iv & vi) with fauxbourdons   *Anon*
            Anthem: There is no rose *Anon. Mediaeval*

FRIDAY   27 JULY
07.30   Mattins and Litany
08.00   Holy Communion
12.30   Organ Recital by Peter Sirak
17.00   Evensong   Psalms 126, 127, 128, 130, 131   *Byrd* Responses
            Daniel Purcell in E minor
            Anthem: There is no rose *Joubert*

SATURDAY   28 JULY
08.00 & 12.30   Holy Communion
10.00   Mattins   Venite 6   Psalms 132, 133, 134, 135
            Te Deum/Jubilate   *Tomkins* The second Service
            Anthem: In the Lord put I my trust   *Silas Standage*
17.00   Evensong   Psalms 136, 137, 138
            Henry Purcell in G minor
            Anthem: There is no rose *Gerald Hendrie*
            Hymn 571 (AMR)

MICHAEL BECK, Succentor

My final week at St. Paul's Cathedral

the Dean's aisle when Frank Harvey, the Archdeacon of London, started to talk to the choir about my leaving. He was more than surprised when all the vicars choral walked away leaving him in mid-sentence. The choir parents arranged a tea party at the choir school, while I went to the west front of the Cathedral to do an interview for BBC television, and then on to the choir school for farewells and photographs.

We returned to Amen Court exhausted, but content that up to the last I'd given everything I could to the Services at St. Paul's. Ten years ago they had asked me to come, and I hoped that ten years on I was leaving the choir in a better state and spirit than I had found it. Tuning into the BBC television nine o'clock news, we were quite surprised to see my departure mentioned in the opening headlines, later followed by a full report.

The next day *The Guardian* newspaper carried one letter I have always kept in my personal files, written by Cyril Taylor, the former St. Paul's alto vicar choral who had helped us out so much in those early days at Guildford:

Sir, — Barry Rose, in a Radio 4 News item about his "dismissal" from St Paul's Cathedral as master of the choristers, was asked what he would miss most. He replied unequivocably: "Evensong."

I had served for more than 30 years as a lay singer (vicar-choral) in four cathedral choirs consecutively until, in 1981, after the royal wedding, I was at the receiving end of the cuts at St Paul's. I am sure I would not be alone in my profession if I were to say that Barry Rose puts more love and care into a daily evensong than anyone I have ever known.

It also happens that with that love and care goes a very considerable expertise and rapport with the junior treble line, the like of which I have not met elsewhere, and which will be sorely missed at St Paul's. — Yours sincerely,
Cyril Taylor.
Crayford, Kent.

This chapter of my musical pilgrimage was over. It was time to move on.

19

To the Cradle of English Christianity
Canterbury 1984–1988

I t was Monday 30th July 1984, and in any of the previous nine years I'd have been waking up to the prospect of five weeks' holiday before the Cathedral choir was back on duty again. This year was entirely different. It was time to look to the future.

Having persuaded Rowland Sidwell to come and babysit for us, Buffie and I set off to Canterbury to meet Canon Peter Pilkington, Headmaster of The King's School. Sitting in the train that morning, we were amused to see that the man opposite was reading the *Daily Telegraph* with the page facing us carrying a full report of my departure from St. Paul's the day before.

Emotional swan song for choirmaster

By GRAHAM JONES

AN immaculate rendering of "Bridge Over Troubled Water" by 30 schoolboys in the practice hall of St Paul's Cathedral Choir School was the final, impromptu farewell yesterday for Mr Barry Rose, their ousted choirmaster.

Parents, adult choristers, and visitors listened transfixed as they took in the fact that this was Mr Rose's last moment with the choir.

Then they burst into spontaneous and prolonged applause for Mr Rose, 50, who was asked to leave by the Dean and Chapter after 10 years at St Paul's, following personality clashes.

The Daily Telegraph,
30th July 1984

In Canterbury we were entertained to lunch by Peter, and I immediately warmed to him. As his later obituary would put it: '*His approach to every issue was refreshingly direct, and he had an unerring ability to cut through the waffle and go straight to the point.*'[1]

How different to what we had known at St. Paul's!

Peter was very keen that we should move to Canterbury; timetabling could be slotted around my BBC commitments, and a more than generous salary would be offered, coupled with accommodation for the whole family. Would we like to see the accommodation? We got into his car.

Just over two miles north-east of Canterbury lies the village of Sturry, home to Milner Court, the Junior section of The King's School, and it was there, adjacent to the church and the old mill pond, that we first saw what would become our home for the next four years: Mill Cottage. Built in the 16th century, and Grade II listed, it was a basic two-up two-down dwelling, extended at the back with a small dining room, bathroom, and separate toilet, and the roof space converted into two very small bedrooms. The two main bedrooms on the first floor were more spacious, whilst the small living room and kitchen had a great deal of olde worlde charm, with their low ceilings supported by sturdy oak beams. The garden was tiny, but Peter was quick to offer us a large lawned space just across the lane that would be solely for our use – and we wouldn't even have to mow it.

Mill Cottage

The first thing we realised was that the cottage could not house any of our larger furniture and that there was no space for an office. Peter was equal to the challenge, ferrying us back to the centre of Canterbury and to St. Augustine's, the former Theological College, now occupied by two of the school Houses.

St. Augustine's Abbey, Canterbury

1   From the *Daily Telegraph*, 14th February 2011.

There, above the ancient gatehouse, he showed me a large room, which I could have as an office. That would solve all our storage problems, including my desk, filing cabinets, the heavy upright piano, and even the large sofa from our sitting room in Amen Court.

The last bit of the jigsaw was getting Peter's agreement to wait for four months for me to start, in January 1985. A lot of work was needed to make Mill Cottage suitable for family accommodation, and that would give time for it to be carried out. John Dean, the school's Clerk of Works, would liaise with us about that, and I would negotiate with Norman Robinson, the School Bursar, about all the practical details, including our move. It was an attractive offer, and we decided to accept.

My legal agreement with St. Paul's had given us the use of No. 4 Amen Court for a further six months, and though we were staying on there as a family until the end of December, we would be visiting Canterbury occasionally to sort out schooling for Julia, as well as keeping up to date with the work being done at Mill Cottage.

As it turned out, we also needed to sort out future schooling for Tim. Having left St. John's College School, Cambridge, in July, Tim had gone on to Framlingham College, Suffolk, as a Music Scholar, but had not settled there. Part of that may have been the usual transitional problem faced by many cathedral choristers after they leave the comfortable surroundings where they are the accepted high achievers, only to find themselves as nobodies in a much larger and strange environment. It culminated in Tim running away from school, and us being woken in the middle of the night to collect him from a remote Suffolk village.

We talked about it with Peter Pilkington, who immediately offered Tim a virtually free, unconditional place at King's. This would be in Marlowe, one of the two day-boy Houses, though, as we were later to find out, Peter hadn't run this by Housemaster David Reid as a possibility. After five years of boarding, perhaps a spell of living at home would be good for Tim, and without any further academic examination, he would be accepted at the country's oldest public school.

Back in Amen Court, the press got news of my appointment, and the *Daily Telegraph* published another article.

St PAUL'S OUSTED CHOIRMASTER WINS CANTERBURY JOB

By KENNETH CLARKE

MR BARRY ROSE, ousted choirmaster at St Paul's, has accepted a new position, as Master of Choirs at King's School, Canterbury, which has a strong musical tradition and is famous for its annual festival of music.

Mr Rose, 50, takes up the post in January. With his wife and three children, he will be moving house to the village of Sturry on the outskirts of Canterbury.

Daily Telegraph, *11ᵗʰ September 1984*

In Canterbury, the headmaster and his wife, Helen, hosted a beginning of academic year party in the dining room at St. Augustine's, a few steps from my new office. As well as the staff, we also met and had a warm personal welcome from Robert Runcie, the Archbishop of Canterbury.

Meanwhile, the new academic year had begun at St. Paul's Cathedral Choir School. Whether or not with his agreement, the Chapter had decreed that Christopher Dearnley would take back the training of the choir, with organ accompaniments for the Services now being played on a more regular basis by John Scott, Andrew Lucas, and the then organ scholar, Simon Lole. It was an arrangement that was not to last, and within a few months John Scott had been appointed as full-time Sub-Organist with the responsibility of conducting the choir, albeit under Christopher's direction. This was the very arrangement that had triggered my refusal to sign the new contract all those months before.

I was still in contact with several of the vicars choral, and one of them, Nigel Beavan, told me that shortly after the new term had begun, and after the end of a particularly bad Evensong with some dire singing from the boys, Frank Harvey, the Archdeacon of London, visited the local pub to join the men, saying, 'We made the wrong decision, didn't we?' Nigel and I were to remain close friends until his untimely death, and he later confided that former lawyer and Cathedral Treasurer Canon Graham Routledge, who was spearheading a move amongst Chapter to oust Alan Webster, the Dean, wanted them to approach me to return to the Cathedral. His plans came to nought when he was struck down with an extreme form of progressive cancer and died at the early age of 61.

We wouldn't have accepted anyway, and now, free from any cathedral duties, Buffie and I were able to go to Venice for a relaxed holiday.

The choirs at The King's School were in the capable hands of David Flood, the Assistant Organist at the Cathedral. He and I would be working closely together since the school was responsible for Matins in the Cathedral on most Sunday mornings.

Back at St. Paul's, Nick Ware and I took over the Cathedral for three nights in October to make the first recording of John Scott on the organ. Previously, Christopher Dearnley had refused to let John do this, but we had built it into the legal agreement I had made with the Chapter over my departure, so this time it went ahead. In his inimitable way, John played perfectly, and halfway through the third evening had recorded all the music scheduled for the LP. Coming down to the control room in the crypt, he suggested that he might use the rest of the available time to record the Elgar *Sonata in G,* and that it 'wouldn't take long'. John was as good as his word. Less than an hour later we had a perfect performance, and even though there wasn't room to include it on our record, it was later issued by another company, and is still used as a benchmark by many organists. The Guild Records LP opened with the *Grand Choeur Dialogué* by Eugène Gigout, using the startling sound of the new West End trumpets. When John and I met up in later years, he always said that it was his favourite of all the organ recordings he'd made.

The reviews were ecstatic. Marc Rochester in *The Musical Times* wrote:

> *Barry Rose, the record's producer, knows the building well and has managed to capture the atmosphere without sacrificing clarity. That John Scott has been able to coordinate the West End trumpets with the dome and chancel divisions of the instrument so perfectly is incredible enough; that the recording captures it so vitally almost defies belief.*

Christmas came, and there were a few nostalgic moments when the choristers made their annual visit to Amen Court to sing carols to the residents. They seemed genuinely pleased that we were still living there, though we weren't allowed to invite them in – and anyway, that wouldn't have been possible since most of our belongings were now boxed up, ready for the post-Christmas move to Canterbury.

Early on the morning of 29th December 1984, a large removal van arrived at the entrance to Amen Court. Despite our advice to the Whitstable-based removal firm, they sent too big a vehicle and there was no way it was going to get close to No. 4. In the end it was parked round the corner near No. 1, thus blocking one entrance to the Court. Much of the day was spent carrying everything from No. 4 to the van, and the extra time this took meant that it, and we, left much later than originally planned.

By late afternoon we had arrived in Sturry and the unloading began. All went well until it came to our double bed. It was too big to fit through the small front door of the cottage and up the narrow stairs. The only way to get it in would be by splitting into two and then re-assembling it in our bedroom. It was already dark, and all the other large furniture needed to be taken back into Canterbury and up the stairs to my new office over the gatehouse at St. Augustine's. Our bed would have to be left outside in the front garden of Mill Cottage overnight until we could arrange for someone to come and sort it out for us. We would spend the night sleeping on the mattress. It began to snow, and by next morning the bed was looking very sorry for itself. Later that day it was dismantled by a local craftsman, taken up to our bedroom and re-joined.

All too soon the start of the school terms arrived. Nicola would be going to a near-by playgroup, whilst Julia, due to take the 11-plus exam in a few weeks' time, would be at the local primary school. Tim and I headed off to The King's School. For both of us it was to be a new experience – he as a day-boy, and me, for the first time in my life, working with girl singers (although primarily a boys' school, King's had recently accepted girls into the sixth form).

The Old Synagogue, Canterbury

Full choir rehearsals took place away from the main part of the school, in the Old Synagogue which had been bought by the school in 1982.

Situated in nearby King Street, the full choir rehearsal was after lunch on Fridays. There were also short sectional rehearsals, on Tuesday morning for lower voices, and Friday morning for the upper voices while the rest of the school was at congregational practice. Many of the members were music scholars, and the soprano line was mixed – girls and some younger boys, though there weren't many trebles whose voices were still intact at the age of 13 plus.

Two days after our first rehearsal together they would be leading Matins in the quire of Canterbury Cathedral in front of the whole school and staff, and we would need to have some sort of anthem prepared by then. But what? It was Epiphany, and it needed to be a piece that would make some sort of immediate impact, preferably accompanied. Trawling the choir library, I managed to find Haldane Campbell Stewart's setting of *On this day, earth shall ring*. At our Friday rehearsal I was encouraged by the speed with which the choir learned the notes. With any luck we might have time to polish it and put some real interpretation into it on Sunday morning.

The Synagogue was small – used by the school as a chamber music recital room – and didn't demand any real vocal projection from the singers. Things were *very* different in the Cathedral quire, and on Sunday morning at the pre-Service rehearsal I was immediately struck by just how small a sound the choir was making. However, with David Flood's encouragement on the organ, they gave a spirited performance in the Service, appreciated by many, including the headmaster and several members of staff who sought me out afterwards.

There was no time to talk to the choir – most of them were in the school orchestra whose rehearsal started just 15 minutes later. One thing was certain: if we were to make real vocal progress, we'd need to rehearse in a much bigger space. The Synagogue was far too 'comfortable'.

A month or so later, the choir had to provide the music for a Confirmation Service in the Cathedral, singing some sections of the Communion Service. Again I trawled the choir library and dug out the copies of the *Mass in G* by Franz Schubert, hoping that we'd be able to learn the *Sanctus* and the *Agnus Dei* in time. The *Sanctus* is scored for full choir, and the *Agnus Dei* requires two very able soloists – a soprano and a baritone. At one of our rehearsals I asked if anyone would volunteer to try out the solos in the *Agnus Dei*. None of the girls came forward, but a sixth form boy stood up and offered to have a go. My heart sank. He had the build of a rugby player and spoke in quite a gruff voice. He opened his mouth to sing and out came a lovely warm and musical baritone sound. I discovered that he was Joe Wrench, a former chorister at Salisbury Cathedral, and from the way he phrased his singing, it was obvious that he'd sung the piece there as a treble.

The next time I rehearsed with the girls, one of them did offer to sing the soprano solo, and it was to be the start of a three-year musical partnership which would lead her to both radio and television appearances. Sara was the daughter of Martha and Bob Bee who were then in charge of Luxmoore House. She had been at the local Simon Langton Grammar School for Girls and had come on to King's for two years in the sixth form the term before I arrived. A day-girl, I got the impression that she hadn't really settled into the ethos of the school and hadn't made any friends in the choir, but as soon as she started to sing, I could sense that here was a real golden voice, naturally and beautifully produced. We started to work together on the Schubert and it soon became obvious that she had a real gift for performing, and after the Confirmation Service everyone was asking 'whoever was that wonderful soprano soloist?'

I started offering free singing lessons to anyone in the choir who wasn't already receiving them as part of their music scholarship. The school employed three professional singing teachers: the operatic bass Dennis Wicks; soprano Geraldine Hackett-Jones; and former King's pupil and current Cathedral lay clerk Clifford Lister; and it was they who taught the Music Scholars. I began with several sixth form girls from the choir, as well as some changing boys' voices, hoping to find out how to cope with any vocal problems as we went along.

In addition to the Chapel Choir, my other main responsibility as Master of the Choirs was to rehearse the school Choral Society, a non-auditioned group open to pupils and their parents as well as members of staff and friends. Rehearsals were held each Thursday lunchtime in the large school hall – the Shirley Hall (named after a previous headmaster, the Reverend Canon F.J.J. Shirley). Every other year, alternating with a staged musical, the Choral Society would present an oratorio concert in the Cathedral, and this year it was to be *Solomon* by G.F. Handel. Paul Neville, the school's Director of Music, would conduct the concert, but I had the responsibility of preparing the choir in these Thursday rehearsals, and also supervising a couple of extra Sunday morning sessions nearer the date of performance, at which we were joined by members of the choir from the local Simon Langton Grammar School for Girls.

My working relationship with Paul was professional, though not that close. I think he slightly resented the fact that I worked directly to the headmaster and independently of him. As Lieutenant Colonel Neville OBE RM, Paul had been Director of Music at the nearby Royal Marines School of Music at Deal before being appointed to King's, and from his background he understood the world of orchestral music far more than anything choral or academic. Paul's attitude to his staff was coloured by his many years of military service, and he was used to everyone obeying orders without question. It didn't always make for the happiest of relationships with them; Bill McConnell had served under him as a violinist in the Royal Marines orchestra, and their relationship still seemed to be very much of officer and bandsman.

Early in my first term, the headmaster told me that the BBC would be broadcasting some Daily Services from Canterbury during the second week of May, and he asked if the Chapel Choir would sing the music for four of them? These were to be live broadcasts from the crypt chapel in the Cathedral on Monday, Tuesday, Thursday and Friday, with a recording on the Wednesday for transmission the following Saturday evening. We would have about two weeks to rehearse everything after the school had re-started following the Easter break, and one of the Services would be sung by the boys from King's Junior School. The presenter would be the school's Senior Chaplain, the Reverend Peter Allen.

The Reverend Peter Allen

Energetic, dashing, and pastorally gifted, Peter was a former pupil of King's who had returned to the school in 1967, not just as Chaplain, but also as rowing coach. Housemaster of Linacre and a gifted instrumentalist and singer, Peter was among the first to welcome me to the Common Room where he and I would sit in a corner over coffee and plan informal musical entertainments for King's Week and other occasions.

We chose hymns and anthems to match the themes for each day, and on Monday morning, 6th May (1985) Peter, the Chapel Choir, David Flood, and I assembled in the crypt of the Cathedral to rehearse, do a balance-test, and at 10.45 a.m., broadcast live. Although they sounded slightly nervous, everything went well. I was fortunate to be working with my colleagues from the BBC Religious Broadcasting and Outside Broadcasts Department, and I had the luxury of a whole week when I didn't have to make those early morning journeys up to London.

On Wednesday we made the recording for transmission on the following Saturday evening – there was no live Daily Service that day since the Service commemorating the 40th Anniversary of the end of the Second World War was being broadcast from Westminster Abbey that morning.

The next day we took a break while the boys from King's Junior School sang the broadcast, leaving us to finish the week on Friday morning – much more confidently than we'd started.

It had all gone well, but there was no time to relax – the school Choral Society concert (*Solomon*) was taking place later that month and all of the Chapel Choir would be involved, either as singers or members of the orchestra. This was my first experience of a large-scale concert in the Cathedral with raked seating at the head of the nave. The choir was big – our non-auditioned Choral Society and the choir from Simon Langton Girls' School. The soloists were all connected with King's in some way, either former pupils or current singing teachers. Paul Neville had prepared the orchestra thoroughly and the chorus was also ready. It was a memorable and successful evening, even if the Chapel Choir sounded 'sung-out' at Matins the following morning.

10.45 Daily Service
from the Crypt of **Canterbury Cathedral**
led by **The Rev Peter Allen**
with
the CHOIR OF THE KING'S SCHOOL
Institution of the Eucharist
Praise to the holiest in the height (BBC HB 88);
I Corinthians 11, vv 23-29;
Bread of the world, in mercy broken (Ridout);
In Christ there is no East or West (BP 38)

Radio Times *billing: BBC Radio 4, Friday 10ᵗʰ May 1985*

The school was then gripped by exam fever, and attendance at choir rehearsals dropped off. But now there was another deadline – King's Week – and we needed a choir for that. Described by the school as '*a unique festival of music, drama, art and recreation that has been held every year in the last week of the Summer term since 1952*', it features instrumental and choral concerts in the cloister area of Canterbury Cathedral, the performers in the east walk of the cloister garth, with the audience sitting on the central grassy area.

The advice I received was to use a small group of singers, and if possible, those who would not be taking their A-levels, since there was no way they could attend rehearsals. But what to sing? Obviously not sacred repertoire. The choir library had several madrigals and part-songs, and it was Peter Pilkington who gave me the idea for the final item. Peter had long expressed his appreciation of all things musical from the Victorian era, so as a finale, and especially for him, I arranged the famous Carrie Jacobs-Bond song *A Perfect Day*, featuring our two 'star' soloists, soprano Sara Bee and baritone Joe Wrench. Overwhelmed by tumultuous

Canon Peter Pilkington, Headmaster of The King's School, Canterbury, 1975-1986

applause, we had to sing it again. It looked as though I would have to come up with something similar for next year, but that was a long way off, and we now had some family business to deal with.

Getting to our seaside home in West Sussex had been a short 50-minute journey from Guildford, and though much further away from London, it had still proved a godsend to Buffie and the children. Now, living in Canterbury, it was a long and slow journey of 117 miles, so maybe the time had come to look somewhere nearer for a property. Living in tied accommodation for the past 25 years had meant that, so far, we'd always had a roof over our heads, though I was always aware that should anything happen to me, the family would need to vacate wherever we were then living. I talked to Peter Pilkington who recommended that we buy a property in Canterbury which could be let to tenants as long as we were resident in Mill Cottage. We found a suitable modern house on the east side of the city, and our Wittering property was sold on to Buffie's sister and her husband. Our Canterbury house remained tenanted for the next 11 years, and it was the sitting tenants who purchased it from us in mid-1997, enabling us to buy our house in Somerset.

Moving into an 11-plus area at the beginning of 1985 had meant that Julia would sit the exam without any time for preparation. In London she had been at a progressive primary school and had not been prepared for the exam. We weren't surprised when she didn't pass, and that meant she would be going to the local Frank Montgomery Secondary School in September. Buffie went to look at the school and was not impressed. She then visited St. Edmund's School, where David Gahan, the master in charge of the Junior School, was very helpful, telling her that there was a reciprocal arrangement with The King's School. If Julia went there, and since I was now a member of the King's staff, we would receive a handsome reduction in fees. Julia was accepted and spent three happy years at St. Edmund's, whilst Nicola, who had been at the local playgroup, started at St. Anne's Convent, Sturry, at the same time.

Back at King's, September was the time to find and audition new members of the Chapel Choir. The focus of Sunday morning Matins had now been moved from the quire to the head of the Cathedral nave, with the choir sitting on the raised steps. So that they could get used to the larger space, I moved as many Friday lunchtime rehearsals there as I could, relying on the duty verger's cooperation, and gradually we were able to be more ambitious with our choice of anthems.

It was soon time to work towards the annual Christmas Carol Service in the Cathedral at the end of the second week of December. From then on it would be a completely new experience for me – for the first time in 38 years I'd have no musical duties in the run-up to Christmas, or on Christmas Day itself. We decided to take a pre-Christmas family holiday in the Canary Islands, returning on Christmas Eve.

As we landed at Gatwick the snow started, and by the time we reached the M25-M2 junction to head towards Canterbury, it was a complete white-out. After a nightmare journey we were able to spend a relaxed Christmas Day together at home.

Late in 1985 I'd had an approach from my colleagues in BBC television about a series of programmes they were planning about cathedrals and their mu-

Mill Cottage in the snow, Christmas 1985

sic. As the Department's Music Adviser, I said I'd be happy to help in any way possible, though I hadn't bargained on being the presenter of the programmes. Somehow, and maybe for budgetary reasons, that happened, and we decided that a good place to start would be Canterbury Cathedral (see page 141). The Organist, Allan Wicks, and I came up with several musical items, all with a connection to Canterbury, and I linked them together, on screen, from various parts of the Cathedral.

Filming took place early in 1986, and the first programme was transmitted on Good Friday, 28th March. To help me get used to talking to a camera, the school's Cinematographic Society provided invaluable help by filming and playing back some of the links before the BBC camera crew and producer arrived for the real thing.

NEW SERIES
4.20 Close Harmony
The first in a series of festival visits to English Cathedrals. Each great church provides a magnificent setting for the sounds of a living choral tradition, prepared every day in the Song Room.
Barry Rose, formerly Master of the Choir at St Paul's Cathedral, starts in the Cathedral Church of Christ in Canterbury, the mother church of English Christianity. He introduces the choir and the music specially written for them to sing in praise of God over the centuries.
The choir is conducted by the cathedral organist, DR ALLAN WICKS, and is accompanied by the assistant organist, DAVID FLOOD.

Radio Times *billing – BBC 2 television, Good Friday, 28th March 1986*

It was around that time that Buffie and I were invited to an evening drinks party in the neighbouring village of Fordwich. Our host said, 'There's a musician who lives in our village that I'd like you to meet.' That musician was Colin Towns, self-taught composer and later well known for his incidental music to *Brother Cadfael* and the *Doc Martin* television series. Colin and I found out that we both came from East London, and we formed a close musical friendship which resulted in the choir of St. Albans Abbey (where I would go after The King's School) recording the incidental choral music for *Brother Cadfael*.

King's Week soon came around, and with it the task of finding more madrigals and part-songs for what I now called The Serenade Choir. For Peter Pilkington

I made a double-choir arrangement of *Love's Old Sweet Song* (*Just a song at twilight*), again featuring soloists Joe Wrench and Sara Bee. It proved to be as popular as last year's *Perfect Day*, and we repeated it as an encore.

David Flood, the Cathedral's Assistant Organist, had been appointed to Lincoln Cathedral, and in September his place was taken by Michael Harris. Michael would later take over the Sunday morning Crypt Choir (who sang at the Communion Service there on some Sundays), and was always our accompanist at Matins in the Cathedral.

Another new experience for me would be the school musical – *Guys and Dolls*. Although Paul Neville would be the musical director, I had the responsibility of coaching all the principal singers as well as training the chorus – hard work, especially in *Sit down, you're rocking the boat* with its complicated choreography.

The Chapel Choir was now moving among the musical elite. One of our newer members was Sir Georg Solti's daughter, Gabrielle, who also played the harp. There was a story that Stewart Ross, the Housemaster of School House, had welcomed Lady Solti and Gabrielle as they arrived at the school. Enquiring about the harp, Stewart asked Lady Solti when it might be arriving, to which she replied, 'That all depends on the Maestro.' 'Oh,' replied Stewart brightly, 'I've got a Maestro, and it will easily fit in that.' Lady Solti frowned – she was talking about Sir Georg, who was always referred to as The Maestro – and not to the Austin five-door hatchback car! The Chapel Choir was later filmed singing *Happy Birthday* for the television programme *This is your Life* celebrating his 75th birthday.

There was also an approach from Southern Television for the choir to appear in Sir Harry Secombe's *Highway* programme for Remembrance-tide. Sara Bee and treble Julian Sturt were the accomplished soloists in Andrew Lloyd Webber's *Pie Jesu*, filmed at the University of Kent with picture windows overlooking the Cathedral in the dis-

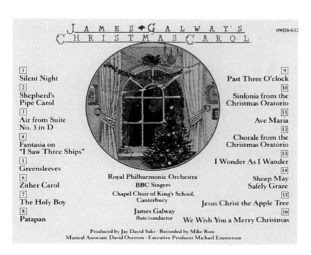

tance. Sir Harry was so impressed with Sara's singing that he invited her to sing as a soloist in another of his programmes. Sara also featured as soprano soloist in Capital Radio's Christmas concert in Holy Trinity Church, Sloane Street, London, where she was accompanied by The Wren Orchestra.

We also had an invitation to make a Christmas record with James Galway, though it meant a trip to London to do so. On a

Sunday, after Matins, we travelled to the RCA Studios in London where we joined James Galway, the Royal Philharmonic Orchestra, and the BBC Singers for an afternoon recording session. The choir sang three items on its own and the CD was issued in time for Christmas 1986.

The Choral Society sang Mendelssohn's *Elijah* in the Cathedral, and there was a nice personal connection with soloists David Johnston (tenor), who had been our first soloist with The Jacobean Singers, and Mark Peterson (baritone), former boy chorister from my time at Guildford Cathedral. The performance also included a group of senior girls from Benenden School, who sang the angelic trio *Lift thine eyes* facing away from the audience as I conducted them from the highest point of the raked seating.

The next school musical was Gilbert and Sullivan's *Iolanthe* for which I was again vocal coach to the soloists, all from the Chapel Choir, as well as training and rehearsing the chorus.

Now accustomed to school life and routine, Canterbury was very much suiting us as a family, though early in 1988, that would all change when I was asked to give some advice about a new Master of the Music at St. Albans Abbey.

Up until then I had given up any idea of ever returning to cathedral music...

The Rose family, 1987

20

Canterbury to St. Albans
1988

The cathedral city of St. Albans lies 25 miles due north of London. Named after Alban, the country's Protomartyr (first martyr), the huge Abbey church bearing his name sits on a small hill, impressively visible from a distance, though from the city, hidden behind the shops and streets that surround it. Once the home of a prestigious and prosperous Benedictine monastic community, the building, including Alban's shrine, was pillaged and desecrated in 1539 during King Henry VIII's purge of all similar foundations, and left in a ruinous state. It was later sold to the townspeople and such parts as were habitable became their parish church, whilst the lady chapel was used as a grammar school.

It was not until over 300 years later that local amateur architect and wealthy benefactor, Lord Grimthorpe, took over its restoration from George Gilbert Scott, re-roofing and making safe England's longest nave, and adding a new west facade in a flamboyant, and later much criticised, Victorian gothic style.

Designated as a Cathedral in 1877, having previously been part of the Diocese of Winchester, it assumed the title of The Cathedral and Abbey Church of St. Alban.

I had visited the city and Abbey as a schoolboy, as well as attending Evensong on that day in 1960 when I had been interviewed for the job at Guildford. Through a succession of highly skilled Masters of the Music, the choir had earned a glowing reputation, widely known through its broadcasts, recordings, and the later St. Albans International Organ Festival (IOF), founded by Peter Hurford, Master of the Music from 1958 to 1978. Its choristers were all local, drawn from different schools in and around the city, though their routine was similar to many of the established choral foundations. On four weekday

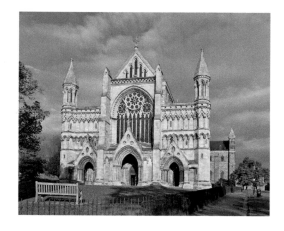

mornings they rehearsed at the Abbey before school, returning to sing Evensong on their own on Monday, Tuesday and Thursday. On Friday evening there was a practice for the full choir, and the boys and men sang Evensong on Saturday, together with two or three Services each Sunday. This was the pattern that Peter had inherited from his recent predecessors, Meredith Davies (1947-51) and Peter Burton (1951-57), and would be continued by his successors, Stephen Darlington (1978-85) and Colin Walsh (1985-88).

Stephen had been organ scholar at Christ Church, Oxford, under the legendary Simon Preston, who had previously run the St. Albans choir for a year while Peter Hurford was away in the USA. Although I had heard Stephen's recordings as accompanist for the Christ Church choir, the first time I met him was in Canterbury Cathedral where he was then Assistant Organist. The occasion was one of the weekly BBC Choral Evensong broadcasts, and in conversation afterwards, I sensed that Stephen was ready for a move and wanted to run his own choir.

One day the phone rang in my BBC office. It was the Very Reverend Peter Moore, Dean of St. Albans. Peter Hurford was stepping down from his Abbey appointment to pursue his already flourishing career as a solo organist. The Dean said, 'You see a lot of young organists as you travel around producing Choral Evensong – who should I be thinking of as Peter's successor?' Top of the list of names I mentioned was Stephen: 'ambitious and ready for a move' was how I described him. The Dean had obviously taken other soundings, and with his own connection as a graduate of Christ Church, Oxford, he must have been very gratified when he appointed Stephen as his next Master of the Music – someone who had started his musical career at the same college ('The House' as it is also known).

Over the next seven years, Stephen brought new life and vigour to the choir, at the same time becoming the conductor of the St. Albans Bach Choir – a post usually held by the Master of Music. In 1984 he was invited to return to Christ Church as Organist and Director of Music. Again the Dean rang me, both at the BBC and at home, but this time he already seemed to have a favoured candidate, and I sensed he was seeking my approbation rather than advice. Colin Walsh was another former organ scholar of Christ Church, and had since moved on to be Assistant Organist at Salisbury Cathedral. What did I think about the possibility of him becoming the new Master of the Music at St. Albans? I was hesitant about giving any opinion; I'd not seen Colin at work since his days in Oxford, and then only as a university organ scholar. Also, I knew that the choral set-up at Salisbury, where the boys were all boarders at the Cathedral's own school, was very different from St. Albans.

It may have been the connection with 'The House' that swayed the Dean, and Colin was duly appointed, taking up residence in St. Albans in September 1985. Two and a half years later, on successive days in March 1988, I visited the Abbey as the BBC's producer of Choral Evensong. The first day was a Tuesday, recorded for future transmission, and the following afternoon was a live broadcast at the usual time of 4.00 p.m. Both Services were sung in the enclosed quire area, and my immediate impression of the choir was of a tightly knit and efficient musical team, but one that produced a much smaller and more restrained sound than I had remembered from Stephen Darlington's days. I also sensed some sort of undercurrent among some of the more experienced lay clerks who seemed to want to be allowed to sing out in a more full-blooded way. Whatever their views and feelings, the choir gave us two first-rate broadcasts.

It was at the end of the second evening that I learned that Colin had just left St. Albans to travel to Lincoln Cathedral, to be interviewed the next day for the post of Organist and Master of the Choristers. From some of the St. Albans lay clerks I gathered that all was not well with relations between them and Colin; the Dean and Colin; and the St. Albans Bach Choir and Colin. Perhaps the interview at Lincoln had come at the right moment – for all parties. He was appointed, and whilst talking about another BBC matter with David Ireson, the senior lay clerk at St. Albans, I expressed the hope that Colin's successor might perhaps be a little more experienced than previous appointees.

It was now Holy Week, and term had ended at The King's School, Canterbury. I had agreed to accompany the Fauré Requiem in the chapel of Bramdean School, Exeter, on Good Friday. The day before, I was practising alone in the chapel when the headmaster walked in to tell me that there was a phone call for me. It was the Dean of St. Albans. Evidently he'd rung home and had been told where I was. Did I have any names to put forward as a possible successor to Colin Walsh? It was not an ideal time to have a long conversation, so taking the same line as my conversations with David (who I later learned had put my name forward to the Dean), I suggested that perhaps the time had come for someone who had already run his own cathedral choir to come to St. Albans, rather than an assistant organist, as on previous occasions. The Dean's response was immediate: 'Well what about you,' he said, 'would you consider it?' Somewhat taken aback, I said I'd need to talk to Buffie.

Our three children were settled at schools in Canterbury, and I was very happy with my job at The King's School and its much shorter terms than cathedral choirs. There was the downside of the early morning commute to the BBC on two or three days each week, and I didn't quite have the same rapport with new headmaster, Anthony Phillips, as I had enjoyed with Peter Pilkington.

We decided to visit St. Albans during the post-Easter break, spending time with the Dean who intimated that he'd very much like me to take the job. We also visited the three-bedroomed Master of Music's house at No. 31 Abbey Mill Lane which, although in an attractive situation, was too small for a family whose three children were at the age where they now needed a bedroom of their own. 'That's no problem,' said the Dean, 'I will arrange for an extra bedroom to be added to the house, and at the same time, an en-suite bathroom for the master bedroom.' And less than two years later he was as good as his word.

Throughout the whole of this process I was totally unaware that the post had already been nationally advertised, a short-list drawn up and dates for interviews and auditions arranged. Inevitably there was going to be some justifiable resentment from the shortlisted candidates over my appointment, but that was something that the Dean would need to deal with – and did.

I gave my notice at The King's School and was surprised to receive a personal hand-written note from the Archbishop of Canterbury. Robert Runcie had been Bishop of St. Albans before his translation to Canterbury, and his note intimated that my move could well hasten his retirement back to St. Albans (he had always been a great supporter of The King's School Choir when we sang in the Cathedral, and often came to find us to say thank you).

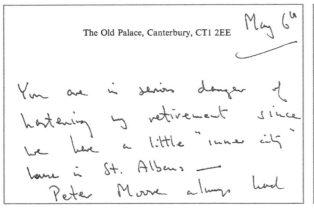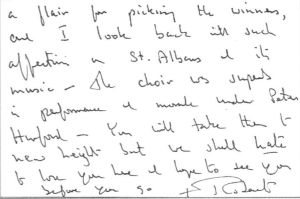

'You are in serious danger of hastening my retirement since we have a little "inner city" house in St. Albans – Peter Moore always had a flair for picking the winners, and I look back with such affection on St. Albans and its music – The choir was superb in performance and morale under Peter Hurford – You will take them to new heights but we shall hate *to lose you here and hope to see you before you go. +Robert'*

Our last term at King's finished with the traditional King's Week concerts, culminating in Speech Day, which this time I had to attend since there were gracious farewell speeches about members of staff who were leaving.

Meanwhile at St. Albans, Andrew Parnell, the Assistant Master of the Music since 1977, was also due to leave. I gathered that his contract had come to an end and that it was not going to be renewed. Knowing Andrew's experience and skill, not just as an organist but also as a choral director, I hoped I could persuade him to stay on in a new musical relationship in which we would work harmoniously together.

We met and I explained that as far as I was concerned we would be equal colleagues, and that we'd make an ideal musical team. I would need his experience and wisdom when I started. Much to my relief he agreed to stay, and I persuaded the Dean that he should be re-appointed. As well as choosing all the choir music for my first month in office, Andrew became the musical director of the St. Albans Bach Choir for the whole academic year. This gave me a chance to get used to the life of the Abbey, as well as continuing with my job at the BBC, now a much shorter train ride than I'd been used to for the past three and a half years. It also avoided clashing with the Monday evening rehearsals of The Singers of London, though I would need to step down as their conductor in a year's time.

From my first days at St. Albans, Andrew and I shared the musical duties almost equally, whilst he combined his work at the Abbey with his teaching post as Director of Music at nearby St. Albans School. We were both assisted by an organ scholar; Nicholas Robinson had already been appointed and arrived at the same time as me, early in September 1988. A former head chorister at St. George's Chapel, Windsor, where his father was Organist, Nick was starting his first year at the Royal Academy of Music. He would play for some Evensongs each week, including those that Andrew directed, and would also be the official accompanist for the St. Albans Bach Choir.

We moved to St. Albans in August 1988. Julia and Nicola started their new schools a couple of weeks later – Julia to St. Albans Girls' School, and Nicola to the Abbey Primary School, just across the way from our house. Tim, now 17, went to the local Oaklands College for a while to take some GCSE exams.

It was time to become a cathedral musician – again.

21

Getting Started (Again)
St. Albans 1988–1990

My first rehearsals with the boys were a voyage of discovery, both for them and me. Morning rehearsals began at 7.50 a.m. and ran until 8.35 a.m. when there was a quick exodus by those boys who were at schools some distance away from the Abbey. They were usually ferried by one of their parents, who sat patiently in the car after dropping them off some ten minutes before the rehearsal began. Any boys who attended St. Albans School or the Abbey Primary School, a stone's throw away, were able to take their time leaving.

The established morning pattern was that the boys would first assemble in the Abbey song school. At the start of the practice, a register was called by the head chorister or one of the choir 'prefects' (known as Woollam Scholars). Wearing older practice cassocks, they would then make their way down the 50 or so steps into the Abbey and to the nave choir-stalls, between which we'd already set up the piano. I was very keen to use the nave as often as possible since it was a big space to fill with sound, and it would give them the chance to gain more vocal projection. Colin Walsh had moved Sunday Evensong into the enclosed quire, and since all weekday Evensongs and Sunday morning Eucharists also took place there, that had only left the fortnightly Matins and any diocesan Services being sung in the nave.

There was no shortage of experience or musicianship amongst the boys I inherited, though there were some rather odd vowel sounds being produced by the leaders, and I was anxious that these did not get passed on to the younger boys. Their physical well-being was looked after by long-serving Mistress of the Robes Carolyn Lewis-Barclay, assisted by Margaret (Miggi) Sharp, mother of Chris, one of the newer choristers. Rehearsing in the nave left the song school free for probationers' practices. These were equally shared by Andrew, the organ scholar and myself, and since there was a Friday evening practice for the choristers, that left me free to work with the probationers alone each Friday morning – I used to call it the most important practice of the week, for here was the future of the choir. Friday evenings were a long sing for the boys, beginning with a 45-minute rehearsal in the nave. They were then joined by the 12 lay clerks (the men of the choir), and after 15 minutes or so of full choir rehearsal, they took a short refreshment break, returning for another 30 minutes before leaving around 8.30 p.m.

My first full choir practice on Friday was an extremely quiet affair. I got the impression that the lay clerks were summing up this man they'd heard so much about, to see if he could actually live up to his reputation of being an able choir trainer. The atmosphere was a lot more relaxed when we repaired to the pub after rehearsal, and gradually as the weeks went by, we struck up a musical and personal rapport which gave them the confidence and the opportunity they'd been seeking to sing out a lot more, especially in the great spaces of the nave.

There was a wide range of ages and vocal experience among the lay clerks. Some were in commerce, some were teachers, and one was starting a career in singing. On my arrival I found that there were two vacancies (one tenor and one alto), and these places were quickly filled: Ian Wicks, the tenor, was a teacher and also an accomplished organist, whilst Gavin Rogers Ball, the new alto, was a first study singing student at the Royal Academy of Music. Of the other ten, basses David Ireson, Kenneth Burgess and Simon Gaunt were also teachers, whilst altos Graham Barton, Simon Blake, and Tony de Rivaz, David Martin-Smith (tenor) and bass Roderick McPhee were all in commerce in one way or another. Senior tenor, Tony Edwards (known to us all as T), worked for the public transport section of the County Council, whilst tenor Vernon Kirk was making his way as a professional singer.

Throughout the process of my appointment, we were helped and encouraged by the Reverend Christopher Collingwood and his wife Sue. Although holding the title of Precentor, and officially responsible for the Abbey's ceremonial and singing the priest's part in the Services, the post was quite a lowly one in the clergy hierarchy, not even warranting a Minor Canon's title.

The Abbey was (and still is) an incredibly busy place, both as a Diocesan Cathedral and a flourishing Parish Church, and it was for the Sunday morning Parish Eucharist that there was another group of singers known as the 9.15 Choir. Each Saturday they rehearsed in the song school from midday onwards, usually taken by the organ scholar. I decided otherwise, and with Andrew, started to take their rehearsals. We hoped this would give them more of a sense of official musical identity, whilst also knowing the way we worked when they teamed up with the boys and men on occasional Sunday mornings. They were not an auditioned group, though several of them had, and still did, sing elsewhere in other church choirs. Initially they practised and led the hymn-singing, but it wasn't long before they were learning short motets to be sung either at the Communion or occasionally as a featured anthem. We were also to spend some family time together since both Buffie and Nicola joined the choir. It was Nicola's first choral experience, and was to lay the foundation for her audition and acceptance as one of the first members of Salisbury Cathedral girls' choir in September 1991.

In our first few months at St. Albans I made a few minor changes over rehearsal routines and in which part of the Abbey the choristers and lay clerks would sing Services. But the most obvious change, both for choir and congregation, would be at the annual Nine Lessons and Carols Services. These were held on two successive evenings, and I was told that they always began with the choir singing *Eia, susanni* from the *Oxford Book of Carols*. I don't know how this tradition had begun, but it seemed that both St. Albans and Guildford Cathedral shared the wish not to start with the usual *Once in Royal David's City*. My reasoning for not doing at Guildford was purely musical. People were so used to hearing the perfection of the King's College, Cambridge, choir on Christmas Eve, and we, as a new choir, would never be able to reach those musical heights.

At St. Albans I decided to re-invent the start of the Carol Services, with an unaccompanied solo treble singing the first verse of *Silent Night* from the organ loft, and the choir answering with verses two and three from the south presbytery aisle. That would immediately be followed by a short organ fanfare and straight into the congregational hymn, *O come, all ye faithful*. I'd always regarded this hymn as an Invitatory, rather than being placed, as it usually is, at the end. After all, in the first verse of the hymn we all heartily sing *O come ye, O come ye to Bethlehem*, and that ties in so well with the words of the traditional Bidding Prayer near the beginning: '*and in heart and mind to go even unto Bethlehem...*'

But there was also a practical reason for this move. So large were the congregations at both Services that they spilled over in the quire and even into the lady chapel, so it seemed only fair that they should not only hear, but also see the choir at close quarters before we processed under the organ screen into the nave.

Easter 1989 also brought innovation: a long-awaited choir tour, and a new musical composition for a Good Friday gathering of Sunday School children in the refectory while the three-hours Service was taking place in the Abbey. Organised by Sub-Dean, Colin Slee, and Mark Bonney, the Chaplain, they brought in an electronic keyboard to accompany the singing. Colin asked if I could set the text that both he and I had seen pinned to the door in the Precentor's kitchen: *Risen Lord, give us a heart for simple things, love, laughter, bread, wine and dreams...* It would need to be melodically simple since the children would learn and perform it during the 90 minutes or so that they were there. They had a keyboard player and Mark played the flute, doubling the melody.

It was rather poignant that Colin, who died in 2010 whilst he was Dean of Southwark, specifically requested that it be sung at the end of his funeral, for which I

made a new arrangement for SATB choir, and was privileged to conduct the Southwark Cathedral choir singing it.

In March I was elected as one of the 300 Fellows of the Royal Academy of Music. The moving spirit behind this honour was the Principal, Sir David Lumsden, with whom I had worked on a few occasions when he was Director of Music at New College, Oxford.

One of the first things I'd learned about the Abbey choir was that there had been a projected tour to Denmark, scheduled to take place just after Easter the previous year (1988), but that had been cancelled. Christopher Collingwood, the Precentor, had made some contacts in Holland and had allayed the choir's disappointment by helping to arrange a trip there immediately after Easter (1989). Most of the venues were already in place by the time I arrived, and I learned that we would be based in the village of Schellinkhout, a small town in North Holland, whilst giving concerts or singing Services there and in several large churches, including Naarden, Hilversum, Leiden, Amsterdam and Haarlem. Travel to and from Holland would be by plane from nearby Luton airport, and we would have a hire-coach to ferry us around when we got there.

On the Tuesday after Easter we set off. The next six days were hectic, the busiest day being Sunday (Easter 1), which as far as we know still remains a record output for any choir on tour – before or since! We wanted the whole choir to have one day free of singing, so we decided to cram three things into that Low Sunday: in three different cities. The day began in the Roman Catholic Cathedral in Haarlem, where we rehearsed with the boys from their choir school before jointly singing the morning Mass. Leaving the Cathedral to a standing ovation, everyone piled into the coach, eating sandwiches etc. as we made the 20-mile journey to Amsterdam.

Once there, the coach dropped us near the maze of canals in the inner city, and carrying cassocks, surplices and music folders, we made our way through the narrow alleys of the Red-Light district towards the Oude Kerk (the Old Church). Needless to say, there were very mixed reactions to the ladies sitting in the windows, scantily clad and displaying their obvious physical assets! Several of the lay clerks hung back, admiring the views, whilst we quickly shielded and shepherded the boys towards the church.

After an hour-long Eastertide Festal Evensong, there was a mad rush to pack cassocks, surplices and music, carry them back to the rendezvous point with the coach, and quickly find a seat and relax on the 28-mile journey to the university city of Leiden. There we were set down outside the huge Hooglandskerke, easily the largest church building we had seen in the past week. There was no time for a meal – that would have to wait until later on in the evening – and although we were singing the same Evensong music as in Amsterdam, the church choirmaster had also asked for a short recital at the end of the Service, so those items had to be rehearsed, especially the accompanied ones. Andrew Parnell managed the ancient and none-too-well tuned organ masterfully, perched up on high in a very small gallery.

Every member of the choir showed incredible stamina, both musically and physically, and exhausted but elated, everyone dispersed for a relaxed dinner afterwards. We'd done it – four Services, three concerts, and a Saturday morning masterclass for choir directors and singers. Tomorrow would be that well-earned day off before returning to St. Albans and the remainder of the choir's Easter break.

If the spring of that year had been a change from routine for all of us, so it was to be in summer, especially for me, with the Dedication of the re-glazed north transept rose window, my first BBC Evensong in June (on the eve of St. Alban's Day), my first International Organ Festival, and the much talked about annual choir camp.

The rose window at St. Albans

Lord Grimthorpe's large rose window in the north transept had been filled with clear glass for over 100 years, and the Dean and Chapter had commissioned Alan Younger to create new coloured glass – a project that would take him nearly two years to complete.

Sponsored by the international chemical company, Laporte Industries Ltd., the themes of the window were the Trinity – God the Father, God the Son, God the Holy Ghost – and the four elements – Earth, Fire, Air, and Water. A special Service was planned for early June, to be attended by Diana, Princess of Wales, and we needed some special music.

Our immediate neighbours in Abbey Mill Lane were Ray and Hazel Ward. Ray was an executive at the Luton headquarters of Laporte and also a keen amateur organist. Through that connection we were able to commission Alan Ridout to write a set of pieces to match the themes of the glass. Entitled *Canticle of the Rose*, part of the work was played by Andrew Parnell on the day of the Dedication, with the final fanfare leading neatly into an unaccompanied festive Anglican chant setting of Psalm 150, sung by the choir in the north transept immediately following the Dedication.

It was a great day in the life of the Abbey, and the Service was followed by a celebratory lunch to which both Buffie and I were invited. Despite having provided the music at her wedding in St. Paul's eight years earlier, I had never met Princess Diana. Today Buffie and I were on the same table and were able to chat with her over lunch. Interestingly, she told me that her favourite piece of music was the Requiem – evidently she had taken part in the Fauré setting whilst at boarding-school in Kent. Eight years later, following her untimely death, a section of the Requiem was sung at her funeral in Westminster Abbey – not the Fauré, but the larger-scale setting by Verdi – someone else may have simply heard her say that her favourite piece of music was 'the Requiem'. I still reckon they got it wrong.

There was no time to relax as it was straight on to Albantide (22nd June) and my first broadcast Evensong with the choir on Wednesday 21st June. Unlike the two previous BBC Evensongs the year before, during Colin Walsh's time as Master of the Music, we decided to broadcast from the nave, choosing music on quite a large scale. The Magnificat and Nunc Dimittis were sung to the double choir setting in F (*Collegium Regale*) by Charles Wood, and the anthem was *Light out of darkness*, a chorus from Edward Elgar's oratorio *The Light of Life* (*Lux Christi*).

Just 21 days later it was time for the IOF. Founded by Peter Hurford in 1963, the St. Albans International Organ Festival was intended as a showcase for the then newly built Harrison and Harrison organ. Originally an annual competition in solo playing and improvisation, it was now held biennially, and a more recent innovation had been a Three Choirs concert in which the Abbey choir was joined by choirs from two other cathedrals or collegiate choral foundations. Those invited for the July 1989 Festival were Christ Church, Oxford, and Chichester Cathedral.

I gathered that the format for the concert would include each choir singing on its own, spaced out at various points in the nave, joining together in polychoral items (at that extreme distance apart), and the second half taking place at the front of the nave with all three choirs grouped together. In correspondence and later meetings with Stephen Darlington (formerly of St. Albans and now at Christ Church) and Alan Thurlow (Chichester), we settled on a programme that would include Zoltan Kodály's *Missa Brevis* as the second half.

Previous Masters of the Music, including Stephen, had also been the Artistic Director of the International Organ Festival, but they had already appointed someone for the 1989 Festival by the time I arrived, and anyway, I was not considered to be a recital organist of national or international standing. I thought it might help dispel that view if, apart from directing the three choirs in some items in the concert, I actually played a solo item. I decided on Sigfrid Karg-Elert's *Third Symphonic Canzona* to end the first half. Scored for organ, solo violin and off-stage four part upper-voice choir, Andrew Parnell conducted the choristers and some altos from Chichester, Christ Church and St. Albans under the organ loft and out of sight of the audience. The solo violin part, also in the distance, was played by Maurice Brett, formerly co-leader of the BBC Symphony Orchestra, who was then living nearby in Hatfield. The effect of the choral sound fading away was achieved by gradually closing the door of the pulpitum, behind which the choir was standing.

All of the music had to be rehearsed on the afternoon of the concert, the visiting choirs arriving around lunchtime. There was an interesting moment in Alan Ridout's 12-part *Corde Natus* when, in one of the tutti sections, the Christ Church choir at the west end of the nave appeared to be singing something totally different from Chichester and ourselves. After a few minutes' cacophony we stopped, and on comparing scores, found that Christ Church had a complete page missing from theirs!

Andrew Carwood, their choir librarian, made a hasty trip to the Administrator's office to photocopy the page, and like true professionals, the Christ Church choir sight-read the missing part.

⁓

My first IOF safely negotiated, it was now time for Buffie, Nicola and me to face the delights of choir camp. These days the word camping can have several meanings, but this was the original, basic version – ex-army tents in a field, washing in a stream, and a toilet which was a deep pit over which you stood or sat on a wooden plank, heaping earth on to whatever had passed from your front or rear end. The place was the village of Luccombe in rural west Somerset, and I gathered that attendance was compulsory for all choristers and probationers; expected, often more in hope than ful-filment, by the lay clerks; and virtually obligatory for the Master of the Music. Camp always took place at the end of summer term, after a couple of days of pre-rehearsing for the boys, and usually lasted a week – beginning on a Saturday with the 150-mile journey in a hired coach.

The choice of Luccombe as the venue could well have had something to do with the fact that Peter Hurford had often played at the village church during his school days. It was also the place to which the former Dean, The Very Reverend Cuthbert Thicknesse, had retired in the late 1950s. Peter Hurford had been born in Minehead, and there is a story that when the boys were singing the Walford Davies setting of *God be in my head*, Peter would ask them to find the copy of *God be in Minehead*!

On the first day of the 1989 choir camp my niece was getting married so we would have to make our own way to Luccombe, arriving there late on Saturday evening. To save disturbing the boys after lights out, we arranged to stay with the local vicar, close to the church where, the following morning and afternoon, we would sing the Services. Andrew Parnell and his wife Sally had taken over the whole organisation of camp, and that included recruiting an advance party of ex-choristers who had gone down two or three days before, unpacked the army-surplus tents from the local barn where they'd been stored, and erected them in the field.

By the time the boys' coach arrived, everything (including the hole in the ground) was ready. Andrew had also rehearsed the men and boys of the choir in church on the Saturday evening, so all I had to do on that Sunday morning was to turn up in my best suit for a short run-through before we sang the Eucharist. After that it was back to the field for lunch, and then to the church again for rehearsal and Choral Evensong. That was the only formal part of the week – it was now time to dress very casually and take part in the activities and walks. The activities included soccer and baseball matches on the field, whilst the walks were up to the top of Dunkery Beacon, along

St. Albans Abbey Choir, September 1989

the precipitous coastal path towards Porlock, and on the penultimate day whilst camp was struck (dismantled), to Minehead. Each of these had a sort of carrot on a stick at the end: cream teas after Dunkery and the coastal path, and fish and chips and slot machines in Minehead.

The last night of camp was always special. All the tents had now been cleared from the field, so there was a general sleep-over in the church using every possible available space, both at pew and floor level. The following morning the boys and their supervising adults piled back into the coach, returning to St. Albans at the beginning of August and the start of a five-week holiday from choir.

In September 1989, as we re-assembled for the new term, I made my first acquaintance with the St. Albans Bach Choir as their new conductor. Our first concert was to be in November, treading a traditional path with the repertoire – Gabriel Fauré's Requiem and *Cantique de Jean Raçine*, with Haydn's *Nelson Mass* as the second half.

Around the same time, the boy choristers were working with Andrew Parnell, taking part in a concert performance of Carl Orff's *Carmina Burana* in London's Royal Festival Hall, with the London Philharmonic Choir and Orchestra conducted by Franz Welser-Möst. A week or so later they recorded it at the famous Abbey Road

Studios, while I started to prepare the Bach Choir for the annual Saturday afternoon and evening carol concerts which each year raised several thousands of pounds for chosen charities.

Meanwhile, we'd had an informal approach from Sky TV to see if there might be a possibility of filming a Service of Christmas Lessons and Carols in the Abbey. Sky had started transmissions in February 1989, and this was to be their first Christmas on television screens across the U.K. We guessed that they were looking for something very traditional, maybe akin to the BBC's annual TV transmission from King's College, Cambridge. The Dean agreed that we could mount a special Service, to be recorded live in the week leading up to Christmas, using the quire and other parts of the east end of the Abbey.

We worked out a programme of music that would dovetail with the carols we would be singing at our own Nine Lessons and Carols, and also invited the St. Albans Bach Choir to take part. Television sound is not always well balanced when it comes to choral music, so I arranged that the sound-producer would be Chris Rees, one of my colleagues at the BBC who had occasionally worked on the weekly Choral Evensong. He would give us the best possible balance.

A few days before the transmission, the Abbey resembled a building site rather than a church, with scaffolding being erected for the lights, and sound engineers slinging wires for suspended microphones in the quire, the crossing, and the north transept. The evening before the recording there was an extended rehearsal and balance-test, and the following evening, in the presence of an invited congregation, the Service took place, filmed exactly as it happened.

It was not perfect, either technically or musically, but there was a real sense of occasion that came across in the transmission, as though the viewer was eavesdropping on a Service that was already taking place. We watched the transmission in a local pub (we didn't have Sky TV at home), but didn't really get much of the effect of either the music or the speech because of the noise in the bar. There were some good close-up shots of lesson readers David Ireson and Rory Lumsdon, as well as soloists Richard West (treble), Vernon Kirk (tenor), and basses Simon Gaunt and Rod McPhee.

Rod was due to stand down from the choir at Christmas and I needed to find a comparable replacement. After the IOF rehearsal in July 1989, Michael McCarthy, one of the basses in the Christ Church, Oxford, choir had introduced himself. In the course of our conversation I gathered that he came from Sudbury, near Wembley (not too far from St. Albans), and could well be interested in singing with us should a vacancy arise. It was to be the start of a very happy association for both of us – Michael taking Rod's place as Decani Bass 2 in January 1990, as well as vocally coaching some of the probationers and junior choristers. That work was to lay the foundation for Michael's later distinguished career as a choral director, founding and directing the treble-line Schola at London's Oratory School, and from there moving on to the prestigious post of Director of Music at the National Cathedral in Washington, D.C. in the USA.

A former first-study singer at London's Guildhall School of Music, Michael had a pleasing and technically accomplished baritone voice. A few weeks after he arrived, in late January 1990, we began recording sessions for a Lammas Records CD. Entitled *A Crown of Light* and sponsored by Laporte Industries, it was to include some music associated with the newly re-glazed rose window, including Alan Ridout's complete organ suite, *Canticle of the Rose*. Michael was more than slightly taken aback (as were his colleagues) when, in one of those sessions, I asked him to sing the extended baritone solo in Ernest Walker's *Lord, Thou hast been our refuge*. He had never sung the piece before, and it was not made any easier by some meant-to-be-helpful comments over technique and interpretation from some of the other lay clerks, as well as a sort of silent resentment from some of his bass colleagues, each probably thinking that they should have been the soloist. In the end it was beautifully sung, catching the mood of the text and music to perfection.

With such a talented back row in the choir it was inevitable that there would be future changes, and one of the delights of what could have been a difficult situation in finding suitable replacements was to welcome former St. Paul's choristers from my time there, all now experienced and accomplished adult singers: alto Jeremy Burrows (former choral scholar at New College, Oxford), tenors Steven Harrold and Ben Knowles (both former choral scholars at St. John's College, Cambridge), and Christopher Head (former choral scholar at King's College, Cambridge). Other arrivals included Justin Lee (tenor), and also, in 1993, tenor James Outram, who was singing with the choir of Magdalen College, Oxford, when they joined us for the IOF Three Choirs concert. Both Graham Barton and Simon Blake had moved on from the alto line, and I was able to offer one of the places to Neil Baker from All Saints' Church, Hertford. He would later be joined by another Baker – Simon – who had been singing at Norwich Cathedral. We had also welcomed local alto Tim Blinko, though because of other commitments, Tim didn't stay long and was replaced by Roger Mullis, a barrister, who had previously sung at Christ Church, Oxford.

22

Spreading Our Wings
St. Albans 1990–1992

If our 1989 Eastertide trip to Holland had seemed busy, the October half-term break in 1990 was to make that seem like any other little local outing. This time we were heading much further afield – to the USA!

Tom Whittemore and Peter Conte, two musical friends I'd first met five years earlier, suggested that the choir might like to visit the Philadelphia area, where they both held organist and choirmaster posts. Tom was at St. Peter's Church, Pine Street, a historic building in the old and now regenerating part of town, and Peter at Valley Forge Memorial Chapel outside the city, at the site of the long encampment of George Washington's army over the winter of 1777. Both Tom and Peter had boys' choirs and offered us an opportunity to sing with them, as well as giving concerts on our own. The local branch of the American Guild of Organists was also prepared to sponsor a joint concert in Daylesford Abbey in which Peter's choir would join with us to sing the Duruflé Requiem with orchestral accompaniment. The concert was scheduled for a Sunday afternoon, with a combined rehearsal the day before. I arranged for all the St. Albans boys to be off school on the Friday, and the full choir flew to Philadelphia that day.

The cost was enormous, but no-one paid a penny towards the air fares. In the weeks before the tour there were fundraising recitals as well as special events organised by the choir parents, two of whom, together with the Mistress of the Robes, would accompany us as chaperones for the boys. I had also appealed to members of the Abbey congregation to sponsor a specific chorister – the only pay-back being that the chorister concerned would send their sponsor one or two postcards while we were away.

The morning after we arrived, the boys and lay clerks assembled at the Washington Memorial

Drawing by Helen Hughes

245

Chapel for an extended rehearsal. Later that day I worked with the orchestra, and in the evening the lay clerks sang Compline by candlelight. On the Sunday, after singing the morning Service in the Memorial Chapel with Peter's choir, we were all transported the five miles or so to the impressive church at Daylesford Abbey. The concert was enthusiastically received by a large and attentive audience, after which we were all treated to a pizza supper.

Other events included concerts at St. Peter's School, Philadelphia, and the Cathedral of the Incarnation, Long Island, New York. From there we travelled to Bedford NY, where we gave a concert in the Presbyterian Church, and the following day sang Evensong at Christ Church, Greenwich, with their choir.

After that hectic schedule, we were able to relax on the 4½-hour train journey aboard the *Connecticut Yankee* from Stamford, Connecticut, to Washington, D.C. In Washington we sang a Saturday evening concert and also the Sunday morning Eucharist at St. Paul's, K Street, as well as an informal Sunday afternoon concert in St. Matthew's RC Cathedral, before running out to the coach, still in cassocks, to get to Dulles airport in time for the plane home.

There was a slightly uneasy moment at the reception at St. Paul's, K Street, on the Saturday evening, 31st October. We arrived to find the hall candle-lit and beautifully decked out with Halloween decorations, but, apart from the ladies in our party, not another female in sight. I began to feel uneasy – these men were to be our hosts for the night, including boys aged 9 to 13. They served us a wonderful meal, and after the usual thank you speeches, I gathered the boys around me and, as delicately as I could, explained possible problems of being hosted by just men. 'That's OK, sir,' they chorused, 'we'll be fine. See you tomorrow morning.' And fine they were, returning to church the next morning to sing the joint Eucharist with the resident choir.

Back in St. Albans, we all found it difficult to knuckle down to the daily routine of practices and sung Services, and when a week or so later, on Remembrance Sunday, we sang the Duruflé Requiem again – this time liturgically – it was nowhere near as good as it had been in the Daylesford Abbey concert. Gradually everything settled down, and soon it was time to lay plans for 1991, starting with a memorable BBC Choral Evensong on 30th January.

If there's a problem in broadcasting at that time of year, it's usually to do with seasonal illness – colds, coughs etc. This time, however, we managed to assemble the full choir and they sang quite beautifully. Waiting for us at the end was the BBC producer. Rather than saying the usual thank you, he calmly announced that not a note of the Service had been broadcast – there had been a power failure just as we were about to go on-air, and there was no time to switch to an auxiliary supply. Immediate reactions were mixed, ranging from 'well, I hope we'll still be getting a fee' to 'at least we sang

Evensong'. We never found out the cause of the power failure, though one of the choir parents said that they'd seen a verger disconnecting some wires from a mains outlet as he closed the doors at the west end of the Abbey just before the Service began. The BBC mobile studio was parked just outside...

That wasn't the only unusual happening for me as far as the BBC Choral Evensong programme was concerned. On Monday morning, 11th February, two days before Ash Wednesday, the phone rang. It was Dr. George Guest, the distinguished choir-master of St. John's College, Cambridge. Could I help him out? Much of the country had been blanketed with snow for the past few days, and it had come down whilst George was visiting rural Wales. 'I'm snowed in and can't get back to college for the boys' rehearsals this evening and tomorrow morning. Could you go and take them and also conduct the choir in the Ash Wednesday broadcast Evensong?' The roads around St. Albans had been cleared, so I set off for Cambridge. The boys assembled in the song school and we rehearsed the setting, the anthem, and bits of the Allegri *Miserere* for Wednesday's broadcast. The following morning I did the same, and was passing the porter's lodge adjacent to the chapel when one of the choral scholars came by and said, 'I've just seen Dr. Guest in First Court walking towards the chapel.' I raced over and found George, who graciously suggested that since I'd taken the rehearsals, I should also conduct the broadcast. 'Not a bit of it,' I said, 'it's your last Ash Wednesday before you retire. You must direct your own choir, and I'll be happy to go home and listen on the radio.'

During the late May half-term, Nicola and I were able to get away and take a short break in Wittering. Buffie was away in France with the New London Singers, whilst Julia and Tim both stayed behind in St. Albans. On the way home I took Nicola to Salisbury Cathedral. It was to be a fateful visit – in the best sense of that word.

Since the beginning of the year, I had known that Salisbury were planning to es-tablish a girls' choir at the Cathedral – we had heard the news from headmaster-elect, Christopher Helyer, and his wife Helen – Christopher had been a lay clerk at Guildford during my time there. Showing Nicola around the Cathedral and Close that afternoon, I asked her if she could imagine herself there as a chorister. The answer was an enthu-siastic yes, so I said we'd need to discuss it with Buffie and then write to Christopher Helyer to see if there were any auditions available. I was not the most popular person in the world when we told Buffie where we'd been. Her younger daughter being sent away to boarding school? – never! Undaunted, I contacted Christopher, who replied that although the first 16 places had already been filled, they would be happy to see Nicola. We took her down to Salisbury, and after an audition with Richard Seal, the Cathedral Organist, she was offered a place in the choir and the school from September. It was a golden opportunity we simply couldn't refuse, even though Buffie still had misgivings about her nine-year-old daughter moving away from home.

Nicola had no such worries, and in early September she would have the unique opportunity to be one of the 18 pioneer girl choristers at Salisbury – a move that would give her a wonderful grounding for her later career as a professional musician.

Before all that, we were hosting a very special Three Choirs concert at the IOF, with Stephen Cleobury and his choir from King's College, Cambridge, and the choir of St. John's College, Cambridge, with their director, Dr. George Guest. Since his first visit to St. Anne's church, Chingford in 1955, I had been befriended and encouraged by George, and now, in 1991, he was going to bring the St. John's choir to sing in

Nicola, leaving for Salisbury Cathedral, September 1991

St. Albans, two weeks or so before his official retirement after 40 years at the College.

For us it was a great coup, and we planned an ambitious programme, with the Duruflé Requiem as the second half, conducted by George and accompanied by Stephen, a former organ scholar at St. John's. It was the St. John's choir who completely stole the show that evening with their exquisitely sung Bruckner motets in the first half. The audience, and the King's and St. Albans choirs, were spellbound by the vocal quality and musicality of what was still the country's finest church, cathedral, or collegiate choir.

At this busy time of the IOF we were pleased to welcome the boys of Peter Conte's choir to St. Albans, where they sang some of the statutory Services with great beauty and efficiency, before moving on to Peterborough Cathedral.

By now the St. Albans choristers were beginning to make the sound that I'd hoped for, and aside from the all-important sung Services, we were able to think about another choir trip, as well as a follow-up CD to *A Crown of Light*. But first I needed to get over a shock. A letter had arrived from the City University saying that I had been elected to the degree of Doctor of Music (*Honoris Causa*). Some behind the scenes research led to Dean Peter Moore being the moving spirit behind this honour, and on 2nd December I became Dr. Rose at a Graduation Ceremony in no less a place than

the City of London's Guildhall, processing from there to St. Paul's Cathedral
for a celebratory Service in which John
Scott played music of my choice. Back
in St. Albans, the choir celebrated with
a post-Evensong party in the refectory.
I'd now have to get used to being called
'Doc' by the men of the choir!

Early in 1992 Franz Welser-Möst
invited the boys to sing at the Royal
Festival Hall in a performance of
J.S. Bach's monumental *St. Matthew
Passion*. It was to be sung in German,
and I found a local language coach to
guide us through the pronunciation.
Franz came to the Abbey to rehearse
with the boys, immediately endearing
himself to them by arriving in what

*Receiving the honorary degree of Doctor
of Music in the City of London Guildhall,
2nd December 1991*

looked like a West Bromwich Albion football shirt. He seemed very happy with the
way they were singing, and in the concert they were placed on a raised level behind
the main choir, the sound of just 16 boys coming across loud and clear.

One of the advantages of recording in the Abbey was that Lammas Records was
very local. Founded and run by Lance Andrews, a member of the congregation and a
former BBC television sound supervisor, we were able to schedule occasional sessions
rather than the usual three or four consecutive evenings that an 'outside' organisation
would want. This time we would have no sponsorship, so any recording fees for the
men would need to be met from my own Abbey Boys' Choir bank account, and the
CD would need to be popular enough to get some, if not all, of that back.

In the end we settled on carols, sung by both the Abbey choir and the St. Albans
Bach Choir, calling the CD *Christmas at St. Albans*. The all-important role of recording producer was taken by Lee Ward, our organ scholar, and we were so impressed
by his encouragement and perceptive criticism that we invited him to return to do the
next CD with us.

On the evening of one of the choir sessions there was a very heavy snowfall, and
some of the boys and men could not get to the Abbey. We still went ahead, altering the
repertoire as we went along, including the last-minute insertion of a couple of items for
men's voices – Peter Hurford's *The Holy Son of God most high*, and Walford Davies'
arrangement of *What child is this?* to the ever-popular *Greensleeves* melody.

In June, the St. Albans Bach Choir spent two evenings recording six items, including John Rutter's famous *Shepherd's Pipe Carol*, with soloists Ken Burgess (baritone), and chorister Nicholas Crawley who was later to carve out a career as a distinguished opera singer.

The CD was issued well in time for Christmas 1992, and the Abbey's own gift shop soon sold out the original run of 500 discs.

In July, in Guildford Cathedral, I was given the degree of Master of the University (*Honoris Causa*) by the University of Surrey. Aside from returning to Guildford, an added pleasure was that I had been sponsored by Dr. Sebastian Forbes, Professor of Music at the University, who introduced me on the day. Sebastian and I had been in Hampstead Parish Church Choir together – he as a treble and me as a bass – as well as fellow students at the Royal Academy of Music.

Honorand and Professor, 17th July 1992

23

Times of Change
St. Albans 1993–1997

The year 1993 was special at St. Albans – the Abbey was 1200 years old. During the year, the Alban Shrine would be re-dedicated in the presence of HM The Queen Mother, Dean Peter Moore would retire, and our IOF Three Choirs concert would break new ground.

But before all that, we were going on another USA trip! This time it was to be a February visit to sunny and warm Florida. What we hadn't bargained for was the wintry weather in the northern part of the USA, and having just made a precarious snowy landing at Boston Airport, we learned that the plane that was due to take us on to Tampa had not made it into Boston; our flight would be delayed for several hours.

Having ultimately arrived in Tampa, we were hosted by members of Eleanor (Ellie) Taylor's choir at St. John's Church, where we sang the Sunday morning Service with their choir and gave a concert the same afternoon.

Processing in the sunshine from Morning Service – Tampa, Florida, February 1993

The following day was free, and on the Tuesday we gave a concert in Orlando Cathedral. You can't be in Orlando without visiting Disney World, and we managed to get free entry by singing an informal concert in the American Adventure Pavilion at the Epcot Center. The following day, the boys (and men) were also able to enjoy the delights of The Magic Kingdom.

Our last stop was at Bethesda-by-the-Sea Episcopal Church in West Palm Beach, whose Organist, Hal Pysher, I had met several years earlier at one of the Valley Forge RSCM courses. We sang a Service with Hal's choir and gave a short Sunday afternoon concert, after which everyone piled into the coach to Miami Airport and the overnight flight home. A very tired group arrived back in St. Albans the following morning; the boys missing their first day back at school, whilst those of the men who were teachers had to go straight back into the classroom.

Now it was time to think about the re-dedication of the Shrine, other celebrations of the Abbey's 1200th Anniversary, and the IOF.

The Alban Shrine is situated behind the high altar and restoration work had been under way for several months. The re-dedication took place on 6th May with HM Queen Elizabeth, The Queen Mother, in attendance. At that point in the Service, we (the choir), the clergy, and the Queen Mother processed to the Shrine area, and standing in the nearby lady chapel, we sang Anton Bruckner's motet *Locus Iste.*

I had not realised how early the Abbey had been founded until one day, when I was doing something for the BBC at Westminster Abbey, Dean Peter Moore casually remarked, 'Oh, I see you're off to the young Abbey today.' History tells us that King Offa of Mercia had founded a monastery at St. Albans in 793, so it seemed right that the present Abbey should celebrate with a series of 1200th Anniversary events in June 1993, and all the more so since Dean Peter was due to retire around that time. We scratched our heads to think of something musical that might be suitable, and came up with the story of the Abbey to be told in words and music. It needed to be custom written, and since I would have to arrange the musical illustrations, it was suggested that I too, as Master of Music, might like to write the script.

Once I'd got over the initial shock, I wrote a narrative as seen through the eyes of one of the 8th century monks, starting with him lamenting the fact that here he was, working in the fields and hearing the distant Abbey bell, realising he'd just have time to dash back in time for the next of the seven daily Offices. Always one for dramatising the readings at Evensong, Canon Bill Ritson was the obvious choice as narrator, which he did with inimitable enthusiasm and panache. The music, ranging from Gregorian chant to 20th century canticle settings, was sung by the Abbey choir, the St. Albans Bach Choir, and the local Fayrfax Consort conducted by their founder David Ireson.

The choirs of Salisbury Cathedral, Magdalen College, Oxford, and St. Albans Abbey rehearsing for the IOF Three Choirs concert, Monday 12ᵗʰ July 1993

The 1200ᵗʰ celebrations were immediately followed by the IOF, and it was here that the Three Choirs concert broke new ground with the inclusion of the girl choristers from Salisbury Cathedral. Our younger daughter, Nicola, had now been in the Salisbury Cathedral girls' choir since its inception nearly two years ago, and with their high profile in the now growing girls' cathedral choir movement, it seemed to be the right time to ask them to take part in the Festival. At first, Richard Seal, their choirmaster, was reticent; the choir was still very new, and it would be their first concert appearance at such a high-profile event. In the end we persuaded him, and they were joined by the choir of Magdalen College, Oxford, under the direction of their Organist and Informator Choristarum, Bill Ives, with whom I'd worked closely at Guildford Cathedral some 20 years earlier.

Similar to 1991, the concert began with the combined choirs singing on the presbytery steps, mainly for the benefit of the members of the audience who had not been able to get a seat in the nave. From there, the three choirs processed to their places, singing Gregorian chant alternating with organ interludes – on this occasion, Magdalen College to the west end of the nave; St. Albans to the north side, about half-way up; and pride of place on the staging at the front being given to the 18 girls and 6 men of the Salisbury choir.

Aside from the extended polychoral items, each choir sang two or three individual items in the first half, with a second half in which all three choirs were together at the front of the nave. The programme included the 1981 Royal Wedding anthem, *Let the people praise Thee, O God*, by William Mathias, sung in the first half by the Salisbury girls and men. The second half included Philip Moore's extended setting of *All wisdom cometh from the Lord*; William Harris's eight-part unaccompanied *Faire is the Heaven*; and as a finale, the *Collegium Regale Te Deum* by Herbert Howells.

Both for Nicola and us, this was a most special occasion, since here she was, back in the very place where she had first started singing with the Parish Choir, and now a chorister in the country's first all-girls cathedral choir.[1]

The IOF had been conceived around the Abbey organ, built by Harrison and Harrison in 1962, but there was also a small one-manual pipe organ in the lady chapel. With just six stops and without any means of expression, it was woefully inadequate for the regular demands of a weekly Roman Catholic Mass, a monthly Lutheran Service, and most important of all, the venue for all weddings. Musical consultations with the couple who were to be married often turned out to be embarrassing: 'Please can the bride enter to the *Trumpet Voluntary*?' – No, not possible. 'May we leave to Widor's *Toccata*?' – No hope of that either, or of any other suitably festive music… But how to resolve the situation?

We had recently hosted a well-attended concert by the American concert organist, Carlo Curley. Promoted by the English branch of the USA-based Allen Organ Company, they had installed a large digital organ in the nave, and although the Harrison and Harrison organ was used in the concert (with the player out of sight on the central stone screen), having the console of the Allen organ in full view of the audience allowed his adoring fans to see Carlo playing, often raising a hand mid-piece to encourage the audience to clap in time. He was the ultimate showman.

After the concert, in conversation with Jeremy Meager, former Abbey chorister and now working for Allen, we came up with a plan to install a small two-manual digital organ in the lady chapel, on the understanding that Allen could bring possible customers to hear it in an ecclesiastical setting, rather than in the sterile surrounds of

---

1   Salisbury was not the first cathedral to have girls in the choir. Back in the 1970s, Harrison Oxley had added girls to the existing choir of men and boys at St. Edmundsbury Cathedral, an arrangement later discontinued on the orders of the Provost.

a showroom. The advantage for the Abbey was that there would now be a really flexible instrument to accompany the regular Services, and also allow suitable music to be played at weddings and funerals. It was a win-win situation, though the installation needed the approval of the Cathedral Council.

With Colin Slee, the Sub-Dean, we came up with a plan which might convince them – and also surprise them. One quiet day (and there were precious few of those at the Abbey), we arranged for the organ to be delivered and installed at the west end of the lady chapel. After many hours of tonal adjustment, we left the building, but not before I had played the first few pages of the famous *Toccata* from the Fifth Symphony by Charles-Marie Widor into the recording facility on the console. A few evenings later, the Cathedral Council met in the lady chapel, where I was able to say a few words about the instrument and invite the Sub-Dean, who had never played a note of music, to 'give us a tune'. With the keyboards out of sight, he pressed the replay button. Making sweepingly grand gestures, he pretended to play, as the impressive sound of the Widor *Toccata* echoed around the chapel. They were gob-smacked, and after a truthful explanation, there was a unanimous decision that the organ should remain in the chapel as long as the Allen Organ Company was prepared to leave it there. There was always the possibility that they might want to remove it, but it became a permanent fixture when a member of the congregation offered to buy it as a memorial to his late wife, commemorated by a small brass plaque on the back of the console bearing her initials. Since then it has been used for recordings and recitals, and is also a useful practice instrument, with the facility for the player to wear headphones.

At the same time, we decided to make one tonal alteration to the main organ: the Swell Mixture. Originally voiced to the tonal design of Ralph Downes, it had never really been usable due to the high-pitched screaming of the upper notes. We gathered that when this particular stop was installed, Mr. Downes had lost some of his upper hearing, and he had insisted that the top notes should sound brighter and brighter until he himself could hear them. Whatever the truth of the situation, Mark Venning of Harrison and Harrison agreed that it was time we should have a stop we could actually use, and he himself expertly voiced it, whilst Andrew Parnell and I sat in the nave nodding our approval.

~

1994 saw our third trip to the USA, a one-off celebrity concert, and the arrival of Christopher Lewis as our new Dean.

Christopher was installed on Saturday 26th February. Formerly a Residentiary Canon at Canterbury Cathedral, he had invited a large number of guests from there, and we knew that the Abbey would be crammed – nave, quire, presbytery and lady chapel. The form of Service was Evensong, but with a slight difference: it would start with the opening preces sung by the choir from the Michael Staircase in the south transept. Realising that a single voice intoning the priest's part would not be heard at the extreme ends of the Abbey, I composed a fully choral set of preces, from 'O Lord, open Thou our lips' to 'The Lord's name be praised'. Having sung them, we processed through the lady chapel, presbytery and quire, ending up in the nave choir-stalls for the legal formalities in the first part of the Service. During the Office Hymn we moved into the quire, and the Parish Choir took our place in the nave choir-stalls, from where they sang the rest of the Service.

The new Dean soon made his presence felt in a positive way by involving some of the great-and-good of the county in the creation of the St. Albans Music Trust – a way of ensuring that the cost of the Abbey's music could be underwritten in perpetuity. One of the excitements at its launch was the sight of the Dean abseiling from the top of the Abbey tower, whilst the choristers waited at ground level, singing *He that is down needs fear no fall* to a melody I'd specially written for the occasion.

Fundraising for the planned October half-term trip to the USA was now a priority, and two special events helped raise most of the money we needed. I celebrated my 60th birthday in May with a concert in the Abbey nave, and in a mixed programme of sacred and secular music, members of the choir sang and played solos, together with items ranging from Byrd to the Beatles.

The second event was the brainchild of the musical parents of one of the choristers. Alexander Lewis was the son of Patricia and Michael, at that time living in Wheathampstead. Michael was a professional opera singer, and Patricia had been a member of the BBC Singers, where she had been the soloist in the first performance of John Tavener's extended work, *Ultimos Ritos*. Both of them had a connection with the distinguished piano accompanist, Geoffrey Parsons. Patricia and Michael said they could persuade Geoffrey to come and give us a fundraising concert, and that he would bring with him some of the singers with whom he worked. On a July evening, the Abbey was packed to hear Geoffrey and four singers, including soprano Felicity Lott (later Dame Felicity Lott). Each of the artistes sang a selection of songs, and after the choir had sung a few pieces, we finished with John Rutter's *The Lord bless you and keep you*. Unknown to me, Felicity Lott was so moved that she burst into tears whilst we were singing it, making her way up to the song school after the concert to say how much she enjoyed it. In conversation, she graciously offered to come and sing a concert with the St. Albans Bach Choir without a fee – a promise she was to keep in November 1997.

Together with other fundraising lunchtime concerts, we were able to book the air tickets for our October half-term trip. This time the destinations would be

Philadelphia, Washington, Baltimore, Princeton, New York, Long Island, and New Haven, Connecticut.

We started by giving a concert in St. Peter's Church, Philadelphia, moving on from there to sing in Washington National Cathedral, Old St. Paul's Church in Baltimore, and Princeton University Chapel. Singing in the National Cathedral was a challenge. A huge building, situated on Mount Saint Alban, our full-scale concert was scheduled for the evening. We had a full rehearsal during the afternoon, after which our boys attended Evensong, sung by the Washington Cathedral choristers who later were in the audience at our concert. It may have been the spot where we were standing or the sheer size of the building that made it difficult for the various parts of the choir to hear themselves. It was not the best that we had ever sung.

In New York we were graciously sponsored by my old friends, Bill and Irene Miller, for a concert in St. Bartholomew's Church, Park Avenue, a huge barn of a building without the slightest hint of any reverberation of audible reward to the singers. So problematic was it that during the rehearsal I had to ask the men to leave me alone with the boys while we re-learned most of the programme, omitting the commas and natural musical breaks usually included when we sang in the Abbey. It wasn't easy and we were relieved that the next venue, the Cathedral of the Incarnation, Garden City, Long Island, had a more rewarding acoustic.

Our last stop was at Trinity Church on the Green, New Haven, for a Saturday evening concert. Director of Music, Walden Moore, already had his own skilled choir of men and boys and we sang the Sunday morning Service with them, after which it was time to head to the airport and home.

Back in St. Albans it was once again the Opus Dei that took priority, though there was plenty of forward planning to do for the following year, including the July International Organ Festival and the exciting possibility of starting a girls' choir.

Since the formation of the Salisbury Cathedral girls' choir in 1991, similar choirs had been set up at other cathedrals, including Wells and Exeter. Colin Slee, our Sub-Dean, was keen that we should give an opportunity for girls to sing in the Abbey, and we settled on September of the following year, allowing ourselves nine months to sort out all the practical details. The first of these concerned the crucial decision of who should run it. My suggestion, unanimously agreed by the Dean and Chapter, was that Andrew Parnell should be the musical director, and that his salary should be enhanced to reflect that extra responsibility. The organ scholar and I would be his assistants and would play and take rehearsals as and when required.

Before that, 1995 saw the tercentenary of the birth of Henry Purcell, an event celebrated by the BBC, including one broadcast of Choral Evensong each month of the year in which a Purcell verse-anthem would be featured, with strings. We were asked to do the March date, and I chose the setting of Psalm 111, *I will give thanks unto the Lord*, in which we were joined by the distinguished viol group Fretwork. A work I had previously recorded with the Guildford choir, our soloists were Ian Wicks, Ken Burgess and Simon Gaunt. The rest of the broadcast included music by John Blow (his setting of *Salvator mundi, salva nos*, sung as an introit), the *Short Evening Service* by Richard Ayleward, and, preceding the final Purcell organ voluntary, Pelham Humfrey's *Hymne to God the Father*, sung by the boys, in which the opening solo was sung by George Corbett, accompanied by the chamber organ.

In June, just before the IOF, we were able to complete another choir CD for Lammas: *Over the Rainbow*. Lance Andrews was willing to fit in with the evenings we could find for recording, and again we asked former organ scholar, Lee Ward, to be the producer. In some ways this was the best record the choir made in my time there, and it featured a wide range of 20th century repertoire, from the traditional to the popular, ending up with the men singing the Beatles' 1967 hit *When I'm Sixty-Four*, arranged by local musician Nicholas Hare, whose son William had recently become a chorister. Michael McCarthy sang solo in the men's version of *Is you is, or is you ain't my baby*, whilst Ken Burgess was a stunning baritone soloist in Philip Moore's *All wisdom cometh from the Lord* – one of its first commercial recordings. The album took

its title from Martin Pickard's SATB arrangement of *Somewhere over the rainbow*. Martin had grown up in nearby Harpenden and had made the arrangement whilst he was organ scholar at Corpus Christi College, Cambridge.

I hoped that there would be a good return from the sales of the CD to help with the costs of yet another USA trip, planned for February 1996, so I approached the Friends of St. Albans Abbey to see if they would sponsor the recording. The answer was yes, until Christopher Lewis, the Dean, decided against it. There must have been some heated discussions since the Secretary of the Friends resigned over the issue, but not before the promised sponsorship money had been given to us.

In the IOF Three Choirs concert we were joined by the boys and men from Guildford Cathedral and the mixed voice choir from Trinity College, Cambridge, in which the second half was a performance of Ralph Vaughan Williams' *Mass in G minor* with some of his organ music between the sections. The evening was made all the more special with a world premiere of a new polychoral piece by Alan Ridout. Entitled *Salve Regina*, Alan had set it for four choirs, the fourth being a separate group of trebles. It was a great success, repeated in 1997 when our own newly founded girls' choir took part.

The Abbey held a Flower Festival in September 1995, the opening Service being attended by HRH Princess Margaret, and in the same month Andrew Parnell started recruiting the first girls for the new choir. Having filled the places, the girls and their parents assembled in the crypt on a December morning to meet each other and hear how their timetable would work. At the end of the morning, Andrew decided that the girls ought to sing something, and the only thing they all seemed to know was *Happy Birthday*. That hesitant offering began a new and now invaluable part of the Abbey's musical life, and they made their first appearance at Evensong just twelve weeks later.

～

1996 got off to a busy start. Christopher Herbert, the new Bishop, was to be enthroned on 20th January. In our discussions about music for the Service, he expressed a wish that the words attributed to St. Patrick – *Christ be with me* – should be sung three times, using different endings – *Christ be with us*, and *Christ be with you* – all to be sung in different parts of the Abbey. Searching around, I could only find two musical settings, so I decided to write the third one myself. It followed a hymn, and to cover the noise of the large congregation settling down, I added a quiet eight-bar introduction in which the four parts of the choir each sang two bars on their own.

I'd also had an approach from a television production company who were making a series of eight short programmes for ITV on the history of church music, to be called *Heavenly Voices*. I knew producer Sarah Rutty from her time at the BBC, and she asked if she and the director of the company could come and see me. I thought it would be for advice, but instead they asked if I would choose and arrange the music as well as present the programmes on screen. It turned out to be a mammoth task, travelling and filming in venues up and down the country, though we were able to feature the St. Albans choir in some of the musical excerpts. Each of the programmes featured a group of eight professional singers, as well as a short interview with a celebrity. We started filming in March and finished in the early summer, just before the first programme was transmitted.

Meanwhile, on our USA trips we had got to know many church musicians, and it was Tom Whittemore (from St. Peter's Church, Philadelphia) who suggested that a group of them might come to St. Albans in May. They rented a house nearby, attended all the boys' practices and organ recitals, as well as singing with the lay clerks in several Services. Welcoming them was the least we could do in return for all the hosting and hospitality we had received over there.

And there would be more of that in our upcoming October trip to the USA – this time back to Florida. Flying to Tampa via Washington, we started by giving a concert in St. John's Church. The following day we took the boys to Busch Gardens theme park. Expecting the usual warm weather, they and the adults were not dressed for the sudden cold snap, and it was a shivering and none-too-well group of boys that arrived back in Tampa at the end of the day. The next evening we gave a concert in Orlando Cathedral, going on from there to Bradenton and the coastal resort of Sarasota where we not only sang, but had time to relax on the beach in what was now warm sunshine. Another concert in Epcot Center gained us free admission as well as to The Magic Kingdom. The tour ended with a Sunday morning recital and singing the Service at Orlando Cathedral. Everyone breathed a sigh of relief when were safely back in St. Albans. We'd now done the USA four times!

In November we broke new ground in our Choral Evensong broadcast, singing an anthem by Robert Walker that required two organists. *Dance, my heart* had been premiered on an RSCM course from York Minster a few years before and I'd always wanted the choir to learn it. In the broadcast it was played by Andrew Parnell and organ scholar Peter Dyke, and for those who preferred their music to be more traditional, we included the *Magnificat and Nunc Dimittis in B flat* by Henry Smart. Quite a contrast!

❧

At the beginning of 1997 I made the big decision to retire at the end of the year. By then I would be 63 and would have completed over nine years at the Abbey. Before the start of the January term, I broke the news to the lay clerks at the usual choir meeting. They expressed the hope that I would stay on, but I explained that the decision had been made and we'd started to think about where we might live. Forget December – the music at the Abbey throughout this year would be as normal.

Well, it would have been normal, but for another invitation to visit the USA. Could we do it? Five times in eight years? I talked to Andrew Parnell and the lay clerks, who seemed very keen, and then with the boys. Their surprisingly dismissive reaction was 'Oh, not New York again'. How blasé can you get?!

Undeterred, I went ahead with the planning, concerned as to how we'd find the money for the air fares this time. I need not have worried, the choir parents rallied round, even producing a one-off fashion show. On the musical front we fundraised at a series of lunchtime concerts in which families associated with the choir took part.

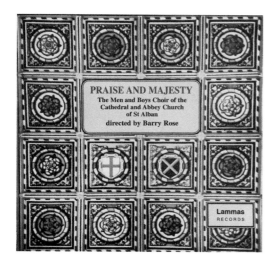

Meanwhile, we were keen to make one more CD before I left, and in March we slotted in a couple of recording sessions during our Friday evening rehearsal times. There were a few items left over from the 1991 and 1995 sessions, and to those we added ten more pieces, giving the finished record the title *Praise and Majesty*, after Mendelssohn's setting of those words on the first track.

The reviews were all effusive, a typical quote (from *Church Music Quarterly*, October 1997) being: '*What more can be said about Barry Rose? – one is left with the impression that something is going on here that other choir trainers rarely even glimpse. Buy it, enjoy it, and wonder how it's done.*'

Summer was busy with another International Organ Festival, to which we welcomed the choirs of Winchester Cathedral and St. John's College, Cambridge, for the Three Choirs concert.

On the Saturday before the concert, the St. Albans Bach Choir opened the Festival with a performance of Elgar's *The Dream of Gerontius*. I spent a lot of time wondering if I was the person to conduct it, and in the end, with the choir's affirmation, I asked Christopher Robinson if he would do it. Christopher knew the work intimately from conducting it several times at the Three Choirs Festival when he was Organist of Worcester Cathedral. It was an excellent performance, with the new Abbey girls' choir singing the part of the Angelicals. Two days later they also took part in the Three Choirs concert, in the second performance of Alan Ridout's setting of *Salve Regina*. The rest of the programme included Philip Moore's unaccompanied *Three Prayers of Dietrich Bonhoeffer* (Winchester Cathedral Choir) and William Walton's *Where does the uttered music go?* (St. John's College, Cambridge); our contribution included the St. Albans *Jubilate Deo* by Richard Shephard and Robert Walker's *Dance, my heart*.

For the second half, the combined choirs sang Josef Rheinberger's double choir *Mass in E flat*, the conducting being shared by David Hill (then at Winchester) and me. Christopher Robinson, now back with his choir from St. John's College, rounded off the evening with Stanford's *Te Deum in B flat* as an encore.

Part of our summer had also been taken up with house hunting. During half-term, which coincided with my birthday, Buffie and I had gone different ways, she to Somerset, and me to Hampshire, where I was looking at properties in the Southsea area. After a lot of searching, it was Buffie who found a house in the Somerset village of Draycott, and in August we were able to collect the keys on the way home from our last St. Albans choir camp.

In September the interviews and auditions for my post took place, the Dean being advised by Dr. Roy Massey, the Organist of Hereford Cathedral. Roy was so impressed by Peter Dyke's playing at the Services he attended that he invited him to be his assistant at Hereford. The Dean and Chapter appointed Andrew Lucas, Sub-Organist of St. Paul's Cathedral, to succeed me as from February 1998. Andrew and I had known each other through working together at St. Paul's, and he was in the audience at our eve-of-tour concert in October, taking the time to search us out afterwards to wish us *bon voyage*.

The boys' prediction was right. It was New York – again! We flew there, giving concerts in Ridgewood, New Jersey; Grace Church, New York; a return visit to Garden City, Long Island; on to West Hartford, Connecticut, and Newport, Rhode Island; and finally, Boston and Worcester, Massachusetts. In Boston, at a harbourside restaurant, I was able to host a farewell thank you lunch for the men, though it was not yet quite time for farewell speeches – they would come in December.

Back in England, the Queen and the Duke of Edinburgh celebrated their Golden Wedding, and at St. Albans Abbey we held a special Service at which Golden Wedding couples from the county were guests of honour. The boys were quite surprised when, in the Service, they got a round of applause for their singing of *Count your blessings one by one*, a song made famous many years before by the Luton Girls' Choir, at a time when most of the couples were getting married.

November also saw my final concert with the St. Albans Bach Choir in which we reprised the programme I had first done with them in 1989 – Gabriel Fauré's Requiem and *Cantique de Jean Raçine*, with Franz Josef Haydn's *Nelson Mass* as the second half. True to her promise three years earlier, Felicity Lott came and sang the soprano solos and was joined by three other excellent soloists – Robin Blaze (countertenor), Ian Wicks (tenor), and Michael George (bass).

At the beginning of December we broadcast Choral Evensong, and on the following Sunday, Evensong in the nave was sung by an augmented choir, including men who had sung with me at Guildford and St. Paul's. The guest preacher was Canon Christopher Collingwood, Precentor at St. Albans when we arrived, and then Precentor of Guildford Cathedral. The choir parents arranged a reception afterwards at which there were songs and speeches, and the same happened two weeks later when the St. Albans Bach Choir had sung their last carol concert. Among the gifts they presented was a large, framed sheet signed by all the members, reading WE TRIED TO DO IT YOUR WAY.

*At a farewell party in
the Abbey refectory,
December 1997*

On 23rd and 24th December there were the two Festivals of Lessons and Carols, and at the end of Matins on Christmas Day morning we processed out to find a large 'Bye-Bye Barry' banner draped across the south transept.

That was it. At the age of 63 it was not just the end of nearly ten exciting and fulfilling years at St. Albans, but also the end of my life as a cathedral organist. It would be hard to leave all this behind – the Abbey, the many friends we'd made, and also the city itself. As far as the music in the Abbey was concerned, none of it would have run smoothly without the invaluable friendship and wisdom of Andrew Parnell, together with a succession of talented and able organ scholars who have now gone on to distinguished musical careers: Nicholas Robinson, Sean Farrell, Robert Sharpe, Lee Ward, Richard Tanner, Nigel McClintock, Christopher Betts, Peter Dyke – and, of course, every boy and every man who'd ever sung in the choir.

Somerset beckoned, and on 29th December we moved to the village of Draycott, and retirement – though the City of Wells and its cathedral was only five miles from our new home...

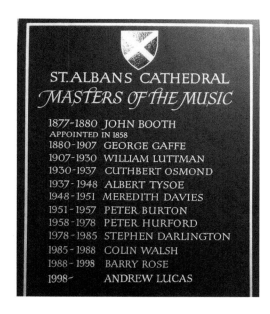

ST. ALBANS CATHEDRAL
MASTERS OF THE MUSIC

1877-1880	JOHN BOOTH
APPOINTED IN 1858	
1880-1907	GEORGE GAFFE
1907-1930	WILLIAM LUTTMAN
1930-1937	CUTHBERT OSMOND
1937-1948	ALBERT TYSOE
1948-1951	MEREDITH DAVIES
1951-1957	PETER BURTON
1958-1978	PETER HURFORD
1978-1985	STEPHEN DARLINGTON
1985-1988	COLIN WALSH
1988-1998	BARRY ROSE
1998-	ANDREW LUCAS

24

Retirement – What's That?
1998–2010

Slippers – armchair – newspaper. That's the way to start a long-awaited retirement.

No chance! On 29ᵗʰ December, we'd not been in our new house in Draycott for more than a couple of hours when there was a knock at the door. Standing there was Malcolm Archer, Organist and Master of the Choristers at Wells Cathedral. Malcolm had just become a father, and Alison, his wife, was still in hospital with newborn Nathaniel. Would we like to go out and get something to eat at the nearest inn? So began a long and fruitful musical association both with Malcolm and Wells Cathedral, which would see me producing several of their choir recordings, playing recitals, singing in the choir as a deputy bass, taking the occasional boys' practice, and even preaching at Evensong. We also wrote and presented our double act, *Two of a kind strike back,* in Wells and at other venues.

Draycott is a small village, and word gets around quickly. Someone must have told the vicar, John Hall, that we'd moved in, and he soon made contact to ask if I would play at the local church. The answer was yes, and that association has continued for the past 24 years. Whenever possible, I've played the small organ in St. Peter's Church for their Services, as well as giving many concerts, and even making some recordings.

But before I could play in church for the first time, and just two days after we moved, I waved goodbye to Buffie, leaving her surrounded by heaps of unpacked boxes. My destination was Australia and New Zealand, where I'd been invited to direct the RSCM's Australian summer school in Newcastle, New South Wales, going on from there to New Zealand for their summer school in Christchurch. In Australia I met up again with Christopher Dearnley, my ex-colleague from St. Paul's, then living in a nudist colony, and in New Zealand I visited Auckland, Nelson, and some of the well-known tourist sites in both the South and North Islands.

Back in Draycott, and away from the daily routine of choir practice and Evensong, it was time to take stock. What should this retired Cathedral musician do? Aside from the pleasure and relaxation we get from canal boating, three things came to mind: teaching, travel, and pens.

T for teaching. Everyone who runs a choir is a teacher, and though I'd never been through any sort of formal teacher training, over the years I'd worked out a way I could pass on what knowledge I had, encouraging people of all ages to sing. It's an interesting thought that organists of my generation did all their own voice training – there were no visiting singing teachers either at Guildford or St. Paul's Cathedral, though we did have some expert help later on at St. Albans. The psychology of teaching had always fascinated me, and it wasn't just with my own choirs.

One day in 1981 my phone had rung in London. It was the headmaster of a small independent school in Exeter, who asked if I would go down to work with their choir and direct them in an Evensong. That was the start of a near 30-year association with Bramdean School in which I acted as an adviser, temporary choirmaster, organist, and singing teacher. A brand-new and spacious chapel had been built in the school grounds, and in the days when it was a boys' boarding school, a Service was sung there on each of the five school day afternoons, as well as over some weekends. Directed by Donald Hanson, the boys' choir was exceptionally good, and as editor of BBC Choral Evensong programme, I was able to include them in our broadcast schedules on at least two occasions. In its later years (the school finally closed in 2020), it had become co-educational, with just day pupils, and the choir had become mixed. Trained by a succession of choirmasters, from 2010 onwards I spent a good deal of time working with the choir on a regular basis, driving down in the early mornings to take the daily pre-assembly choir practice as well as directing them in their sung Evensongs. I also offered individual singing tuition to any member of the choir who showed interest. From those who took advantage, we discovered several promising soloists, both in the upper and broken voices. The school provided some choral scholarships, and I remember one audition just before Christmas 2010, when an eight-year-old girl came into the chapel, played the violin, and then sang most beautifully. Here was a young musician we simply had to have, and I persuaded Headmaster Tony Connett to offer her a scholarship. What a wise decision he made, for all of us, since that young lady, Helena Paish, went on to win the BBC Young Chorister of the Year competition at the age of 12, singing in the great spaces of St. Paul's Cathedral, London. In 2015 she became a founder member of the girls' choir at Truro Cathedral, going on from there to Trinity College, Cambridge, as a choral scholar. Helena and I worked together for more than ten years, as did another young Bramdean singer, flautist and pianist, Catherine Stoyle, with whom I am also still in contact during her university days.

In March 1998 it was a real surprise to receive an official-looking letter saying that I had been awarded an OBE (Officer of the Order of the British Empire). Totally unexpected, these things don't just happen, and behind the scenes I gathered that many people associated with St. Albans Abbey had put in nominations. A few months

later, Buffie, Tim, Nicola and I went
to Buckingham Palace where I had the
honour of being invested with the medal by the Queen herself, after which we
went for a celebratory family lunch at
the Royal Festival Hall. Although I'm
the one wearing the medal, the honour really does belong to everyone I've
worked with throughout my musical
career.

Just before leaving St. Albans at
the end of 1997, I had an approach
from Leslie East, the Head of Choral
Publications at Novello and Co. Ltd., to
see if I might be interested in assembling
an anthology of music for upper voices.
Leslie had been a chorister with me at
St. Andrew's Church, Kingsbury, and
it was good to link up with him again.
With the help of my editor, Elizabeth
Robinson, we started to assemble possible items, some of which would appear
in print for the first time.

OBE day, June 1998

In mid-1998 the collection was published under the title *High Praise*, and it was
at about that time I joined a panel of choral advisers. My colleagues were Ralph
Allwood, Suzi Digby, David Hill, and Brian Kay, and we met at Novello's London
headquarters. Over the next few years each of us concentrated on a particular aspect
of the choral repertoire, mine to find and edit the material for eight more collections,
including *High Praise 2*, *Sing Low*, and *More than Hymns* volumes 1 and 2, now in
many church and cathedral choir libraries.

Cathedral choirs were to come back into my life, not just in nearby Wells, but
also in the Essex town of Chelmsford, where the Organist and Director of Music,
Dr. Graham Elliott, was leaving to take up an appointment in the USA. Might I be
available to move to Chelmsford in late October 1999 to run the Cathedral choir until
his successor was appointed? It would be back to teaching mode.

Being an interim is never easy, and that proved to be so at Chelmsford. The boys
seemed to be sullen and resentful that their choirmaster had 'deserted' them. I got the
impression that they had been held on a very tight rein in choir, and they couldn't get

used to a more relaxed approach where they themselves were expected to be responsible for their own attitude and behaviour. It may not have been the best time for either the boys or me, but working with the men of the choir was a delight, and over those few months we had some great musical and social times together. Among the changing voices were three ex-choristers who would later go on to make their own special mark in the musical world: Tim Mead to the choir of King's College, Cambridge, and on to the world of opera; Tim Wayne-Wright as an alto in the world-famous King's Singers; and James Kennerley, now Organist and Director of Music at the only Roman Catholic choir school in the USA in Cambridge, Massachusetts. I stayed on at Chelmsford until mid-February 2000, when the new Organist, Peter Nardone, took over.

2001 dawned for me a long way from home – as guest Director of the RSCM summer school in Johannesburg. I had flown out to South Africa soon after Christmas, linking up at Heathrow airport with organist, Simon Morley, who was to be our expert accompanist for the week. Although apartheid had ended six years earlier, the centre of Johannesburg was still an unhappy and unsafe place to be on your own. There was strict security and some tension in getting us to and from the Cathedral safely, though the opposite was true at St. John's College where everything was delightfully relaxed.

Well, it would have been relaxed, but for a looming musical deadline. A year or so earlier, we'd been visiting Rowland and Nicola Sidwell in Guildford. At that time, Nicola was working for Guildford Borough Council as the general manager of the Guildford Philharmonic Orchestra, and was planning the following season's concerts. Would I like to do a choral concert in the Cathedral in March 2001, and if so, what should we include in the programme? Having decided on an audience pleasing Fauré Requiem in the first half, we then started to discuss the second half. Realising that it was the eve of Passion Sunday I casually remarked, 'Well, we could do the orchestrated version of John Stainer's *Crucifixion*', assuming there would be a version in the publisher's hire library.

I should have kept my big mouth shut! There was no orchestration, but with Nicola's enthusiasm for the idea I felt I couldn't backtrack on my suggestion. I'd have to orchestrate it myself. Easier said than done; I knew as much about writing for an orchestra as a glider pilot knows about flying a jumbo jet. Still, there seemed to be a lot of time until the date of the concert, and with a bit of study and advice it should be possible.

Now in Johannesburg, just 16 weeks before the concert, here I was looking at a vocal score open at page one and a huge blank sheet of manuscript paper. Mild panic was setting in. It had to be completed well before March so that the instrumental parts could be prepared. I grabbed my pencil and began. There was no chance of getting beyond the first two or three movements in the time I had available here, but at least it was a start.

Four weeks later, in Norwalk, Connecticut, USA, at the home of Vince Edwards and Rodney Ayers, I persuaded them to clear their dining room table and leave me alone for several hours while I made the supreme effort to get as near to completion as I could.

By the end of February it was finished, and the printed orchestral parts were carefully prepared by Graeme McCullough, who was then singing bass in Wells Cathedral Choir. The full score would have to remain in my pencilled handwriting, but at least I would be able to read it.

On the morning of Friday 30th March 2001, the orchestra, with soloists Robert Johnston (tenor) and Stephen Charlesworth (baritone), assembled at a central London venue for rehearsal. Although the work was well known to the soloists, it was completely new to the orchestra, and our allotted three hours flew by. In that time, we'd managed to get through most of the movements – though tomorrow, all the hymns, apart from the specially orchestrated last one, would be accompanied by Stephen Farr on the organ.

The following evening, Saturday 31st March (the 100th Anniversary of Sir John's death), the world premiere of the orchestral version of *The Crucifixion* took place in Guildford Cathedral in the presence of an appreciative, capacity audience. Less than two years later, starting on a snowy January afternoon, we were back in Guildford Cathedral to record it, this time with soloists Peter Auty (tenor) and Roderick Williams (baritone), with Malcolm Archer as our recording producer. Issued as a CD just before Easter, I was more than apprehensive as to how it would be received by the critics; after all, Stainer intended the work solely for liturgical use, with just organ accompaniment. It was quite a relief to read this review from John Quinn in *Music Web International*:

> *I must say I was a little perturbed to find that this recording was in a new orchestration by Barry Rose. It concerned me that orchestral dress was bound to change the essential nature of the work and make it into an inflated concert hall work, something which it emphatically is not. In the event I need not have been concerned at all. Yes, the use of an orchestra inevitably imparts a different character to the work. However, Rose has done his work with such skill, sympathy and understanding that the result is never less than convincing. Indeed, while most performances of The Crucifixion will remain the preserve of organists (and rightly so), Barry Rose has added a new dimension and I sincerely hope his orchestral version will be taken up and widely performed.*

Across the Atlantic

T for travel. For many years now, I've been going back and forth across the Atlantic on a regular basis to work with choirs in the eastern part of the USA. It all began in Guildford way back in 1973, when Gerre Hancock, the Organist and Choirmaster of St. Thomas Church, Fifth Avenue, New York, came to stay with us for two weeks. Gerre had been appointed to St. Thomas' in 1971 at a time when their school, the only Episcopal choir school in the USA, was threatened with closure. The church had sought an organist who was a brilliant improviser, and Gerre was singularly talented in that field. A year later, the Reverend John Andrew, Rector of the parish church in the city of Preston, U.K., was appointed as Rector of St. Thomas', and immediately decided that the choir school would not be closed, under any circumstances. It was John who suggested to Gerre that he should take some time in the summer of 1973 to visit the U.K. and hear English boys' choirs at work. Gerre arranged to visit David Willcocks at King's College, Cambridge, to observe the choir at rehearsals and in Services. At the end of his time there, Gerre asked David where he should go next, and was told, 'Go to Guildford.' For the next two weeks, Gerre attended every one of our choir practices and Services, even coming on tour with us when we sang in Boxgrove Priory and Arundel Roman Catholic Cathedral. As a result of that visit, I was invited to be guest director of the very first official Choirmasters' Conference at St. Thomas' in May 1974 – something I would do another eight times over the next 40 years.

In 2004, Gerre was succeeded by John Scott, with whom I'd worked so closely at St. Paul's, and soon after his appointment, John invited me back to St. Thomas' to direct another Choirmasters' Conference. I told John I'd only come if we could work

With John Scott at St. Thomas Church, New York

together again in one of the Evensongs, (they are usually accompanied by one of the assistant organists). Luckily for me, he agreed. It was quite like old times.

St. Thomas' may have music of a cathedral standard, but just as exciting had been the invitation in 1985 to work with the combined parish choirs of St. Peter's, Philadelphia, Christ Church, Greenwich, and St. Peter's, Morristown, New Jersey. Arranged by Tom Whittemore, Organist and Choirmaster at St. Peter's, Philadelphia, we got through an ambitious programme of music over the weekend, helped and encouraged by Peter Conte's superb organ playing.

In 1988 it was Tom who masterminded the first RSCM summer school to be held at the Valley Forge Military Academy in Wayne, Pennsylvania. Whilst it may have been musically of a high standard, the same couldn't be said about the facilities, which included spartan dormitories, communal washing facilities, and toilets with no doors! A loyal following returned for the next two years, after which the course moved to King's College, Wilkes Barre, where today it remains the most popular and best attended of all the RSCM courses around the country.

Among the many other invitations to work with choirs was one from St. Catherine's Girls School in Richmond, Virginia. Nick Stephenson, the Director of Music, had a choir of which he could be justly proud, and in the first of my visits they, with boys from nearby St. Christopher's School, gave an exciting performance of Edward Elgar's large-scale anthem, *Give unto the Lord, O ye mighty*, with Nick playing the demanding organ part. When the St. Catherine's girls visited the U.K. we were able to host them for an Evensong at St. Albans, and on a later tour with the boys of St. Christopher's, I had the opportunity to work with them in the chapel of Emmanuel College, Cambridge. Over the following years I went back to St. Catherine's and St. Christopher's on several occasions, and in more recent times, Greg Vick, the Organist at St. Christopher's, and I linked up for another choir rehearsal at the school, as well as a reunion lunch with Nick Stephenson.

In summer 2003, Michael McCarthy, former bass lay clerk during my time at St. Albans Abbey, was appointed as Director of Music at Washington National Cathedral, and I was invited to direct them on a couple of occasions on their first tour under Michael's leadership – mainly in and around New York, where the venues included St. Thomas Church for Evensong and a pre-Mass recital in the church of St. Mary the Virgin, near Times Square. Since then, Michael has welcomed me to his home and the Cathedral where, on one occasion, I was handed the scores of some music I'd never seen before, to direct with the girl choristers in Evensong that same afternoon!

Meeting any choir for the first time can often be a daunting prospect for both the visiting director and the singers. To achieve optimum musical results, there needs to be some sense of continuity, and the start of my longest continuing association with church choirs in the USA had begun on a snowy evening in January 1996 when I arrived at Boston's Logan airport. The occasion was to be the very first of a Three Choirs Festival weekend with the boys and girls from the choirs of St. Paul's Church, Fairfield, First Congregational Church, Milford, and St. James Church, West Hartford, where the Festival was taking place. Because of the snow, road travel was impossible, so I stayed the night in an airport hotel, meeting the choirs for the first time at a rehearsal in West Hartford the following evening.

More than 50 young singers looked expectantly at me – and I at them – each wondering where to begin, and each of us having no idea that we were starting something that continues 25 years later. The three choir directors, Vince Edwards, John Abdenour and Brian Carson, had left it to me to suggest some upper-voice repertoire for a Saturday Evensong and a Sunday morning Mass. Somehow we got through it all in that first rehearsal, leaving time the following morning for the boys and girls to build on what we'd started the evening before, but more importantly, to feel that they now knew the choir director (a little), and what he might be asking of them. Those early days were not just pioneering, but also challenging, as we tackled bigger and bigger repertoire, now including altos, tenors and basses. Some might feel that the zenith was when Johnson Flucker and Bruce Neswick invited us to hold the Festival in the great spaces of the Cathedral of St. John the Divine, New York, though I tend to think that we were at our most musical in the following ones at St. Thomas, Fifth Avenue, New York, and in All Saints Church, Worcester, Massachusetts, where those most important elements of Evensong, the psalm singing and the responses, were at their most cohesive and communicative.

At St. Thomas Church, New York, for one of our Festival Evensongs

Philadelphia has long been a second home to me, during Tom Whittemore's tenure at St. Peter's Church, Matt Glandorf's time at St. Mark's, Locust Street, and with Peter Richard Conte at St. Clement's Church. On a personal level I've cherished the friendship and support of Peggy and Denny Hatch, who first hosted me in their

Gaskill Street home when the St. Albans choir visited in 1994, and since then have regularly revived and housed this ailing and wan choir director when he has appeared on their doorstep at all hours of the day and night.

At St. Peter's I have not only worked with the choirs, but also written an anthem for them, whilst at St. Mark's, I've rehearsed and conducted the choir, and also been part of a church music seminar. The 12-voice professional choir at St. Clements has carefully guided me through the complicated Orders of Mass for High Days, whilst I've enjoyed making the best of unaccompanied polyphony and Gregorian chant with them.

Perhaps the icing on the cake has been playing the mighty Wanamaker organ in what is now Macy's store. Resident organist, Peter Richard Conte, is always so gracious when I visit, allowing me to play one or more of the lunch-time or evening concerts, though as I tell him each time, 'I'm not really a concert organist', and I certainly won't do it unless he chooses the stops and tells me which of the six manuals to use!

With Peter Richard Conte at the Wanamaker organ, Philadelphia

And then there's Trinity Church on the Green in New Haven, Connecticut, where the long-standing tradition of their first-class boys' choir has now been joined by a more recent girls' programme. Long-serving Organist, Walden Moore, is among the most highly respected and gifted choir trainers I know, and every time I take one of their boys' practices I marvel at their maturity and professionalism – an example to so many choirs.

❧

P for pen. What's all this about pens? Surely you write with a pen, and that's all? Not so – there are avid pen collectors all round the world, and I've been (and still am, up to a point) one of them. In the mid to late 1940s, most children used a fountain pen at school; the sort you either filled with ink by a side lever, or by pressing a button on the top of the barrel. Although superseded by the Biro, fountain pens were still available in the latter part of the 20th century, the ink now being supplied in more convenient cartridge form.

So how did I start collecting? I remember the day well. It was while I was teaching at The King's School, Canterbury. One morning I was asked to help at a House assembly, and arriving there I threw down my jacket before starting to play the piano. After the assembly, on the train to London, I reached into my pocket to use my rolled gold Parker 61 pen. It had gone! Either I'd dropped it somewhere, or a light-fingered boy had taken a fancy to it. That Monday evening I was walking through Covent Garden Market where there were stalls selling antiques and collectibles. On one of the stalls was an array of colourful fountain pens. I bought one – a Conway Stewart – and passing through the Market the following week I bought another. So began a collection that ended up with nearly 2,000 items, making it the most comprehensive Conway Stewart collection anywhere in the world.

On the way I acquired several new 'pen friends' with whom I've remained in contact ever since. In a coffee bar in London's Brompton Road, I first met Graham Jasper, who opened a wallet and showed me several Conway Stewart pens, some of which I couldn't resist and bought on the spot. Graham was later to be instrumental in finding and supplying many of the choicest items in my collection – it would be quite usual for him to phone me from some pen-show in the USA to see if I wanted to acquire this or that rare item. One of the first contacts I made when we moved to Somerset was Brian Toynton, living in Weston-super-Mare. An expert in all aspects of pen repair and restoration, Brian and I are regularly in contact, often visiting each other's workshops and homes. Always helpful, especially with his research and advice about Conway Stewart pens, is Steve Hull. His published book on the history of Conway Stewart pens is a must for any enthusiast and collector, and many of the pens shown in it were from my collection, photographed by Andy Russell, who would later add to that history with his own book about the Conway Stewart Dinkie pen.

Like most collections, mine grew like topsy, and in the early days I even travelled to Hull for two days of expert tuition in how to restore pens. It may seem strange, but in stressful times of making music, I found (and still find) working with the pens to be so calming and therapeutic. Blackbird, Burnham, Conway Stewart, Mentmore, Onoto, Parker, Swan, Waterman's, Wyvern – you name it, and I might still have one (or several) here in the workshop. Though my own collection has now passed on to a new owner, I still search out more, even as far away as New York, making sure that, when possible, I visit the Fountain Pen Hospital in Lower Manhattan – though music still comes first.

25

Postlude
2010-2021

Back in 2001, we had moved further afield with our Three Choirs Festival – from Connecticut to New York. One venue was the historic Plymouth Church in Brooklyn, where Peter Stoltzfus was then Director of Music, and another Festival took place at St. Bartholomew's Church on Park Avenue, where Vince Edwards was now running their chorister programme. I had recently written an upbeat setting of Psalm 150 for Vince and his choristers, and we were able to include that as one of the anthems.

Patrick Allen, the recently appointed Organist and Master of the Choristers at Grace Church, Lower Broadway, invited us to sing our Saturday Festival Evensong there in 2002. I had previously met Patrick when he was Associate Organist at St. Thomas Church, Fifth Avenue, and a few years after that visit, he suggested that Grace Church might start an annual concert for the novices and junior boys and girls of their choirs, and would I like to direct it?

The first of these was in 2009, and it began a pattern that has continued ever since. Singers of all ages need to learn the art of performing – giving yourself to the words and music, and then communicating both those elements to your congregation or

*With Grace Church choristers
in rehearsal*

audience. And what better age to start learning that skill than eight, nine or ten? Over the years, Patrick and I have established a pattern of post-school afternoon rehearsals on four successive weekdays, together with a full Saturday morning in church, with the concert on Sunday afternoon. That's a lot to ask of young children, especially after a long day at school, but the benefits they get from it are far more than just musical: the discipline of teamwork, the concentration, self-confidence, the excitement of doing something really well, an appreciation of beautiful texts – the list goes on. Over the years we've had expert help from senior mentors who have been through the programme as novices and juniors, and their example has helped us to find new young soloists to make their debut at these concerts.

It was in 1997 that I had first visited Grace Church, when the St. Albans choir gave a concert there, and I was immediately struck by the graceful proportions of the build-

*Stops on the Swell organ –
Grace Church, New York*

ing, both in length and height. What wasn't so pleasing was the church organ, then in dire need of restoration, though that didn't stop guest organist Peter Richard Conte giving a roof-raising performance of his own transcription of *Danse Macabre* by Camille Saint-Saëns. In the end, the church commissioned a brand-new four-manual instrument from Taylor and Boody, dedicated at a special choral concert in 2013 at which I was honoured to be the guest director of the choirs. I happened to be staying with Patrick when the tonal finishing of the instrument started, and with his encouragement I helped set the sound of the softer stops on the Swell organ, around which the rest of the instrument was voiced. Imagine my surprise when the 8-foot flute was named as the Rose Flute!

Life in New York has not always been about work. Buffie, Nicola and I have had some wonderful social occasions, a memorable one being a surprise lunch in 2014 celebrating my 80th birthday and attended by many musical friends from as far afield as Boston and Washington.

One regular social fixture across the years was with Bill Miller, with whom I always made a point of meeting up for lunch or dinner when in town – our friendship went back a very long way. William (Bill) Miller CBE was one of three brothers, two of whom (John and Donald) used to sing at Kingsbury and with The Jacobean Singers. Bill and I had first met in 1958 when he was working for Pfizer at their U.K. base in Sandwich, and we were later to link up again in New York in the early 1980s when he was Vice-Chairman of the board of Bristol-Myers Squibb. Through his life-long interest in music, and with his wife Irene, Bill sponsored the arts in the city, including the Metropolitan Opera where he was Managing Director, and also the Manhattan School of Music, where he received an honorary doctorate and do-nated the William R. and Irene D. Miller Recital Hall. I introduced him to St. Thomas Church in the early 1980s, af-ter which he regularly worshipped there

Lunch with Bill Miller, 2016

and was a member of the Vestry. His lasting memorial is the recently built Miller-Scott organ, for which he was the lead donor and lived to see and hear the project complet-ed in October 2018.

Further north, an unexpected invitation came from Harvard University to work with their choir. Former Cambridge University organ scholar, Edward Elwyn Jones, has been Choirmaster at Harvard since 2003, and among his other duties, he directs the music in Appleton Chapel where his choral scholars sing the Service each weekday morning. It was a pleasure and privilege to direct them for a whole week, in which the choir also sang Compline and Evensong, and since then I have been a regular visitor, working with the choir on a daily basis.

Being in that area has also enabled me to link up again with Dan Moriarty, Choral Director at Groton School. Dan and I met regularly in Philadelphia several years ago when he was Organist and Choirmaster at The Church of the Redeemer, Bryn Mawr, and he often invited me to take his afternoon choir rehearsals. At Groton I've worked with the choir in rehearsals and Services, and also played the organ for some school assemblies.

Another renewed contact has been with Peter Stoltzfus, now Peter Stoltzfus Berton, formerly Organist and Choirmaster at All Saints, Worcester, Massachusetts. While at Worcester, Peter had brought his choir to sing in Gloucester Cathedral, and asked me to direct them. Now in Rhode Island, at the church of St. John the Evangelist in Newport, Peter made contact to see if I might visit, and work with the choir on their 2019 tour to the U.K. I was able to get to Newport for a pre-tour Evensong, and also speak at a fundraising English Tea. A few months later I met up with the choir again in Worcester U.K. where they sang Services in the Cathedral, as well as in Tewkesbury Abbey and Hereford Cathedral. It was a great week with some really first-class singing.

From what you've just read, you may be tempted to think that I spend most of my musical time abroad. That's not quite so. In recent years I've been privileged to play several organ concerts in Wells Cathedral, and courtesy of Stephen Layton, direct the stunning choir at Trinity College, Cambridge in an occasional Evensong. A special delight has been the opportunity to see and hear the growth of the new girls' choir at Truro Cathedral, and also to be given the opportunity to work with them in rehearsals and Evensongs. Through the kindness of Christopher Gray, their director, I was also able to continue to work with Helena Paish, one of the founder choristers, as well as giving a couple of informal song recitals with her.

One of the biggest musical gatherings I've seen in the past 20 years was at St. Albans Abbey on Saturday 14th June 2014. Courtesy of the Dean, and Andrew Lucas, the Master of the Music, we had a Festival Evensong to celebrate my 80th birthday. From my past at Guildford, the BBC, St. Paul's and St. Albans, there was a phalanx of amazing singers who could manage anything musical thrown at them. Together with the boys and men of the Abbey choir they filled the whole quire area – a sound that

Rehearsing for Evensong in St. Albans Abbey, 14th June 2014

had to be heard to be believed. I don't think I will ever forget the quality of the massed altos, tenors and basses singing Franz Biebl's *Ave Maria* as the anthem that afternoon – quite the best and most exciting performance of that piece I've ever heard or am ever likely to hear.

Afterwards, at a reception in the lady chapel, Richard Tanner had organised speeches and presentations, including, from St. Paul's, a replica of one of the choir lamps (this time, complete with lampshade) to remind me of the 1981 Royal Wedding. The day ended with a celebratory dinner and more singing.

≈

Reading this memoir may have seemed like an unending list of places and events, and that's probably the only way of describing a musical career in chronological terms. But alongside all that, there's also been our life as a family, with our three delightful children, now grown adults. How time has flown since Buffie and I first became parents in June 1971.

Tim, our eldest, currently working in Scotland, is easily the most widely travelled of all of us. Beside him, my journeys pale into insignificance. At the age of 12 he had already visited Australia, Spain, Greece, Sweden and Holland with the choir of St. John's College, Cambridge, and maybe that kindled the wanderlust that has since taken him to such countries as Japan, China, Kenya, Egypt, India, Borneo, Myanmar, Iceland, Vietnam, the Caribbean – and these are just a few.

One of three family members to hold a university degree, Tim (B.A.) graduated a year after Buffie was awarded her B.A. in Art and Design, appropriately presented to her in St. Albans Abbey, with her proud husband playing the organ at the ceremony.

The third is our younger daughter Nicola who, somewhat like her father, took a few years to end up in the profession that was calling her – music. Graduating with a B.Mus. from the Royal Welsh College of Music, Nicola now teaches there, as well as living a busy freelance life as an accompanist and repetiteur. There have been many occasions when Nicola and I have been able to make music together, the most far-flung being in Sydney, Australia, in July 2019 for Sydney inSpires – a week-long course for musicians of all ages. We worked together with the boys and girls in an intensive and exciting week that saw them singing for David Hill, John Rutter and Noël Tredinnick, as well as in the Services that I directed.

Julia and her husband John still live in St. Albans with their fast-growing children, Luke, Sam and Libby. Luke, now 18, is already out at work, following his father into the family security firm, and before we know it, Sam and Libby will have left school.

It's such a delight to see the close bond between our three children, and one of my regrets is that I didn't spend more time with them during their early years – though they don't seem to hold that against me. In some ways, I've never been a close family man – the Rose family (my two sisters and myself) usually only meet up for the hatch-match-and-dispatch occasions, though since I've stopped full-time employment, there have been many more times when Buffie, our children and the grandchildren have

September 2020 – with the grandchildren, Buffie, Julia and Nicola after reaching the top of the Foxton lock flight on the Grand Union Canal

been able to meet together. We all share a love of canal-boating, and if you've never tried it, it is the ideal relaxation for anyone who leads a busy life. There you are in the slow lane – no more than four miles per hour, seeing towns and the countryside from a totally different perspective as you glide peacefully along a tiny proportion of the 4,700 miles of the canal system. Apart from the sheer enjoyment and relaxation, it's also a time to stop and think, almost impossible with the speed of life these days. And it's here I ought to be thought-provoking and maybe philosophical – though that's never been me.

But hold on, you've come this far on my journey and are probably still asking yourselves 'how' and 'why'? Some years ago, I attempted to answer that question, and you might now want to skip to the Appendix (page 298), which contains the opening address I gave in Houston, USA, to the 1988 National Convention of the Guild of American Organists.

∾

For those who've stayed here, in the twilight of my life, I can now look back with gratitude at the many musical privileges I've had. Who'd have thought that the 24-year-old who bought a 2/6d brick at the new Guildford Cathedral would one day have the privilege of creating its musical foundation? Who'd have thought that this 11-year-old schoolboy, one of the millions of sightseers to St. Paul's Cathedral would one day have the privilege of directing the music in that great building? Who'd have thought that this keen, young, would-be church musician who tuned into BBC radio Choral Evensongs in the early 1950s would one day end up at the BBC with the privilege of running and producing the programme?

How, and why? There has to be a guiding hand that puts you on life's path, and a voice, that in those early days said to me, 'this is what you *have* to do'.

I introduced this book with a mention of faith and Faith, and it's the latter that has seen me through the good and not-so-good times. The dear old Church of England – top heavy in administration and slowly sinking into obscurity for lack of clergy at parish level – has been my home, comfort, inspiration (and frustration) for the past 75 years. More than half a century ago, Dean Tony Bridge at Guildford had his own strong views about it. He once accused the C of E of '*transforming itself into a bureaucratic annexe to the Welfare State with a few pious and neo-Gothic overtones. Hag-ridden by committees and worm-eaten by synodical government, it has dedicated itself to activism, it has banished prayers, mystery, silence, beauty and its own rich musical and liturgical heritage to a few remote oases in order to make way for hymns written by third-rate disciples of Noël Coward and sung to the strident noise of guitars played by charismatic curates in jeans.*'

Plus ça change, plus c'est la même chose?

Whatever your views, all I can hope is that something of what I learned from so many amazing people might have passed on to those with whom I've worked. Music carries a message, and we musicians are the messengers. In church, our musical message is to convey the Eternal truths – what a challenge, what an honour, and what a privilege.

From harmonium to Heavenly harmony – and occasional earthly strife; I wouldn't have wanted it any other way – *Deo gratias*!

26

More Than a Hobby
Guild Records 1967–1994

The Cathedral choir at Guildford was singularly fortunate to have a contract with the world-famous EMI company, and by the end of 1966 had made four records with them, including two best-selling Christmas discs.

In 1967 the contract came up for renewal, and this time I suggested that we should record the Allegri *Miserere* as a matter of some urgency. John Dexter, our top-C soloist, was then at his peak, and his treble voice would probably not last beyond the end of that year. The response from EMI was that they would think about it, but in the meantime they had other projects they'd like us to take on.

Determined to capture John singing the Allegri, Nicolas Ware (son of the Precentor, and now my brother-in-law) and I met in the Lyons teashop in Guildford High Street to talk about how we could make that happen. Nick was now working for the BBC as a sound engineer and making recordings of the Cathedral choir in his spare time. We came up with a plan to form our own record company. EMI's offer to renew would be declined, though we hoped they would continue to use the choir and the Cathedral for future projects. Sitting at the table in the teashop, we decided on the name GUILD (after Guildford) RECORDS, upturning two empty cups of different sizes and drawing round them, coming up with a large G. This would be our crest, both on record labels and sleeves, in the shade of blue usually associated with Guildford Cathedral.

Dean George Clarkson, who would have signed the renewal of the EMI contract, wished us good luck in our new venture, at the same time stressing that there would be no money available from cathedral funds. To produce any discs, we would need some capital, and it came from alto lay clerk, Roger Lowman. To preserve his investment, a legal agreement was drawn up by a firm of local solicitors.

We decided to begin with three 7-inch EP records, labelling them GRS 301-303 – the S for Stereo, with similar records with an M (Mono) prefix for those customers who did not yet have stereo record players. GRS 301 contained four items sung

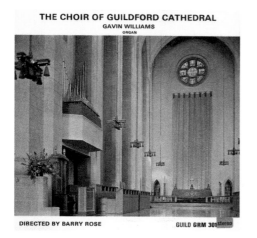

THE CHOIR OF GUILDFORD CATHEDRAL
GAVIN WILLIAMS
ORGAN

DIRECTED BY BARRY ROSE   GUILD GRM 301 stereo

by the full choir: Thomas Morley's *Nolo mortem peccatoris*; the *Nunc Dimittis in F* by George Dyson (bass solo by Phillip Mindenhall); John Joubert's setting of *There is no Rose of such virtue*; and the hymn, *The God of love, my shepherd is*, sung to the tune *University*, with a tenor solo verse by Robert Hammersley. The recording was made in one evening, early in July 1967, on a Revox tape recorder borrowed from Patrick Heigham, one of Nick's colleagues at the BBC.

The following evening the boys alone made the second EP – GRS/GRM 302 – featuring five items, the longest being the first set of *Sacred Songs for Treble Voices* by Alan Ridout. Written two years earlier for the boys of Canterbury Cathedral Choir, this was its very first recording. The other items on the EP were A.E. Baker's arrangement of the French carol *Whence is that goodly fragrance flowing?* Leonard Blake's setting of *And now another day is gone*; the plainsong hymn, *Hail, true body, born of Mary*; and Richard Dering's two-part motet, *Gaudent in Coelis*. Our recording producer was Clifford Mould (then a tenor lay clerk and teaching at Lanesborough School), who gave us a lot of guidance and musical help during the various takes.

Gavin Williams, the Sub-Organist, agreed to make an EP of the organ (I had already made one a couple of years before for the Ryemuse label). What better piece to show off the full organ sound than the well-known *Toccata* from the Fifth Symphony by Charles-Marie Widor? That would fill one side of the disc, and for the other side, Gavin chose a Flor Peeters chorale prelude on *Uns ist geboren ein Kindlein*, and we both played the Thomas Tomkins *A Fancy for Two to Play*.

The whole object of founding Guild Records had been to record the Allegri *Miserere*, and though we planned to do that at the July sessions for the EP records, we ran out of time. John Dexter said he would stay on in the choir for an extra term (he was leaving Lanesborough School to go to the Royal Grammar School), so the recording could wait until after the summer break. The comforting thing was that John, now just 13, was quite small in stature and would almost certainly keep his treble voice intact until Christmas 1967 when he would formally leave the choir.

Our immediate priority was to assemble the master-tapes of the three EP recordings and start to prepare the necessary paperwork for the Mechanical Copyright Protection Society, without whose official permission no records could be made – they represent the interests of composers and authors on recordings and collect and distribute royalties on their behalf.

The next step was to find a company that would produce the master lacquer discs. From these, the stampers could be made from which the discs would be pressed. Orlake Ltd. had been founded in 1963 and was located in Dagenham, Essex, from where they produced discs for several independent record companies. As new customers, we were required to pay up-front, and it was then a case of waiting for a few test-pressings; though, since we were not just new but small customers, our order had to fit around the thousands of pop-records that Orlake were pressing each week.

The test-pressings arrived, and Nick, Roger and I were able to play them on our home equipment. The quality was variable, and often there were clicks and bumps. We logged each fault and sent the details off to Orlake, hoping that the finished records would be perfect.

In the end, we had no option but to accept whatever they produced, not least since we had an October 1967 date for the launch of Guild Records and had taken advertising space in the national magazines, *Gramophone*, *Records and Recording*, and *Gramophone Record Review*. We contacted the record department in Harvey's, our local department store, and they agreed to give us a full window display at the beginning of October, provided we could produce some montages of record sleeves etc. That was something we'd have to make ourselves, but first we needed the sleeves. With cover photos taken by Nick, they were printed by the West Surrey Printing Company in Byfleet and delivered in late September.

The launch day came and went, and as well as selling records at Harveys, we were able to offer them to the choir and chorister parents at a discounted price. Copies were sent out for review, and we were delighted with the positive response. Kenneth Long, writing in *Records and Recording*, was exceptionally complimentary:

Barry Rose must be proud to realise that Guildford choir now takes its place amongst the very finest choirs in the country; it runs rings round places like Westminster Abbey and St Paul's. The boys' tone is clear and round and their phrasing beautifully smooth and effortless, even at the top of their range. The full choir possesses all the virtues of good choralism — an impeccable technique (precision, blend, balance, tuning, etc.) coupled with a sensitive response to the music they are singing.

Buoyed by this success, the choir re-assembled on three evenings in early December 1967 to record the Allegri *Miserere* as part of our very first LP – *Music for Passiontide*

(GRS 7001). John Dexter was still in fine voice for the top Cs in the Allegri, ably supported in the solo verses by second treble Roderick Taylor, alto Michael Barry, with David Gibbs and Clifford Mould on the lower part. First, we recorded the full choir verses, plus the last verse, in which the solo group is juxtaposed against the full choir. All the boys, apart from John and Roderick, then went home, and when all was quiet, we recorded the tenor and bass plainsong links between the full and solo verses. That done, just five people remained. Although the treble singing the top Cs usually gets the plaudits in the piece, it is really the second treble who holds the key to much of the tuning, and Roderick Taylor was always one hundred percent reliable with his pitch.

One hour later, all five solo verses had been successfully recorded. We'd done it, and this would be only the second Allegri on an LP – the first being the already famous Argo Records Ash Wednesday Evensong by the choir of King's College, Cambridge, with Roy Goodman as the high treble soloist.

Would ours be as good? We weren't so sure, but maybe we could do something slightly different? We decided to re-record the final solo verse, and this time John Dexter changed a couple of the notes from naturals to sharps. The result was so good (and certainly different) that we all agreed this should be the version to appear on the disc. As a relaxed end to the evening, everyone changed parts for one of the solo verses, albeit a tone lower – Michael Barry taking the top treble part to a high B flat, Clifford Mould on the second treble part, whilst the two boys and David Gibbs filled in the alto and low tenor part. The result had to be heard to be believed!

Although in separate sections, we now had the complete Allegri on the same recording tape. It was a puzzle that Nick needed to sort out, with a razor blade – the usual way of editing recordings in those days – and we spent half a day in his bedroom at No. 3 Cathedral Close to assemble a final 'performance'. Having decided which take of each verse to use, Nick cut it out from the master tape, put it on one side and re-joined the tape so we could go on listening.

Some hours later, spread out over the bedroom carpet were rows of small pieces of tape that had been cut from the master – full choir verses on the left, plainsong verses in the centre, and on the right, the precious solo verses. Neither of us dared move for fear of treading on one of them. Painstakingly, each was spliced together, and when complete, we played it through, hoping there would be no dropouts at the joins (usually caused by the razor blade becoming magnetised). We were immediately disappointed. Several of the edits went through with an audible 'plop', and somewhat dejectedly we switched off the equipment and retreated for a cup of tea, wondering if that was the end of our Allegri project.

The next day we played the tape again, and this time it was perfect – almost as though there'd been some Divine intervention. With the addition of several more items,

Music for Passiontide was now complete, though it would be another 12 months or so before it would be ready for release. We had other recordings to make elsewhere.

~

The first of these was at Wimborne Minster in Dorset where Michael Austin had taken up the post of Organist and Choirmaster and was keen to record the recently restored organ. One advantage of an EP record is that it can be recorded in one evening, though a good deal of that time is often spent in finding the ideal positioning of microphones to convey not just the clarity of the instrument but also the size of the building. Michael had chosen an eclectic mix of pieces, the first of which, by Francis Jackson, showcased the new Orchestral Trumpet stop which pro-

truded horizontally (*en chamade*) high above the front pipes.

Having found the right recording balance, Michael played the Jackson *Fanfare*, a Bach Trio, and the *Final* from Louis Vierne's First Organ Symphony quite brilliantly, and we left Wimborne that evening with little or no editing to do. It was a great success with the critics, being singled out in *Audio Record Review* as one of the records of the year (1968).

For the second EP we travelled just 13 miles to Farnborough Abbey, and this time I did the playing. Noel Mander had loaned the Abbey one of his 'Hoxne' model organs and suggested that we might like to record it at his expense. With four pieces from the 18th and 19th centuries, we called the disc *English Organ Music (1700-1850)*. Issued only in mono, it was favourably reviewed by Geoffrey Cuming in the April 1969 issue of *Gramophone* (left).

Music for Passiontide, our first LP, would be ready for distribution and sale early in 1969, and we decided on a release date to coincide

ENGLISH ORGAN MUSIC. Barry Rose (organ). Guild Ⓜ GRM304 (7 in., 13s. 11d.). Played on a Hoxne Organ, Farnborough Abbey Church. Guild Records, 1 Cathedral Cottage, Ridgemount, Guildford, Surrey.
English Organ Music: **James.** Voluntary in A minor. **Camidge.** Gavotte in A minor. **S. Wesley.** Air and Gavotte in F major. **Travers.** Cornet Voluntary.

The instrument is a two-manual organ with 15 stops, designed and built by Noel Mander. Normally used for continuo work, it is ideally suited to music of the kind presented here, and it records very well in the favourable acoustics of Farnborough Abbey. The company has decided to issue the record in mono only, as it was felt that the stereo gave a larger-than-life impression; the organ is only 4 ft. 3 in. wide! Barry Rose gives a delightfully neat performance of these pieces, which is all they require.

with Ash Wednesday (19th February). For the sleeve illustration we trawled some of Buffie's art books, choosing the Raphael painting of *The Crucifixion* hanging in the National Gallery in London. We needed their permission to use it, paying a fee and signing an agreement that there would be an acknowl-

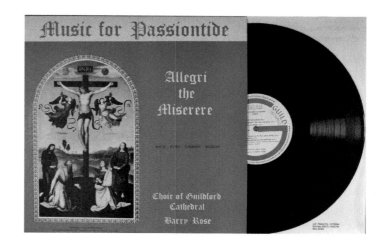

edgement of the permission on the sleeve.

Now we needed to find a printer. Looking at sleeves from the major record companies, we had spotted the name of Senol Printing Ltd., a family-run business in Croydon. Somehow we persuaded them to print 1,000 copies of our *Music for Passiontide* sleeve, though they did point out that our small job would have to fit around much bigger orders.

The test-pressings arrived, and this time the quality was quite acceptable. There was the occasional small click, but there wasn't time to complain and ask Orlake to start again. Much of the music was out of copyright, so this time there were only small payments to make to MCPS. The records were ready for Ash Wednesday 1969, and we were left to wonder what the critics would say.

Some of the reviews were mixed, and this time, Kenneth Long, who had been so kind about our first EP recordings, was a bit critical:

It is courageous of Guildford to challenge King's on their own ground and to record Allegri's *Miserere* again, complete with *abbellimenti*, and there is no denying that John Dexter makes a splendid job of his top C's. Indeed the whole performance is very good indeed, yet somehow it lacks the sheer magic of the King's version. Perhaps this is because the King's recording has a far greater feeling of peace and serenity: it all seems so effortless that the voices, almost disembodied, seem to float. Not only is Guildford a shade faster, but the flowing lines of polyphony are constantly disturbed by an irritating habit of exaggerating consonants. Listen, for example, to the initial h on the very first word; t's are particularly bad. This fault spoils much of the rest of the record too.

Nevertheless, as I have often said before, Guildford is undoubtedly one of the finest cathedral choirs in the country, and a well chosen programme of great music sung by them can hardly fail to give pleasure, in spite of the minor criticisms I have listed. The recording is satisfactory, balance is good, and the silent surfaces set a shining example to some of the mammoth companies.   K.L.

Records and Recording, *March 1969*

Meanwhile, we'd had another approach from Noel Mander – might we be interested in recording his recently restored Renatus Harris organ in the City of London church of St. Botolph, Aldgate? The church had been damaged by fire in 1966, and on its re-opening later that year, John Oxlade, then in his early 20s, had been appointed as Organist and Choirmaster. Noel offered to cover all the costs of the recording, and in mid-1968, Nick and I spent three nights recording in the church – late, since we wanted to avoid as much traffic noise as possible.

The finished record was released in mid-1969, bringing our LP catalogue to two. We needed to think about another. Francis Jackson, the distinguished and long-serving Organist of York Minster had played the opening recital on the new Guildford Cathedral organ in October 1961, and early in 1969 he asked if we might be interested in recording him on the historic organ in Downpatrick Cathedral, Northern Ireland. The idea had come about through Francis' friendship with Lord Henry Dunleath, a keen amateur organist who lived nearby at Ballywalter Park. We wasted no time in responding positively – Guild Records would now have an internationally-known concert organist on its label.

In late summer, Nick and I took the boat from Liverpool to Belfast, motoring on to Downpatrick where we booked into a local guest house, while Francis stayed with Lord Dunleath. Over the next three days, Francis recorded works by Charles Wood, Charles Villiers Stanford, Felix Mendelssohn and Samuel Sebastian Wesley.

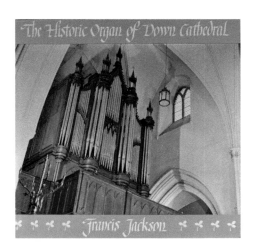

Back in Guildford we edited the finished tapes, and a few weeks later were able to send a test-pressing to Francis for his comments. Everything seemed acceptable – even the quality of Orlake's pressing – and after completing the usual MCPS forms, the discs were manufactured.

In the meantime we needed a sleeve, and what better predominant colour for an Irish disc than green? Living near Guildford was an expert calligrapher, Anthony Gardner OBE, who had written many headings etc. for royal occasions. We engaged him to write the script on the front of the sleeve, framing one of Nick's photos of the organ.

One choral and two organ LPs – where would we go from here? In the end the decision was virtually made for us, following a suggestion that we might record the two forthcoming Diocesan Choirs Festivals. The Festivals took place in the Cathedral each year on two Saturdays in October, and the discs would be available for purchase by everyone who took part.

The repertoire for 1969 contained one really ambitious item – a Harvest anthem, specially written for the occasion by Derek Bourgeois (1941-2017) who was then doing his teaching-practice at nearby Cranleigh School. One of his colleagues in the school's preparatory department was English teacher, Ian Freegard. Ian was a regular member of the Cathedral congregation at most weekday Evensongs, and at some stage when we were talking, I lamented the lack of good anthems suitable for Harvest. It might have been that conversation that spurred Ian to write a new and imaginative text, opening with a 20th century slant:

> *The plum and wasp is boiling in the kitchens, great nets spawn silver into trawlers' hulls. The cannery and brewery are working round the clock. The honoured altar-bread and chaliced wine with grateful glow are set before the Kindly One who planned this harvest, and parents bring their quiversful of children to marvel at the marrow and the sheaf-shaped loaf.*

> *Loving Lord of the green fingers, look now upon our harvest-shaven fields, The window-plants, the dahlias in cottage gardens, and hear the honest voices 'plough and scatter' in thanks for blessed ripeness You have sent.*

> *And with their thanks, men pray for wisdom, for charity, that all may share in your harvest of plenty.*

Derek agreed to set it to music, and to say that the result was a challenge for parish choirs is one of the understatements of all time. Brilliantly conceived, with so many deft musical touches painting the text: the insistent clatter at *the cannery and brewery are working round the clock*; the hushed reverence at *the honoured altar-bread...*; and even, in the accompaniment, a quote from the melody of the well-known Harvest hymn, *We plough the fields and scatter*, when the *honest voices plough and scatter* is sung. Added to the adventurous choral writing was a challenging accompaniment that was way beyond the ability of ninety-five percent of parish church organists. However, we were lucky. We would have Gavin Williams to play it at our two Festival Services.

At that time, the Cathedral choir did not take part in the Festivals, so every note and phrase of the *Harvest Anthem* had to be sung by the participating parish choirs.

It was not easy – most of the singers struggled with the new idiom, and added to that, there was no printed version – the large and clear original manuscript was now small and cramped after it had been reduced in size to fit the Festival booklet. Everyone found it difficult to read the handwritten text, let alone get the notes right... and in tune... and in time.

Rehearsals were painful – grinding out the notes and learning them parrot-fashion – but somehow, at the two Festivals, we got through the new piece, though we were not so sure if any of it, or any of the other pieces in the Services, would be worthy of perpetuating on an LP record. On the two Saturdays in October 1969, Nick recorded the Festivals exactly as they took place, both speech and music. A week or so later we met up and listened to the results, choosing a combination of music and speech from both Services.

Now we had our fourth LP for Guild Records – GRS 7004 – not for public sale, but available to every choir member from the Diocese who took part in the Festivals.

THE 1969 GUILDFORD DIOCESAN CHOIRS FESTIVALS

GAVIN WILLIAMS—Organ   Directed by BARRY ROSE   **GRS 7004**
stereo

SIDE ONE.

a) **Alleluia! A. T. Ola-Olude, Ora Elese T'oku** Arranged by Fela Sowande.
(Soprano Soloist: Penelope Cave (Pyrford))
(4th October).

b) **Opening Responses** and the **Lord's Prayer.**

c) **As the watchman longs for dawn** (Psalm 130) Music by Gregory Murray and Joseph Gelineau.
(Shortened version of 4th October)
(Soloist: The Precentor of Guildford Cathedral)

d) **Reading:** Isaiah, Chapter 9, vv. 2, 6, 7.
—Dr. J. B. Gurney Smith.

e) **Chorale: Zion hears her watchmen's voices.** Music by J. S. Bach.
(18th October).

f) **Reading:** St. Matthew, Chapter 1, vv. 18—25
—Mr. Frank Sharman.

g) **Nativity Carol**—Words and Music by John Rutter.
(4th October).

h) **Reading:** St. John, Chapter 3, vv. 12—17
—Dr. J. B. Gurney Smith.

i) **Hymn: My song is love unknown** (verses 1, 2, 3 & 5)
Words by S. Crossman. Music by John Ireland.
(18th October).

j) **Anthem: The strife is o'er.** Words Anonymous 17th Century. Melody by Melchoir Vulpius, arranged by Henry Ley
(18th October).

SIDE TWO.

a) **Hymn: Our Lord, his Passion ended.** Words by F. C. Burkitt. Music by Harold Darke.
(4th October).

b) **Reading:** The Acts of the Apostles, Chapter 2, vv. 1—4a
—The Dean of Guildford.

c) **Anthem: O Lorde, the maker of al thing.** Words by King Henry VIII. Music by John Joubert.
(4th October).

d) **Be thou my vision, O Lord of my heart.** Words translated from the Ancient Irish by Mary Elizabeth Byrne. Music—Traditional Irish Melody.
(18th October).

e) **Responses** (said).

f) **Harvest Anthem**—specially commissioned for these Festivals. Words by Ian Freegard, Music by Derek Bourgeois.
(18th October).

g) **Hymn: All my hope on God is founded.** Words by Robert Bridges. Music by Herbert Howells.
(Verses 1, 2 and 5—4th October.
Verses 3 and 4—18th October).

Sales were good. It was time for another project. But what?

～

We'd long been aware of the fame that Vernon Handley was bringing to Guildford as conductor of the Guildford Philharmonic Orchestra, and I had already worked with him in a concert in the Cathedral. Tod, as he was affectionately known, had formed a young peoples' choir which he named The Proteus, and he was keen for them to make a recording – would we be interested? The answer was yes, and one evening in January 1970 the choir assembled in the Cathedral to record two works by Ralph Vaughan Williams – *Valiant for Truth* and *Silence and Music*. Issued later in the year, with a striking silver sleeve featuring a pen and ink drawing of Mr. Valiant-for-Truth drawn by Tod's wife, Barbara, it was the first of two records that the choir would make under his leadership.

With more music from the 20th century, our next recording was by the Cathedral choir. Among the large-scale anthems now in the repertoire were Sir William Harris's eight-part unaccompanied *Faire is the Heaven* and E.W. Naylor's demanding and dramatic *Vox dicentis: Clama*. Tenors Robert Hammersley and Clifford Mould had both sung *Vox dicentis* at King's College, Cambridge (for whom it was originally written) when they were trebles in the choir, and kept pressing me to do it at Guildford. No-one, apart from King's, seemed to have any copies, so I wrote to Curwen's, the original publishers, who sent me a copy, together with a letter saying that I could copy it as much as I wanted, with no payment to them. I'm still not quite sure why they said that, but I persuaded our local printing firm to replicate 250 copies which we later sold to other cathedral choirs in aid of the Guildford Choir Fund.

With these two anthems, and Alan Ridout's *Third Set of Sacred Songs*, we had the

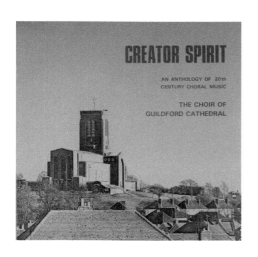

nucleus of our 20th century anthology. To these pieces we added the recently composed *Festival Te Deum* by William Mathias, two Alan Gray pieces from his *1914* sequence of settings of Rupert Brooke poems, and the Derek Bourgeois *Harvest Anthem* written for last year's Diocesan Choirs Festivals. Also included were Brian Easdale's *Ubi caritas et amor*; and Bernard Naylor's unaccompanied *Creator Spirit*, giving the album its title. Unlike earlier and later recordings when the choir sang on the steps facing the west end, this time they sang in the stalls, giving a more definitive audio separation between the two sides in the double-choir anthems.

The LP was released early in 1971 and the reviews were both positive and enthusiastic:

THIS ANTHOLOGY of 20th-century British choral music, entitled 'Creator Spirit' after Dryden's verses set by two of the composers here represented, is an excellent production from all points of view. The programme is varied and interesting, consisting as it does entirely of pieces currently unavailable on other labels; and the standard of performance is consistently high.

The Choir of Guildford Cathedral shows itself to be a highly accomplished body: disciplined, clear of diction, technically almost flawless, and never less than intensely musical.

Records and Recording,
April 1971

Our next venue was Chester Cathedral. The organ had just been rebuilt by Rushworth & Dreaper Ltd. (who had also installed the organ in Guildford Cathedral), and they were keen that their work should be publicised. I had known Roger Fisher, the Cathedral Organist since my boyhood days in Chingford. By the time we made the recording he had been at Chester for three years, and he chose a programme of three contrasting pieces that would demonstrate the wide range of sounds on the newly refurbished organ: *Noël* by Henri Mulet; J.S. Bach's chorale prelude on *Wo soll ich fliehen hin*; and the sparkling *Toccata in G* by Théodore Dubois.

There was a special excitement for us with this project since EMI had agreed to press our records. Sales were good on Chester Cathedral's bookstall, and now that we had also acquired a trade distributor, it was available at a number of record shops around the country.

A year later, on a Saturday evening in September 1971, we were in Blackburn Cathedral to record the recently installed J.W. Walker organ, high up in the newly built extension at the Cathedral's east end. John Bertalot, the Cathedral Organist, played an eclectic programme ranging from

Henry Purcell's *Trumpet Tune and Air* to the impressive *Variations de Concert* by Joseph Bonnet. Coupled with John's imaginative playing and the stunning new acoustic, this was easily the best organ recording we had so far made.

Blackburn Cathedral organ

Now with a current but small catalogue of LPs and EPs, we didn't make any new recordings in the period 1972-1974, apart from a private recording of Patience Strong reading her own poems, illustrated by suitable organ music recorded in Guildford Cathedral, and played by Hilary Davan Wetton, then Director of Music at Cranleigh School.

By early 1975 I was busy with my new work at St. Paul's Cathedral, so when a request came from Rushworth & Dreaper that we might record their new organ in Mold Parish Church (North Wales), Nick undertook to do it on his own, acting as both producer and recording engineer. The result was an LP of 17th century German organ music, stylishly played by Geoffrey Knowles, the resident Organist, which included works by Bach, Buxtehude, Walther, Lübeck, and Krebs. The sleeve design was entrusted to Martin Palmer, one of Nick's students from the Guildford College of Art. Martin would later design artwork for several more of our sleeves, and went on to found and run his own record company, Prelude Records.

Our future recordings would be in much grander ecclesiastical and concert hall surroundings – St. Paul's Cathedral, Westminster Abbey, Salisbury Cathedral, St. Patrick's Cathedral Dublin, the Grote Kerk of St. Bavo, Haarlem, and St. Laurens, Alkmaar, as well as London's Queen Elizabeth Hall. From modest beginnings, Guild Records had really arrived!

Early in 1978, the London Bach Orchestra had recorded the Schubert *Mass in G* with us in St. Paul's Cathedral, and although he wasn't present at the sessions, their founder and artistic director, Martindale Sidwell (my former choirmaster at Hampstead Parish Church), sent a message about the possibility of Guild Records making a disc of Bach works with the orchestra. Their monthly mainly-Bach concerts at the Queen Elizabeth Hall were drawing capacity audiences, and with Martin's help, we worked out a plan to record the orchestra in the Hall itself. On three afternoons in September 1978 we were able to use the Hall, recording the orchestra playing four contrasting

Bach works – *Sinfonia* from the *Easter Oratorio*; *Brandenburg Concerto No. 3 in G*; *Suite No. 2 in B minor*; and the *Ricercare* from *'The Musical Offering'*.

Although we had plenty of photographs of the sessions, we were keen that the front cover should contain a panoramic view of the Hall itself. Nick and I spent some time looking for good vantage points and decided that the best shot would be from Waterloo Bridge at dusk, just as the Embankment and the Hall were being illuminated.

An ideal picture would also have the distant Houses of Parliament and Big Ben floodlit, but we noticed that those lights didn't come on until much later. Nothing ventured nothing gained, we wrote to the 'keeper of Big Ben' asking if, on a certain October evening, the lights could be switched on a couple of hours earlier. That evening we waited apprehensively on Waterloo Bridge, camera at the ready, and as if by magic, the lights on the Houses of Parliament and Big Ben were switched on at the appointed time, giving us the ideal shot.

The record was so well received and reviewed that two years later, we made a follow-up Bach disc with the orchestra.

In addition to our choral recordings, we were also anxious to continue to record as many organs as possible. We had linked up with a small record-distribution concern in Holland, run by Willem Smit and Frits Baan, who owned and ran STB Studio in the North Holland municipality of Huizen. Through that connection we met the world-famous organist, Piet Kee, and were able to record him on what must be two of the most famous organs anywhere in the whole world – the Bavo Kerk in Haarlem, and the Grote Kerk in Alkmaar.

We will never forget the impact of the size and space at Haarlem when we first entered the building – and the cold! It was so huge that it seemed to have its own weather. The famous Müller organ is situated high up in a west gallery, and there was no way we were going to be able to sling microphones on a wire from one side of the church to the other. Nick had already thought of this and had borrowed some tall stands which gave us a perfect close balance which we then coupled with carefully placed space microphones. The recording sessions took place late in the evening and into the dead of night. It was a slow process, not least because on this organ the player is not able to manipulate the drawstop knobs himself and needs an assistant each side to do so. There were very long periods of silence between the takes, and we were left wondering if Piet was explaining the stop changes to his assistants or had nipped out for a smoke, a drink, or even a call of nature!

Whatever, the finished result was acoustically stunning, and we were able to issue the record in a splendidly designed double sleeve, complete with photos of both the organ and Piet, taken by Nick.

Both Piet Kee and the critics were impressed with the recording, *Hi-Fi News* of September 1979 giving it A* for both performance and recording:

With Piet Kee celebrating the conclusion of the Haarlem recording

> *The richness of this organ has possibly never been captured better than it is on this disc, where it is allowed to breathe in the warmth of the large building.*

A few months later, Piet suggested that we might like to record him on another of the most famous and revered Dutch organs: the huge Grote Kerk of St. Laurens, Alkmaar. Situated in the centre of the town, the church houses two historic organs – one high up at the west end originally built in 1646, and the small choir organ on the north side of the church, which dates from 1511 and is the oldest organ in playing order in the whole of the Netherlands. The sessions took place across two late nights in September 1980, continuing until first light each morning. To prevent any ambient traffic noise, either Piet or Willem Smit had persuaded the civic authorities to close the roads around the church on the nights when we were recording. The finished result was available a few months later with a handsome double sleeve, complete with plans of the siting of the two organs and photographs taken by Nick.

Although the cost of the whole project was underwritten by STB Studio, there was a later *quid pro quo* when Frits and Willem brought a large mixed-voice choir over to London for a weekend, complete with their own organist and recording equipment. One Saturday evening, I let them into St. Paul's Cathedral where, in a few hours, they managed to make a complete LP of hymns and chorales.

We'd also been to Dublin in 1980, to St. Patrick's Cathedral, where John Dexter (former Guildford chorister and organ scholar at St. Paul's Cathedral) was now Master of the Music. Over three evenings John recorded six items, including the first modern recording of Dublin-born Charles Villiers Stanford's three-movement *Sonata Celtica* and John's own arrangement of the ever-popular *Londonderry Air*.

Our next recording venue was St. George's Chapel, Windsor Castle, where in early January 1982, we made an LP. Since his arrival as Organist and Master of the Choristers seven years earlier, Christopher Robinson had transformed the Chapel choir into one of the finest in the country, and had arranged that they would return from their post-Christmas break two days early to make the recording. Making a recording in the Chapel can often be spoilt by aircraft noise, either as they take off from nearby Heathrow airport, or approach to land. We had not been in the Chapel for more than an hour when heavy snow started to fall. It blanketed the whole of southern England, closing Heathrow to any flights, a situation that was to last until two mornings later, just as we were about to complete the last take. Surely someone 'up there' must have been on our side!

∾

Although a hobby for both Nick and me, Guild Records was not only taking up a lot of our time but was also expensive. Since those early days at Guildford, we had paid the standard professional fees to organists, choristers and lay clerks, so we were glad when, in July 1984, we were offered the opportunity to record with Anthony Froggatt and his choir at Portsmouth Cathedral, with full sponsorship from the nearby U.K. head office of IBM. With that financial help we were also able to use a brass ensemble in some of the items, and *Portsmouth Remembers* (GRSP 7021) was issued later in the year in a handsome double sleeve, the front cover featuring a locally painted watercolour of Old Portsmouth and the Cathedral.

Another sponsorship, this time from Exxon Chemicals (a division of the international oil and gas company), enabled us to make our 1986 LP in Canterbury Cathedral with Allan Wicks and the Cathedral choir. Having been appointed in November 1961, the recording was a celebration of Allan's 25th Anniversary, and featured music associated with the Cathedral and also York Minster (where Allan had begun his career as Sub-Organist). Entitled *A Canterbury Celebration*, it was our first recording to be issued in just CD and cassette format – LP records were no longer selling in any quantity.

One of the great buildings in which we'd not so far recorded was Westminster Abbey. Assistant Organist Andrew Lumsden had moved there from Southwark Cathedral in

1988, and he and I often worked together on the BBC Daily Services. In 1990 Andrew offered to record for us on the Abbey organ, and with a programme of music associated with royal occasions at the Abbey and elsewhere, we issued the CD with the Guild logo in 'Royal Red' rather than the usual blue colour.

A Grand Chorus was one of the last location recordings we would make, though not the last CD. We'd been able to retain ownership of the St. Paul's pop-style recordings originally issued on the K-tel label, and now they were transferred to CD, together with other solo recordings by Paul Phoenix, entitled *Golden Favourites from St. Paul's*. We also issued a second compilation CD – *Great Occasions at St. Paul's* – featuring the 1978 and 1980 recordings of the Schubert *Mass in G* and Haydn's *Nelson Mass*.

Early in 1993 we had an unexpected approach from a member of the staff of Chandos Records and his business partner from Switzerland to see if we'd like to sell Guild Records. During the protracted negotiations that followed, we had set up a recording to be made in Salisbury Cathedral with the boys, girls, and men of the Cathedral choirs. It would be the first appearance on record by the girl choristers, and we settled on the appropriate title of *Canticum Novum* (*A New Song*). Would we like to make the recording for the new owners of Guild?

The sessions took place over three summer evenings in 1994, and since Nick was already committed to be working elsewhere, Brian Roberts made the recording, whilst I acted as producer, also taking the opportunity to spend a little time with Nicola who was now Precentor's Chorister.

27 years had passed since that afternoon in the Guildford teashop when Nick and I had first talked about starting Guild Records. Since then, we'd both enjoyed every aspect of making all the recordings, though the time had now come to say farewell to what had been a fulfilling, if time-consuming and expensive, hobby.

In March 1995 Salisbury's *Canticum Novum* was issued as the first release of the new Guild Music Ltd. – definitely a new song for them, whilst for us, another track on the record seemed rather appropriate: Richard Shephard's setting of *The Old Order Changeth*.

Appendix

What's It All About?

The opening Address to the National Convention of the American Guild of Organists, Houston, USA, June 1988.

The other evening, I was having a conversation with my 14-year-old daughter Julia. Those of you who have 14-year-olds will know just how difficult that can sometimes be. 'Daddy,' she said, 'what are you going to do in America?' I replied, 'I'm going to preach a sermon.' And with that she fell about in uncontrollable laughter. 'Organists don't preach sermons,' she said. 'Oh, very well,' I said, 'I'll compose a fugue in words. Will that be all right?' She nodded.

Well, whatever this is going to be – a sermon, an address, or a verbal fugue – I must begin by saying how honoured I am to be in this pulpit. What a feeling of power as you stand up here. There you all are, waiting to hang on my every word. But I need to be a bit careful, because yesterday morning in St. Paul's United Methodist Church here in Houston, the minister, the Reverend Wayne Day, told us in his sermon that he and Bob Brewer, his organist, had come to an understanding: that the minister wouldn't attempt to sing if the organist didn't attempt to preach. Now my presence in the pulpit this morning is not the green light for all the clergy to leap to their feet and burst into song.

First of all, let me say how delighted I am to be with you at this Convention and to see so many old friends, as well as making so many new ones. I bring you warmest good wishes from many English organists and choir directors, and how well I remember our visit to the 1980 AGO convention in Minneapolis and St. Paul with the St. Paul's Cathedral choir. I'll never forget what a thrill it was for us to sing with such a musically appreciative congregation. I've always thought that your hymn singing was among the best I've ever heard, even if you remember that the last Matins was at the early hour of 8.30 in the morning.

It's the *best* that I am going to talk about today, because this address is based on the organist and choir director and their relationship with Worship – the best we can offer to God. As this morning's first hymn aptly put it, it's 'in our music that God is glorified'. That is why you and I play or conduct in church. We are, to take the words literally, 'proving our worth(ship).' So let me take a subject for my verbal fugue, and it comes from Psalm 96 verse nine, which reads, 'O worship the Lord in the beauty of holiness'.

I want to begin with a rather silly story, but it does have a point. An organist died, and in due course he arrived at the pearly gates of heaven. There was St. Peter waiting to greet him (when I say *him*, ladies, throughout this address I do, of course, embrace *her* as well). 'And what were you on earth?' said St. Peter. 'Well, I was an organist.' 'Oh, we don't have many of those up here, you know. Now, let's see, we've got a spare heavenly chapel you can use, complete with four-manual tracker organ, of course – low wind pressure, of course – where you can practise your trio sonatas in eternity. Come on, I'll take you there.' As they wandered through the heavenly landscape, they passed several other chapels, each with the door slightly open. Out of the first could be heard the strains of a Bach prelude and fugue majestically played, but at a rather slow speed. 'Who's that?' asked our organist. 'That,' said St. Peter, 'is the great Albert Schweitzer.' 'Oh, I know all about him,' said the organist, 'what scholarship.' On they went, and in passing the next heavenly chapel, there was the most scintillating and sparkling performance of Bach's *Fugue in D major* drifting through the door. 'That,' said St. Peter, 'is the master himself, the great Johann Sebastian Bach.' 'Oh, I know all of his chorale preludes,' enthused our organist, 'perhaps he'll teach me one day.' They continued, and there coming out of the next chapel was a Bach trio sonata, superbly played and twice as fast as our organist had ever been able to manage. He couldn't resist a peek around the door when St. Peter wasn't looking, and much to his astonishment caught the back view of the organist playing one part on the manuals and the other two on the pedals. Absolutely astonished, he turned to St. Peter with an inquiring look. 'Oh, that's Virgil Fox,' said St. Peter. 'Oh, I know all about him,' said the organist, 'what a technique.' On they floated, and suddenly they were outside the most beautiful chapel, superb in architecture, with the most poised and polished performance of Bach's *Fantasia and Fugue in G Minor* you've ever heard in your life, perfect in every detail of articulation and phrasing. 'That's it,' said our organist excitedly to St. Peter, 'the greatest playing of all. I must know who it is.' 'That,' said St. Peter grandly, 'is God.' 'Who's he?' said the organist.

However you look at that story or however you decide to adapt it to your own local situation, it does point us to the only possible reason for our being in the church – that we should lead the hearts and minds of our listeners to God through our music. In his opening address in the 1982 AGO convention in Washington, Paul Hume reminded you of the power of music to 'take people's hearts and minds to God as nothing else could,' and he said that you musicians hold the keys to the citadel of heaven. Well, you certainly deal in heavenly harmony, but what about the earthly strife? You know the sad stories and situations as well as I do, and like me, some of you may know them from firsthand experience. There didn't seem to be much godliness around in the vestry of a great church in the east of England on a Sunday morning not so long ago when

the organist arrived only to be told, after many years of loyal and devoted work, that
his services were no longer required. Would he pack up his things and leave there and
then. That's a story which could be repeated for many different locations throughout
this country of yours and certainly in England and elsewhere. The scenario is all too
familiar, and the shame of it is that music and liturgy should be on the same track,
with clergy and musicians creating a close partnership on what must be equal terms,
at least at the practical level. But the fact remains that the church organist and choir
director is a highly skilled employee sometimes treated like an unskilled employee,
subject to pre-emptory dismissal, often unappreciated, unloved and certainly under-
paid. What is the church thinking about when it advertises an important town church
post in England at a salary of $1,800 – no, certainly not per week, and, regretfully,
not per month but, believe it or not, per annum. Whatever happened to chapter ten of
St. Luke's Gospel about the labourer being worthy of his hire? I know we don't do it
for money, and you know that. We don't necessarily need to be appreciated, so why
are we still drawn to making music in church? I put it to you that we are called – in the
best sense of that word – called just as much as anyone else who finds their vocation,
their purpose in life. We are, to use modern terminology, practitioners in the ministry
of music. Don't let anyone underrate the value of music in Worship.

On my 21st birthday I received a set of volumes of J.S. Bach's complete organ
works. They are now in a very tatty condition, but the flyleaf of the first volume still
has its inscription, 'Music is the speech of angels.' How right that is, even if some
of the results that I've heard – and delivered – have left the angels sitting there with
their fingers in their ears for much of the time. A few years before that birthday,
the Archbishops of Canterbury and York had commissioned a report from a distinguished panel of musicians and clergy entitled *Music in Church*. The report tells us
that 'throughout the centuries, music has found a welcome and almost essential place
in church, and there must be few churches today in which music is not accepted as
the indispensable companion of prayer and praise.' As ministers in music, it's your
function to hold hands with that indispensable companion to bring people closer to
God; you do it by the way you play and the way you train your choir, all very practical things which need hours and hours of preparation – as I well know – and careful
planning and rehearsal, often in cold, dark and empty churches.

The report goes on to stress that another essential in Worship is silence, perhaps
something musicians and clergy don't think about often enough. Silence is no longer a
desirable commodity in our modern liturgies. The late Canon John Collins, who was
one of the most distinguished priests ever to serve St. Paul's Cathedral, lamented this
lack of silence. He'd say, 'We're not allowed to communicate with the Almighty, either
we're having to shout out some response or else we're jumping up and down shaking

each other's hand or cuddling each other.' And I know what he meant. Nowadays we're so conditioned to overactive participation that we never face up to the challenge of silence for meditation. It's positively embarrassing if there's a silence in the service. I've even heard the priest use a loud stage whisper to say to the organist, 'Play something... now!'

This is where our fugue subject enters again, but like all good fugue subjects, it's now inverted, for as I see it, the role of the organist and choir director is not just to help those who listen to 'worship the Lord in the beauty of holiness', but to help them worship the Lord in the holiness of beauty. To do that you need inspiration, skill, perseverance, sensitivity, adaptability and the patience of Job. And all for what? A congregation that talks loudly and clatters around during a quiet voluntary, or even worse, church officials who do the same; clergy, perhaps, who show no sensitivity whatsoever to the way music and speech should interlink within the dignity of a well-ordered Service; the use of music for getting from one place to the next as a sort of background effect, what someone once described as 'holy pre-ambulations' – no wonder the organist feels unloved and unwanted, tucked away there behind the console or in some remote corner of the chancel or gallery. His music has been the first thing to be heard in the Service and it will be the last, and probably has filled more than fifty percent of the time that we've been in church, unless of course the sermon is a long one like this one. There we're not blameless or sensitive enough to the value of speech. 'Sir,' said one of the choirboys one morning after a Service, 'I do wish that sermon hadn't been quite so short.' 'Why is that?' I asked, thinking that some great wave of holiness had descended on this normally over-lively twelve-year-old. 'Well, sir,' he said, 'the boy next to me was telling me about his aunt and an overfriendly cab driver, and now I shall never know what happened.'

No matter what his or her professional qualifications through diplomas or, better still, experience, the organist is the resident musical expert and, as such, needs to be physically involved in all musical decisions that affect the church Services. I don't know about your experience, but too often I've been handed the list of hymns, which is fair enough, and then been given a list of specific instructions about which tune will be sung, almost as though it was a vote of no confidence in the resident musician's ability to match the words and music together in a sensitive way. It's often in that way that we musicians are landed with music that was described in a recent English church journal as 'being written, I suppose, by adults with a starry-eyed concept of childhood, probably frozen at about the age of five.' The trouble with this, the article goes on, is that jelly-bean hymns – which is what the author called them – 'are liable to leave children with a lasting impression that Christian Worship is only intended for the under-sixes. Once they've seen through the lyrics – and that doesn't take long

– they properly assume that the truths and aspirations of Christianity are on much the same level.' And, of course, they're not. It is part of our ministry to guide and educate musically, whatever the occasion or situation. As the Collect says, 'when two or three are gathered together in thy Name,' perhaps in a room in someone's house, then that is not the place for formal music making, any more than a great church building lends itself to what Erik Routley once described as the 'cultivation of a brutally contrived informality in the liturgy – a music that is monotonously juvenile.'

Here we musicians have a problem – the problem is that there are now so many diverse styles of buildings and liturgies, that what works in one place isn't necessarily going to work in another. It isn't the case of going in with preconceived ideas that what worked in your last appointment is going to be right for this one. That, I'm afraid, often applies more to the clergy than the musicians.

I always remember my arrival at St. Paul's Cathedral in 1974, having come from the Cathedral in Guildford, some 25 miles south of London. Both buildings were so different. Guildford is modern, slightly austere, but greatly conducive to Worship, while St. Paul's is massive in its almost Baroque-like splendour, never silent with its throngs of visitors, and perhaps justifying that rather apt description by William Morris, who called it 'God's railway station'. But our musical aim in both places was the same – only the best will do in the worship of Almighty God. Yes, only the best would do, though the way we achieved that best was different in both places. Buildings dictate such mundane and yet vitally important musical matters as the speed we take hymns and anthems, the sort of vocal quality our choirs will produce and, of course, the amount of volume it must put out. We have to be adaptable. What suits a tiny, enclosed quire area in a small Cathedral isn't going to have any telling effect in the great spaces of a building such as your own National Cathedral in Washington. What suits the crypt of Canterbury Cathedral isn't going to match what suits this building here today.

But back to my arrival in St. Paul's. The senior member of the choir was quite blunt in his speech, something we associate with those who come from the county of Yorkshire. He took me aside soon after I arrived and said, very wisely as it turned out, 'If I were you, I wouldn't make any decisions about changes until the building has had a chance to talk to you.' About five years later I said, 'Owen, is it all right if I make a decision now?' But he was right. I learnt as we went along. And you – my friends and musical colleagues – you also learn; if you ever stop learning, then is the time to cease to hold musical office.

One of my duties and privileges throughout the week is to direct the music in the BBC's broadcast Daily Service, a 15-minute act of Worship which includes two hymns and a psalm. This is the world's longest running radio program. Can you believe that?

Here I am in Texas, and we've got something that's longer running and bigger and better, but it *is* the world's longest running radio programme. It was 60 years old last Friday morning, just three days ago. Compared with my two illustrious predecessors at the BBC, Sir Henry Walford Davies and Sir George Thalben-Ball, I'm just a beginner, having only been there for 17 and a half years. But I'm learning all the while, and I hope my understanding is still improving. The whole point of telling you this is to underline this great fact, that we never stop learning. For 35 minutes we rehearse those two hymns and that psalm, when we could well sight-read them, and in doing so we learn about that most vital piece of the choir director's basic skills, the interpretation of words. As a hymn puts it, 'We have a gospel to proclaim', and we're not going to do that if our singing becomes a meaningless jumble of ill-framed and perfunctorily delivered words. Ours is the monumental task of telling the listeners, whether they be on the other side of the microphone or a few rows away in this church, that here is a message just for you, and this is it. Have you ever analysed the awesome responsibilities placed upon your singers? In my more light-hearted moments at The King's School, Canterbury, where I still am for a few days longer, I tease the boys and girls about the difference between making music orchestrally and vocally. It's not meant to be too serious when I tell them that the orchestral player has only got half the work to do as the singer. But there's a certain truth there, isn't there? – as they well know, because they're also all very talented orchestral players as well. Singers not only recreate the vision of the composer, but also that of the author, and like any other musician they do it with their whole being. For a singer, it's two-dimensional and very demanding to do properly.

Our choir motto at St. Paul's was drawn for me over a heraldic shield by a young man who just happens to be here this week as a choral scholar with the King's College choir. I wonder if he still remembers the deep meaning of those words, which I used to quote endlessly at St. Paul's Cathedral Choir: 'It is not enough to make a noise.' Think hard about that, and then realise that those simple words contain the clue as to how you and I must respond to our music in church if we're going to proclaim the eternal truths through what we do, day by day, week by week.

Technical expertise and perfection are admirable and I, like everyone else, strive for it – I never get there, mind you – but there's no guarantee that any technically perfect piece of music making is going to lift the hearts of your listeners to a level which is above everyday things. The truth is, you're probably going to bore them stiff. Our music needs humanity and warmth, and it needs executants who give of their whole selves in that music making.

Someone who once sat close to the world-famous violinist Fritz Kreisler while he was playing a concert wrote that he 'suffered for all of us on his instrument,' and you can see that for yourselves in the faces and movements of many of the world's greatest musicians. So it is in church, where we meet together in the name of one who suffered for all of us on Calvary, as we fulfil our ministry, if you like, our calling. We play the King of Instruments in the service of the King of Kings. What a responsibility! What an honour! And what a challenge!

You come to this convention for the renewal of old friendships and the making of new ones, but above all for comradeship, inspiration and, if you're like me, a re-charge of your spiritual batteries. I've come over 5,000 miles to bring you words of comfort, words of encouragement, words that I hope will challenge. Don't lose sight of your standards. Maintain musical integrity – no-one else will if you don't. Stand firm against the second- and third-rate. As the prayer says, 'Hold fast to that which is good'. But also be adaptable. A little giving can be hard, as I well know, but pays such dividends in return. Above all, be thankful that you've responded to that special calling to help lead people in the worship of the Lord in the beauty of holiness, whilst also showing them the way to worship in the holiness of beauty.

So ends my verbal fugue, and let me close with these two verses from a modern hymn which sums up so much of what I've been saying. Yes, there are some splendid modern hymns – we've been listening to some this morning – and this is another of them, written by the Reverend Caryl Micklem, the minister of a United Reform church in London. Its subtitle seems so appropriate to all of us who make music in church – 'Staying Power'.

Give to me, Lord, a thankful heart
and a discerning mind;
Give as I play the Christian's part,
the strength to finish what I start
and act on what I find.

Jesus, with all your church, I long
to see your kingdom come;
Show me your way of righting wrong,
of turning sorrow into song,
until you bring me home.

Amen.

Index